WINES OF THE NEW SOUTH AFRICA

THE PUBLISHER GRATEFULLY ACKNOWLEDGES THE GENEROUS
SUPPORT OF THE GENERAL ENDOWMENT FUND OF THE UNIVERSITY
OF CALIFORNIA PRESS FOUNDATION

WINES OF THE NEW SOUTH AFRICA

Tradition and Revolution

Tim James

UNIVERSITY OF CALIFORNIA PRESS

Berkeley   Los Angeles   London

University of California Press, one of the most distinguished university
presses in the United States, enriches lives around the world by advancing
scholarship in the humanities, social sciences, and natural sciences. Its
activities are supported by the UC Press Foundation and by philanthropic
contributions from individuals and institutions. For more information, visit
www.ucpress.edu.

University of California Press
Berkeley and Los Angeles, California

University of California Press, Ltd.
London, England

Library of Congress Cataloging-in-Publication Data

James, Tim (Timothy James), 1954 –.
    Wines of the new South Africa: tradition and revolution / Tim James.
        p.   cm.
    Includes bibliographical references and index.
    ISBN 978–0–520–26023–8 (cloth : alk. paper)
    1. Wine and wine making—South Africa.   I. Title.
    TP559.S6J36   2013
    663'.20968—dc23   2012048632

Manufactured in the United States of America

22   21   20   19   18   17   16   15   14   13
10   9   8   7   6   5   4   3   2   1

The paper used in this publication meets the minimum
requirements of ANSI/NISO Z39.48–1992 (R 2002)
(*Permanence of Paper*).

To Louise and Eben

CONTENTS

MAPS

PREFACE AND ACKNOWLEDGMENTS

It will quickly become clear to any reader of this book that my approach is often colored by a consciousness of the history of South African wine. The title, of course, suggests that the focus is on one particular slice of history—the most recent—but that is so only insofar as I am always aware of the past informing the present of the new South African wine industry. This is, after all, one of the oldest wine industries of the so-called New World, and the only one that, with the wines of Constantia, made a notable contribution to the greatness of wine before the twentieth century. The notorious politics and social structures of the past still have less-attractive echoes today, but I have effectively defined the "newness" that is my focus with a date that most immediately has a sociohistorical significance: 1994, the year of the country's first nonracial parliamentary election. That was, of course, the event that allowed the reentry of Cape wine into the world markets, after many years of boycott and isolation, and precipitated the vinous revolution that rolls on yet. The wine lands are redolent of the recent and the older past, which are inevitably embedded in the change and growth of the past few decades. I look forward to there being one day a comprehensive and readily available history of South African wine; meanwhile, in a thoroughly unspecialist way and in a general book, I offer here what little I can of it, as part of an attempt to characterize and account for the present.

I do not venture the wineries profiled as a definitive list of the best producers of South African wine; to do so would make me even more vulnerable to criticism than I will be in claiming these as among the best. (Other interesting wineries are also mentioned in the introductions to the various regions.) Many are an ineluctable choice, of course, but there were sometimes competing claims to be weighed, in the context of space limitations.

Perhaps the category of producers that is most egregiously missing is that of garagistes (some of them the personal labels of winemakers at larger properties), and that is because many of them might and do make fine wine but in tiny quantities and with little breadth of distribution. Some of them have perforce given way here to larger, more "significant" wineries whose wines I might personally value a little less, or even to producers whose greatest claim is sentimental, because of past prestige or a long history. A further consideration: lexicographer Samuel Johnson wrote, "No dictionary of a living tongue ever can be perfect, since, while it is hastening to publication, some words are budding"; books about wineries and wines are similarly doomed. Because of the way the South African wine industry has changed over the past few decades and is continuing to change (though now at a slower rate, perhaps), these winery profiles are something like a photograph of a moving object, and that has its implications for coverage of both the broader picture and the details. That all said, I can't evade the fact that my own taste (and probably my own imperfect information and experience) inevitably prompted some inclusions and omissions. In brief—I am aware that some good producers are probably neglected. It should be noted that the maps that accompany the chapters devoted to the different areas indicate only the wineries that are mentioned in the text—approximately a quarter of the total.

The wine world I know in South Africa is a gregarious, sharing, discussing one, so that the views and judgments in this book always owe something to others, as do whatever information and understanding I have picked up. Nonetheless, any errors are mine and when they are pointed out I will have to refer to Dr. Johnson once more and say, as he reportedly did when asked how he could possibly have made a particular mistake in his dictionary: "ignorance, Madam, pure ignorance." So: thanks to winemakers and viticulturists, to fellow wine journalists, to those with whom I often drink wine and talk and argue happily about it. More specific thanks to friends and colleagues who've encouraged this project, who've read parts of it and given opinions and advice: Angela Lloyd (who was particularly helpful with some of the winery profiles), also Michael Fridjhon, Melvyn Minnaar, John Platter, Mark Solms, Cathy van Zyl, and Philip van Zyl. And thanks to Blake Edgar of University of California Press for many useful observations. Those who, like me, gleefully seek out statistics in South Africa are fortunate that SAWIS (South African Wine Industry Information and Statistics) is in one respect an old-fashioned institution as well as being a formidably efficient one—it believes that its function is to assist inquirers, and Yvette van der Merwe and her colleagues have been unstintingly helpful. André Matthee of the Wine and Spirit Board has been similarly obliging with matters of regulation and law.

Some scattered sentences in this book have appeared on my Web site, and a few in the pages of that excellent journal *The World of Fine Wine*, to whose publisher and editor I am grateful for allowing me to recycle my words.

INTRODUCTION

What is South African wine? Rather, ask first: what are South African vineyards, and what do they mean?

Inland from the Atlantic, some three hours' drive from Cape Town, we eventually found the farm called 't Voetpad—an old Dutch name meaning "the footpath." The landscape is mountainous, beautiful but hard, with few signs of habitation. Wheat and rooibos tea are the main agricultural pursuits. But at the end of one of the large valleys, next to a homestead, an ancient barn, and a cluster of trees, was the neglected vineyard about which an ambitious winemaker, looking for old vines, had learned.

The nearest vineyards to this are far away, across at least a mountain or two. These few hectares of tangled vines were mostly planted some one hundred years back. They grow as untrellised "bushvines," with no irrigation despite heat and little rain. Though planted after the phylloxera infestation had laid waste the Cape's vineyards in the late nineteenth century, requiring almost universal replanting with resistant rootstocks, these vines grow on their own roots: this was too remote a corner, perhaps, for the insect to bother with. In other ways, too, this vineyard could have been planted three hundred years ago. The half-dozen grape varieties growing here in random promiscuity were already established in the early years of the Dutch East India Company's little settlement at the foot of Africa.

Rationally, the vineyard should have been uprooted years ago, but the farmer's mother felt sentimental about it, so the vines were dutifully if minimally maintained and the grapes sold for a pittance to the nearest cooperative winery, where they disappeared into some nameless, cheap blend. But why were they planted in the first place, so obscurely, so isolated from any obvious market? This was surely not originally a commercial vineyard, but rather one of a type that must have been, for a few hundred years, scattered across the old Cape Colony: planted to make wine for domestic consumption and to sell to neighboring farms. In the early twentieth century the notorious "tot system" was still widely and unembarrassedly used by landowners, who doled out frequent rations of liquor to their farmworkers (descendants of slaves and the indigenous population) as part of a system of low pay and social control. Other farmers within easy reach by ox-drawn wagon would have also wanted wine for their laborers and themselves—no doubt it was a useful source of nutrition, too, as wine was for the peasants of old Europe.

This rare old vineyard, which evokes so much of the history of the Cape wine lands, has been saved for now, and finds a fascinating expression in a wine.

Closer to the heartland of the South African wine industry, there's another unirrigated vineyard of bushvines where I have stood and wondered. It is on the slopes of the Paardeberg, a granitic mountain with trailing skirts of vineyards, that rises suddenly among wheat lands and under the enormous skies of the Swartland. Although the summer sun is hot, cool breezes reach from the Atlantic some twenty kilometers away. There were already farms hereabouts by the end of the seventeenth century, one of them granted to a French Huguenot escaping religious persecution in Europe, but these large vineyards of Chenin Blanc were mostly planted in the 1960s to feed the brandy industry and a new market for fruity white wines recently made possible by cold-fermentation technology. Now many low-yielding old vines are scarcely viable commercially, and most are being ripped up and replaced. These gnarled vines are most carefully tended, however, and their wine goes into a highly regarded white blend, of a new and uniquely South African type.

To an unsympathetic observer this is a scruffy, scrubby, and unlovely vineyard, not to be compared with what can be observed on an adjacent hillside. There, vines in trellised rows are lush and deep green in the bright light under cloudless midsummer January skies—also Chenin Blanc, but young and vigorous vines of a high-yielding clone, irrigated and intelligently farmed with all the resources of well-capitalized modern agriculture and the unstinting (though expensive) support of the agrochemical industry. The grapes are sold to a wholesaler to make unexceptionable wine at a low price, mostly for the supermarket shelves of Europe.

There are few scruffy, dry vineyards that I am aware of in the long, broad inland valley of the Breede River. Endless stretches of the other kind may be found, though, with high-yielding vineyards vastly outnumbering the few farmed to produce high-quality wine. Growing vigorously in alluvial soils, these vines would not survive long in the heat without copious irrigation; they would not look as lavish and rich as this, so heavily laden with large bunches of luscious grapes, without water pumped from the river and its dams, without chemical controls for the diseases that breed in those thick canopies of leaves. The spaces between the rows of vines are blasted clean with herbicide, and down them move the tractors and the mechanical harvesters.

In the Stellenbosch region, we find vineyards that are also mostly fairly young at one of the grandest properties there—although vines have been planted on the farm, and wine has been made, for more than three hundred years, since an early Cape governor established a huge estate and fine homestead for himself. There is still splendor and high expenditure, as the estate is a showpiece of a major multinational company, but there's even greater determination to make the best possible wine. These vineyards are more closely monitored than most in the country, and among the few that can be claimed to be free of the damaging leafroll virus, rampant in South Africa. The price of that freedom is continual vigilance; any vine showing signs of developing virus is pulled up, destroyed, and replaced. But the vines are not the only vegetation here—even Stellenbosch is not quite a vinous monoculture. The alien vegetation that, along with modern agricultural industry and urban expansion, threatens the Western Cape's incomparably rich indigenous plant life is itself being systematically attacked on the 3,500-hectare estate. The reestablishment of indigenous vegetation, and its penetration up to and sometimes right into the vineyards, seems to be playing a part in eliminating pesticide applications and dramatically reducing fungicide and herbicide use on these vineyards.

In the less imposing, bleaker landscape of Elim the wind seems to blow unceasingly. Here, near the southernmost tip of Africa, scattered vineyards have been planted. For a while, long ago, there were some vines grown by Moravian missionaries at their station, which took in freed slaves after 1838, but all those one can see now were planted after 1992. That was the year when, at long last, the authorities abandoned the system that imposed quotas on production, which effectively prevented the opening up of new wine-growing areas. Now some of the country's best Sauvignon Blanc comes from these vineyards, where the vines must struggle against voracious grape-predating birds as well as the cool, but often vicious, salt-laden winds off the oceans that meet at Cape Agulhas.

With all this diversity of origin, and not even taking into account how the grapes are turned into wine, one must be reluctant to make easy generalizations about "South African wine." The multifariousness of wine comes primarily from two elements other than different vine varieties: the land and the human beings who have interacted with it. In winegrowing terms they have been doing so for more than 350 years, since roots of the Eurasian vine *Vitis vinifera* were first brought here, to be planted and tended by small-holders, servants, and slaves. All these landscapes and all these vineyards (just a few of which have been sketched above) have a human history as well as a natural one. As vineyards, they are where they are, and how they are, because of human decisions and actions. The land can speak through that history and express diversity—unless it is muted by farming that has no interest in nuance, or muted by sheer ignorance of how best to let it speak. Learning the language of the land is part of the adventure of the most ambitious South African winegrowers today.

But the landscape is physically and conceptually shaped by human culture—and increasingly by an international culture, for what is grown here at the foot of Africa, and how it is grown, is partly shaped by the decisions of, say, supermarket buyers in Amsterdam and Berlin and grander importers in New York and London.

The past too is part of the informing fabric of the present. When it comes to the simple question of old vines, that is a good thing; and another good thing about modern South African wine is the persistence of some of the independent traditions and understandings established though the decades of international isolation. These—the best of them at least—mean that there is something different about good South African wines, a difference culturally as well as geographically informed.

More troubling elements of the past also persist. The land was appropriated in the first place, to have new ideas of ownership thrust upon it and upon those who had long been using it for pasture and hunting. Later, when many people around the world refused to drink South African wine because they could taste in it the bitterness of apartheid, they were not wrong. Looking closely at the vineyards I have sketched above, one can observe that above all they are all possessions, and their owners are all white men, or multinational corporations redolent of established power. One can observe that most of those who work on them, harvesting in the heat and pruning winter vines with cold hands, are black or—given the subtleties of racial classification achieved here—"colored," people of mixed race in the Western Cape, descendants of imported slaves, of the indigenous Khoikhoi and San people, and of the Europeans who settled here, and ruled and destroyed and created, starting in 1652.

All this history; all this beauty of mountain, valley, and space (as so many have observed, there is no wine land anywhere more lovely than the Cape); all this complexity; and all this potential is in the vineyards. It is a landscape and a diversity worth exploring—physically, intellectually, and, above all in the context of wine, sensually.

A note on Southern Hemisphere vineyard seasons: Harvesttime in South Africa varies according to the local specificities of the climate, of course, as well as depending on the variety (and to an extent on the philosophy of the winegrower). In the warmest parts it is likely to start in early midsummer, often in late January. February is generally the hottest month. By the end of March, summer might have an autumnal touch, and most farmers will have already brought in their crops, but in cooler parts the grapes will still be ripening and picking will linger at least through April. In May, winter is definitely approaching, the rainy season in the Cape (with any luck some rain will already have fallen on the exhausted vines in dryland areas). Pruning will follow in winter, July and August, and within another month or two the new growth will be greening the vineyards. By November, myriad tiny flowers will show the shape of the bunches of grapes to come.

1

WINE AND THE NEW SOUTH AFRICA

In 1994, in a hopeful time as a new democracy came to the land of apartheid, South African wine ventured out into the world—a world of which it was terribly ignorant, and which, in turn, had largely forgotten about it during years of boycott. Perhaps, though, an atavistic memory clung from the eighteenth and nineteenth centuries, when wines from Constantia were welcomed among the world's greatest. Now, a figure shrunken from long years of isolation, South African wine blinked in the light, a little tentative but with more confidence than was justified—as was to be demonstrated, when the international wine market made it clear that it was going to demand more than just the reflected glow of Nelson Mandela in the background.

Marketers and makers of Cape wine saw and tasted what was selling in London, Amsterdam, and New York, and the alert among them might have realized a problem. But many were slow, reluctant, or complacently ignorant of any problems, while international wine-lovers, still curious and generous about the "new" South Africa, were being indulgent. One moment that can be seen as symbolic, as well as having had an actual salutary effect, came in 1995 when South Africa was trounced in a comprehensive wine competition against Australia, held in Cape Town with judges from both countries. Producers were shaken, many disbelieving: something was undoubtedly wrong, but surely not their wines!

Various industry bodies seem to have then put pressure on SAA, the national airline that had supported the competition, to abandon its three-year sponsorship. Another international competition that had been planned—against Argentina and Chile—never took place. Winemaker André van Rensburg (whose Stellenzicht Syrah had beaten the

5

famous Grange in the match against Australia) reacted trenchantly to this sulky refusal to face reality: "If a winemaker is scared of competing against Chile, he should stop making wine and grow vegetables. The objections of the better-known estates are based on their unjust reputations earned from wine writers who have been too kind to them."

Fortunately for South African wine, the estates continued to farm grapes rather than turn to broccoli and carrots. Meanwhile, the most important competitions took place when the buyers for supermarkets, national monopolies, and wine shops around the world made their choices. Too many Cape wines were, for example, clearly made from stressed fruit off virused vineyards where the grapes struggled to ripen; too many were overacidified, in accordance with the abstract dictates of the local university enology department, which encouraged safety above all; oaking was not always carried out in a sophisticated manner—and there was some suspicion that the barrels themselves were not always of the highest quality. Furthermore, tastes had changed in the larger world of wine, in ways many in South Africa were only coming to realize.

The local wine industry seized upon the few years of indulgence it was granted; lessons were learned, and the pace of transformation was astonishing. Some changes could come quickly—in the cellar, especially, and some aspects of vineyard management. Other changes—such as finding the land best suited to particular varieties, improved viticultural practices, and working with better and cleaner plant material—would take longer. Those longer-term changes, whose effects would be observed only ten years later, were to constitute something like a second stage in the South African winemaking revolution. But all these effects were part of a more fundamental shift in quality, particularly at the most ambitious end of Cape winemaking.

Other than the swift adaptation to what the world demanded of a modern wine producer, something else was astonishing. In one way, it was precisely the opposite of adaptation, although it did not rest on complacency. Within the arrogant response of producers to their humiliation in the test match against Australia had been a few grains of truth that might become useful and valuable if properly understood and used. It was not certain that the ripe fruitiness that had made Australian wine the darling of the vital British market in particular was entirely something to aim for at all costs. More important was to recognize and assert an independent tradition and some older-fashioned virtues that should not be too hastily discarded. The Cape had nearly 350 years of winemaking behind it. In some of the urging to modernize in order to compete effectively on the international market a demand could also be heard to abandon tradition and the claims of a specific winegrowing landscape in favor of the blandness of internationalist winemaking competence and globalized fashion.

Even in the recent decades, when South Africa's isolation had undoubtedly led to provincialism, a (small) number of fine wines had not quite fitted what seemed to be demanded by those for whom the new-world standards were provided by Australia and California. Those were the days of Australian ascendancy in the United Kingdom, South Africa's largest market. Forward fruit and a touch of sweetness seemed to beguile everyone there, from the supermarket customer to the lofty critic. The makers of some apparently old-fashioned Cape wines had endured sniffs and sneers, but they resisted stylistic demands while striving to improve the quality of what they were creating. There was a vague but not unjustified idea abroad, which encouraged them, that South Africa's natural position in the world of wine was somewhere between the respective styles associated with the New World and the Old. But if ripeness was all for some enthusiasts of modern wine-making, the old-fashioned were not always right, either. There were winemakers for whom defense of tradition was associated with hard, overacidified reds kept too long in barrels of dubious quality, insipidly flabby or too-acidic whites, or ultrasweet fortified wines.

In the introduction to the 1995 edition of his annual *South African Wine Guide,* when the revolution in local wine was scarcely under way, John Platter described what was happening in tones different from those of his introduction of the previous year, when recession and poor-quality exports had edged his words with despair. He wrote percipiently in his necessarily enlarged *Guide:*

> The stampede of new wines—nearly 400 this season alone—is neither a completely chaotic second-coming, nor a chase into the unknown. South Africa has had a foot in both the Old and New worlds of wine. In reclaiming the past—and past overseas markets—the re-launch of the Cape was always going to be steadied by its long traditions, its ease with wine. The old profile of Cape wine would be swiveled a bit on its plinth, to catch different beams of light, to offer new outlines. But the soils and climates and many of the ways of the Cape remain inimitable and impose a continuity too.

Platter might not even have apprehended the extent of the change that was just starting, but he was perceptive in his conclusion: "Often, the Cape's youngest wines are its best. And the finest have not yet been bottled."

In one of the most important developments of all, many in a remarkable younger generation of winemakers (sadly, only a few viticulturists as yet) traveled the wine lands of the world, not just to learn new-world cellaring techniques, but also to taste and marvel at and seek to understand the classic wines of Europe. They brought home reminders of the great fundamental that the finest wine is true to its origins, the soil and climate in which grapevines are nurtured. There was undoubtedly a qualitative leap in Cape wine in the late 1990s, but another, more profound change—precisely, the emergence of increasing numbers of authentic wines—seems to have happened in the first decade of the twenty-first century. In fact, that is why a number of the wineries profiled in this book are so young. John Platter's point in 1994 remains perhaps more clearly true now: a significant proportion of the best South African wines today were not being made in 2000, and many of what are now recognized as the finest wineries were not yet established.

It is worth stressing the point: the reentry of South Africa into the world since the early 1990s has meant a growth in international sophistication for its wine. At its best, that has meant not the imposition of a bland "international style," but the emergence of the local story, better told.

Here is an example that works as an argument for this claim, and for the previous one about the more recent deepening of transformation in South African wine, as well as for an illustration of the rich dialectic between local and international in that reinvigorated transformation. For many observers, the class of South African wine that today comes closest to excellence is that of blended whites. In fact, one should say *two* classes, for two distinct styles are emerging. In the cooler areas, many blends are based on the Bordeaux-blessed marriage of Sauvignon Blanc and Sémillon, taking the classics of Graves as their model. This style was inaugurated here with a Vergelegen wine as recently as 2001, the second style a year later with Sadie Family Palladius. Their successors—and competitors—are now numerous. The second style emerged under the wide, warm skies of the Swartland and has at its core the old-vine Chenin Blanc of the region, with a diverse range of partners. (There's more Chenin in the Cape than in its Loire homeland, but it was long despised, or at best tolerated for its willing service.)

Of course, such wines are a tiny proportion of South African production and a tiny part of the rebirth of the country's wine industry, however appealing they may be as signs of achievement and possibility. For the larger picture, statistics of change can serve well (a synoptic table listing many of them appears in the appendix). The most remarkable index of international acceptance is the increase in wine exports over the period from 1993 to 2011, from nearly twenty-five million liters to well over four hundred million. In 2011, exports, having fallen a little over the previous few years in the adverse international financial climate, amounted to 43 percent of total wine production. (It was 6.2 percent in 1993!) That was perhaps just as well, considering that domestic per-capita consumption of South African wine is low and declining, at just seven liters annually. Getting the domestic black population to drink wine at all levels is a challenge the wine industry wants to meet—although it is being a trifle lackadaisical about it. Beer, including traditional African beer, has more than 60 percent of the market share of alcoholic beverages based on alcohol content; wine has little more than 15 percent, somewhat less than spirits.

The most significant political context of the rebirth of South African wine has been the reentry into the world market. (Repercussions of socioeconomic relations within the industry are discussed later in this chapter.) But an important enabling feature has been the unshackling of Cape wine from certain restrictions, which coincided precisely with a situation in which the industry could benefit from greater freedom. Chapter 2 will discuss the effect, through much of the twentieth century, of the all-powerful KWV, which began its life as a national producer cooperative, the Koöperatieve Wijnbouwers Vereniging, but rapidly acquired substantial statutory powers in managing the industry. In the context of the continuing deregulation of other parts of agriculture, which had already taken place before 1994, and faced with further governmental policy changes, the KWV from the early 1990s started to reconstruct itself as a more conventionally commercial force without national administrative duties or powers. For an organization like this, which had been so cozily intertwined with the apartheid government, the prospect of an African National Congress government was not encouraging.

When the KWV applied for permission to convert its legal status from a cooperative to a company, the government opposed the court application until the KWV agreed to make available, in a trust set up for various wine industry purposes, some 477 million rand (the notional value of the benefits to the KWV of its statutory functions). By the time permission was granted, in 1997, the KWV's abandonment of two of the most important parts of its rule had started having a major effect on the industry: the "quota system," which, in the name of preventing overproduction, had disallowed expansion into promising new winegrowing areas; and the guaranteed minimum price for wine, which had been part of a system that effectively encouraged production for quantity rather than quality.

It must be said that the KWV left behind it a system that manages well the bureaucratic needs of the wine industry, where control is unquestionably in the public interest. The appellation system that was introduced in the early 1970s, and its associated certification process, work efficiently under the Wine and Spirit Board, the control function contracted since 1999 to SAWIS (South African Wine Industry Information and Systems). Some of the funds wrested from the KWV went to research and generic promotion, and these are also generally well handled. And the industry flourished in the new regime of regulatory freedom, despite the lack of a continuing body to represent and strategically manage the industry. The South African Wine and Brandy Company was formed in 2002 to implement a strategic outline called Vision 2020. It lasted, without apparently achieving much, until 2006. Out of its "restructuring" emerged the South African Wine Industry Council, which was intended to deal with major wine-industry issues, from socioeconomic transformation to streamlining relations among the industry, government, and other relevant stakeholders. It, too, lasted only a few years before being abandoned. There is, at present, no pretense that any body is guiding, or even representing, the industry at the highest level.

THE WINE PRODUCERS

There's a lot more South African wine about these days than there was in 1993— approximately half as much again. Total production (along with total vineyard area) has only increased by not much more than 20 percent, but now less of what the vineyards yield is doomed to distillation or diversion to unfermented grape juice. The 2011 vintage produced a record 831 million liters of wine, which was about 80 percent of the total wine-grape crop—the remainder going for brandy, distillation, or juice.

More important is the basic quality, and one useful indication of improvement here is the amount that is certified. In South Africa, no wine may carry any information on its label about vintage, origin, or grape variety unless it has undergone a rigorous process of certification. This involves a good deal of record-keeping and paperwork, as all stages of production are monitored to see that the basic sums add up: if so many tons of Cabernet grapes were produced on a particular farm in a particular year, producing so many liters, the authorities will get very anxious if a different volume is bottled. For a wine to be certified it must also meet a minimum level of quality, as adjudged by official tasting panels. In 1993, just 12 percent of wine was thus certified, but the proportion rose steadily each year to about 57 percent in 2011—showing a major increase in ambition.

The classic tourist image of the South African wine farm is of the whitewashed homestead and sturdy outbuildings sheltered by oaks at the foot of purple mountains, with grape pickers bearing (no doubt cheerfully) their boxes of golden or purple fruit to the crusher. But as the tourists (also hopefully cheerful) make their harvesttime way around the wine lands, they will inevitably have to wait occasionally behind slow-moving trucks piled high with grapes, and might see them turn down a side road toward what looks like a small oil refinery or industrial plant. With any luck the trucks will not have to stand too long in line there, with the sun beating down on their fragile freight, awaiting their turn to deliver the crop to the crusher. By far the larger proportion of wine, both certified and uncertified (destined for the distillery), is made at such places—unromantic, perhaps, but immensely impressive, with their miles of coiling or rigid pipes, dials and switches, hardworking attendants, and rows of gleaming and enormous stainless steel tanks, some containing a million liters of wine.

Most of these are the country's cooperative wineries and the wineries that used to be cooperatives before converting to companies. There are still fifty-two of these "producer cellars," as they are officially known collectively. More and more cooperatives have been commercialized since the early 1990s, largely because of the demand for higher-quality wines. Older arrangements of paying for members' produce, with acceptance of everything guaranteed, are not feasible in today's tougher and more exacting market. The KWV is no longer there to take, in its turn, anything unsalable by the cooperative—the national minimum price arrangement, which guaranteed an income, was finally abandoned in 1995. Now the former co-ops are generally owned, as companies, by the farmers who supply them with grapes; the latter's income, however, now depends much more than before on such matters as grape variety and quality of fruit delivered to the crusher, because there is no longer an obligation to accept substandard or unmarketable material.

The producer cellars crush more than three-quarters of the entire wine-grape harvest—in 2011, 82 percent of the white grapes (some of which are grown specifically for brandy) and 72 percent of the red. Many of them have raised their game significantly, with increased attention to viticulture as well as to what happens in the cellar. A few of them now market single-vineyard and other prestige bottlings—more as a way of encouraging farmers to aim for quality and to build the general reputation of the winery, perhaps, than to maximize income. Generally they bottle and sell under their own label an increasing but still fairly small proportion of their own wine; the larger part is sold off to supplement the needs of private cellars or (most of it) in bulk to the wholesalers and exporters.

The wholesalers and specialist exporters—now including giants like Distell and the KWV—have a long and important history in South African wine. Before the rise of the private estates and of direct sales by the cooperatives, it was the wholesalers who were responsible for the overwhelming proportion of wines on the market, while the KWV had a virtual monopoly on exports. Wholesalers continue to market South Africa's biggest brands locally and internationally, though they no longer have things all their own way. There are also far more of them around than there were in the ultracentralized days before the revolution of the 1990s. There were fewer than half a dozen bulk buyers in the early 1990s; now there are more than a hundred, many of which buy wines solely for export under labels that South African wine-lovers would not recognize.

Many such merchants are fairly small, of course, and none is anywhere near as large as Distell, which accounts for up to a third of all South Africa's still and sparkling wine production. Distell was the result of a merger in 2000 of Stellenbosch Farmers' Winery and Distillers Corporation. They had, in fact, been united for some years as Cape Wines and Distillers until 1988, when government decreed their separation; in 2000 there was no opposition from the Competition Board to the merger. And in fact the improvement in some of the well-known brands offered by Distell has paralleled the country's general improvement, with labels like Nederburg and Fleur du Cap offering excellent quality at different levels. Distell does own some vineyards and crushes some of its own and bought-in grapes, as well as having some joint ventures with important estates; but the great majority of its wine, especially of what it produces for the middle and lower parts of the market, comes from the producing cellars. The wholesalers that crush at least some of their own grapes account for about 7 percent of the total harvest each year.

While the larger producers have increased their penetration of the fine wine market, the sort of wine that is the main concern of this book, which approaches the level of artisanal rather than industrial, comes mostly from the cellars of private producers. Their share of the total crush rose to 17 percent in 2011, but their numbers have grown even more substantially than their share of the crush, from 170 in 1993 to more than 500 by 2011. This is a total that will still seem surprisingly small, however, to someone who knows that the young wine industry of Washington state, for example, has many more wineries than this, despite a much smaller area under vine. The discrepancy is explained partly by the average price reached per bottle of wine and partly by the presence of many more wealthy people in and near Washington to buy the wine and—at a different level of wealth perhaps—to invest in wineries. It seems inevitable that the number of "lifestyle" farmers in the United States would be much greater than here—though certainly some of the new wineries and estates in the Cape have been established by wealthy outsiders willing to do what one of them, banker G.T. Ferreira of Tokara, self-deprecatingly described as seeking "return on ego" rather than "return on investment."

Furthermore, of course, the cooperative tradition in South Africa is a drag on the number of grape-crushing facilities. Although the number of grape farmers has declined in recent years, largely because of consolidation in tough economic times, there are more than 3,500 of them—many more than in Washington state. A minuscule proportion of these grape farmers has either converted entirely to producing their own wine or has started diverting some of their grapes—sometimes from their best vineyard blocks, separately farmed for quality rather than quantity—into bottles under their own labels. That would account for some of the rise in the number of private wineries. Many of these producers are small, though few are as tiny as Bein, which makes good Merlot off its 2 hectares of vines; and they range up from there. Koopmanskloof (in Stellenbosch, like Bein) has 520 hectares, while Willie Dreyer harvests more than 1,100 hectares of vines on his four farms in the Swartland and Voor-Paardeberg, most of the grapes going elsewhere for vinification.

THE CHANGING VINEYARD

A more important contribution to the development of South African wine since 1994 than grape farmers being tempted into making wine for their own labels has been the appearance of entirely new wineries. Many of them have planted vines on virgin land— occasionally in the traditional wine lands, but more in new areas that have opened up since the early 1990s. To taste the Berrio Sauvignon Blanc, grown amid the salty bluster of Agulhas, or a Crystallum Pinot Noir from Hemel-en-Aarde, and realize that they were simply not permissible before 1992 adds a bizarre note to the pleasure. That was the year that the KWV abandoned the quota system, freeing would-be winegrowers to spend their money as foolishly as they wished, driven by ambition to make fine wine.

This expansion has been one of the most exciting aspects of the history of South African wine in recent times. There has even been growth as far distant from Stellenbosch as the subtropical province of KwaZulu-Natal. But new vineyards have also usefully extended the range of such well-established areas as Constantia and Stellenbosch. On the other hand, much of the significant change to the vine landscape has come about, first, through better viticultural practices, and second, through replanting. Sometimes the same vineyard has been replanted with a more suitable variety or better combination of variety and rootstock; sometimes an estate has abandoned the vineyards in the rich alluvial soils of a warm valley floor and dragged the vines, as it were, up the lower slopes of the mountains to cooler sites where lower yields will come from the poorer soils. Virgil knew that vines love hillsides *(Bacchus amat colles)*, and would have nodded approval of the changing view from a good vantage point in Franschhoek, Stellenbosch, or Constantia—seeing those high verdant patches.

Because of the dramatic changes to South African wine, one might have expected more absolute growth than has in fact happened. Australia and Chile, for example, have enormous new plantings, while the net growth in the total wine-grape vineyard area of South Africa in the fifteen years since 1996 (from 95,721 to 100,568 hectares) has been minimal. Much of that 5,000 hectares is accounted for by vineyards intended for high-quality wine in the recently opened cooler areas. In terms of the total production of wine, South Africa ranks eighth in the world, recently overtaken by Chile. In the early 1990s South Africa's vineyard area and wine production were far ahead of Australia's (and, even more, Chile's). But Australia's international success was accompanied by great expansion of vineyard area and production: the latter rose by something like two-thirds in the decade and a half to 2011 (something now regretted by many, of course). Chile's production much more than doubled in the same period. Such spectacular growth did not happen in South Africa, for various reasons: a less overwhelming international success, less interest in investment by local or foreign forces, but also, significantly, the lack of irrigation potential, which means that South Africa is close to its limit of irrigable vineyard.

Faltering exports in a time of world economic sluggishness, together with depressed local demand, have even led recently to a reduction in the total vineyard hectarage. Since 2003 the number of hectares newly planted has been declining, and since 2006 it has been exceeded by the hectares uprooted or abandoned. The troubling aspect of this trend is its implication that vineyards are not being renewed as often as is generally thought desirable for the health of the industry: while carefully maintained older vines are frequently good news for high-quality production, an aging vineyard is not conducive to economically viable higher-yield production. Furthermore, there is every likelihood that in hard times for farmers, more and more vineyards are not being cared for as assiduously as they should be.

The expansion that has occurred over the past decades has brought continuous development of the pattern of official appellations. South Africa's Wine of Origin (WO) system, which covers origin in terms of vintage and cultivar as well as appellation, is the most established and elaborated of any wine-producing country outside Europe. It was initially promulgated into law in 1973 (details of its workings are given in chapter 4). Although the WO system does not stipulate such things as viticultural and cellar practices, it is becoming increasingly refined, through subdivision of larger appellations into smaller ones, based on identity of terroir (soil and mesoclimate particularly). This in turn is both an expression of and encouragement for a degree of specialization—at least marking an emerging association between particular areas and grape varieties or styles of wine: Elgin, Constantia, and Elim for Sauvignon Blanc, for example; Hemel-en-Aarde for Pinot Noir and Chardonnay; Stellenbosch for Cabernet Sauvignon; and the Swartland for Syrah and a particular approach to white blends. While this process is starting to happen and is likely to continue, the associations are as yet necessarily tentative and exploratory, and far from exclusive, let alone definitive. The dominant practice remains for wineries from large to small to produce a fairly wide range of wine, although this is also starting to change, as individual estates discover what their climates and soils do best and concentrate on that. But as many will claim, some climates and soil serve a diversity of cultivars, and the large ranges persist, though generally on a less extensive scale than in the 1980s.

If the total size of the South African vineyard did not change drastically in the first fifteen years of the new South Africa, that is not true of its nature, particularly in terms of varietal composition—precursor, of course, to changes in the wine being made. The most obvious shift has been from the overwhelming preponderance of white grapes: in 1993 white grapes occupied 81 percent of the total vineyard area, much of the harvest destined for distillation. International demand required more red wine than the Cape was producing, especially of the best-known varieties, and the pattern started changing rapidly. There was even something of an overcorrection. In 2005 the white grape percentage was down to 54.3, but it rose again, to 55.6 percent in 2011. Especially because a good deal of the white grape crop goes into brandy and comes from high-yielding vineyards, the proportion of white wine to red is higher than the proportion of the respective vineyard areas: white wine is now 62.4 percent of total production.

The prime grape victim in the great color shift was Chenin Blanc. At just over 18 percent it remains by far the most planted variety, down from about 33 percent in 1993 (its high point was five years previously). Patterns of change are discussed more fully in chapter 3, but it is worth noting here how planting patterns have responded to the demand of international markets for wines from the best-known varieties, especially red wine grapes. In terms of vineyard area Cabernet Sauvignon grew from 5.5 percent of the total in 1993 to 12 percent in 2011, Syrah from 1.0 percent to 10.3 percent, Merlot from 1.8 percent to 6.4 percent. Of the important white grapes, Sauvignon Blanc went up from 4.5 percent to 9.6 percent and Chardonnay from 3.2 percent to 8 percent.

As for managing these vineyards, viticulture has improved greatly in recent years. For one thing, there are now many more professional viticulturists than there were, although it must be said that they are unfortunately generally less appreciated than winemakers, are sent abroad less often to gather expertise, and are less well paid. Francois Viljoen, from the country's most important viticultural consultation service and one of the country's foremost viticulturists, points out that when he started work in 1986 there were some twenty-five trained viticulturists in the Cape; the number rose to probably more than forty by the turn of the century; today he estimates there are about eighty—not including those formally untrained but with great local and international experience. And the latter category is, in fact, vital at the most ambitious end of wine production, for it's certain that most of the Cape's best producers have a closer link between cellar and vineyard work than ever before. Nonetheless, the cult of the winemaker is as established a religion in South Africa as it is elsewhere in the New World. At wine competitions it is invariably the winemaker called up to receive the medal and then, usually, to mouth platitudes (which he—usually he—possibly even believes) about "wines being made in the vineyard." In fact, in many of the foremost wineries, and certainly the smaller ones, it is nowadays common for the cellarmaster and viticulturist to be one person: the traditional vigneron of Europe, in fact (and the traditional wine-farmer of South Africa too, for that matter, though now hopefully on a rather more convinced and convincing level).

So far, so good, but two important negative factors in South African winegrowing must also be mentioned. While the shift in the vineyard to superior varieties is an undoubted improvement, bringing South Africa more in line with its international competitors, the limited choice of clonal material and the limited availability of less mainstream but high-quality grapes are problems. It is one of many shortcomings that can be ascribed to poor leadership from the KWV in its days of overlordship. Through much of the twentieth century in South Africa not only was clonal material sought and developed with the aim of maximizing yield rather than quality, but there was little useful experimentation in finding varieties well suited to the Mediterranean climate of the Cape. The difficulty of obtaining good and sought-after vines was made particularly clear in the 1970s and 1980s, when ambitious producers felt obliged to resort to illegal smuggling in response to a lack of suitable available material and to long bureaucratic delays in bringing vines though quarantine. Chardonnay was the variety most famously involved, and there was even a governmental commission of inquiry into the matter.

Systems were subsequently streamlined, but leadership, at least, remained lacking, and a number of varieties that should be available—from similar climates in Italy and Portugal above all—are not. This remains a big problem in taking development forward. Diversity within the vineyards is sorely lacking: the five most planted varieties occupy more than 60 percent of the vineyard area, the ten most planted occupy more than 85 percent. Most producers with ambitions to produce high-quality wines limit themselves to the same "big five" that the rest of the world also dutifully worships (and of course the market demanding what amounts to brand names is a real problem): Cabernet Sauvignon, Syrah, Merlot, Chardonnay, Sauvignon Blanc. Chenin Blanc and Pinotage are the most significant local additions to this depressingly small list. (See chapter 3 for further considerations on varieties and varietalism.)

Somewhat ironically, the marketing body Wines of South Africa (WOSA) uses "Diversity is in our nature" as a central slogan in its international campaigns. This diversity refers, of course, not to imported vines but above all to the Cape floral kingdom, the world's smallest and incomparably richest: the Cape botanical region has 1,385 species per ten thousand square kilometers (the standard measure), while the second highest figure is 340, for the Neotropic floral kingdom (the Americas from the southern parts of North America southward). Generally difficult growing conditions and a wide range of topographical and climatological factors give rise to this diversity, and since this is where most of the wine lands are situated, WOSA not unreasonably encourages a perceived alignment between the natural beauty and biodiversity of the wine lands and the image of South African wine. The link has been made more profound since 2004 through the Biodiversity and Wine Initiative, a partnership between the wine industry and important environmental bodies that encourages wine farmers to set aside land for encouraging natural flora, in a situation where invasive plant species as well as agriculture and urban creep have severely compromised the natural environment. The program seems successful, with 174 members formally conserving more than 130,000 hectares of land by 2012. One of the largest (and richest) participants, Vergelegen, in 2004 began an ambitious ten-year program to clear alien vegetation from 2,000 hectares of its land and restore the natural flora and fauna to a pristine state; leopards and honey badgers are among the more spectacular creatures caught on Vergelegen's infrared camera installations these days. But a rare plant or bird secure in a hectare of wetland whose preservation in pristine condition the program has encouraged is as heartening.

Another expression of concern for the environment in the Cape wine industry has been the continuing and developing success of the voluntary Integrated Production of Wine scheme since 1988. Certification according to established international wine industry environmental sustainability criteria is carried out by an office responsible to the Wine and Spirit Board, which evaluates and audits members' practices in vineyards and cellars. A seal for the bottles of qualifying members was introduced for the 2010 harvest year.

At least as significant a problem as the lack of varietal diversity in the Cape and the lack of investigation into the most suitable varieties for its conditions is the continuing wide-spread presence of leafroll virus. A major dereliction of the KWV's duty as industry leader in the twentieth century was its lack of assiduity (to put it generously) in attempting to solve the problem. To the casual wine-lands visitor in late summer the problem, in fact, looks nothing other than charming, as it spreads the loveliness of autumn coloring across the landscape. But unfortunately the color change is spreading rather earlier than the season warrants: virus-affected vines will not ripen fruit as well as clean vines with green chlorophyll surging in their leaves. While a little retarding influence on ripening can in some vintages be a useful thing (while infection levels are low), the wine made from heav-ily affected vines is not immune from unattractive associated flavors—stewed rhubarb, perhaps! The useful life of infected vines is much more limited, too—farmers are lucky if they will produce commercially viable crops until they are twenty years old, which would give them only twelve to fifteen years of good-quality harvests. Frequent replanting adds greatly to the expense of grape farming; it also denies the possibility of making wine from old vines, which are often associated with concentrated and finer flavors.

The problem is a large and complex one, but recently there has been significant prog-ress in developing techniques to eliminate the virus and to at least ensure that virus-free material (both rootstocks and vines of the desired variety) can be supplied for planting. After that, it is up to the farmer to control the almost inevitable reinfection (which is spread mostly through the agency of the mealybug). Prevention of leafroll virus is some-thing that requires determination, dedication, and hard work in South Africa, and is only now becoming widespread. Few vineyards can genuinely be claimed as "virus-free" (though heavy infection is greatly reduced)—and only vineyards subjected to continual scrutiny, careful preventive measures, and ruthless replacement of any infected vine are likely to remain so.

THE SOCIAL LANDSCAPE

Understandably, considering South African history, the social structure of the wine industry here is more closely scrutinized than in most parts of the world. And if slavery cast a long shadow over the wine industry after its abolition in 1834, so too has apartheid after the arrival of formal democracy in 1994. Most laborers, but precious few people at more exalted levels, in the wine cellars and vineyards of the reborn industry were and remain, in the fine racial distinctions that South Africa developed, "coloreds"—that is, of mixed race, mingling in themselves much of the industry's human history. For wine industry workers (as for all engaged in agricultural labor), there was little protection from the apartheid-capitalist state. Wages were generally very low and housing poor. Accom-modations were mostly on the farms; employees and their families were doubly depen-dent on the farmer.

The tot system (alcohol given to workers partly in lieu of wages, partly as a tactic of social control) goes back to the early days of slavery, and not everyone is convinced that it has disappeared even now—certainly it lasted long after it was legally abolished in 1962. Unquestionably its legacy does live on in the wine lands, in the endemic alcoholism that causes untold misery, and in the widespread fetal alcohol syndrome that blights so many lives. The wine industry is largely responsible for this legacy and has never adequately taken up the challenge of trying to address it—although, of course, it is a problem inextricably bound up with larger structures of poverty and degradation and requires a broad social solution, something much more thoroughgoing than moralizing, charitable patches, or simplistic attempts to medicalize the issue.

John Platter mused wryly on some of the social ironies of the wine industry in the new South Africa, in an "assessment of prospects in a sanctions-free world" in his 1996 *Guide:*

> For connoisseurs of such things, the piquancy of how the new black government saved the white owned wine farming industry from growing insolvency is exquisite. It took a virtual teetotaling President Nelson Mandela—and an ANC-led government with a largely non-wine drinking, beer-thirsty African constituency—to bale out wine growers, mainly Afrikaner, mainly Nationalist Party voters who supported the 27-year incarceration of the man who opened the door to a sanctions-free, export-led recovery. No signs, of course, of discomfiture among the rescued—politesse deems it uncivil to even mention it.

The issue of "transformation" (a concept immediately understood by all South Africans to have racial connotations) is complex and sensitive, and it is impossible to do more here than highlight selected points within the complexities. But it is hard to avoid the conclusion that in most aspects of social relations, the wine industry is less transformed than many other sectors of South African society, despite some specific pockets of change and some broader areas of improvement. This is true at all levels, from the question of who owns land to the situation of the often unmotivated, inadequately trained people working on it.

In the absence of a radical national land agenda and because of the high value of most vineyard land and the high cost of working it, it is unsurprising that there has been virtually nothing in the way of land redistribution to alter the pattern of white ownership. A few ultrarich black individuals or black-involvement consortiums have acquired direct interest in or ownership of wineries: left-wing-politician-turned-capitalist Tokyo Sexwale, for example, some years back bought a wine farm in Franschhoek (though nothing has been heard of it or its wines since then); and a consortium he leads bought half of Constantia Uitsig. Somewhat less rich (as most people are, of course), former cabinet minister Valli Moosa now produces the Ecology range off his Bot River property, Paardenkloof; and members of the more modest Rangaka family have a vineyard in Stellenbosch and a brand, M'hudi, with the wines made at Villiera Estate.

Of rather more relevance to broader transformation, some significant "land and brand" projects have been undertaken. These are generally joint ventures between farmers and their workers, with the latter acquiring in various ways (government-sponsored or farmer-facilitated) part ownership of land and winery businesses, usually indirectly through shares or trust units. Examples of such partnerships include Thandi (vineyard ownership, with the brand part-owned by the large Company of Wine People), Tukulu (a joint venture among Distell, black entrepreneurs, and a workers' trust), Thokozani (a brand with a 30 percent shareholding in Diemersfontein), and Solms-Delta (a passionate individual project of restitution).

Black ownership or part ownership of wine brands (without vineyard or winery), with wine sourced from established producers, is rather more common. Ses'Fikile, for example, was funded by Flagstone Winery (now part of the massive international Accolade, formerly Constellation Wines); its name, incidentally, means "we have arrived in style"! Yamme is a brand owned by a consortium of black women, as is Women in Wine. There are perhaps more than a dozen black-owned brands, aligned through the Black Vintners Association, which was founded in 2005.

This brings us closer to what has become the real focus of transformation in the wine industry: the Black Economic Empowerment (BEE) program, which has evolved to mean little more than equity ownership by black shareholders (whether capitalists or workers) in wine businesses of all sizes. A process toward drawing up some sort of charter for the industry was under way in the late 2000s. Drafts indicated that access to land would be a minor component of the charter, but any redistribution of such substantial assets was not in question. Also largely absent were matters affecting the majority of black people in the industry, such as working and living conditions.

Even without the existence of a formal charter, many large wineries and companies have already embarked on BEE deals, generally involving both employees, via a trust, and, proportionately more important, black investment companies. A highly controversial deal gave a black shareholder consortium 25.1 percent of the KWV—no doubt a pleasant symbol of the new South Africa, considering the deep implication of the KWV in its previous incarnation in the old South Africa. The controversy largely involved the role of the South African Wine Industry Trust (SAWIT), which was a body charged with, among other things, facilitating social transformation in the industry. SAWIT handed over its fund to a group of black entrepreneurs and others in order for them to buy the KWV stake. The money had originally come from the KWV, as the price it paid for being allowed to convert into a company, so there are some nice ironies here too: the KWV, in the end, in this way simply funded its own claims to political respectability through its acquisition of such a fine BEE component. As a result of becoming technically insolvent, SAWIT was no longer able to do much (it had never done much, in fact) in the way of wider empowerment of the poor and powerless within the industry. Meanwhile, the BEE package put together by Distell, while rather more "politically correct," also involved a shareholding deal with outside investors as well as its own employees.

SAWIT had failed from the start to develop the skills of farmworkers and generally somehow "empower" them as it was supposed to. Other wine industry initiatives now tend to focus their transformation efforts less on need than on simple notions of "blackness" through BEE. This is a much more comfortable and easy process than grappling with the real problems faced by the majority of those involved in the industry—permanent workers and the temporary grape-pickers of harvesttime. But in some ways at least, the situation of all agricultural workers improved after a democratically elected government came to power after 1994. Notably, for the first time such workers were included in developing basic legal provisions to protect employees (health, insurance, work hours, leave, etc.), and a mandatory minimum wage (a very modest one) was promulgated. Of course, there are a number of relatively progressive farmers and businesses whose employment practices exceed basic legal requirements, but there are undoubtedly a number of others that fall short of meeting them. The Wine and Agricultural Ethical Trade Association (known as WIETA), which has various categories of membership, conducts audits prior to full accreditation, and this experience has shown just how little it can be assumed that national employment legislation is always complied with. Furthermore, as yet only a small proportion of wineries undergo WIETA's audits—although this should change when the new "ethical seal" initiative, described below, is launched.

In the wine industry as a whole it is also clear, however, that some of the more positive aspects of rural paternalism are breaking down (partly in response to protective legislation, ironically): providing housing to workers on farms, for example, is becoming less common. So too is permanent employment—casualization of labor is increasing, as well as the use of labor brokers, some of whom are responding usefully to the seasonal nature of vineyard work, but others are simply making exploitation of workers more efficient by sparing farmers the trouble of grappling with the consequences of employing people. There is little effective trade unionism in the wine lands; organizing farmworkers is notoriously difficult.

Something of a breakthrough, perhaps, came in 2012, as a direct consequence of the previous year's scathing report into the fruit and wine industries of the Western Cape by the respected international monitor Human Rights Watch. That report concluded (confirming what many knew, of course) that there remained significant human-rights problems for cellar and vineyard workers in the wine industry. It particularly blamed the state for not adequately monitoring its own laws and regulations. The anecdotal nature of much of the report's evidence and other methodological inadequacies were arguably insufficient to support the generalizations it made and made it vulnerable to defensive attack. If there were real problems, it was a question of bad apples in the barrel, ran a common countering line.

A more thoughtful, positive response than the industry's outrage came in early 2012 with the announcement of a new "ethical seal" that wineries complying with certain criteria can affix to their bottles. The scheme is being implemented under the aegis of WIETA, which announced that the purpose of the seal is "to acknowledge and accredit wineries and farms that follow ethical practices and to protect them from any potential negative publicity resulting from those who flout the law." Already some major importers—notably Systembolaget in Sweden, but even supermarkets in the United Kingdom and elsewhere—had long been making demands that producers provide some proof that the conditions of workers met basic international standards. Fairtrade Foundation accreditation had been the most important indicator of this, but the new initiative should make adequate accreditation cheaper and easier. Most of the big players in the industry supported it, as did a number of nongovernmental organizations active in the area as well as the leading farmworker trade union. There seems reason to hope that the "ethical seal" will effect some improvement in worker conditions where it is needed.

PAST, PRESENT, FUTURE

The shadows—above all, perhaps, the racially informed inequality, but also problems like still-rampant virus—dim the brightness of the new world of South African wine, but do not obscure it. With a bit of perspective gained, it has now become possible to see and understand the developments that have taken place, and also to be not so overwhelmed by the brightness as to be unaware of the challenges. The context of South African society is indeed one of them, as is the international wine market and its demands. And there are other problems and opportunities that are local, even if they are not all entirely unique to here.

The history of South African wine is a long one by new-world standards—more than 350 years—and it contains within it the story of a great wine, Constantia, which remains something of an inspiration to modern South African winemakers, not least as an affirmation that high quality is possible at the foot of Africa. This does not exactly qualify as a wider tradition of greatness, however, and in fact the tradition of the Cape vineyards and wine business is above all one of poor-quality wine, heavily dependent on exports to a metropolitan market and always tending to overproduction—and overproduction of mediocrity. Without a great tradition, the task of building a great wine industry is daunting.

All the more remarkable, then, after so many years of mediocrity, was the rapidity of improvement at all levels since 1994. The change has largely been credited to the demands of a newly interested international market and the willingness and ability of South African wine-producers to respond, but that ability and willingness bear a little interrogation.

The ability is to a great extent the actual winegrowing potential of the land and the climate. This is the fundamental aspect that we sometimes vaguely call the terroir—the infrastructure, as it were, of viticulture, which interpenetrates with the human beings without whom terroir has no meaning beyond *abstract* potential. A useful sign of the potential is when "style" changes and quality remains. There are, for example, undoubtedly people who think that many Rustenberg Cabernet Sauvignons of that generally dull decade for the Cape, the 1980s, were (and even remain) very fine wines. Regardless of whether they are finer than the bigger, bolder, riper Rustenberg Peter Barlow Cabernet Sauvignons of two decades later, few who have drunk both would deny that both styles reveal a soil and a mesoclimate capable of producing good wine.

There seems to be something meaningful in the idea alluded to earlier, that the Cape is somehow naturally poised between (to employ reductive generalizations) the restraint and finesse of classic Europe and the powerful, fruit-driven exuberance of the New World. To an extent, as suggested earlier, it is a matter of winemaking traditions, but these traditions seem prompted by climate and soil. The assertive, sometimes flamboyant fruit that is found in California and Argentina, for example, is not easily found here, but nor is the equally forceful restraint (if that is not too much of an oxymoron) of France, while modesty in its best sense seems to come more easily here than it does in Australia—although, again, one needs to look beneath winemaking. A quality that many critics have noticed in many modern South African wines that are not pushed to excessive ripeness, especially whites, is a genuine freshness—and minerality for those who'll countenance that description—connected to acid balance. This question of acid structure is particularly noteworthy, as it can point to the need to explore ways to understand and articulate a winegrowing potential. In the 1980s the academic insistence on understanding wine through analysis meant that virtually all local wines were routinely acidified—always to the point of technical safety and often to the point of hardness and imbalance. It was a given thing that the Cape's acidic soils meant that the wines they produced were correspondingly lacking in acidity. But improved viticulture as well as more sensitive winemaking, the latter often achieved partly through the experience of working in Europe, means that now many of the Cape's best wines go unacidified, and their natural balance—with a fine acidity—is all the better for it. This acid structure is one reason that white wines, where tannin is less of a vital component and acidity is more structurally exposed than in reds, are widely considered (by me for one) to be the stronger category in South Africa.

So much for inherent potential. The willingness of winemakers to learn to respond with new understanding—not just those who were young in 1994, but also many who had been making wine for twenty years or more—was much more than a technical response to a marketing challenge. It was part of, enlivened and encouraged by, a changing culture marked by huge social dynamism, which in certain ways carried along with it even the largely conservative individuals of the Cape winemaking establishment.

The larger bodies in which that conservatism found its most relevant wine-industry expression did, in fact, take longer to respond. The KWV was obliged to do so rapidly in terms of renouncing its dictatorial powers, but it took some fifteen years for it to show real signs of cultural and winemaking modernization in the best sense of that vague idea. Distell, the enormous wholesaler, which often still seems too monopolistically large for South Africa's winemaking and wine-drinking good, changed more quickly, and started making better use of the range of vineyards at its disposal.

Nonetheless, it is to a few large private estates with uncompromising devotion to quality and, perhaps especially, to the small growers that one must inevitably look for innovation and real excitement at the highest levels of ambition. There are young—some very young—winemakers in areas like the Swartland who are trying radical experiments: a few fascinating barrels of old-vine Chenin Blanc fermented on its skins, or wines from rather despised grapes like Cinsaut and Carignan, picked unfashionably early, light-colored, and lacking massive concentration—and nevertheless rather profound and undoubtedly making for satisfying, pleasurable drinking. First-rate and fascinating wines have been made from old vineyards whose small yields had previously been lost in the massive anonymous vats of a cooperative. This is a trend of great significance, in indicating both an interest in the past and, even more, further recognition of the primacy of vineyard over cellar in producing fine quality. One of the Cape's youngest wineries, Alheit Vineyards, declares its aim as being "to vinify extraordinary Cape vineyards," and Chris and Suzaan Alheit have sought out old vines around the wine lands: "We love these old blocks not only because of their undeniable quality, but because they represent our heritage."

So there is still fresh excitement in South African wine. It became apparent maybe fifteen years after the first important developments initiated in the early 1990s that a second, renewed qualitative shift had been taking place since the early 2000s. If the first phase of the vinous revolution basically involved catching up with accepted international standards and practices of growing and vinifying grapes, the second was predicated on responding to larger aspects of the Cape wine landscape: taking advantage of the new areas opened up to viticulture by the abandonment of the KWV quota system (Elim, Elgin, Cape Point, etc.) and reinventing and reinvigorating some of the old areas (Tulbagh, Swartland); making a useful start with the matching of terroir and grape variety; and forging styles of wine that accorded with what was offered by the (different) areas. A third phase of the revolution is now under way. One sign of it is the "discovery" of many scores of those old vineyards, because essentially this latest phase involves a crucial turn to detail—not in the winery, but among the vines. There are more professional viticulturists in the country than ever before, but of greater significance for the finest wines is the international experience brought to bear on local traditions of what we can no longer call straightforward winemakers—they are winegrowers, or vignerons, in the European tradition, uniting the processes of growing grapes and vinifying them, always with the emphasis on the former. An analysis of the real elite of Cape wine producers would show that the majority of them demonstrate this continuity between cellar and vineyard, often with the same person responsible for managing both.

Chris Alheit is "dead certain that the golden age of Cape wine is ahead of us." Thanks, he suggests, to the pioneering work of figures like Eben Sadie and viticulturist Rosa Kruger (the woman responsible for tirelessly seeking out and "rescuing" so many old vineyards), "the Cape has never been so loaded with promise." Another of the younger generation of winemakers remarked to me recently: "We have prepared the soil of the future, and we have made the roadway to it. Now, just the same as with democracy in this country, we still have to move forward to get somewhere really good."

2

A BRIEF HISTORY OF SOUTH
AFRICAN WINE TO 1994

BIRTH AND MATURING OF THE INDUSTRY: 1652–1795

The origins of winegrowing in South Africa can be fixed with unusual accuracy. A crucial moment was recorded on 2 February 1659 in the logbook of Jan van Riebeeck, commander of the tiny settlement at the foot of Africa. It was nearly seven years since he and his expeditionary force of some ninety men had gone ashore at Table Bay, intent on establishing a revictualing station. The Cape of Good Hope had been known to Europeans since Bartholomew Diaz had rounded it in 1488, but circumstances in international trade suggested its usefulness to the Vereenigde Oost-Indische Compagnie (Dutch East India Company).

"Today," wrote van Riebeeck, "God be praised, wine was pressed for the first time from Cape grapes . . . mostly Muscadel and other white, round grapes, very fragrant and tasty. . . . These grapes, from three young vines planted two years ago, have yielded about 12 quarts of must, and we shall soon discover how it will be affected by maturing." Wine production was probably not originally envisaged among the "needful refreshments" to be provided by the station, but van Riebeeck's early enthusiasm about this potential addition to the company's garden, in what is now the heart of Cape Town, made sense to the practical minds of the ruling Lords Seventeen in Amsterdam. Wine not only keeps better than water but could also help prevent scurvy among sailors making the long voyage between Europe and the company's possessions in the East Indies. Moreover, if production could supply even just the needs of the European residents at the Cape, that would help reduce the "overwhelming expenditure" that the administrators back home were to continually abhor.

At any rate, van Riebeeck eventually got his grapes. The first rooted vines seem to have arrived rotten in 1654, but at least some of a subsequent shipment were successfully planted, and other cuttings followed. The commander also asked Amsterdam for wine-making equipment and information. Before leaving in 1662 he had learned not only something about winemaking but also some of the natural forces against which viticultur-ists must contend: in that year the crop was virtually destroyed by a plague of birds. Incidentally, it later became clear that one means the settlers used to evade this particular problem was to pick the grapes before they were ripe enough to please the birds, with depressing effects on the wine made from them.

By the time van Riebeeck left, the principal vine plantings were no longer in the original company garden. An initial farm on flat coastal land nearby was too battered by wind, and in winter the lake overflowed and drowned the vines. The settlers established a new substantial farm farther down the peninsula and allotted an area to vines. The commander clearly had leanings that would have appealed to biodynamic viticulturists three centuries later: he recorded in August 1658 that he, "with the aid of certain free burghers and some slaves, took the opportunity as the moon waned of planting a large part of Bosheuvel with young rooted vines and cuttings."

That is a significant account for other reasons than its reference to lunar influences, however, with its allusions to the labor of free burghers and slaves—the forces by which the wine industry was established. The free burghers were former Dutch East India Company servants granted land, along with rations and tools to be later paid for in wheat, in an attempt to stimulate agriculture and reduce expenditure. Initially, private farming was little concerned with wine—meat and grain were the pressing needs of the company—but Bosheuvel was soon bought by a free burgher and became as viticulturally significant as Rustenberg, the company farm at Rondebosch. Soon more free burghers were developing small vineyards; by 1686 production of some 80 leaguers was recorded as originating from them, compared with a quarter as much from Rustenberg. (The leaguer was 152 Dutch gallons, equal to nearly 127 Imperial gallons; about 577 liters.)

Although colonization was not the company's original intention, the Dutch (and many German) free burghers were already providing the basis for the later colonial conquest of the land, and settlement on the grazing and hunting grounds of the Khoisan provoked a first war (1658–1660). The Khoikhoi ("Hottentots" to the Dutch), according to the now customary analytical division of the indigenous people of these parts, were herders of cattle and sheep; the San ("Bushmen") were hunters, with no herds. The boundaries between the two groups were flexible and complex, however, and the academic portman-teau word *Khoisan* reflects this.

The settlement was expanding physically, as the free white population grew and the company, always driven by the logic of its account books and now also partly by concern that the warring English might try to capture the Cape, transferred more agricultural production to private farmers. It was looking increasingly like a nascent colony more than a mere victualing station. To supply the farmers with labor, more slaves were imported, from the East or from elsewhere in Africa. The local people were not enslaved but did increasingly get pressed into service as their land was appropriated and their traditional ways of life became impossible, and any resistance was crushed. In the year the first wine was pressed, there were already 187 slaves—outnumbering the total of soldiers, company officials, and burghers—and their numbers would grow until the end to the sorry business in 1834.

Resistance from the indigenous people delayed expansion into the hinterland, but the need for more grain and meat was imperative. After a period of apparently lackluster leadership in the Cape, the commander who arrived in 1679 accomplished more, and was to have great influence on the development of the Cape's wine industry. Within weeks of his arrival, Simon van der Stel (he subsequently became the Cape's first governor) had initiated a settlement in the valley on the other side of the dreary, sandy Cape Flats, and thirty families were living in the Stellenbosch area by 1683. Another settlement was founded at De Paarl on the banks of the Berg River in 1687. Soon agriculture outside the Cape, as the area roughly comprising the Cape Peninsula was generally called, provided the larger part of production, including of wine. Plantings of vines increased rapidly, to a million and a quarter before the end of the century—too many altogether, thought van der Stel: "On account of the vine flourishing here so well, many persons are inclined to neglect other farming and to plant large vineyards."

A notable addition to the farming community came during the few years after 1688, in the form of Huguenots who fled French Catholic persecution and were offered assistance as emigrants by the Dutch East India Company. Only about two hundred ventured so far south. They constituted about an eighth of the colony's white population and have left an enduring social legacy in the Afrikaner population, but their contribution to wine culture has often been overrated. While some had worked as vineyard laborers, there is no evidence that more than (at best) a few had the winemaking skills that van der Stel had hoped for. Most of them were settled, interspersed among the Dutch, in the inland Drakenstein area: they named the upper end of the Drakenstein valley Le Quartier Français, the French Quarter, but within a generation the name changed to Fransche Hoek (now Franschhoek), reflecting the settlers' rapid absorption into the dominant culture. As their recent historian Eric Bolsmann notes drily, despite many romantic claims and assumptions about their role in the development of a winemaking culture, "details of their specific contributions are conspicuously lacking."

While keeping in mind that the objective for the settlement at the Cape was not to build a major wine industry, the governor took account of the growing significance of wine to the little society and its economy. He encouraged the use of new varieties, and perhaps introduced the Pontac and Muscat de Frontignan that were going to be important in his personal adventure in wine; he imposed some controls over sales (again, the company's interests, needs, and revenues were paramount); and he attempted to improve quality. He had long found local wine to be "exceptionally harsh," and was aware that slovenly and ignorant practices in vineyard and cellar were to blame. He tried to do something about the problem of lack of ripeness at harvest; a committee was established to visit wineries and ascertain that the grapes were adequately ripe before they were pressed.

Early exports had already foundered because of poor quality. The first tiny export seems to have been to Batavia in 1679, and some samples also braved the journey back to Amsterdam, where the Lords Seventeen found it "not bad," but expensive in comparison with Canary and Spanish wine. But there were complaints from Holland and Batavia, and in 1688 the Cape was told firmly not to send any more. If exports were not going to supply the company with income, however, sales at home were starting to do so, through licenses, taxes, and excise duties. English buccaneer and author William Dampier was pleased to find in the 1690s, "The country is of late so well stocked with Vineyards that they make abundance of Wine of which they have enough and to spare, and do sell great quantities to Ships that touch here." The no doubt more respectable Reverend J. Ovington noted in 1696 that an "exorbitant Fine upon the Tavern and Tipling Houses makes them exact extravagant Rates from the Guests that drink the Liquor."

Van der Stel's most significant contribution to winegrowing was the tradition of excellence he established at the large estate he was granted, called Constantia. Even today the past of Constantia is important to the present, something that the industry as a whole can invoke with pride—and relief, for without Constantia, the older history of South African wine would be a much more depressing story. The land there was transformed into a flourishing farm through its owner's "salutary zeal" and, one must presume, even more so through the zeal of his many slaves; farm buildings, slave quarters, and a house were built; the vineyard was larger and more carefully planted and tended than any other in the Cape at the time. By 1700, the year after he retired to live at Constantia, further additions and grants had given him a virtual empire in the Cape Peninsula, where he farmed wheat and cattle on a large scale, as well as vines. The "Governor's wine," made in the sweet, liquorous style then most in demand, soon established a reputation for excellence in the Cape and even beyond, first in Batavia (where it was found that "the wine from Constantia is of a much higher quality than any sent out so far") and Holland, and then farther afield. Numerous accounts survive of more or less distinguished visitors to the Cape, who frequently called in at the principal estates. French traveler François Valentijn visited first in 1705, and gave "principal praise and honour" to van der Stel and his son (at Vergelegen) "since, although before their times there were already vines here, and wine had already been pressed, it is certain that the old Heer van der Stel brought to his outstanding country estate many sorts of vine stocks from Germany and elsewhere, previously unknown here; also that until now there is no wine to be compared to the red Constantia wine."

This is perhaps the place to note that in fact, up through the nineteenth century, it is impossible to be sure what varieties were grown. Bewildering numbers of names are mentioned by travelers—mostly carrying little conviction to modern readers, on account of some strange names and stranger associations (Pontac as "the great grape of Côte-Rôtie," for example), and there is little more than frustration to be had from learning that Vergelegen at the end of the seventeenth century had "Russelaar, Pottebakker, and a

Persian long white variety, as well as varieties from Avignon, Champagne and Burgundy."
We can be sure, however, in that the first century of Cape viticulture, more or less
important contributions were made by Greengrape (Sémillon), White French (Palomino),
Steen (Chenin Blanc), a few Muscats, and Pontac (a grape of the teinturier type). In fact
it does seem that white grapes have dominated the Cape vineyard, with little real competition until the twentieth century brought demand for more red wines on the local market.

Simon van der Stel died in 1712. The outlying properties reverted to the Dutch East
India Company, and Constantia itself was divided into three portions and auctioned off.
The tradition of Constantia wine was continued and developed particularly on the portions
known as Groot Constantia ("large Constantia," the home farm, with the estate buildings)
and Klein Constantia ("little Constantia"—but not the same as the present estate of that
name). It was Johannes Colijn, into whose hands Klein Constantia soon passed, who
established the large export market for Constantia, to such an extent that in the 1730s
demand had outstripped supply. Fortunately, Groot Constantia, after a period in which
its potential had been somewhat neglected, acquired a new owner, and a long and profitable partnership arrangement between the two properties was initiated. It continued
through some ownership changes—during which it seems the quality of the wine fell off
somewhat—until Hendrik Cloete acquired Groot Constantia in 1776 and inaugurated a
renewed and perhaps heightened period of excellence in the wine of Constantia, soon
coinciding with the new marketing possibilities that were to emerge with the passing of
the Cape into British control.

Simon van der Stel had been succeeded as governor in 1699 by his eldest son, Willem
Adriaan, who confused more culpably than his father the distinction between serving his
private interests and performing his duties. In the history of South African wine he is
remembered now as the founder of another great estate, Vergelegen, acquired almost as
soon as he took office. As Louis Leipoldt, in his *300 Years of Cape Wine*, notes, "no expense,
either on his or the Company's part, was spared to make it a most imposing undertaking."
As well as establishing fruit orchards and cattle and sheep stations, and having a mansion
built that reportedly required the services of very many of the company's slaves in its
construction, he also planted substantial vineyards. Despite this, there is no account
of the wines being comparable to Constantia's. There was, in fact, little time for the
vines and wines to reach their potential. An arrogant—not to say illegal, torturous, and
brutal—confrontation with some of the wealthier burghers, who objected to Willem
Adriaan's attempts to monopolize for his own profit various parts of trade including
the export of wine, led to his downfall. In 1707 he was exiled, and soon thereafter the
splendid estate was broken up.

Meanwhile, the colony expanded ever-farther outward from Cape Town, as farmers
sought new grazing lands not exhausted by their cattle and new sources of cheap meat
once they had shot the wild animals with which the plains had teemed on their arrival.
The settlement was growing—largely through natural increase, as the company thought
that economic circumstances precluded absorbing more white immigrants as some had
proposed (the alternative, considering labor needs, was to bring in more slaves, which is

what was done). But expansion in the eighteenth century had little effect on wine production: wine lands that would become economically viable once roads and railways were built were still impossible to develop. The only way a farmer could take his barrels of wine to sell in Cape Town was expensively and laboriously by ox-drawn wagon, which meant that wine was produced only within a few days' journey of the market. Transportation even for those farmers was a problem; a new hard road across the sandy Cape Flats reached Klapmuts near Paarl only around the middle of the nineteenth century, when it almost halved the transport costs of farmers in that region.

In 1752 a Swedish traveler, Anders Sparrman, noted that after leaving the areas of Stellenbosch and Drakenstein the only vineyard he found was one for domestic use at Swellendam. In those two areas and in the peninsula, however, production and planting grew steadily during the eighteenth century. It much more than doubled between 1700 and 1750, by which date nearly four million vines were producing about 3,000 leaguers of wine. By 1794 these figures had increased by about 150 percent; Drakenstein (the larger Paarl area today) was responsible for more than half of production, followed by Stellenbosch; the "Cape" contributed less than a tenth.

Who bought and drank this wine? Export possibilities remained limited, largely for reasons of poor quality—apart from the growing interest in Constantia. The company generally kept a monopoly on trade. At home it wanted wine for its hospital, slaves, local company officials, and use on company ships, as well as for the East Indies. Through the first half of the eighteenth century particularly, as both production and demand continually shifted—before settling into the dominant pattern of overproduction—the company sometimes tried to find external markets for wine; and sometimes it disallowed private sales to ships when its own needs met supply. In 1793 the company bought about 13 percent of the total production. The rest would have been sold on the local market, and to visiting ships when possible.

FROM 1795 TO 1910

In the internationally war- and revolution-ravaged decades around the close of the 1700s the little outpost of Europe at the foot of Africa changed hands three times, with great implications for it—and its wine industry. As the vines were coming into leaf in 1795, Dutch East India Company rule was ended by the first British occupation. This was maintained until 1803, but the subsequent period of Netherlandish rule lasted only until the British occupation of 1806, which led to the cession of the Cape Colony to Britain in 1814.

War, and specifically the change of regime, was good for the wine trade here: commercial and naval shipping traffic and the British garrison presence prompted a substantial increase in plantings and production. The population also exploded about this time. The Khoisan were not counted, but the number of Europeans rose from 7,736 in 1770 to more than 20,000 by the end of the century and more than double that by 1820; the slave population rose from 8,200 to nearly 32,000 in that total period. That figure inevitably includes a lot of wine drinkers, even apart from the Khoisan (laborers and slaves were given rations of wine, largely as part of a system of social control, in a precursor to the notorious tot system).

Just under ten million vines were recorded for 1795, and the number more than doubled over the next decade, particularly in the Stellenbosch and Paarl-Drakenstein areas. Many of the grander rural examples of Cape Dutch architecture—those lovely whitewashed and elaborately gabled buildings—date from this time of prosperity for the larger and more successful farmers.

The economic health of Britain's new colony as a whole was not robust, however. The colonial masters sought a viable export commodity in order to generate local revenue and address the chronic trade deficit. They decided to foster the Cape wine industry even though there was already awareness of problems of quality: apart from what they tasted themselves, they knew that other export markets had been lost when Cape wines had been rejected. In 1813 duties payable on Cape wines imported into Britain were substantially reduced, as Governor Cradock was to announce "with the most lively satisfaction." A short-lived golden age for Cape exporters had begun. It ended in 1825 when the preferential tariffs were reduced—Cape wine was still to be charged lower duties than most others, but the major incentive was gone, particularly when transport costs and the quality problem were taken into account.

By 1825 there were more than 31 million vines planted, a threefold increase from 1795—most of them Greengrape (Sémillon, that is), for reasons discussed in chapter 3. Wine production varied remarkably from year to year, but generally rose steadily over the period: in the five years 1821–1825 it averaged just under 17,000 leaguers. Production of infamously bad Cape brandy was fairly static at little more than 1,000 leaguers. The expanding home market remained hugely important, though exports increased. In 1813, just 200 leaguers of Cape wine went to dubiously delight palates in the new mother country, less than a tenth of that year's exports. This figure rose dramatically: the average export of ordinary wine to Britain for the period 1821–1825 was 5,416 leaguers, approximately three-quarters of all exports. Total wine exports in these five years amounted to about 40 percent of output. At their height they contributed more than half the value of the Cape's total exports; only in the 1840s did wool become more important. Wine farming, particularly in the arable southwest of the Cape, remained the prime economic activity for some decades.

Grapes, even before the boom years, had been a profitable activity for many farmers. As a group, wine producers were comparatively wealthy members of the colonial population, but inequality among them had (as for all farmers) intensified during the eighteenth century, and this process continued. According to an official list compiled in 1823 there were 374 wine farms in the Cape Town and Stellenbosch-Drakenstein regions, owning three-quarters of the colony's vines and responsible for 85 percent of its wine production. Mary Rayner, in her study of wine and slaves in the first half of the nineteenth century, calculated that a majority of these were marginal or small producers, with fewer than 69,000 vines; at the other extreme, just thirteen had more than 150,000. In addition to producing absolutely more wine, the larger farms were relatively more efficient, with higher yields per vine.

By the time the wine-export boom was ending, two-thirds of the wine farms were heavily mortgaged, suggesting that the image of wine-farmer prosperity at the time should not be too blandly generalized. William Bird, in his *State of the Cape of Good Hope in 1822*, noted that overly enthusiastic planting had led to a production surplus and lower prices—not for the first time or the last in South Africa. A problem farmers faced (and made many complaints about) was an increasing labor shortage—although it should be pointed out that the main sufferers of the shortage were undoubtedly the harder-pressed laborers, the slaves on whom the industry still depended. In the early nineteenth century, owners of wine farms possessed, on average, sixteen slaves. Britain had ceased trading in slaves in 1807, though many were brought into the Cape Colony after that date. Rayner has pointed out that wine farmers "were confronted with a paradoxical situation of being encouraged to raise productivity by a colonial government which, at the same time, had acted to cut off the major source of labour for the wine farms." As Rayner puts it, "the burden of the wine boom must have been carried by a diminishing number of aging slave men." No doubt owner-family labor also increased at the time, including child labor. The labor shortage continued, to be made worse by the abolition of slavery in the colony in 1834 (with a four-year transition period thereafter). A contemporary newspaper noted a claim that a farm that might once have had seven or eight male slaves by 1840 might have only one—now a paid laborer, of course.

It was not simply a matter of labor power. P. D. Hahn, discussing the labor shortage in a government report later in the century, noted that "farmers found themselves not only without the usual supply of labour, but also without that thorough practical knowledge of viticulture" embedded in the more skilled slaves. The lives of "free" laborers were very hard too: the British abolition of slavery argued no softness for workers, as the draconian Masters and Servants Act of 1856 made clear. While farmers had to learn to deal with wage labor, massive inequality and by now institutionalized racism continued.

The move away from preferential tariffs in 1825 was a severe blow to the colony's wine industry. Exports to Britain immediately started falling. The five-year period 1831–1835 saw imports from the Cape just two-thirds of the average for the corresponding years of the 1820s. Some minor new export markets were found, but these did not compensate, nor did they endure. Equally serious, the price of exported wine declined steeply: in 1824 it was approximately £23 per leaguer; after 1839 the average price varied between £9 and £16. Local prices would also have declined. The colonial economy was much impoverished, as were many individuals, and the number of insolvencies rose. Governor Bourke wrote in a letter, "The culture of the vine is not in the increase, the low prices of wines in the last years having caused great discouragement."

London was implacable. There were repeated (and, as always, perfectly justified) suggestions that quality should be improved—the Cape had, after all, been given a fine opportunity to establish an export market. Murmured the undersecretary of state for the colonies in Manchester School tones: "If the wine trade of the colony cannot be profitably conducted, let it be abandoned, and the capital employed in it diverted into some other channel"—which was rather more easily said than done, when most of the capital was small-scale and heavily mortgaged, and other channels somewhat less than numerous.

There was a sudden sharp increase in exports to Britain in the late 1850s because of oidium-decimated European crops, but that was a temporary respite, and matters became worse still after 1861, when a British trade treaty with France reduced duties on that country's wines. All supplier countries to Britain were now to be treated equally, with duties being differentiated only on grounds of alcoholic strength—a further blow to the Cape, whose wines were routinely heavily fortified to help them withstand the rigors of the sea voyage to Europe. In 1862, Cape wine exports to Britain were down to 356 leaguers, less than they had been in 1814.

Britain, in the years of preferential tariffs, was taking some three-quarters of the Cape's wine exports. The absolute total exports sometimes varied as wildly from year to year as did total production. For example, in 1816 total wine production (excluding brandy) was 15,398 leaguers (50 percent more than in the following vintage); total exports were 3,647 leaguers (of which 70 percent went to Britain). In 1823 production was 21,147 leaguers (5,000 more than in the previous year) and exports 7,013 (not much different from the previous year). In the years when exports to Britain were falling, there were renewed attempts to strengthen other markets—including the United States, which was a moderately successful outlet for a time, with an average of 23 leaguers going there annually in the 1835–1854 period. The basic problem, apart from import duty anomalies, seems to have been, as so often, that Cape wine could not compete on a quality level with suppliers from Europe. But in the nineteenth century, Cape wine was exported to a remarkable number of countries (if not consistently), from Jamaica to Australia, and from India to Sweden.

Despite undoubted hardships for many wine farmers, the wine industry somehow more than survived the problems occasioned by falling exports. In 1865 the number of vines was over 55 million (there were 31 million in 1825), and production rose significantly, at least helped by a burgeoning population. An increasing proportion of the surplus was diverted to brandy over the following century. Cape brandy had been, according to an anonymous writer in 1820, "one of the worst and most pernicious spirits ever produced." Now there were concerted attempts to encourage an improvement, both to make it more widely salable and to make it acceptable for fortifying wine: most dealers with any ambitions for quality used imported French brandy for that purpose. Quantities as well as quality rose: in the twenty-five years before 1860 production nearly quadrupled, to about 4,000 leaguers.

There was less improvement with wine. Authorities and commentators continued to blame and lament the quality of Cape wine (Constantia always excluded) and insist on the desirability of raising standards—an "imperious necessity" Governor Bourke called it. In fact, reading many of the contemporary accounts, one wonders how the stuff ever got sold at all, let alone drunk. In 1824, at the height of exports to England, a Cape newspaper noted, "With regard to Cape Madeira, and the Wines in General of this Colony, it is a fact which is acknowledged by everybody, that nothing is so bad in England as the Wines of the Cape." Descriptions abound of "miserable trash" that is "villainous," "execrable," "filthy," and so on—with, as well as "an undisguised taste of brandy," a frequently observed "earthy taste." Too often and too easily Cape wine "turned sour" in transit and arrived at its export destination undrinkable. A frequently occurring complaint was that Cape wine was sold too young: it would appear that it required at least a year's maturation, preferably more, before it was palatable.

What were the types of wines being made in the Cape in the first half of the nineteenth century, and why hadn't quality been improved? Mention has been made of the near monopoly of the vineyards by Greengrape, later identified as Sémillon. As to types of wine, it is impossible to penetrate behind most of the various names and usefully ponder how Cape Malaga, Vintint, Moselle, Hock, and Vin de Graves were discriminated, and how they differed from Cape Madeira. It would seem that a turn from sweet wines at the beginning of the century (Cape Madeira, Steen, and Hanepoot seem to have been sweet) to predominantly dry wines by the middle of the century is ascribable to British taste. Virtually all these wines (though probably not usually Constantia) were to some degree fortified.

Blame for their poor quality was, unsurprisingly, disputed. A few perceptive observers noted viticultural problems, while "slovenly" winemaking was frequently cited; many noticed wine farmers picking unripe grapes and including leaves, earth, and rotten grapes, allowing the wine to ferment at too high a temperature, the misuse of sulfur, dirty casks (there seems to have often been a severe shortage of suitable containers, many of which might have been used for highly unsuitable contents in their journey to the colony)—and, above all, a general dirtiness. But if the wine farmers were negligent, and frequently excoriated by the Cape Town dealers who took in most of the colony's wine production, many implicated the dealers, too. One commentator spoke of them as treating the wines they purchased from farmers "as raw materials, to be altered and fashioned according to their own taste and judgement. An injudicious tampering with it has deteriorated instead of improving the commodity." Furthermore, it was rather convincingly suggested, "the wine boers were encouraged to make the greatest possible quantity of wine, with entire disregard for its quality." Dealers in England did not go unblamed either, as many travelers noted that Cape wine tasted better in its land of origin, and ascribed this to "altering and fashioning" in London more than to the sea voyage between the two places.

Generally, however, it was clear that the primary need was to improve winemaking techniques. Many attempts were made by government as well as private individuals and bodies to improve matters. Farmers were offered information through newspaper articles, pamphlets, and handbooks about the best viticultural and winemaking methods; Governor Cradock promised "premiums and rewards . . . for the production of the best Wines," and established an office of Wine Taster intended to control the quality of wine bound for export. Regulations attempted to ensure that wines were sufficiently aged, and suchlike. A Cape Wine Trade Committee representing growers, manufacturers, and merchants was established in 1826 in the wake of the export market's collapse. Unfortunately, because of the structural impediments for most farmers of a lack of capital and a lack of price incentive, all these attempts proved futile. Most Cape wine—and even more, Cape brandy—remained "damnable poor stuff."

Accounts of winemaking at the Cape right up to the end of the nineteenth century seem to indicate a fairly standard approach—probably the most significant difference would be the state of the grapes when picked, the cleanliness of the cellar, and the state of the casks used for fermenting and maturing the wine. Otto Mentzel, a German resident in the Cape in the 1830s, describes the standard means of pressing: "A 'balie' or barrel, (usually a leaguer cask cut in two) which is pierced at the bottom and along the sides with many holes made with an half-inch drill, stands on a trestle in a second larger barrel, without holes except for a bunghole, through which the must that is trodden out, passes into a pail or barrel placed beneath it. A slave stands in the perforated barrel, holds onto a short piece of rope stretched above him, and treads the grapes with which it is filled with bare feet." Carl Thunberg, traveling in the Cape in the 1770s, also observed this basic process, adding, "the must that runs out is put into large high vessels to ferment." Then "the trodden grapes, before they are farther pressed, are put, stalks and all, upon a coarse strainer (or the bottom of a bed) made of rattans, on which they rub the fruit with their hands, till the husks go through it, the stalks in the meantime remaining behind, which are now separated and thrown away, as they are supposed to make the wine austere and bitter. The husks are then put into the fermenting-vessel, which the next morning is in full fermentation."

Rather more horrified, Baron Carl von Babo, the government viticulturist toward the end of the nineteenth century and a passionate advocate of improved winemaking methods, spoke in a government report of "a number of half-naked coloured men" trampling the grapes with feet carrying "acetous germs" from the wine-splashed floor, not to mention dirt and sweat: "Although this does not perceptibly increase the quantity," Babo noted, "it certainly imparts a most objectionable bouquet to the wine." He added, "Juice, husks and stalks are thrown together into the fermenting tubs, and the astringent harsh tannin is thus extracted."

Making the best red wine, Mentzel suggested, requires removing the stems before the grapes are crushed, after which "they are left in this state in a vessel for four or five days without further treatment, so that the whole mixture may ferment for a while with the husks. . . . [Then] it is pressed out again with a press." Mentzel described the wines being repeatedly racked into further barrels. Tubs were often painted with lime, Babo said, giving the wine "that flat, insipid taste of acetate of lime"; or else they were simply so dirty and tainted that there was a good chance of the wine "turning bad the first year." Finally, as per Mentzel, the "tightly corked" barrel is "left undisturbed for a few weeks, when it may be sold or transferred to smaller barrels for personal use."

For white wine, Mentzel observed, "The new must is now poured into a barrel impregnated with sulphur. . . . Fermentation is in full swing the very next day and if the wine is desired mellow and sweet, it should soon be drawn off into a newly-sulphurated barrel, which process could continue daily until the wine quietens down. . . . Every second or third day all wines are drawn off and poured into other newly-sulphured vessels. . . . When the wine has been . . . drawn off and settled it is left undisturbed for a few weeks."

Through all the time of boom and bust in the wine trade, however, the wines of Constantia were locally and internationally praised and sought after (until suddenly Constantia went bust too)—showing perhaps that, with adequate capital resources and labor and with the attention to detail prompted by ambition and encouraged by high prices, the Cape could make fine wine. Some outline of Constantia's story is important to complete the sketch of a turbulent time for Cape winemaking. Through the eighteenth century, Constantia had built on the reputation established during the earlier period of Simon van der Stel's ownership, before the property was divided. From the 1770s—after a few decades in which quality had perhaps slipped somewhat—it acquired further international luster, with Groot Constantia now in the hands of Hendrik Cloete. There are numerous accounts by eminent visitors telling of the vineyards and the winemaking cellar, and noting the great care taken in the production of the famous wines.

The larger part of the production of the Constantia farms went abroad to the ruling classes of Europe, and famously, for a time, to the emperor gloomily exiled on Saint Helena, while the victor of Waterloo stocked his Apsley House cellar with the same liquor. In the middle decades of the nineteenth century, when production of Constantia wine generally varied between 20 and 30 leaguers (out of a Cape total of, say, 16,000 leaguers), the value of its exports was 3 percent to 6 percent of the total value of the colony's wine exports. Perhaps, as for so many cult wines today, the price was inflated, and there are occasional accounts of wine lovers asserting the equal merits of some other wines. John Barrow, writing at the end of the eighteenth century, claimed that at some farms in Drakenstein, "Muscadel" was pressed into wine "equally good, if not superior, to the Constantia, though sold at one-sixth part of the price; of such importance is name."

But Constantia did have the name, and had earned it. The wines—the four most important being a white and a red, a Muscat de Frontignan, and a Pontac—were of a sweet and unfortified style increasingly rare in the Cape, as British tastes turned drier through the nineteenth century. The general collapse of prices after 1825 affected Constantia wines comparatively little. But their fashionability in Europe was declining, and it seems that this, combined with the reduction in size of the important farms through deletions and with comparatively high labor costs, contributed to financial crises by the 1870s. When Jacob Cloete of Groot Constantia died in 1875, the estate was insolvent. Commentators, even Jose Burman, the meticulous historian of Constantia, seem at a loss to explain the sudden decline of the most prosperous and prestigious of the Cape's winegrowing regions. It was certainly not, as Burman suggests, the scourge of phylloxera that made "Groot Constantia's future look bleak," for phylloxera arrived there only at the very end of the century. Clearly there was an inability to adjust to the new realities that forced themselves on the wine industry in the last decades of the century.

Whatever the causes, the sudden and precipitous decline of Constantia marked the end of an era. Fortunately for the sake of the birth of a new one, the government bought Groot Constantia in 1885. A model and experimental farm was envisaged, along with a training school for winemakers. But suddenly the most urgent need was for a place to grow millions of vines of a very different kind from the ones that had made Constantia famous throughout the wine-drinking world; for in 1886 it was established that phylloxera had started its depredations in the Cape vineyards.

For long, the most significant disease in Cape vineyards was anthracnose, a fungal infection. Powdery mildew, *Oidium tuckeri,* was an import from northern America into Europe that did much damage there in the 1850s before sulfur was established as a satisfactory preventive treatment, but there seems to have been little alarm about it in the Cape, and when oidium started having noticeable effects in the greening vineyards of late 1859 it was not immediately identified. The disease spread fast, but once a local shortage of sulfur was resolved, the problem was eased, with only a few harvests significantly affected. Things would not be so easy with the next plague.

Also imported from North America into Europe, the small vineroot-feeding aphid relative now scientifically known as *Daktulosphaira vitifoliae* announced its effects there as early as 1863, and within three decades had started spreading a swath of destruction around the winegrowing world. *Phylloxera vastatrix* (the devastator) it was initially called, and many desperate treatments were tried as the vignerons of France watched their vineyards die—even after it had become increasingly clear that the only viable response was to grow the wine grapevine on rootstocks of American origin: evolution had ensured that these were immune.

There was some moderate watchfulness at the Cape at the time, but little real preparedness to deal with phylloxera by the time it became clear that the pest had already arrived. It was the French consul in Cape Town who—presumably having seen ravaged vines back home—in early 1886 alerted the authorities to signs of it in a vineyard in Mowbray, not far from the earliest Cape vineyards. It was revealed that the vineyard was indeed affected by phylloxera and, moreover, had been showing progressive deterioration for four years. The government immediately sent scientific inspectors to look at as many vineyards as possible. Through 1886 more farms were discovered to be affected, and then the pest reached the more outlying areas, until most were affected. Constantia was among the last, in 1898 (strangely, since it is within ten kilometers of Mowbray). The insect continued its remorseless progress despite government programs to combat the spread. Unlike in Australia, for example, the winged form of the pest appeared here, and there was no escape from its depredations. During the 1890s at least a quarter of the Cape's vines were destroyed—while expensive chemical and other antidotes were also tried in vain. European experience showed that replanting on American rootstocks was vital and unavoidable; this proceeded, with a number of "American vine plantations" established through the wine lands to produce rootstocks, and research was undertaken to learn the best methods of grafting, as well as rootstock affinity.

Right through the 1890s there were insufficient supplies of rootstocks, however, and replanting was not as rapid as is sometimes supposed. Mr. C. Mayer, a German viticulturist at Groot Constantia, estimated in a 1900 "Retrospect on Phylloxera" that just fewer than two million grafted vines had been planted (out of a Cape total of more than

87 million), and "now at least one million grafted vines are being annually planted." Many destroyed vineyards remained unreplaced, and there was, in fact, a useful turn toward the planting of fruit trees in areas where this was possible. The vineyards of Cape Town (other than those at Constantia), including the one where phylloxera had first been found, were swallowed by the encroaching suburbs; particularly during the early twentieth century, as many farmers as could do so turned to farming ostriches and alfalfa (lucerne) to feed them. Oudtshoorn in the Eastern Cape had five million vines in 1875; in 1909 it apparently produced no wine at all. Today virtually the whole of the Cape vineyard is planted on American rootstock; only the occasional vineyard in sandy soil successfully chances its luck.

Much hardship was caused to wine farmers by phylloxera, despite some governmental compensation. Altogether, in the decades following the near-total collapse of the export market and widespread damage to the vineyards, Cape viticulture was perhaps at its lowest ebb yet—though things were to get worse as the century turned and brought imperialist war in South Africa, followed by depression. Looking at contemporary accounts of wine-lands problems, the wonder is that the industry survived. Not only that: bizarrely, production increased during the difficult years. In 1860, when one would have thought that wine farmers would have already turned to something else if they could, or at least have ceased planting, there were 55 million vines planted; in 1875 there were nearly 70 million. The league table for that year shows Paarl ahead as usual with some 21 million vines, followed by Stellenbosch with 16 million. Then come some areas that had not featured before in this story, and had become viable through improved communications within the colony, particularly the railway lines—and it is presumably these new plantings by hopeful pioneers that account for the overall increase: Oudtshoorn, Robertson, and Worcester each had more than 5 million vines; the Cape, Malmesbury (Swartland), Tulbagh, and Riversdale about half of that number.

Although reliable statistics from this time are hard to come by, a government report notes that in 1882–1883 wine production was nearly 40,000 leaguers, up from 25,000 in 1860. Brandy production had proportionately grown even more, to more than 11,000 leaguers, reflecting the one pale gleam on the winemakers' horizon: the possibility of exports to the hard men and no doubt equally hard women in Kimberley, where the diamond rush had begun in 1866. In 1888, about 4,905 leaguers of spirits were sent to Kimberley, something like half of the total production. From the late 1880s the goldfields of the Transvaal also offered the prospect of some profit to those toiling in the vineyards of the Western Cape. Dr. Hahn, in a report of 1882, was emphatic that, taking into account local costs and quality and the price of wine in Europe, "the idea of exporting Cape wine to Europe at present must be altogether abandoned"; the diamond fields, the Transvaal, and the Orange Free State were much more likely prospects, with drinkers perhaps rather less discriminating than those in England—or indeed, than the English in the Cape Colony, where much more wine was imported than exported at the time and certainly not enough of the local product was drunk to please the farmers and merchants.

Less than ever was there doubt in the minds of the authorities (and of drinkers!) that the quality of Cape wine was also very low. In 1887 yet another report to a concerned Parliament stressed, "The production of wine is still increasing but ... there is no demand for the increased production. The price for wine has therefore gone down considerably, especially of the inferior kinds, of which some are almost unsalable, as they are unfit even for making spirits." In 1885, after Baron Carl von Babo was appointed as government viticulturist, his first report, which included scathing views of winemaking techniques, recommended the founding of the model farm and viticultural school at Groot Constantia.

In fact, the viticultural school there never seems to have amounted to much, in the face of the pressing need for the farm to produce wine in commercial quantities to satisfy the Treasury as well as enough American rootstocks to satisfy phylloxera-ridden farmers. This is a great pity, as there were signs that a deal of good might have been achieved. Viticulturally, for example, apart from planting with better varieties, there were useful trials of different trellising and vine-spacing practices, and successful experimental treatments for pests like the snoutbeetle (a pernicious weevil). In the cellar, among other investigations, inoculated yeasts were tried and observed. And the benefits of the "attemporator" or "cooling worm"—basically a coil of pipe carrying cool water through the fermenting must—did in fact reach far beyond Constantia. But a later viticultural expert, Raymond Dubois, pointed out the inadequacies of even Groot Constantia as a model. Australia, he said, has "better buildings, more advanced and fitted with modern machinery and time and labour-saving implements," while "there is not one cellar in the whole of the Colony fit to guarantee good wine." Unfortunately, his 1905 report indicates little continued progress in experimental work or establishing a teaching institution. The straitened financial state of the colony, suffering a severe depression after the wars between Britain and the Boer republics, was blamed.

So severe was the effect of the "prevailing depression" on the wine industry that various commissions were appointed to look into the condition of the wine districts. A 1905 inquiry "established beyond a doubt that the Wine and Brandy Industry is at present in an alarming state of depression." A lengthier 1909 commission report gives a useful overview of the state of the industry. The great majority of wine farms were mortgaged, the commission noted, and in most areas land values were greatly depreciated. No longer was there a labor shortage. The commission remarked that "the wages paid have decreased considerably, and ... the condition of the labouring classes generally is a deplorable one ... ; the grower has been forced to confine himself only to the most necessary of work on his farm." It quotes a farmer in Paarl saying, "It used to be very difficult for us to get coloured labor, but now if you hold up your finger you can get hundreds."

But production was, as ever, excessive. The average harvest in 1907 and 1908 yielded nearly 45,000 leaguers. The 1909 harvest was apparently a very poor one, however—"a decided blessing in disguise, seeing that, as far as can be ascertained, considerable stocks of wine and spirits of the previous vintage were still on the hands of merchants, farmers and certain of the Wineries at the commencement of this year." In fact, there is some evidence that the area of the colony's vineyard had decreased. The commission noted that census returns for 1904 had given the total area under vines as 16,610 morgen (a morgen being about 0.85 hectare), while for 1909 it appeared to be 10,120 morgen. This major decline doubtless reflects the depredations of the assiduous phylloxera: in 1904 there were some 19.25 million grafted vines and still 58.5 million ungrafted ones—presumably many of the latter had succumbed by 1909 and not been replaced.

But more than the total production, perhaps, it is interesting to note the proportions of the different varieties given for 1909. Greengrape was still by far the largest contributor to the total, but down from its near-monopoly to 40 percent. Steen (Chenin Blanc), White French (Palomino), and Red Muscadel (Muscat) were high on the list, but Cabernet Sauvignon and Sauvignon Blanc now featured (Syrah was not listed, but was planted at Groot Constantia in the 1890s). More significant was the rise of Cinsaut (called Hermitage). It appears to have been brought into the country about 1880 and in 1909 was third only after the two popular white grapes. The commission in fact specifically connected Hermitage to a factor it identified as contributing to excess wine production, the racial prohibition that had grown up in southern Africa: "Before the imposition of restrictions on the sale of liquor to Natives in the Transvaal, a large demand existed among the Natives on the mines in that country for Hermitage, sweetened and slightly fortified"—thus accounting for the growth in those plantings. The commission noted that in the Transvaal and the Orange River Colony, "the sale or supply of liquor to any coloured person is prohibited"; an essentially similar situation prevailed in Natal, and "in most districts of the Cape Colony itself restrictions prevail against the sale of wine and spirits to the aboriginal native." These were all British colonies, and it hardly needs pointing out, of course, that racism did not leap forth new from the head of the National Party when it came to power in 1948 and formalized apartheid.

One response to the severe crisis was producer cooperation. The 1905 government inquiry had recommended the establishment of cooperative wineries to enable more effective use of machinery and lower costs, as well as to realize the benefits of collective marketing. With substantial government financial support, nine cooperatives were established, the Drostdy in Tulbagh being the first in 1906. Four of them, however, were not to survive long in the continuing conditions of slump and overproduction. But a man called Charles Kohler was already starting to work on his conviction that only a centralized, unifying body could resolve the crisis. The organization that was born from the crisis and Kohler's work was to change fundamentally the course of Cape wine production. "South African wine production" we should call it now, in light of the political uniting of the two defeated boer republics (Transvaal and Free State) with the two British colonies (Cape and Natal) as the Union of South Africa in 1910. That unity was to also affect the wine industry, which was henceforth, after its earlier central importance in the Cape's economy, to be just one struggling agricultural sector among others in the eyes of a national government—all needing, at this period, to capitalize in order to survive.

THE KWV YEARS: SOUTH AFRICAN WINE TO 1994

For the greater part of the twentieth century the character and conditions of South African winemaking were shaped by the organization that came to be known simply as the KWV. Its origins were in a particularly severe episode of the Cape's perennial overproduction that hit the wine industry in the early decades of the twentieth century. The initial aims of the organization were limited to resolving that problem, but its ambitions grew, and it was granted progressively more regulatory power by a succession of governments. Particularly close ties with the National Party and other forces of Afrikaner capital ensured that it was something more than influential in any legislation concerning the industry. This centralized power did have positive benefits for the industry (apart, that is, from guaranteeing an income for wine farmers), such as allowing a relatively smooth transition to an effective appellation and certification system. On the other hand, its strategies did much to discourage the making of fine wine, and left some crucial aspects of the industry very weak by the time its grip was fully relaxed in the 1990s, almost simultaneously with the collapse of the apartheid state.

Desperation, rather than visions of power, was behind the first steps toward producer unity in the early twentieth century. A few of the new cooperatives were surviving; others had collapsed. Joint action also came about at different times in protest against government increases in excise duties. In 1916, after representations on this issue failed to move the authorities, Charles Kohler, who had been for some years active in organizing wine farmers, presented plans for an industrywide cooperative that would control supply and thereby regulate the prices at which wine and brandy would be sold to wholesalers. A draft constitution was put forward, and a Viticultural Union held its first meeting in Paarl in December 1917; the following year it was floated as a company under the name the Koöperatieve Wijnbouwers Vereniging van Zuid-Afrika Beperkt (Cooperative Winegrowers' Association of South Africa Limited). The KWV, as it became universally known, was registered as a "mutual cooperative society" in 1923. Its aim was to "direct, control and regulate the sale and disposal by its members of their produce" in order to "secure or tend to secure for them a continuously adequate return for such produce."

The overwhelming majority of wine farmers signed up—with just a few in Constantia and Stellenbosch opting out on the grounds that they had no trouble selling high-quality wine. Deals were made with "the trade": the merchants would buy only from the KWV, which would not compete with them in the local market, but rather concentrate on exports. The prices paid to farmers rose significantly for a year or two, with the KWV at that stage converting the surplus into ethyl alcohol, but soon old patterns of overproduction were on the rise again. The system was not working well, but government intervention created a turning point for the KWV's fortunes. Against the objections of the wholesalers, the Wine and Spirits Control Act of 1924 gave the KWV the power to fix annually the minimum price to be paid to farmers for distilling wine; for the time being, "good wine"—that is, wine not intended for distillation—was not included. This was just the first step in the arrogation to the KWV of great power.

At the same time, the KWV made plans to develop and improve the brandy industry by centering its distillation on the production of mature, pot-stilled brandy; it was, in fact, to become one of the world's largest brandy producers. Quality of winemaking, too, began to improve. No doubt the support of the Department of Viticulture and Enology at the University of Stellenbosch (it was founded in 1917, though teaching in these subjects had been undertaken for nearly two decades already) was useful. The department's first director was the eminent Dr. Abraham Izak Perold, who had already made a useful contribution to Cape viticulture by importing a number of new varieties and doing a good deal of viticultural research. That research was to lead to his publishing a *Treatise on Viticulture* (in Afrikaans in 1926 and in his own English translation a year later), as well as to the almost incidental creation of Pinotage, the most significant new variety produced in this country. Perold became the KWV's chief research scientist in 1927. Among other activities he wrote numerous articles on improved winemaking techniques in the *Wine and Spirits* magazine founded for the benefit of wine farmers.

Perold was later joined at the KWV by another scientist, Charles Niehaus, who was responsible for establishing the local sherry industry, which was to be very important for some decades. The making of table wines also benefited, though at a very basic level: there is little indication that there was much to excite the serious wine lover in the 1920s and 1930s at least. It is symbolic that the lackluster vineyards of Groot Constantia, the onetime focus of a winegrowing effort that had proved the Cape could produce fine wine, were at this stage being leased out to a private producer. The government wine farm, which had actually done some useful experimentation and encouragement of better winemaking methods in the years around the turn of the century, had largely abandoned any pretense of educational usefulness by the time the historic manor house burned down in 1925.

But if quality was discouraged by the system of minimum pricing, production continued to rise implacably, as a ten-year sampling shows (with figures drawn from contemporary issues of *Farming in South Africa*): in 1919 there were 114,128 leaguers of wine produced; ten years later, 159,722; in 1939, 290,308; in 1949, with farmers no doubt still encouraged by a great demand for brandy during World War II, production was up to 452,879 leaguers. Exports generally—effectively monopolized by the KWV—had grown well during these decades (though insufficiently to match production), largely because of preferential treatment given by Britain to countries of the British Empire, which system had recently been reestablished.

The KWV took another crucial step in 1940 when the Wine and Spirits Control Act—with Parliament again resisting merchants' objections—extended its control to setting minimum prices also for "good wine" (seldom very good, in fact, but intended for drinking as such rather than for distillation). The whole wine industry was to be covered, and all transactions between merchants and producers were to be monitored by the KWV, which would be the medium for all payments. The act also introduced powers for KWV to impose production limits. A government commission in the mid 1930s had noted clearly that the KWV's minimum pricing policies led to more wine production, and more wine of lower quality, and that statutory control over all aspects of wine production was necessary—and who better to do this than the KWV itself?

Plantings of vineyards had continued apace. Although lower prices were paid for the volumes that the KWV decided were "surplus," they were usually sufficient to amply reward the overproducer: the more overproduction, the greater the income. Farmers had, essentially, no responsibility for marketing their produce, they were there to grow grapes; the cooperatives and the KWV were there to sell the wine. There was certainly little incentive for most farmers to improve their viticulture except to make it more productively efficient, and little reason to experiment with new varieties or clones. Quite the opposite in fact, as most funded research into grapevine improvement in the twentieth century in the Cape went into development of clones that gave better yields rather than higher-quality grapes. It was only in the 1960s that there started to be a significant (though still tiny) number of estate owners with real ambitions for their wines. Nonetheless, it is important to note that a few excellent wines were produced even before, as merchants started to develop some premium brands. For example, vintages of Chateau Libertas from as far back as the 1940s, made by the Stellenbosch Farmers' Winery, have been drinking splendidly (the few treasured bottles remaining) seventy years later.

These middle decades of the century saw the start of the wine industry's major expansion into the inland parts of the country, where warmth and irrigation, generously supported by the offerings of the agrochemical industry, secured heavy yields. It was also the time when the number of cooperatives grew enormously, as farmers needed cellars in which to produce the "good wine" (at standards not incompatible with heavy cropping) that earned a premium over distilling wine—although sometimes the prices for the two were remarkably close, again reducing incentives to quality production. The war years saw the number of cooperatives increase from 6 to 19; by 1950 there were 30, by 1955 there were 46. The introduction of expensive technologies, including cold fermentation, further discouraged the private producer. One of the great names of the time, Zonnebloem, became the property (it seems by means of an unattractive process) of Stellenbosch Farmers' Winery (SFW) when the farm was unable to afford the cost of modernizing its cellar; Zonnebloem became an increasingly dull brand rather than the name of a few fine wines. The need for expensive capital equipment encouraged the move to cooperatives, and by 1975 there were 69.

Cold fermentation—a technology that the KWV had studied in the 1930s but advised the farmers against—was experimented with after the war, notably by N. C. Krone at Twee Jonge Gezellen in Tulbagh, and by an immigrant German family, the Graues, on their farm Nederburg, near Paarl. Nederburg, which started building its reputation during the 1950s, especially after the arrival of Günter Brözel as cellarmaster in 1956, was to become part of SFW in 1966. This was fitting, as it was SFW that made the most spectacular use of the new possibilities brought in by cold fermentation for making fruity white wine in a warm climate. In 1959 SFW launched a semisweet wine, mostly made from Chenin Blanc, named Lieberstein, which was to effect something like a revolution in Cape wine—and the drinking habits of South Africans, more of whom were prompted to turn to wine.

It was the first wine to be marketed nationally here, and the huge new domestic market it created meant that by 1964 Lieberstein for a while claimed to be the largest-selling bottled wine in the world. And of course it prompted imitators. The KWV itself built a modern cellar with cold-fermentation facilities in time for the 1962 harvest. Plantings of Chenin Blanc increased hugely, numerous wine cellars were modernized, and the Cape tradition of producing more white wine than red was reinforced.

But overproduction—thanks to a system of rewarding it, and to improvements in viticultural efficiency, including better pest control—had once more become a significant problem during the 1950s. The question of whether it was not, rather, a problem of underconsumption came to the fore again. This no doubt helped motivate the government's appointment of the Malan Commission of Inquiry into the General Distribution and Selling of Intoxicating Liquor. Its report led to legislation in 1962 that allowed for unrestricted sale of liquor to all races. The comprehensive Liquor Act of 1928, which governed the trade and industry, had confirmed the almost total prohibition of the supply of liquor to blacks (with severe limitation on sales to "coloreds" and "Asiatics," while making provision for the application of the tot system in the Western Cape). As the commission noted, there had been illicit trade on a scale that "surpasses the wildest flights of imagination" (though wine would have played a comparatively minor role, except to the "coloreds" of the Western Cape).

The abandonment of an official racially based prohibition was motivated by both economic and political considerations. The government had many intimate links to the KWV and a close relationship with Cape wine farmers, whose capital was useful to the growth of Afrikaner nationalism, and it was keen to resolve the overproduction problems. Another factor was the usual state hunger to gain tax revenue. Moreover, the government was aware that resentment of prohibition and consequent police actions played their part in the anger increasingly being expressed by black people—as most dramatically in the demonstration that had led to the Sharpeville massacre (in which police killed sixty-nine demonstrators) and the defiant response in Langa in 1960. So consumption was allowed, but licensing sales outlets to blacks was quite another matter.

More significant in the KWV's ostensible but paradoxical struggle against overproduction was legislation in 1957 empowering the KWV to set production limits for individual farms. The "quota system" essentially preserved the status quo—it made no distinction between high-quality wine production (where there was in fact generally a shortage and potential for growth) and bulk production, and it protected current growers. A crucial effect quotas had on the South African wine industry until their abandonment in 1992 was that they effectively vetoed the development of new wine regions where ambitious producers might seek to make high-quality wine. There were occasional amendments to the quota regulations, especially ones that allowed for expanded mass production in areas like the Northern Cape: total quota volume grew from 7.4 million hectoliters in 1957 to 12.5 million in 1990. The mass of legislation relating to the KWV was replaced and consolidated by Parliament in Act 47 of 1970, the "KWV Act."

A highly publicized instance of the quota system's thwarting winegrowing ambition was to lead to a limited but useful amendment in 1984. Tim Hamilton-Russell had started farming in the Hemel-en-Aarde Valley, planting the then southernmost, coolest vineyards in the Cape. But he had no quota for his important vineyards, and only by some strange and clearly problematical sleight of hand could he produce and sell wine at all— uncertified but increasingly recognized as fine. As Michael Fridjhon says (he tells the story in his *Penguin Book of South African Wine*), the much-reported standoff "was beginning to embarrass the KWV—an organization which ordinarily seemed impervious to criticism and change. It is difficult to assert that your regulations are there in the interests of quality wine production, and then find yourself pilloried for failing to make provision for an innovator with vineyards in Hermanus." The compromise was to amend the regulations to permit the sale and transfer of quota to another producer in the same or an adjacent region.

It's worth taking a snapshot of the production situation around this pivotal period. There were some 300 million vines, at least half of them in the hot irrigated valleys of the Olifants, Orange, and Breede rivers. In 1979 the grape harvest was 6.22 million hectoliters, of which only 40 percent was used for wine, the rest going for juice or distillation. Of the natural wine, perhaps 10 percent could generously be called high-quality. In the vineyard, Chenin Blanc was still increasing its percentage share of plantings, and by 1979 had reached 29.3 percent (these percentages for grape plantings are adjusted from those published in contemporary KWV statistics, to exclude Sultana [Thompson seedless], not used for wine; this deduction has, sensibly, become standard practice in recent years for official statistics). Palomino followed (17.2 percent) but, like Cinsaut (now a mere 14.1 percent, having been overtaken by Chenin in 1968 at roughly 22 percent), it was on a downward path. Pinotage and Cabernet Sauvignon were the only two other red grapes in the top fifteen varieties, with both under 3 percent.

In fact, Cabernet, even at that miserable level, had greatly increased its plantings during the 1970s. The imminence of new legal controls restricting the use of variety names had trebled the price of the grape between 1970 and 1973 alone. Frans Malan of Simonsig, an early official "estate," remarked at the time that it was now starting to be "a paying proposition" to grow more of the "'noble varieties' . . . it has never been so before." It was a decade that saw, as the Hamilton-Russell story indicates, a definite rise in the quota of high ambition in Cape winemaking, and the emergence of some framework to shape it—as well as encouragement from developments in other parts of the New World. The famous tasting of American and French wines in Paris in 1976 fed the confidence and ambition of more than just Californian winemakers. It must be said, however, that there was more conservatism and complacency in the Cape than there was acquaintance with the wines or the winegrowing and winemaking practices of other countries, a situation that was not going to improve much until the 1990s. However, although the focus of the serious consumer was increasingly on the estate wines and their claims about provenance, the merchant houses too were supplying some remarkably good wines, notably in the leading brands of SFW. Some of the Nederburg wines of the 1970s were still drinking very well more than thirty years later, particularly the selections made for the annual auction that Nederburg inaugurated in 1975, which has taken place every year since then. The auction was in itself a boost for quality, although it no longer plays the vital role it once did in bringing fine wines to the attention of the wine lover.

The best of the merchants' wines certainly should have been good: they were able to draw on grapes and wine from some of the finest vineyard sites in the country, even if these were hardly performing at the limits of their potential. In 1966 a book was published called *Fairest Vineyards,* by Kenneth Maxwell, claiming to be the first to give a virtually complete catalog of Cape wines. A large percentage were fortified but, looking at the list of table wines, it is clear that the majority of even these were the blends of the merchants: just a handful of names are of the estates that were to become much better known in the next decade: Delheim, Muratie, Twee Jonge Gezellen, Schoongezicht, Rustenberg . . . and precious few others. Ten years later, another book was produced: *Estate Wines of South Africa,* by Graham Knox. It profiled forty estates that were producing their own wine, and an "Estate Wine Record" at the end listed a few hundred such wines.

The "estate" was a concept legislated by Parliament as part of the Wine of Origin (WO) Scheme, which came into being in 1973 (see chapter 4). The aims of the scheme were twofold: it provided an appellation system to assist with continued exports to a Britain now joining the European Economic Community, and responded to the demands of the small producers. In 1971 the Cape Estate Wine Producers' Association started meeting with the governmental committee of inquiry into the production and marketing of estate wines, feeding into the process that resulted in the first version of the WO scheme. Controls over claims as to origin, variety, and vintage were to play an important part in the marketing and growth of the independent producers during the 1970s and beyond. They gave registered estates, defined then as the smallest units of the scheme, an enormous cachet—and also lent that cachet to other independent producers even if they did not meet all the requirements of estates or wish to register as such. It became established that, as Knox noted in his book, "not all Estate wine is fine wine, nor is it all necessarily superior to the produce of the wine merchants' cellars, but the best wines of the country are grown and made on the Estate principle." Meanwhile, of course, most of the farms now selling wines under their own labels continued to supply grapes or wine to the merchants.

Undoubtedly, much needed to be done if the Cape was to start producing more than a few isolated examples of fine wine, and if the number of smaller producers making serious, terroir-driven wines in their own cellars was to increase. What cellar expertise there was derived more from experience in Germany than in France—which might well have proved useful in making white wine, but was less evidently so for the reds. And as for the vineyards, amid all the Chenin Blanc (a fine grape but treated as a workhorse) and Cinsaut, there was a paucity of varieties internationally recognized as premium. A factor that was to play a role in improving the quality of both viticultural and winemaking practice from the 1970s onward was the extensive research undertaken at the Enological and Viticultural Research Institute. Generally known simply as Nietvoorbij, which was the name of the experimental farm just outside Stellenbosch where it was based, the institute was inaugurated in 1969.

The bureaucrats responsible for controlling new plant material and seeing to the quarantining of imports were less helpful in overcoming the desperate shortage of high-quality planting material. It could take a great many years to get a new clone or variety into the ground. The spectacular result of the steps taken by many of the Cape's leading producers to import material illegally was a public scandal, and the Klopper Commission of Inquiry of 1986 found evidence that "the illegal importation of vine propagating material had started as long ago as the beginning of 1973 and had continued intermittently into the eighties," with at least some knowledge of it on the part of the authorities. The focus of the inquiry was Chardonnay—or rather Auxerrois, as it was revealed that, ironically, this second-rate variety was what had mistakenly been imported and propagated on many of the Cape's best-known properties—but other varieties were also illegally imported. Also imported, it seems, were some of the diseases that quarantining is precisely designed to guard against.

Among the most important figures accused by the Klopper inquiry were Peter Finlayson, the first winemaker at Hamilton Russell, and Danie de Wet, a great innovator at De Wetshof in Robertson and later a pillar of the Cape wine industry establishment. Another was a man who deserves credit for his role in modernizing the Cape vineyard and perhaps even more for his influence on local winemaking. This was Julius Laszlo, who arrived from Romania in 1974, armed with a doctorate in soil microbiology from Moscow. After periods at Nietvoorbij and Boschendal he took charge of technical development at the Bergkelder (meaning "mountain cellar"), part of the large Distillers Corporation. This was not only responsible for a number of increasingly ambitious ranges, but had entered into partnership with a number of leading wine estates (including Meerlust, Alto, and La Motte). The deal involved not just the crucial marketing of wines but also access to some of the best expertise available, as well as maturation (and bottling) in excellent conditions. Laszlo was innovative in, for example, his insistence on cellar hygiene, but is best remembered for introducing new small oak barrels as an important resource for makers of serious red wines.

The situation with regard to such wines was remarkably different at the end of the 1970s from what it had been ten years before. It was a time of innovation and experimentation on the estates even more than in the more ambitious, and better equipped, divisions of the wholesalers, where Julius Laszlo and Günter Brözel were revolutionizing production. The Cape Independent Winemakers Guild was founded in 1983 "to contribute to the advancement of the quality of Cape wines by mutually developing the knowledge, capabilities and horizons of the members." It was instigated by Billy Hofmeyr, a lover of Bordeaux, who was in the process of abandoning his career as a quantity surveyor in favor of developing his recently acquired small Paarl farm, Welgemeend. It was Hofmeyr who brought out, in 1979, not only the Cape's first Bordeaux-style blend, but also its first blend of Pinotage with other varieties in the attempt to make a local interpretation of a classic southern Rhône wine. The Bordeaux blend was to be taken up enthusiastically through the 1980s, but the forerunner of the "Cape blend" was not to be much copied until the 1990s. (The guild was to drop "Independent" from its name and, particularly through its annual auction, arguably put greater stress on marketing its members' wines than on advancing winemaking skills.)

In many ways, the 1980s can be seen as a period of consolidation of the 1970s innovations, as well as preparation of the conditions that helped make possible the massive breakthrough of the 1990s, when political liberation at home opened the wine industry to the world. At this stage, of course, the situation in terms of exports was getting worse for the producers. The informal sanctions that had begun as early as 1963 took on greater, formal force starting in 1985: exports—apart from shady dealings with Eastern Europe—fell between 1964 and 1989 by about two-thirds. Other changes were more positive for the industry. The WO system continued to elaborate itself in terms of both appellations and controls. The limited market in quotas mentioned above did allow a small amount of innovation from the likes of Hamilton Russell, though independent producers of high-quality wines continued to be severely hampered by the quota system. The number of small producers was nonetheless growing, and the manufacturing wholesalers' share of the market was falling. KWV power had severely limited the number of wholesalers from the early years, and complicated restructuring deals in the 1970s had resulted in the amalgamation of the two overwhelmingly largest of them, Stellenbosch Farmers' Winery and Distillers/Oude Meester, into one monopolistic entity, Cape Wine and Distillers. But this marriage was annulled in 1988—in the name of the free market, although the same shareholders retained control of both SFW and Distillers. The only competing companies of note were Gilbey (part-owned by those same shareholders), and Union Wines and Douglas Green (which soon united as Douglas Green Bellingham).

The small local market (in the absence of an international one) for better-quality Cape wine was growing and becoming more exigeant. The indispensable guide to South African wine inaugurated by John and Erica Platter in 1980 rapidly became an annual one. The tenth anniversary edition of the Platter *Guide* briefly looked back at a decade that had seen the number of wines it described rise from 1,250 to about 4,000, and noted:

> Progress and proliferation, yes, both dramatic and erratic. Our first edition recorded one Cape chardonnay. There are now 40. And who would have guessed then that chenin blanc . . . would be overshadowed so rapidly and emphatically, as a dry white wine, by sauvignon blanc, which accounted for four labels then and 121 now. Only one methode champenoise sparkling wine featured in the first edition; there are now 17. The classic (Bordeaux) claret blend, a commonplace today . . . had yet to make its appearance, and amongst its first successful producers was an estate which hadn't bottled a single vintage by 1980. Nor, for that matter, had some of our finest quality cellars in other categories—pinot noir, chardonnay, etc.

Nonetheless, the fundamental situation of the vineyards was changing only slowly beneath this important development. By 1990, Chenin's domination had grown, and it now constituted more than 35 percent of hectarage, while white grapes in general accounted for more than 85 percent of the total. Chardonnay was up from virtually nothing to nearly 1.7 percent, and Cabernet had crept up a little over the decade, to 4.2 percent; Syrah remained below 1 percent. In the early 1990s the surplus pool going to KWV for distillation and fruit juice could still take up 45 percent of the vintage. Another ten years on, and all these statistics were to be dramatically different.

The end of the white minority regime in 1994 allowed for the remarkable changes in the South African wine industry that followed. In the shadow of this structural change came others: the collapse of the KWV quota system in 1992 and of the minimum price in 1994 were notable moments in the gradual dissipation of its once massive control and restrictive powers of regulation; in 1997 the organization was converted into a company. Although the KWV lives on as a large producer—memorably described by critic Michael Fridjhon as now just one hustler among the rest—the KWV era, with its positive and all its negative aspects, was ended.

3

GRAPE VARIETIES AND WINE STYLES

VARIETIES AND VARIETALISM

The history of grape varieties in the Cape is murky, from the time when van Riebeeck failed to specify in his diaries either the origin or the variety of his imports. Early Cape viticulture would have included Greengrape (Sémillon), White French (Palomino), Steen (Chenin Blanc), Muscat de Frontignan (Muscat Blanc à Petits Grains), Muscat of Alexandria, and Pontac. A large number of other varieties, sometimes mentioned to bewildering effect by travelers, were brought in over the years, though only a few of them became in any way established.

Early commentators do not always give us reason to have confidence in their pronouncements. William Bird in 1882 speaks of Pontac (now identified as the original Teinturier) as "the same as the cote-rotie of the Rhone, the pontac of Guienne . . . and the port grape of the Douro"—a bizarre array. Bird also refers to the "steen grape . . . so called from the same grape on the Rhine." This suggestion presumably refers to the many German vineyards including *stein* in their names, and indeed it is far from impossible that some of the grapes referred to as Steen were Riesling rather than Chenin Blanc—which adequately serves to indicate our inevitable uncertainty about the varietal mix of the past.

Any experiments were set aside and things became much simplified, however, during the hurried vineyard expansion during the early decades of British administration in the Cape Colony: Sémillon (Greengrape) came to dominate overwhelmingly. Even so, we cannot be sure of what subsequently happened in terms of varietal planting over the nineteenth century, until some conscious efforts at improvement were made in the last decades, especially through the government farm at Constantia, which raised awareness about varietal identity—particularly when the question of appropriate rootstocks became an issue. The ravages of phylloxera did give producers the opportunity of replanting with superior—or at least recommended—varieties, but the replanting process was slow.

We can, however, start being more confident about which varieties are actually being referred to as of the beginning of the twentieth century. In 1907 the young I. A. Perold, a temporary professor in chemistry at the University of Cape Town who had already shown evidence of his profound interest in wine and viticulture, was sent abroad by the Cape government, which recognized a need to widen the range of grapes available. He was to bring in 177 varieties, which formed the core of a collection that still exists at the Welgevallen Experimental Farm of the University of Stellenbosch (where he became the first professor of viticulture). Perold was also important in identifying various varieties in use locally (and in producing a new one, Pinotage).

But for much of the twentieth century (the KWV years), quantity rather than quality counted. There was little diversification, and a great shift toward the dominance of white grapes suitable for brandy and, later, for fruity table wines. A historical chart of the two most commonly planted varieties after World War II shows a rather gratifying X shape, with Cinsaut's line plummeting downward and Chenin Blanc's as inexorably rising: the lines cross at approximately 22 percent of total plantings in 1968. From roughly this period we are in early modern times, starting to move toward the current pattern—though Chardonnay, for instance, was still to make its impact, and the changes brought about by reentry into the international market in the 1990s were a huge boost to the proportions of the "noble" varieties in general and black grapes in particular, at the expense, mostly, of Chenin Blanc.

More statistics regarding the changes in plantings are given in the appendix, and chapters 1 and 2 have pointed to the major shifts over the past forty years, but before we move to a discussion of the roles of the different varieties it is interesting to note again continuing developments in recent years. The leading ten varieties at the end of 2011 were as follows, with the percentage of total plantings (in terms of vineyard area) given in parentheses, together with the change from the percentage fifteen years earlier:

Chenin Blanc (18.2 percent in 2011, down 12.9 percent from 1996)

Cabernet Sauvignon (12.0 percent, up 6.5 percent)

Colombard (11.8 percent, down 0.2 percent)

Syrah (10.3 percent, up 9.5 percent)

Sauvignon Blanc (9.6 percent, up 4.3 percent)

Chardonnay (8.0 percent, up 3.0 percent)

Merlot (6.4 percent, up 4.2 percent)

Pinotage (6.5 percent, up 2.7 percent)

Ruby Cabernet (2.2 percent, up 1.3 percent)

Muscat of Alexandria (2.1 percent, down 4.2 percent)

These ten make up more than 85 percent of the total plantings as measured by area. (Note that the percentages for 1996 differ from those originally published by the authorities because until 2003 they included Sultana, virtually entirely used for raisins and table grapes; these figures are adjusted to exclude Sultana.)

VARIETALISM, BLENDS, AND LABELS

Varietal naming of wines is currently dominant in South Africa, at all quality levels, as in most of the New World since it emerged as an inexorable practice in the United States in the middle of the twentieth century. This procedure is, of course, not inevitable, and earlier practices and debates in South Africa related instead to the European procedure of identifying wines by geographical origin—although reference was generally to European rather than local areas, except in the case of Constantia. Baron Carl von Babo was not the first to complain when he commented in his first report as government viti-culturist in 1885: "It is entirely useless and misleading to adopt foreign names for Cape wines; such names as Constantia, Paarl, Breede River, and Montagu on the labels of bottles containing properly prepared and manipulated Cape wine will read as well as Sherry or Madeira. . . . Also the name Hock is false and unjustifiable."

In fact, there have long been some Cape wines named for varieties, either wholly or partly and with uncertain accuracy. Most notable were probably Hanepoot (Muscat of Alexandria), Muscadel (Muscat Blanc à Petits Grains), Steen, Pontac, and something called Frontignac (discussed later)—sometimes used together with "Constantia," the only Cape area to have attained sufficient prestige to be really useful as a brand. All of those varieties were to some extent associated with a particular style of wine. But, judging by the insouciance, confusion, and ignorance with which varietal names were handled in the eighteenth and nineteenth centuries (precisely because they were not widely consid-ered to be immensely relevant in themselves but were generally used to indicate a style of wine), varietal naming was inevitably subordinate to a myriad of hopeful associations, such as Mallaga, Vintint, Moselle, Vin de Grave, Rheinwein, Rota, and even Boene—that is, Beaune.

While varietalism is a strong force in South Africa, monovarietalism is a little less so, as there is also a tendency toward producing blended wines. The tendency is notable, for example, in the use and image of the red Bordeaux varieties. A rough estimate, based on the summary of wine ratings in the 2013 edition of Platter's *Guide,* suggests that there are approximately equal numbers of varietal Cabernet Sauvignons and blends using a significant proportion of Cabernet. This seems to be very different from the situation in, say, California and Australia. In the Cape, the authority of the Bordeaux example would appear to be simply greater. In California varietal consciousness appears to imply that if varietalism is good, then monovarietalism is better. In South Africa there can be observed an evident pride in including all five of the main Bordeaux black grapes—more than a few wines even allude to this in their names (De Toren Fusion V, Constantia Glen Five, Raka Quinary, and Gabriëlskloof Five Arches among them), in something of a triumph of tradition over terroir.

This tendency to blend is nothing more than that: there are probably more varietal Syrahs than Cabernet Sauvignons, for example, but fewer blends based on Syrah than on Cabernet. But where an estate produces both a varietal Cabernet (or Merlot or Cabernet Franc, for that matter) and a Bordeaux blend, the latter is likely to be the flagship wine and to take first choice of grapes when it comes to assembling the cuvées. The general rule in the Cape seems to be that wines labeled simply with the name of the property (like Morgenster and Vergelegen) or with an invented name (Buitenverwachting Christine, Mvemve Raats de Compostella) are blends, while the varietal Cabernets are usually named as such.

A factor that must have played some role in all this is that generic naming based on European models was dealt a heavy blow in 1935. In that year the so-called Crayfish Agreement between the South African and French governments involved the dropping here of names and words associated with French appellations in exchange for a commitment to buy South African crayfish. (It's pleasant, incidentally, to note than an exemption was given to Chateau Libertas as it had been on the market since 1932; it is now one of the most venerable of local wine labels—and still spelled without a circumflex on the first *a* of *Chateau*.) The names of German vineyards remained to be plundered, however, and increasingly were—hardly surprisingly, since the German influence on winemaking here has been strong. Even now many popular wines are marketed (only locally, of course) under such long-established names as Kupferberger Auslese and Grünberger Stein. *Stein* even became a generic description for off-dry or semisweet white wine, inevitably causing some confusion because the more general name for Chenin Blanc remained Steen until comparatively recent years. But in *Fairest Vineyards* by Kenneth Maxwell, the first near-complete list and description of all Cape wines, published in 1966, the only French that creeps in is the occasional Vin Rouge, Vin Blanc, and Rosé, alongside a few Chiantis and the Germans. Apart from the many "Sherries," the remainder mostly go simply by the name of the producer either alone or with a varietal appendage or with a more-or-less fanciful name.

Before the Wine of Origin legislation of 1973 there were no controls over varietal naming. Such had been the misuse of variety names that restrictions were introduced gradually; for instance, a requirement that a wine had to include at least 75 percent of a variety in order to be given that variety's name was phased in over a period of years. Today, however, the international standard of 85 percent is observed. When a South African producer wishes to indicate on a label the different varieties that have gone into a blend, this is a matter of bureaucracy and paperwork—meaning that in practice, details of blends are not always given. Where they are, there is no requirement to indicate percentages, but the varieties must be given in descending order according to their proportions: it is not unusual for a producer to have a wine called Shiraz-Merlot one year and be obliged to change the name to Merlot-Shiraz the next, if the majority component has changed. If the varieties are listed, then usually *all* must be listed (though there are provisions for the smallest contributors to be omitted).

RED WINE VARIETIES

THE BORDEAUX BLACK GRAPES

Cabernet Sauvignon

In a brief discussion of Cabernet Sauvignon in the first (1980) edition of the annual Platter *Guide*, it is unquestioningly remarked that it "produces wines hard and astringent in youth. . . . A minimum of seven years ageing should be given a full-bodied cabernet to do it justice." How times have changed! There certainly are some local wines that will benefit from seven years or longer in bottle, but comparatively few that are not made with the hope of giving at least some pleasure when they are released a few years after bottling. In the 1980s and into the 1990s (but seldom nowadays), serious red wines tended to be offered for sale only three or four years from their vintage date, and the advantages of further maturation were obvious to equally serious wine-lovers. Even at a modest level, Cabernets were expected to improve.

It is uncertain when Cabernet was introduced to the Cape vineyard. When it was being grown with some seriousness at Groot Constantia in the last decades of the nineteenth century, the claim was made that it had been growing there for about fifty years. During the first half of the twentieth century it gained a good deal of prestige, even though most of the wines associated with Cabernet were blended—above all with Cinsaut, ostensibly to "soften" the wine, but also to eke out the small quantities available. One of the most famous wines of the mid twentieth century was the GS Cabernet Sauvignon made experimentally in 1966 and 1968 by or for (details remain uncertain) George Spies, production director at Stellenbosch Farmers' Winery. This bore a significant "100%" beneath the name of the variety on the minimalist label, testifying to the unusualness of the percentage, and also probably alluding to what was probably part of Spies's experiment: to show that Cape Cabernet could make a valid wine by itself. The wine is still splendidly alive now—as are some older so-called Cabernets.

Plantings started to increase through the 1970s, but even by 1990 it remained under 4 percent of the national vineyard. Paarl and Stellenbosch had and continue to have the largest Cabernet plantings, but it is to be found virtually everywhere to some extent, such is its comparatively forgiving nature and its reputation for quality. There is a great deal of high-cropping Cabernet churned out, for example, by the cooperatives of the warmest regions (from the Swartland to Robertson); these wines are usually just about acceptable, adequately fruity and ripe, often with the expected pseudo-serious gloss supplied by oak chips but with tannins reined in by clever winemaking. Particularly at that level, no customers expect to have to wait a few years for tannins to soften before drinking their Cabernets.

The same truth applies at more ambitious levels too, in most instances, although some of the most classic, such as Vergelegen's, can be austere in their youth. But the majority of the best, while they should improve with at least five years in bottle, are made to provide satisfaction at release: with forward fruit, ripely smooth, and soft tannin and acid structures. If the expensive new oak is still very obvious, as it often is—well, many of the customers expect that and, sadly, welcome it as a sign of quality, or at least of price. These are, in any case, truths common to all red wines and also hardly unique to the Cape. Tannic or early-charming, Cabernet Sauvignon remains undoubtedly the grandest of the Cape's red wine grapes, its prestige enhanced by its association with some of the finest red blends—though challenged these days by some Syrahs and a few Pinot Noirs.

Cabernet remains comfortably ahead of Syrah as the most planted red variety in the Cape, although at the end of 2011 it was down a little from its peak in 2004, but still more than double the hectarage of fifteen years previously. In 2000, well over 40 percent of the vines were under four years of age; now, as the vineyards mature, that figure is less than 3 percent. There are now more than 12,000 hectares planted, nearly half of them in the Stellenbosch-Paarl heartland.

Merlot

Merlot's critical reputation in the Cape is even more uneasy than it is in, say, California or Australia. Although there are a few good examples, many show an overtly herbaceous element, often expressed as mint, and often combined with an ultraripe lushness consequent on late harvesting that has endeavored to combat the greenness. Like Cabernet, it was widely planted, but proved less forgiving of unsuitable soils and climates. Its supposed tendency to make soft, round, and supple wines when compared with most of the other Bordeaux black grapes means first that it has historically been used in the Cape, as in Bordeaux and elsewhere, more frequently as a contributor to blends than for a varietal wine. Second, where it has been offered alone (sometimes with a stiffening of Cabernet), it has acquired the status of a particularly easygoing *style* of wine as much as a variety—even if not so markedly here as the film *Sideways* showed the case to be in the United States.

It seems that the little Merlot that was around in the 1970s was used for blending, and it was certainly planted by Billy Hofmeyr at Welgemeend in that decade for his Bordeaux blend. It has also worked well as a partner to Pinotage, at Middelvlei for example. Overgaauw is credited with the first varietal bottling for its 1982 Merlot. There are now nearly as many varietal Merlots as there are Bordeaux-style blends, though not as many as there are Cabernet Sauvignons, and they are in most cases less ambitious and less expensive wines than either of those two categories. A few consistently good Merlots are made, including those of Thelema and Bein. As with other "noble reds," but even more than most, plantings of Merlot increased substantially over the fifteen years to 2011, and it now occupies more than 6 percent of the total vineyard, in third place among the reds and seventh overall. There is a wide distribution (cool Elgin has a promising newcomer from Shannon Vineyards, for example), but Stellenbosch and greater Paarl have the largest plantings.

Cabernet Franc

For much of the twentieth century there was a little Cabernet Franc grown alongside Cabernet Sauvignon, gaining more recognition with the rise of the Bordeaux-style blend, of which it came to be seen as an increasingly useful part, adding some perfume, complexity, and even elegance. It was widely observed to perform extremely well in a number of areas (the Helderberg in Stellenbosch has been rather more associated with Franc than anywhere else), and it became ever more used in such blends and started playing a larger role in some of them. It had a parallel career as a solo performer, with Landskroon the pioneer here, and there are now a few dozen varietal Francs, some of them (such as Raats, Warwick, Raka, and Buitenverwachting) very good. It is generally producers aiming at elegance who want Franc, who also delight in its aromatic profile and are not scared (when "herbaceous" tends to be a term of abuse in red wine) to welcome the leafy note that often, but not always, accompanies even ripe Franc grapes. Growth in plantings has been fairly spectacular: there are now more than 1,000 hectares devoted to it, a threefold growth over fifteen years. Franc is most important to the wines of Stellenbosch, greater Paarl, and Constantia.

Petit Verdot

It was long thought that Welgemeend contained Petit Verdot, but this proved to be a misidentification, and the 1996 figure of 10.3 hectares of Petit Verdot might even have been exaggerated. In the years since then, however, from that minuscule base it has seen proportionately the fastest growth of any variety: by 2011 there were 675 hectares. An increasing number of varietal wines have been made—some twenty-five by 2013 (possibly more as experiments than with deep conviction about the suitability of the grape for going solo, and none are immensely convincing)—but undoubtedly the main purpose of its cultivation has been, as in Bordeaux, to use it to complement the other traditional varieties in the blend, adding complexity and sometimes depth of color.

Malbec

What is true of Petit Verdot is also true to only a slightly lesser extent of Malbec, in terms of growth and its role in the blend. But Malbec might well soon outstrip Petit Verdot, not because of its actual or theoretical usefulness in blends but because of its suitability as a varietal wine—with the imprimatur of Argentina. There are already about thirty audaciously fruity and delicious Malbecs made (including Annex Kloof, Paul Wallace, High Constantia, and Diemersfontein, for example) and probably there will be more, as more producers and consumers become aware of the variety's charms.

Other Bordeaux-Related Black Grapes

It might be fanciful to associate Pontac with Bordeaux, just because the name connects it to the well-known historical family from there and therefore with the associated area south of Bordeaux city. But Perold showed that Pontac, so important here in the nineteenth century, was identical with Teinturier (the original "dyer" grape, also known as Teinturier Mâle or du Cher). It seems to have come to the Cape in the seventeenth century (when it was also first noted in France). Its great career in old Constantia had late echoes in a number of fortified sweet wines, and a few table wines were made until the 1990s, but the last heavily virused block has now been pulled out. It would seem the last wine made in South Africa from Pontac was a Cape Vintage port from De Wet Cellar in Worcester; but in fact, it looks as though four Pontac vines were saved by the relevant authorities and cleared of virus, and at least one commercial winegrower is intent on propagating it once more.

It was thought for some time that the local crossing called Roobernet, released in 1990, was derived from Pontac and Cabernet Sauvignon, but tests in 2007 proved the parents to be Cabernet and Alicante Bouschet (the latter is a French crossing with Teinturier in its background, so that Roobernet is indeed related to Pontac). It scarcely matters: there are still only some 140 hectares planted, and Roobernet seems unassured of a great destiny.

Ruby Cabernet is quantitatively much more important, although this high-yielding American cross between Cabernet Sauvignon and Carignan is of no great significance for high-quality wine. There is a good deal of it about—mostly in the hotter areas, particularly Worcester, for which it was bred—and it actually ranks ninth in surface area: at well over 2,000 hectares nearly triple the area it occupied in 1992 (it was first planted here in 1982). A handful of varietal wines are made, but most goes into proprietary red blends, generally sold in boxes.

The Bordeaux Blend

If the continued strength of the Bordeaux blend tradition in South Africa is based on proven success, the tradition was begun on the basis of the authority of the Médoc and an attempt to replicate its strengths in a South African context. Billy Hofmeyr, a land surveyor by profession, became a winemaker initially by avocation, inspired by his love of claret. His Paarl farm, Welgemeend, produced, in the 1979 vintage, the Cape's first commercial classically Bordeaux-style blend. Meerlust and Kanonkop followed rapidly. The success of these wines, in a decade when the estates were becoming increasingly important to fine-wine production, led to a proliferation of the style. It would probably be true to say that most such blends continue to be based on Cabernet Sauvignon, but experimentation with the Bordeaux grapes has led to a great range of cépages. Even Welgemeend soon produced a second version, with Merlot and Malbec predominating. Nowadays, Merlot is the lead variety in, for example, Morgenster; Cabernet Franc leads in an increasing number of examples, of which Boekenhoutskloof's Journeyman is only one of the more recent.

The somewhat abstract determination to include "all five" main Bordeaux black grapes has been mentioned (fortunately for such producers' peace of mind, Carmenère has no presence here). It took two famous Bordelais winemakers, Bruno Prats and Hubert de Boüard, to speak slightly ironically of the authenticity of Syrah in a Bordeaux blend when they released the first vintage of Anwilka, the wine in which they have a direct interest. They were, of course, referring to the older practice of adding sunny Rhône wine to Bordeaux in poor vintages, as well as to some plantings that persist even now in Bordeaux.

Using Syrah is not a necessity, but nor are any rules broken, when making the mix in the Cape, and producers here are far from alone in finding it a satisfactory partnership, especially when they want to bring some early complexity to a wine.

The Bordeaux blend is undoubtedly one of the strongest categories in South African reds—no doubt at least partly because it is one on which many producers lavish the most care. Of producers with both a blend and a varietal Cabernet, it is most commonly the former that gets the best barrels of Cab.

THE RED RHÔNE AND MEDITERRANEAN VARIETIES

Syrah/Shiraz

There is no doubt that the huge growth in plantings of Syrah from the 1990s onward has been prompted by its international fashionability, which in turn was stimulated—initially at least—more by the offerings from Australia at all levels of quality than by the great wines of the northern Rhône. In fact, some authorities have thought it likely that Syrah has been present in the Cape in a small way for a very long time, if not necessarily continuously, and may have been among the earliest plantings. Unambiguous references are in short supply, however, and it is also more than possible that Australia was, more recently, the source. Certainly the influence of Australia on South African Syrah plantings long predated recent decades. Following a visit there toward the end of the nineteenth century, C. T. de Waal, the enterprising manager of Groot Constantia, recommended that the Department of Agriculture (which exercised a monopoly on the importing of grape-vines) should send to South Australia for vine cuttings. Syrah was prime among the imports; known in Australia as Hermitage, it understandably impressed him more than Cinsaut, the local usurper of that great terroir's name.

It must have been this more immediate origin that led to South Africa and Australia sharing Shiraz as a primary synonym for Syrah. Interestingly, although Perold in his 1926 treatise spells the former version in the now-accepted way, during the 1930s the spellings *Schiraz* and *Schiras* are also found. The use of Syrah as an alternative grew once it became an official synonym here after an application by Stellenzicht estate for its 1994 bottling, made by André van Rensburg. Van Rensburg wanted to use the French rather than the traditional name, as he insisted that his wine was different from "old style, sweaty, horsy Shiraz." This excellent wine was perhaps the one that most alerted winemakers and wine lovers to the local potential of the variety.

The grape had made little headway in the Cape in the first seventy-odd years since its (re)appearance here. Although a few varietal wines were made (the first varietally labeled example was from Bellingham in 1957), what little was planted mostly went into good-quality blends with Cabernet and Cinsaut. When the WO legislation was introduced in 1973, there were fewer than half a million Syrah vines in the country. The great leap forward started in the 1990s, and plantings grew steeply to well over 10,000 hectares in 2011. Syrah is the only red-wine grape that has increased its plantings every single year in the fifteen up to 2011, and it is now the fourth most planted grape: more than 10 percent of the total vineyard area, and more than 20 percent of black-grape plantings.

A necessary corollary of all the new plantings is that there are still many youngish vineyards around—although the grape's age distribution profile has changed dramatically in recent years. At the end of 2011 only 35 percent of vines were under ten years old (in 2008 the proportion was 75 percent). On the other hand, only 7 percent were older than fifteen years, and a mere 2 percent over twenty. Fashionability has meant that Syrah is planted heavily in all parts—from cool Elgin and Elim to the hot Klein Karoo. Clearly the picture of Syrah in the Cape will be different in ten and twenty years' time, with more mature vineyards and a better sense of terroirs most suited to it. What is already encouraging is that good wines are coming from many sources, although performance generalizations are difficult, especially as winemaking still tends to dominate.

Syrah is used more as a monovarietal wine than in blends. The modish addition of a dollop of Viognier (a practice ultimately deriving from Côte-Rôtie, though the immediate inspiration is Australia) is perhaps waning, and anyway now done with more subtlety than was often the case in the past. Mourvèdre and Grenache, in the style of the southern Rhône, are more common minor blending partners (not always announced). The Swartland—with the inspiration of first Charles Back's Spice Route and more definitively with Eben Sadie—has emerged as the leader in such blends, but it is far from alone in producing them. Nico van der Merwe, Catherine Marshall, Newton Johnson, and La Motte are among the other sources of fine Syrah-based blends of this type.

The Australian model of Syrah-Cabernet blends has not been compelling here, although Syrah is often successfully used within what would otherwise be Bordeaux-style blends. Rust en Vrede's flagship Estate Wine has long been of this type, as has Rouge from nearby Alto; and this has fostered something of a minor subregional tradition on the Helderberg and Simonsberg slopes (Uva Mira, Haskell, and Guardian Peak among those fitting in). Anwilka's was a more recent high-profile launch of a predominantly Cabernet-Syrah blend.

Cinsaut and Other Varieties Associated with Southern France

Cinsaut is of great historical significance in the Cape. It has been grown here since the middle of the nineteenth century and was known locally as Hermitage (for unclear reasons) until the trade agreement with France in 1935 prevented taking the names of French wine regions in vain. Perold had already made the formal identification with Cinsaut (often spelled Cinsault) of southern France, and that name became widely used. Until the rise of Chenin Blanc, it was South Africa's most planted variety, occupying nearly a third of the vineyard and used for everything from brandy, through rosé, to sweet, dry, and fortified red wines. The quality range was extreme. Records are rare, but apparently even some of the best "Cabernet Sauvignons" and blends of the mid twentieth century included a greater or lesser percentage of Cinsaut. From the 1960s onward, uprootings ensured that it now accounts for less than 2 percent of the total—mostly in the warmer regions, but a surprising amount lingers in Stellenbosch. Some 27 percent of Cinsaut vines are more than twenty years old, and a mere 2 percent are under four.

Some ambitious new producers of the Swartland particularly have sought out old bush-vine Cinsaut for inclusion in their serious Syrah-based blends (Mullineux and Badenhorst, for example). There are some splendid old bushvine vineyards of Cinsaut in that area, and Sadie Family Pofadder is one of very few ambitious monovarietal Cinsauts in the country. But there will undoubtedly be more, and not only from the Swartland, as winemakers come to realize that the results obtainable from well-farmed, low-cropping vines are a world apart from the insipidity of Cape Cinsaut in the late twentieth century. Cinsaut's main claim to fame, or notoriety, in the Cape remains, however, its role in the parenthood of Pinotage.

Carignan, too, lingers in one or two decent wines made from old vineyards, notably Fairview's Pegleg from the Swartland, and it finds its way into a few good blends in that area; but the variety has never been present here in anything like significant volumes. Grenache, like Carignan, is a grape that is originally Spanish but internationally best known for its voluminous presence in the south of France. The original importation into South Africa seems to have been from Spain, and it was established (mostly for fortified wine production) by the time Perold identified it in 1910. Some is now being planted, but as the variety is generally regarded as requiring more vine maturity than most to make decent quality, the tiny volume of older Grenache (notably in the Piketberg area) is keenly sought after by ambitious producers of both Rhône-style blends (especially in the Swartland, but also Ken Forrester's the Gypsy, for example), and monovarietal wines (by Neil Ellis, Vriesenhof, Sadie Family, Tierhoek), of which the numbers are growing. There is also a little of the red *(gris)* and white versions.

Mourvèdre, the French name for the Spanish grape Monastrell, is officially known in South Africa primarily as Mataro, reflecting its importation from Australia at the end of the nineteenth century, though it is invariably referred to by its French synonym. Of the little group of varieties associated mostly with the south of France, it is probably the most fashionable in the Cape, but plantings are still very small. There are some good varietal wines made from it (from Beaumont, Spice Route, and Tobias, for example), but its main role is probably as a minority partner with Syrah—the best known of which blends is Sadie Family Columella.

Tannat, the grape from southwestern France, has risen from nothing to nearly 75 hectares in 2011. As yet it mostly disappears into blends—including Zorgvliet's flagship Richelle, otherwise a Bordeaux blend—but a few rather tough and alcoholic varietal examples are made.

Petite Sirah is officially known as Durif, and exists only in some small plantings made by Charles Back at Fairview and Spice Route. Back is a great believer in the future of Petite Sirah in the Cape, and it would be foolhardy to disagree with the assessment of such a man.

ITALIAN VARIETIES

One might have expected South African interest in Sangiovese, and even more in the varieties of the southern Italian mainland and Sicily, but official indifference and widespread ignorance have dictated otherwise in the past. Difficulties and delays in importing stock are still a deterrent, but interest in the grapes of Italy is growing, and Sangiovese, with 61 hectares in 2011—a huge increase since 1996—is making a modest showing: there are half a dozen varietal examples, and some blends. On a smaller scale, the same is true of the Piedmont-based varieties Nebbiolo and Barbera. Strangely, considering the climatic difference involved as well as the notorious difficulty of succeeding elsewhere with the grape, Nebbiolo was mentioned in Perold's 1926 treatise as doing well in warmer sites in the Cape, but little seems to have been known of it subsequently until it became the first of the Italian varieties to appear on a label here: that of Steenberg in the late 1990s. Steenberg Nebbiolo is now becoming increasingly convincing. The few local producers of Italian extraction have understandably shown interest in making wines from these grapes, but unfortunately the examples from Idiom and Morgenster have generally been subjected to overripeness, precluding them from serious interest. There is also a minor but interesting fashion to blend the three available Italian varieties together in serious wines, which can work very well for Nederburg Ingenuity and for Bouchard Finlayson Hannibal (which contrives to include also Pinot Noir and Syrah). Zinfandel/Primitivo, which has been planted in a small way in the Cape for many decades, has never aroused much interest—although Blaauwklippen has made it something of a feature of its range—and now seems to be on the decline, even while other Italians are prospering.

PORTUGUESE AND SPANISH VARIETIES

As with Italian, the lack of penetration by Spanish and Portuguese varieties is unfortunate to the point of being scandalous in light of similarities of climate and conditions—that is, leaving aside Garnacha and Monastrell, Spaniards that entered the country with French passports. And various port varieties have been here for some time and are increasingly being used for table wines as well as fortified ones, especially by the port producers of the Klein Karoo. Tinta Barocca (the official misspelling of Tinta Barroca) is by far the most extensively planted of them, although it had just 221 hectares in 2011, which is in fact a big decrease from 1996's figure, while the plantings of the finest variety, Touriga Nacional, has quadrupled to 87 hectares in the same period. Eben Sadie is now making a wine from old Tinta Barroca vines, which is bound to increase interest. Other port varieties are grown in a small way, including Tempranillo/Tinta Roriz and Tinta Amarela/Trincadeira.

OTHER BLACK GRAPES

Pinotage

Whether South Africa's "own" grape is ever to provide a unique selling point is surely starting to seem doubtful to even its greatest admirers. While varietal Pinotage and Pinotage-charactered blends do reasonably well in the international market, as they do at home, and a rare few are even lauded, the grape continues to have its implacable detractors, both locally and internationally. There are, of course, many passionate defenders and advocates of Pinotage—but as they are mostly local, there is often some discernible element of self-interest or of patriotic stirrings. Yet Pinotage makes enough good wines to establish that it is certainly not "vile" (as British writer Jamie Goode once called it).

The variety dates to 1924, when Professor Perold successfully crossed Pinot Noir and Cinsaut. The latter grape was known in South Africa at the time as Hermitage, hence the second part of the portmanteau name later given to the cross. Perold, one story has it, planted four seeds in the flower garden of his university-owned house. Two years later he left the university and in 1928 a young lecturer rescued the young plants from a team clearing the garden and took them to Professor Theron at Elsenburg Agricultural College. It is possible that Theron knew about the seedlings if they had, rather, been planted at the university's Welgevallen Experimental Farm. Different accounts persist (Pinotage's most thorough historian, Peter F. May, has been unable to resolve the discrepancies). The young plants were grafted onto rootstocks in either 1932 or 1935 by Theron, who proceeded to evaluate the new variety. He and Perold then selected the strongest of the young plants for propagation and gave it its name ("Herminot" was a possibility, too).

In 1941 the first wine from Pinotage was made at the small Welgevallen winery by C.T. de Waal. The first commercial plantings seem to have been near Somerset West in 1943. But in 1953, Bellevue and Kanonkop also planted this unknown new variety. In 1959 a Bellevue wine made from Pinotage was named best wine at the Cape Young Wine Show. The wine was marketed in 1961 by Stellenbosch Farmers' Winery under the Lanzerac brand, the first label to carry the new variety's name.

Since then, the grape has inevitably had its vicissitudes in terms of producer and consumer popularity. The grape was viticulturally undemanding, and quite widely planted during the 1960s. It came to occupy about 2 percent of the vineyard, but by the early 1990s its hectarage had grown little and it was the second-cheapest red grape in South Africa. The mid-1990s wave of international enthusiasm or curiosity about South African wine added impetus to Pinotage. It seemed an omen when a Kanonkop Pinotage received the Robert Mondavi Award as the best red wine at the 1991 International Wine and Spirits Competition in London. Prices for Pinotage grapes rose dramatically through the 1990s and so did plantings, which reached a high point in 2001 when Pinotage occupied 7.3 percent of the national vineyard. But thereafter plantings fell away (as prices dropped even more than for most other red varieties), and its relative status plummeted. By 2011 its share was down to 6.5 percent. We can presume that this is not the end of the story in the fashionability or otherwise of Pinotage.

Pinotage is grown widely around the Cape, with most of it in Stellenbosch, Paarl, and Swartland. What does seem clear is that the best wines come off older, dryland bushvines—and there are, in fact, still a number of producing vineyards dating from the 1960s; although, as the notable result of such conditions is comparatively low-yielding vines, this is perhaps the essential reason for the higher quality. Such vineyards are mainly responsible for fine Pinotages from, for example, the Kanonkop, Meerendal, and DeWaal estates.

No doubt Perold's hopes were that his cross would have the inherent greatness of Pinot Noir combined with Cinsaut's prolific ease and tolerance of hot days. But strange things emerge in such processes, of course—who would have imagined, for example, that two grapes that tended to produce light-colored wines would merge to produce a grape giving deep color? As to the elegance and finesse characteristic of good Pinot Noir, few would claim that these number among Pinotage's virtues, although there certainly are some more lightly made Pinotages with a perfume and grace that recall this side of the grape's origins, and after the best versions have been ten years or so in bottle, its noble ancestry seems by no means implausible. Many have aged well: tasted in 2010, the Lanzerac 1963 was splendid, lively and fresh with not too much grip and deep, lingering fruit. More recent wines than that, notably Kanonkops, have also shown the ability to mature beneficially over a decade or more.

The problems? There are indeed a few, though it must be stressed that as viticulturists and especially winemakers have learned to deal with the grape these are encountered increasingly rarely. Judicious winemaking reduces to a whisper the sweet acetone pungency (deriving from isoamyl acetate), and the trace—or more—of bitterness that emerged in the 1990s particularly is now rarer, and often even attractive when at a very low level. Pinotage is prone to deliver big tannins, a characteristic exacerbated by the overoaking inflicted by some ambitious winemakers. In fact, there is perhaps more ambition around than a lot of Pinotage can take, and too much patriotic anxiety also, as well as "cultural cringe." Without at all decrying the very good Pinotage wines made by a number of producers (apart from the few already mentioned here, one should add at least Beyerskloof, Grangehurst, Simonsig, and L'Avenir), the great virtues of less-grand wines should be mentioned: lightly wooded, sufficiently ripe, delicious examples like the standard Beyerskloof, now made for an international audience in huge volumes.

Using Pinotage in blends has been a less purist track to the goal of a South African style of wine that will be both unique and compelling. The idea of a "Cape blend" has had some success among eager producers at least, so that the phrase appears on a number of labels at all price levels. The minimum percentage needed for a wine to be considered a Cape blend is a matter of some debate even among the advocates of the idea, and any regulation around the matter is a long way off—not least because there are a number of producers who dislike the idea of one recipe arrogating to itself a name that implies such authority.

In fact, Pinotage frequently works happily with other varieties. The first wine to make a declared virtue of blending it with other grapes was Welgemeend Amadé in 1979, which also included Grenache and Syrah to make an indigenous equivalent of the southern Rhône blend. There was no general enthusiasm for the idea until the first half of the 1990s, when Uiterwyk (now DeWaal) introduced its Estate wine, which took on the Cape blend moniker from 1994; a number of other wineries subsequently took up the idea. Generally both Bordeaux and Rhône varieties feature in such blends. Pinotage tends, in fact, to be the minority component, partly because it tends to dominate. This dominance typically becomes much less pronounced after a few years in bottle—a maturation that is well deserved, as some of these wines have shown (Beyerskloof Synergy, Clos Malverne Auret, DeWaal, Grangehurst, and Kaapzicht among them). In terms of style, as with varietal Pinotage, the blends range from the comparatively restrained to the large, powerful, and lush; from modest, scarcely oaked, graceful wines to august, ambitious wines matured in all-new French oak.

Pinotage also makes a good rosé and does occasional service in other styles of wine, from sparkling to fortified. But the big success story for the "national grape" in recent years, locally and increasingly internationally, has been so-called "coffee Pinotage." Pioneered at Diemersfontein in the early 2000s by its then-winemaker, Bertus Fourie, it basically implies a wine fermented on highly toasted oak staves to give a strong mocha character. There are now numerous big-brand examples—somewhat to the horror of Pinotage's true believers.

Pinot Noir

This famously difficult variety has a short history of real success in the Cape, but has made great, even exciting progress during this century. Plantings are growing but still small, just over 1 percent of the total, and by far the larger part of the Pinot harvest goes into sparkling wine. The number of genuinely good examples of varietal Pinot can be counted on a pair of hands, but the number is growing, and what's more, from varied geographical origins.

Pinot was probably imported by Perold in the second decade of the twentieth century; in his *Treatise on Viticulture* of 1927 he describes it as producing on the university farm "a wine of high quality . . . beautifully coloured, strong, full-bodied wine with an excellent bouquet." Some Pinot seems to have found its way in 1920 to a very short-lived career at Alto (it ripened too early to be easily suitable for blended wine), but it found a warmer welcome at Muratie later in the twenties. For many decades, Muratie's was the only South African example. Perold's interest in the variety at the time was also marked by his crossing it with Cinsaut to produce Pinotage.

The prelude to the modern era of Pinot in South Africa came in the late 1970s, when a number of more ambitious producers planted it and attempted to make a good wine from it—foolhardy and obsessed producers, perhaps, since the prevailing wisdom was that the grape could not successfully transplant from Burgundy. At their inspirational head was Tim Hamilton-Russell and his winemaker, Peter Finlayson, in the Hemel-en-Aarde Valley. The problem that eventually became apparent was that the approved clone was a Swiss one, BK5, developed for sparkling wine. Finlayson soon moved on to another little bit of Burgundy in the valley, and his first Pinot, of 1991, was made from grapes grown in Elgin, where better clonal material had been experimentally planted in the early 1980s. It was immediately apparent to many commentators that this superior clonal material was the only way forward. All significant producers of Pinot with experience in Burgundy have by now replanted to a handful of Burgundian clones.

The Hemel-en-Aarde region and Elgin remain the joint headquarters, as it were, of Pinot production, with a number of good new producers joining the old guard—Newton Johnson, Sumaridge, and Crystallum among them in Hemel-en-Aarde, and Oak Valley (the original supplier to Bouchard Finlayson), Catherine Marshall, and Paul Cluver in Elgin. There are also fine examples emerging from other coolish areas, such as the higher slopes of Franschhoek, where clever work in the Chamonix vineyards has led to a dramatic upcurve in quality. And in the cool heights of the Outeniqua Mountains, Herold is showing what can be done with Pinot in the most surprising places, as is Fryer's Cove up the West Coast. Pinot is among the varieties being experimented with in Super Single's highlying and continental vineyards of Sutherland-Karoo. A few decent examples are made in warmer Stellenbosch, notably Meerlust's.

The growing sophistication of winemakers and viticulturists, well traveled and acquainted with Pinots not only of Burgundy but also of New Zealand and Oregon, is no doubt as significant a factor in quality improvements as is the improvement in clonal material and virus-cleaned vines. Viticultural methods remain varied—Bouchard Finlayson, for example, used high-density planting and Burgundian-style trellising from the outset, but many others adopt more standard South African practices with success. Overuse of new oak remains something of a temptation for some in the cellar, as does an affection for very ripe fruit and consequent high alcohols, and a reliance on extracted tannin rather than acidity for structure; but if these are faults (and they are not so for everyone), they tend to be minor ones these days. Despite the excitement of what is happening with the fickle grape, there is little doubt but that Pinot Noir will always occupy a tiny niche in the edifice of Cape wine, given the dearth of suitably cool locations with enough water for supplementary irrigation.

WHITE WINE VARIETIES

CHARDONNAY

When ambitious estate winemakers in the 1970s turned to Chardonnay, they found only the badly virused and diseased clones at the Stellenbosch University collection. Danie de Wet of De Wetshof in Robertson was one of the pioneers of the variety (he produced the one Chardonnay listed in the 1980 edition of the annual Platter *Guide*), and he says, "From day one we knew that we must get better material." Unfortunately, as described in chapter 2, illegal imports seemed the only way to do this in a reasonable space of time—and unfortunately, too, much of what was brought in proved to be Auxerrois. But better planting material did become available during the 1980s; plantings grew from negligible levels to about 1.5 percent of the total by 1990, and continued to rise.

The style in the early years also tended to reflect the new-world fashion for heavy oaking, though a few producers, like Hamilton Russell and De Wetshof, were making some fine wines even then. But the quality of Chardonnay in the Cape improved at least as much as any other variety in the 1990s, and there is no doubt that now there are some very fine, ageworthy examples. Jancis Robinson was on the judging panel of a local competition in 2007 that awarded a Museum Class trophy to a decade-old Chardonnay Reserve from Chamonix; she asked afterward "where else [other than South Africa] outside Burgundy could field a 1997 in such great condition?"

There is no one recipe for the best wines—some are barrel-fermented, some not; some go completely through malolactic fermentation, some not; lees may be stirred with batons or the barrels may be rolled; increasing numbers are made without acidification and without yeast inoculation. Burgundy is clearly the ruling model here, rather than the Californian "brand Chardonnay" cliché of obvious oak and some residual sugar—although there are, of course, wines in that style, too. The category of unoaked Chardonnay has also grown substantially in recent years, from the time when De Wetshof produced the first such wine with Bon Vallon.

Chardonnay is planted voluminously throughout the Western Cape (there's even some in the Orange River area), and still expanding. With just over 8 percent of total vineyard coverage in 2011, it ranked sixth in terms of vineyard coverage, the fourth most planted white variety (this proportion up from 5.1 percent fifteen years previously). Clearly the ABC brigades (anything but Chardonnay) are not winning, although the new vineyards are particularly serving the burgeoning growth in sparkling-wine production. More than half of the plantings are in the Breede River Valley, but this does not carry the usual adverse implications for quality, as half of these vineyards are in Robertson, where a rich vein of limestone has proved to be well suited to the grape, even if these are not the Cape's most exciting Chardonnays. Paarl and Stellenbosch are the areas next in terms of Chardonnay vineyard area; but there are virtually no districts in which Chardonnay is not to be found, and usually producing at least one decent example. It is difficult, then, to suggest that there is any degree of specialization on the basis of terroir that has emerged over the years, beyond the success of the Robertson soils and of the cooler climates in Hemel-en-Aarde, Elgin, and Constantia, where most of the wineries produce good to excellent Chardonnays. It would be difficult to argue against the claims of Hemel-en-Aarde for preeminence, perhaps, from well-established Hamilton Russell (in 2011 I enjoyed a superb 1989 in fine condition) to the newer Newton Johnson and Crystallum. Elgin might disagree, with my support.

The significance of a greater degree of coolness is also graphically shown in Franschhoek, where Chamonix's is by far the most successful Chardonnay, from vines that are planted at a higher altitude than elsewhere in the valley. Robertson apart, few of the most highly regarded samples come from warmer areas. The best-known Robertson examples come from Springfield, De Wetshof, and Weltevrede. Stellenbosch has a large number of at least decent, often better, examples (including, but not exclusively, Rustenberg, Vergelegen, Jordan, Thelema, and Uva Mira), but Paarl has many fewer (Glen Carlou having shown the best potential).

White blends notwithstanding, Chardonnay might arguably offer the largest contribution to the list of the best South African white wines—which, on the whole, means the best South African wines *tout court*.

CHENIN BLANC AND CHENIN-BASED BLENDS

The story of Chenin Blanc in South Africa tends to invite extremes, along with phrases like "highs and lows" and "splendors and miseries." Today, though far off its quantitative height, it remains by far the most planted variety in the Cape: by area more than 18 percent of all varieties and well over 30 percent of whites. It is spread throughout the wine-producing areas, but inevitably the heaviest concentrations are in the hot, irrigated inland valleys, plantings in marked contrast to the old low-yielding bushvines that produce the finest wines (although old unirrigated bushvines are frequently found in warm parts, like the Swartland and Olifants River). Each year it tends to be the most frequently uprooted as well as the most newly planted variety—with much more uprootings than plantings but with less discrepancy than during the 1990s, when the fashion was to replace as much of it as possible with red varieties. In the early years of that decade Chenin occupied nearly a third of the vineyard area. It was—as it still is to a large extent, along with Colombard—the versatile workhorse of the industry, producing vaguely pleasant wine from heavy-cropping vineyards as well as supplying the grape-juice, brandy, and fortified-wine industries. But with more vines than any other country, and with great quality improvements at all levels of ambition, Chenin is gaining a reputation as a South African signature variety—and a good one, at that.

This is one of the oldest varieties on the Cape, though only in 1963 did Professor Orffer match the Loire variety with what had been known here as Steen. It was also known as Stein; some pardonable confusion and folk etymology made the Germanic connection, and there is even a note in the handwriting of Governor Simon van der Stel suggesting comparability in terms of quality of Steen with German Stein wines, which shows that the duality has been around for a long time. *Stein* has no status as a synonym any longer, and has also largely lost its status as a generic name for off-dry white wine. One theory has it that the Dutch corrupted Listán (a Spanish name for Palomino, another pioneering variety here) into La Stan and then into De Steen, before dropping the article. Now the name *Steen* appears as a synonym for Chenin on only a few defiant wine labels (including two fine ones: one from the tiny producer Tobias in the Swartland, and Donkiesbaai, from Piekenierskloof, made by Jean Engelbrecht of Rust en Vrede). It lingers stubbornly, though, among some growers, who associate the lower-yielding, better-quality—perhaps best-adapted—clones of the grape (there are ten currently available in South Africa) with Steen. It is greatly to be hoped that further research will establish not so much a justification for the name as whether the variety has adapted itself to local conditions in a reproducible clone.

So, with varying reputation, Steen-Chenin has been a continuous feature of the Cape vineyard. It was one of the grapes grown at Constantia in the eighteenth and nineteenth centuries, although its price was far off those of Pontac and the Muscat varieties. By the early twentieth century Steen was advancing, but still some way behind Greengrape. Although the rise in brandy production was undoubtedly responsible for much of the increased planting of Chenin in warm areas, the grape's defining moment came during and subsequent to the 1960s with the huge popularity of off-dry white wines like Lieberstein, and its rise (anonymous to the public) became inexorable.

In the post-1994 Cape wine revolution, destruction might have been more extreme had it not been for the awareness of a few farsighted winemakers that mature Chenin vines might produce better wine than the despised or, at best, taken-for-granted grape was usually credited with. There were the first signs of Chenin being taken more seriously. Walter Finlayson of Glen Carlou blended a little of a rather more prestigious grape into his barrel-fermented Devereux Chenin Blanc–Chardonnay 1994. Then Irina von Holdt introduced her nearly dry Blue White Chenin Blanc in 1995, comparatively expensive and in a striking blue bottle.

The growth in number and quality of varietal wines was undoubtedly furthered by an annual competition, the Chenin Blanc Challenge, expressly dedicated to improving the breed. This revival has been further driven by the Chenin Blanc Association, one of the most active of the variety-based winegrower bodies. To an extent, however, the improvement has come with the price that is paid when competitive blind tastings acquire significance: more winemakers started picking their best fruit ultraripe—with resulting high alcohol levels and often a noticeable degree of residual sugar—and then put the wine into new oak to complete the blockbuster effect. While many of these expensive "show wines" are undoubtedly of high quality, not all of them make for satisfying, refreshing drinking to the bottom of the glass.

As the industry matures, however, and as the market's doubts about such wines grow, more winemakers are relying rather on purity and intensity of fruit. Many of the top-priced Chenins continue to be wooded, but less emphatically so than they were. Any short list of examples would omit many good wines, but labels would certainly include Ken Forrester, De Morgenzon, Raats, Kanu, Rudera, De Trafford, Teddy Hall, and Jean Daneel. Top-end unwooded Chenins include those of Beaumont, Old Vines, Raats, and Vinum, as well as quite a number of new-wave wines from Swartland producers, like Lammershoek. The majority of cheaper, simple and fruity Chenins are unwooded.

The basis of the large volumes of good Chenin at all levels is the old vineyards of, especially, Paarl, Stellenbosch, and the Swartland. The variety's natural good acidity is fully taken advantage of in such viticultural conditions. The market for relatively expensive Chenin is necessarily limited, so old, low-yielding bushvines are still being pulled out, if at a slightly less alarming rate. Nonetheless, the age distribution chart shows more than half of the vines to be older than sixteen years, and nearly 40 percent older than twenty.

Chenin's first moment of South African glory came many decades ago, however, when it was used in Nederburg's Edelkeur, the first of the Cape's unfortified botrytised dessert wines. It still serves Edelkeur, as well as a number of other extremely good versions, including Ken Forrester T, Kanu Kia-Ora, and Rudera Noble Late Harvest.

A new role for Chenin came early in this century with Eben Sadie's Palladius, a blend based on sixty-year-old Swartland vines. While Palladius and similar wines have links with styles emerging also in the south of France and in parts of California, effectively Sadie and the Paardeberg terroir invented the local version—or rather, they are inventing it, as a valid and original expression of the Cape. A few producers have even seized the idea of a Cape blend from the punters of Pinotage, and are suggesting that a Chenin-based blend might well form a valid white equivalent. While the other main kind of white blend pursued locally, based on Sémillon and Sauvignon, tends to originate in the relatively cool areas, the Chenin-based version mostly comes from warmer areas, with the Swartland remaining the center. Blending partners include Chardonnay, as well as such Rhône varieties as Grenache Blanc and Clairette (generally known in South Africa by its synonym, Clairette Blanche), as well as Viognier and the much scarcer Roussanne. Undoubtedly Marsanne, at present undergoing the necessary bureaucratic processes as an immigrant, will soon be coming to this party (if rumors are correct, it is already an illegal gate-crasher).

COLOMBARD

This is the third most planted variety in the Cape, with nearly 12,000 hectares in 2011, 11.8 percent of the national vineyard, mostly in the heavy-cropping hot and irrigated areas. A substantial part of the crop goes toward distillation and grape juice, and much of the rest into cheap, nameless blends, although there are also some varietal blends (the partnership with Chardonnay can be pleasant), and a small handful of modest bottlings labeled Colombard or Colombar—both spellings are used.

MUSCAT VARIETIES

Although various Muscat varieties occupy only a tiny percentage of the Cape vineyard (and much of that goes to raisins and table grapes), it is a historically important category—and a somewhat confusing one, particularly but not only as far as nomenclature is concerned. Jan van Riebeeck caused the first problem, in his reference to "the Spanish grapes" among the first imports to the settlement: it seems likely that these were Muscat of Alexandria—which certainly is one of the longest-established varieties here. Its more popular name is Hanepoot (always used when the grapes are for the table rather than for wine), the origins of which are controversial. In the 1730s Otto Mentzel described this as one of the best grapes for wine and called it "the 'Haanen-Kloote' [Cock's testicle]," but added that it is "called Haanen-poote [cock's foot] by the ladies of Africa." Perold accepted the idea of euphemism as the origin of the name, saying (no doubt with an authority denied to most of us) that "the berry of this variety resembles somewhat in shape and size" the relevant anatomical bit of a rooster. The other common explanation is that the name derives directly from the Dutch for "cock's foot," because the formation of the variety's stems allegedly resembles a spread claw. Whichever might be true, it is undoubtedly the case that adducing "honey-pot" as an origin, by association with the luscious sweetness of the grapes, is an illegitimate bit of folk etymology. As to wine from Muscat of Alexandria, there are very few table-wine varietal versions these days (though it probably finds its way into some blends, and the international fashion for Moscato is likely to change this), and most of the crop that isn't used for table grapes and raisins goes into fortified bottlings as Hanepoot, Muscat d'Alexandrie, or white Jerepigo. Plantings have declined severely, however, since it constituted some 13 percent of plantings in the early 1970s.

The much superior (for winemaking at least) Muscat Blanc à Petits Grains at that time was 3 percent of plantings, but it has also declined to negligible proportions. Even more than Hanepoot, however, it has played an important part in the history of South African wine, both as a white grape and in its red mutation. It too is better known by other names: a French one, Muscat de Frontignan, and two local ones: Frontignac (also used as a synonym for the grape in Australia, and occasionally for the sweet wine from the grape in France) and, more important, Muscadel—to be distinguished from Muscadelle (the similarity of names precludes the use of Muscadel on labels destined for Europe). Under the latter names it was responsible for a good proportion of the sweet wines of Constantia. Muscadel was mentioned by van Riebeeck as among the very first grapes to be harvested at the Cape, in 1659—and we presume he referred to the grape that now has that name.

Mention of Constantia raises (for a few curious people at least) a puzzle. Today Muscadel is officially a synonym for Muscat de Frontignan, but there is no doubt that Constantia produced a red wine called Frontignac in addition to red and white wines that were possibly made from Muscadel. Perold in 1927 maintained the distinction, pointing to the close connection between the varieties while saying that Frontignac/Muscat de Frontignan was the finer. Later tests showed no meaningful distinction between grapes that went by those names in South Africa, but that is very possibly because the "genuine" Frontignac, which might well have been a local fixed mutation of a variety that is notoriously prone to mutation, or even a cross, has disappeared, or at least been lost track of. Could there be some still undetected, somewhere, wasting its fragrance (as it were) on the desert air?

The wine that is being made at Klein Constantia, and now elsewhere in the valley, in an attempt to re-create the great Constantia wines of the past, is entirely from (white) Muscat de Frontignan. Elsewhere in the country, notably in the hotter inland areas where it grows in dwindling amounts, Muscadel is used for the eponymous fortified wine. There is twice as much of the white version as of the red, but together they amount to less than 1 percent of the total vineyard, by far the greater part of the vines being in the Robertson area, where there are some old vines: Rietvallei makes a tiny quantity each year from a single block of (black-fruited) low-sprawling bushvines planted in 1908. Morio-Muskat and Muscat Ottonel are now scarcely planted.

RIESLING (AND THE "CAPE RIESLING" MASQUERADER)

While it might have been thought neither here nor there that Riesling has been a sharply declining feature of the Cape vineyard, the international success of Australian Riesling serves as a reminder of the price paid here for neglect of arguably the finest of all white grapes. Some is indeed grown here, and a few fair wines made from it. Furthermore, there are increased signs of interest from some producers, often spurred by their own love for Riesling. The vineyards that remain (now just 0.2 percent of the total; they were about 1 percent in 1990) are mostly in the more suitable, cooler parts, and are even being expanded there by, for example, Paul Cluver in Elgin and Klein Constantia in Constantia.

The grape has not been well served by the timid bureaucracy of the industry. Not long since, the name *Riesling* was reserved for the grape that was also known as Cape Riesling but is actually the irredeemably minor Crouchen. Meanwhile, the genuine thing was obliged to label itself as either Weisser or Rhine Riesling. The fraud was, we must presume, allowed to continue because of big-business interest in continuing to mass-market Nederburg Paarl Riesling and Theuniskraal Riesling, two vaguely pleasant wines made from Crouchen—the first one now defunct. Most Crouchen (which occupies just 0.6 percent of the vineyard, mostly in Paarl and Worcester, down from 4 percent in 1996) ends up in anonymous blends now. In 2008, a partial victory for quality was finally won: starting with the 2010 vintage, Riesling was able to call itself Riesling, unprefixed; Crouchen, unfortunately, retained the right to use the name Cape Riesling within South Africa (this is now how the Theuniskraal version is labeled), thus still leaving room for confusion.

I recall a visit to the Cape from Rheingau winemaker Hans-Josef Becker in the late 1990s, when he asked me to direct him to some of the best local examples of the grape. I suggested that the best Rieslings in the Cape (as opposed to the best Cape Rieslings!) were the dessert wines—but Becker wasn't interested. If a producer could make a good dry Riesling, he was confident that the sweet wines would be good; as the reverse was not true, he'd prefer to start with the drier versions. Undoubtedly the best Rieslings have been a few botrytised dessert versions—notably from Paul Cluver, Neethlingshof, and occasionally Klein Constantia. Of the nondessert wines, the few good examples have tended to have a little residual sugar (about 10 grams per liter), but with a balancing acidity and a rather higher alcohol than would be apparent in most German Spätlesen. Klein Constantia, whose Rieslings had a track record of aging beneficially for five to ten years, moved from this to a drier, more powerful but perhaps less graceful style, with interesting results. Hartenberg makes a successful version with a little older wood influence. Hartenberg and Thelema offer counterexamples to the suggestion that Riesling will do well in South Africa only in the coolest areas, but it is likely that, if ever the winds of the Riesling Renaissance reach these shores, they will blow most productively in areas like Constantia and Elgin, as well as occasional high-lying tracts elsewhere, such as that producing grapes for Howard Booysen's Riesling in the Swartberg mountains, which makes for a steelier example than those in coastal regions.

SAUVIGNON BLANC (WITH A NOTE ON NOUVELLE)

It is unclear when Sauvignon was introduced to the Cape, but it was certainly planted at Groot Constantia in the late 1880s, and reportedly performed well there. Until the turn to quality and the rise of the estates in the 1980s, however, it did not get much attention. C. J. Orffer in 1979 noted both quality and scarcity, but in fact Sauvignon was then just starting its dramatic quantitative climb. The first varietal Sauvignon on the market was that of Verdun (now Asara) in 1977, with Backsberg and De Wetshof joining in 1980. Within a few years there were many more. Interestingly, many of the early Sauvignons were at least lightly oaked, probably reflecting a hope that Sauvignon could serve the function of Chardonnay, which was performing poorly at the time.

Sauvignon has not ceased its inexorable progress, the only white variety to increase its planting every single year in the past decade and a half. By 1990 there were 3,300 hectares planted, by 1996 nearly 4,500; it overtook Chardonnay by the turn of the century and covered 9,644 hectares by 2011—9.6 percent of the national vineyard. The oldest Sauvignon vineyards in the country are at Spice Route, planted in 1965, and at Bloemendal, planted sometime in the early 1970s. Such is the fashionableness of Sauvignon that it is grown everywhere in the country to some extent. More than a third of the plantings are in Stellenbosch, however. Particularly because Sauvignon is vulnerable to heat waves and can lose its aromatic intensity quickly under such conditions, it generally performs best in the Cape's coolest areas. Nevertheless, total production in such parts is actually minuscule compared with what comes out of hot Breedekloof. It is the most planted variety in Constantia, Durbanville, Elgin, Elim, and the Hemel-en-Aarde, reflecting both their suitability for the grape and the ready market for top-quality Sauvignon at a high price.

If I am enthusiastic about the quality and style of Cape Sauvignon as it has recently developed, I feel the more entitled to be so in light of my many doubts in the past: now, however, it is clear that a small handful of varietal Sauvignons and a slightly larger handful of Sauvignon-based blends are among the country's best wines. But at the mass-production level, too, quality has improved greatly, and a large number of (admittedly virtually indistinguishable) wines show a genuine zestiness and play nicely with both green and tropical notes. Some plump definitively for one or other of those two basic approaches, though the tendency seems to be a move away from the more implacably green style.

A similar polarity marks the more ambitious products too and relates to the development of methoxypyrazines (the "greener" elements like green pepper and grass) and thiols (passion fruit, grapefruit, blackcurrant, etc.). Few show the overt thiol-derived "sweatiness" associated with many New Zealand Sauvignons. An increasing number of serious producers, including Hermanuspietersfontein, Lomond, and Nederburg, now in fact market two (at least) Sauvignons that stress different parts of the aromatic spectrum. To an extent it is a matter of ripeness—and viticulturists and winemakers have become very adept at blending separate pickings at different degrees of ripeness—but it is undoubtedly also a matter of site, and not just because one site might attain ripeness more easily: Lomond's two markedly different versions come from nearby single vineyards, and the one with more green notes is, in fact, usually picked with a higher sugar concentration than the other. It would be difficult to give a brief list of the best, but apart from those mentioned, and almost all the serious examples from the specialist cooler areas, one could offer Fleur du Cap's and Nederburg's multisourced ones, Fryer's Cove and Sir Lambert from the West Coast, Vergelegen, Waterkloof, Jordan, and Kleine Zalze from Stellenbosch, Springfield from Robertson, and Boschendal from the Franschhoek area, among others.

Most Sauvignon is vinified in stainless steel, without any oak influence. Those early experiments with wood soon ceased when Chardonnay came into its own, but recent years have seen more examples of serious Sauvignons fermented and/or matured in oak—seeking an added dimension that Sauvignon doesn't always show, no doubt inspired by some of the Sauvignon-Sémillon blends. Chamonix has long offered a superb oaked version with its Reserve bottling; more recent examples come from Cape Point, Quoin Rock, Reynecke, and Waterkloof.

It is at last being realized by discerning local consumers that good Sauvignon can develop well and interestingly in bottle for at least three or four years. Vertical tastings of leading Sauvignons show that the best vintages will keep beautifully for ten years, and standard vintages will do so for at least five—although enjoyment of old Sauvignon is not universal.

Apart from wines that are presented as blends and contain some proportion of Sauvignon, many apparently monovarietal Sauvignons do, in fact, include a small amount of either Sémillon (for example, Klein Constantia has been doing so for a long time, to add a little weight) or Nouvelle (a cross developed by Chris Orffer between 1958 and 1965). And this is probably the place to introduce Nouvelle, whose role in life is essentially to increase and complexify the grassy, green pepper characters in Sauvignon Blanc wines. Until 2007 Orffer himself suspected it was a cross of Sémillon and Crouchen, but DNA testing showed a derivation from Crouchen and Trebbiano/Ugni Blanc. A varietal Nouvelle was made by Boland Cellar in 2005, and it is no longer quite alone, but the grape's primary destiny remains as a blending partner. As such, plantings have increased markedly in recent years, and with 373 hectares in 2008 Nouvelle was just outside the country's top twenty most planted grapes.

SÉMILLON

As in most non-Francophone countries, in South Africa the name of this variety is generally spelled without the accent on the first *e*. It was for a long time the Cape's overwhelmingly popular grape. Sémillon was probably among the varieties planted in the early decades of the Dutch East India Company's settlement. Then, and for two centuries, no connection was made to the great white grape of Graves, and the variety came to be known simply as Greengrape or Green Grape (*Groendruijf* in Dutch, *Groendruif* in Afrikaans). The reference was not to the color of the grape itself, but to the vine foliage's bright green. When a red (not black) mutation occurred and became widespread, it was referred to as "red Greengrape." And as the variety became extraordinarily dominant it was also frequently known simply as *wijndruijf*, or "wine grape." When William Bird wrote his *State of the Cape of Good Hope in 1822*, he recorded that 93 percent of vines were "the common green grape," a figure that at first seems extraordinary. In fact, between 1795, at the time of the first British occupation, and Bird's book there was a major increase in the size of the vineyard, thanks to war, a burgeoning population, and then the reduction in duties payable on Cape wines imported into Britain. This makes the preponderance of one grape across a fairly large and varied terrain more understandable: buyers had little power of choice, while farmers planted only the vine that was most prolific and most resistant to common diseases.

Certainly by this time the red mutation of Greengrape had emerged and become common. This is clear from some contemporary accounts (cited in a historical article by Perold in 1936). A Paarl farmer, for example, noted that most of his hundred thousand vines consisted of red and white Greengrape, which were interplanted; Charles Marais of Stellenbosch had only Greengrape, and spoke of "ordinary and white Greengrape," implying that the red variety predominated. During the twentieth century, the red version became little more than an increasingly supplanted curiosity that few people (in a wine culture that had mostly forgotten much of its history) could account for. In the Franschhoek area, where there are comparatively many mature Sémillon vineyards, Stony Brook made a few vintages of a dessert wine from it earlier this century. In Wellington, Graham Knox in 2006 took cuttings from the few red-fruited wines in his Stormhoek block of Sémillon (planted in 1972) to make a small new vineyard. Eben Sadie used it consciously in field blends in his Old Vineyards Series made from 2009 onward, and Pieter Euvrard at Orangerie in the Swartland has since made what was certainly the first bottle of wine labeled Red Semillon.

The identification of Greengrape with Sémillon was made around the end of the nineteenth century by J. P. de Waal (manager of Groot Constantia) in Bordeaux. In 2009 DNA testing confirmed that Red Greengrape, too, is genetically identical to Sémillon. It seems it might be a uniquely South African mutation.

Throughout the twentieth century, Sémillon's role in the South African *vignoble* declined steadily. By the late 1970s it was still the fifth most important in terms of volume, but it is now down to 1.2 percent of the total (including a slight upturn in recent years). The largest plantings are in Stellenbosch, followed by Franschhoek—and, perhaps strangely, the Swartland, which produces little varietal Sémillon and whose warmth is not apparently well suited to the variety. Franschhoek has a good deal of old bushvine Sémillon, including one of the oldest vineyards in South Africa, at Landau du Val, where they make a usually first-rate wine off the gnarled, unirrigated bushvines planted about 1905. Other unirrigated, very old bushvines with interplanted red and white versions have recently been made into excellent wines by both Eben Sadie and Johann Rupert's Cape of Good Hope.

More important than absolute quantity is the growth in prestige and prominence of Sémillon. More is now bottled both monovarietally and in important blends, mostly with its traditional partner, Sauvignon Blanc. Used by itself, most ambitious dry Sémillons are oaked to some extent. At Boekenhoutskloof it is in all-new barriques for a year; at

Steenberg, the grapes are usually fermented in barrel but the juice is removed before malolactic fermentation starts—any tendency for Sémillon's fatness to become too oily can otherwise be accentuated. The best examples show better after at least a few years in bottle, and the usual lack of immediate early charm is no doubt a reason for the comparative lack of popular appeal for these wines.

Occasionally a tiny amount of Sauvignon is added to the Sémillon to point the freshness. As noted before, the reverse is more often the case: a number of excellent Sauvignon Blancs include a little Sémillon to give palate-weight and add both length and longevity. There are some nonstandard but well-considered couplings involving Sémillon, such as Adoro's Naudé White blend, which is usually Chenin-based with Sémillon and (less) Sauvignon making up the balance. The substantially growing and exciting partnership, however, is the one based on the authoritative Bordeaux example, discussed separately below.

A few excellent wooded dessert wines are made from botrytised Sémillon, generally in the typical Cape manner somewhere between German Beerenauslese and Sauternes in style. Boekenhoutskloof, Vergelegen, and Nederburg are among the leaders.

SÉMILLON-SAUVIGNON BLENDS

Those wanting to supplement Sauvignon's eager fruit with weight, dimension, and enhanced potential for bottle maturity, and those wanting to bring some Sauvignonesque freshness and further complexity to Sémillon, have found confirmation and inspiration in the Graves model. Here the pairing is establishing itself as a counterpart to the Rhône- and Mediterranean-oriented blends. The white flagship of Vergelegen in Stellenbosch is an outstanding example, and the maiden 2001 was the first to draw substantial attention and extravagant critical praise. It must be said, however, that this has not led to a stampede from even serious wine-drinkers: most locals seem more at ease with blended red wines than with blended whites.

The number of Cape winemakers following the Bordeaux model for white wines grew substantially in the first decade of the new century, as it became clear just how exciting and imitable the Vergelegen experiment was. Cape Point Vineyard's Isliedh soon became another major success story for the genre, and now there are many first-rate examples. Generally the most ambitious blends originate in the more classic and cool regions of the Cape, notably Stellenbosch, Constantia, and Elgin. The Constantia White from Constantia Uitsig, for example, is a fine and serious wine with usually a majority of Sémillon; Groot Constantia's Gouverneurs Reserve white is similar. In Stellenbosch, the elegantly opulent Tokara White tends to be about 80 percent Sauvignon Blanc. In Elgin, Oak Valley's OV blend has so far been made with little oak influence; and this is also true of the excellent Magna Carta from Steenberg, whose maiden 2007 was released as intentionally the Cape's most expensive standard white wine (since overtaken by, at least, Sadie Family Mev. Kirsten); here just the Sémillon component was fermented in new French oak for five weeks, prior to blending. As these examples indicate, there is no fixed pattern of either varietal proportion or winemaking style. What does seem certain is that the Graves-style white blend is responsible for a handsome proportion of the Cape's finest white wines.

VIOGNIER AND OTHER RHÔNE VARIETIES

Viognier's international march to success during the 1990s swept South Africa along from 1998, the first vintage of Fairview's pioneering wooded version. Others followed, and within a decade there were many dozens of varietal Viogniers. From less than half a hectare in 1996, plantings rose by the end of 2011 to 880, widely dispersed but with a stronger showing in the warmer areas, particularly Worcester and the Swartland. As viticulturists and winemakers learn to work with the variety (and discover the need to restrain its exuberance), coupled with the diverse origins there is inevitably a range of styles. Many show the evidence of ultraripe harvesting, with high alcohols and billowing perfume—and, rather too often, some residual sugar resulting from a fermentation whose path to dryness has been thwarted by alcohol. Some are heavily oaked, some fresh from stainless steel, some matured in older oak only, adding to the richness of texture without adding oak notes to the characteristic peachy aromas. It would not be unfair to say that most of the best serious wines have come from the less-hot regions, such as Stellenbosch (Tamboerskloof, Radford Dale, Fleur du Cap, the Foundry, for example), or even cooler areas like Constantia (Eagles' Nest).

It's not just that the market is perhaps a little oversupplied with Viognier that has led to its widespread use in blends—it is a willing and compatible partner with a wide range of varieties, and there are almost certainly more fine Cape blends that include Viognier than there are fine Cape varietal Viogniers. Many come from warmer areas, and Sadie Family Palladius has been a useful trailblazer, with Rhône varieties, Chenin Blanc, and Chardonnay in an autochthonous blend whose prestige has acted as a validation, as it were, for similar or approximating blends in a similar style. A number of Chenin-based wines include a little Viognier. Chardonnay-Viognier is a blend with international precedent and one that has been successful in the Cape, with or without further partners—but in fact, just about anything goes, even at high levels of ambition, so that Kumkani's VVS is an equal mix with Verdelho and Sauvignon Blanc, for example. Solms-Delta's Amalie is a Viognier-based blend with a more authentic Rhône imprimatur, having Grenache Blanc (and more latterly Roussanne) as one partner; but both are vine-dried, giving an immense, rich, and concentrated wine. Viognier is also an occasional very minor partner with Syrah, as discussed elsewhere.

There is no doubt that many producers would be delighted to get their hands on more Rhône varieties, but little is available as yet, though plantings are on the increase. At the end of 2011 there were still fewer than 55 hectares of Grenache Blanc, a few of Grenache Gris and Bourboulenc, and fewer than 50 of Roussanne—though pioneering Rustenberg has been joined by a few other producers with varietal Roussanne). Marsanne was rumored to be present in a few illegal plantings, but there were no official hectares at that stage, with quarantine regulations responsible for the delay. Clairette is a grape far declined from its heights in South Africa a half-century back, when it occupied more than 3 percent of the vineyard, but it still covers nearly 300 hectares. Many of these are of old bushvines and can add freshness to blends: Clairette is used, for example, by Mullineux, Sadie, and Badehorst, among others, in their fine Swartland whites. Probably, however, much of the Clairette crop disappears into vast cooperative vats.

SPARKLING, SWEET, AND FORTIFIED WINES

SPARKLING WINES

Bubblies have long been made in South Africa from artificial carbonation and from second fermentation in tank, but the first made according to the traditional Champagne method of second fermentation in bottle and subsequent disgorgement was done by Frans Malan at Simonsig in 1971. Those early vintages of Simonsig Kaapse Vonkel ("cape sparkle"), as the wine is still called, were made from Pinot Noir, Pinotage, and Chenin and were not, by all accounts, distinguished wines. The first to be made only from traditional Champagne varieties was a Brut 1984 made at Haute Cabrière (then Clos Cabrière), the first—and still one of only half a dozen—Cape producers to specialize in Champagne-method wines. Nowadays the majority of the serious sparkling wines are made from Chardonnay and Pinot Noir, with just a little bit of Meunier too.

With Champagne aggressively protective of its name and unwilling to countenance even any references to such concepts as *méthode traditionelle,* local producers in 1992 settled on the name Méthode Cap Classique, shortened to MCC, for this category of bottle-fermented wines, a term that has settled down comfortably. A producers association was formed in the same year and, says Pieter Ferreira of Graham Beck, probably the Cape's leader in making MCC, by 2012 it included eighty-four of an estimated hundred-plus qualifying producers. The association makes no prescriptions about such matters as variety, but strives to improve quality as well as marketing. According to law Brut wines must have less than 15 grams per liter of sugar, Extra Brut less than 6, and Brut Nature less than 3 (there are also official categories for sweeter versions).

There are many good MCCs, fresh and bright, neither over- nor underripe, and generally with relatively low dosages. Unfortunately, the majority tend to get disgorged and sold very quickly, often after only the minimum nine months on the lees, before there is time to develop complexity (from the end of 2013, the regulations will require a minimum lees contact period of twelve months). A few producers do make versions that are released after some five years on lees, including Graham Beck, Simonsig, the House of Krone, and Villiera—the last of these making a good range of MCCs, including perhaps the best Brut Nature: from Chardonnay, naturally fermented, without sulfur or dosage, and two years on its lees. Leading producers apart from those already mentioned would include the very impressive specialist Colmant, Ambeloui (a tiny winery in the Hout Bay ward), Bon Courage, Constantia Uitsig, and Topiary.

UNFORTIFIED DESSERT WINES

It's ironic, as well as testimony to the deadening hand that a bureaucracy can wield—especially when in the service of entrenched interests—that for a good portion of the twentieth century the Cape was simply not allowed to produce the rich, sweet, but unfortified wines that had been her greatest pride a hundred and two hundred years earlier. Until the 1970s, any wine with more than 20 grams per liter of residual sugar was required to be fortified—a rule hard to account for except as a means of protecting the important industry in spirits and fortified wine. There were occasional experiments with "Sauternes"-style wine even in the 1930s, but little came of them.

When Günter Brözel arrived from Germany in 1956 to start his illustrious career in the cellars of Nederburg, his thoughts tended (as he has often told) to the great sweet, botrytised wines of Bordeaux, Tokay, and Germany, and he wanted to make a South African version. So tests with botrytis were usefully carried out in the laboratory, and Brözel felt ready to proceed with making the wine—but for the prohibitive legislation, which even the power and prestige of Nederburg was apparently unable to challenge. Eventually, a specific, grudging, and limited indulgence was granted by the Department of Agriculture. The first restriction imposed on the Nederburg team was not unreasonable: that the "noble rot" had to emerge in the vineyard rather than in the cellar. In 1964 he started work on infecting a vineyard himself, and spraying it with water from overhead sprinklers to introduce the high humidity that was necessary to make the fungus spread (warmth in Paarl's late summer was hardly a problem).

Then, in 1969, came a spontaneous and suitable outbreak of botrytis on the Chenin Blanc grapes Brözel had decided on as the most promising for his wine. The wine was made—though much to his rage, Brözel was obliged to leave no more than 35 grams per liter of residual sugar. Nonetheless, it was a start, and he reckoned on using success as a spur to the authorities; his relief and pleasure must have been enormous when that maiden vintage of Edelkeur was judged top wine at an international competition in Budapest in 1972.

Establishing a local market for this unprecedented and unlikely wine was the next challenge that Nederburg had to face. The 1969 was auctioned by postal bid. For the second vintage—which came only in 1973, because of unfavorable conditions in the intervening harvests—Nederburg established the annual auction that remains the only original selling place for Edelkeur. Prices for the wine were not remarkable, but Brözel had shown, and was continuing to show, that the Cape could produce a fine unfortified dessert wine.

Nomenclature and styles of dessert wine are strictly monitored and controlled in South Africa. For the more ambitious categories of wine, which may exceed 30 grams of sugar per liter, the significant essentials are as follows:

Special Late Harvest: the grapes must have been harvested ripe; no sweetening agent or fortifying spirit may be used, and the must should not be dehydrated or otherwise concentrated; the alcohol level should be at least 11 percent. There is no limit on residual sugar.

Noble Late Harvest: similar conditions, but the residual sugar content should be above 50 grams per liter, and the wine must show evidence of noble rot.

Sweet Natural (or Natural Sweet): a catchall category, only requiring a residual sugar content above 50 grams per liter.

Wine from naturally dried grapes (often known as straw wine or *vin de paille*): very ripe grapes must be used, with a potential alcohol of at least 16 percent; it must not be a Noble Late Harvest or Special Late Harvest wine.

Some of these categories overlap, it will be seen, and the choice is often up to the producer. In a ratio of quality to quantity, undoubtedly the most important of them is Noble Late Harvest, and it is also the most useful in setting and meeting consumer expectations.

When Klein Constantia's celebrated Vin de Constance was introduced in 1986, avoiding botrytis character, the category of "Wine from naturally dried grapes" was not available, although it could possibly be used now. But Vin de Constance now makes use of the catchall Natural Sweet appellation. The "naturally dried" category was introduced in the mid 1990s, largely to cover so-called *vins de paille,* or straw wines (the first was De Trafford's), made from healthy grapes that have been laid out on, typically, beds of straw or racks, either in the open or indoors, to gain concentration by losing water. The same effect can be obtained equally "naturally" when the grapes are dried on the vines. This is essentially what happens with Vin de Constance, and a handful of other wines; good examples come from Quoin Rock and Zevenwacht, for instance. Apart from De Trafford, good examples of straw wine are made by well over a dozen producers, among them Fairview, Rustenberg, and Mullineux.

Some fifty Noble Late Harvests are made, many very good and a few excellent. It is difficult to generalize about winemaking methods: some use no wood at all, for example, while others use all-new barriques for maturation. The general stylistic goal would seem to be somewhere between Sauternes and the Rhine, in fact: apart from the significant differences in wood treatment, seldom are alcohol levels as low or sugar levels as high as in a Trockenbeerenauslese, even where Riesling is used and the lack of oak marks an orientation to Germanic styles. The arch-experimenter and sweet-wine lover Jean-Vincent Ridon of Signal Hill is probably alone in having made a fine dessert wine according to the methods of Tokay; and the one Eszencia he also produced (not officially a wine, as the alcohol was below 6 percent) was something that those who have been fortunate enough to sip it are unlikely to forget.

A number of varieties are used, too: Riesling and Chenin Blanc are the commonest. Leaders with Riesling would include Paul Cluver, Fleur du Cap, De Wetshof, and Neethlingshof; those with Chenin would include Ken Forrester, Rudera, Nederburg, and

Teddy Hall. Sémillon features seldom, but very effectively in wines from Boekenhouts-kloof, Lourensford, and Nederburg, and Simonsig and Tokara are among the few that follow the Sauternes model in blending Sémillon with Sauvignon Blanc. Sauvignon alone has been used by Klein Constantia occasionally. Chardonnay is not important, but Muscats are a little more so, with wines from Signal Hill and Nederburg (Eminence) among the best (Muscat de Frontignan is, of course, the grape in Vin de Constance, probably the Cape's internationally best known dessert wine).

FORTIFIED WINES

A century back, of course, fortified wine was at the heart of the Cape wine industry. In a hot country, before the days of cool fermentation and of air-conditioned maturation cellars, the chances of a decent fortified wine were much higher than they were of an acceptable dry white. Exports of such wines were less problematical and, all in all, this sort of thing was what the metropolitan countries expected of the wine-producing colonies. In the middle decades of the twentieth century, too, most South African exported wines were fortified, though sales declined from the late 1960s.

Fashions have changed, and production has declined steeply (though the quality of port has improved, and only this category of local fortifieds now has any real cachet) to the point that there are, for example, more varietal Viogniers made in the Cape than Muscadels. It is in many ways a pity, in part simply because it is the decline of a great tradition (one suspects that in many cases Jerepigos are made almost as a defiant assertion of that tradition rather than to meet a market need that is worth the effort in terms of financial reward), and in part because there have been some brilliant examples, and fine ones continue to be made and could give much pleasure.

Port

Some sort of history of port in South Africa has been traced to the early nineteenth century, but it became significant when local port and sherry were the mainstays of KWV exports. Particularly from the 1940s onward some delicious if not always entirely orthodox ports were made (also by merchant houses, notably Monis), some still drinking well today. Serious work went into improving the standards: in the early 1940s KWV and Stellenbosch University's Agricultural Sciences Department were experimenting with growing nine different varieties imported from Portugal on a Stellenbosch farm chosen for (they said) having much in common, in terms of terroir, with the lower Douro valley. However skillfully and successfully these wines were made, though, they tended to be made in a nontraditional style that the current producers rather sneer at as being too high in sugar and too low in alcohol: more fortified dessert wines than the real thing. Something like a port revolution was inaugurated by the appearance of JP Bredell Vintage Reserve Port 1991 (actually from the same farm where the KWV's experiment took place, and which had been for decades producing vast quantities of fortified wine for KWV; unfortunately JP Bredell Wines has not released any new wines, fortified or otherwise, for five years up to 2013).

The Bredell was the first of many fine wines of this type with more traditional analyses: alcohol levels approaching 20 percent, residual sugar around 100 grams per liter. At one stage this looked like a particularly promising category of local wine, with some excitement and the emergence of a core group of very good producers, particularly those based in the Calitzdorp area of the Klein Karoo, including Boplaas, De Krans, and Axe Hill. But the market for such wines is very limited and sadly the best examples, which do achieve reasonable prices, remain more of a *succès d'estime* than anything else. There is still only a handful of top producers—though quite a number of wineries, especially in the hotter areas, produce fortified wines ostensibly belonging to the category.

Matters have not been helped, of course, by the denial of the name "port" to local exponents: the Wine and Spirits Agreement, which formed part of the Trade Development and Cooperation Agreement between the South African government and the European Community, precluded it from appearing on any exports from 2007 onward and on the local market from January 2012. (De Krans put on the market, just before the prohibition came into effect, a wine labeled "The Last Cape Vintage Reserve Port"!) In fact, while the generic name for such wines remains a real problem—the Port Producers Association has declared it will continue to refer to the wines as port—it has been accepted that the names of the established Portuguese categories may be used, prefixed by "Cape": Cape Vintage, Cape Tawny, and so on.

The association has attempted to bring order and coherence to styles and labeling, and identifies seven styles: Cape Vintage and, for the best years, Cape Vintage Reserve for wines aged in wood for one year or more; Cape Late Bottled Vintage for wines aged for three to six years (at least two in oak); Cape Ruby for young port; Cape Tawny and Dated Tawny for wood-matured wines; and Cape White.

The finest wines have been in the vintage style, but a few excellent tawnies have also emerged in recent years (including some old wines from the KWV cellars), notably from Boplaas. Calitzdorp and Stellenbosch remain the sources of the choicest examples of local port. The focus nowadays is very much on the Portuguese grape varieties, with increasing amounts of Touriga Nacional, and Tinta Barroca and Souzão the other most commonly used grapes.

Jerepigo and Muscadel

If sweet fortified wines have generally had a rough time internationally in recent decades, even more so have the Muscadels and Jerepigos of the Cape. Immensely sweet, sometimes brandishing their spirit a little too bravely, and associated with rusticity and lack of sophistication, they have lost their general appeal as well as the appreciation of connoisseurs that the best deserve. For there are, indeed, some fine examples that can stand alongside good fortified wines anywhere in the world. Unlike the celebrated Australian Muscats, however, these are mainly unoaked and sold within a year or two of the vintage.

The word *Jerepigo* (alternatively Jeripego, Jerepiko, Jeropigo, and the like) is from the Portuguese *jeropiga*, a term used for grape must that has been prevented from fermenting by mutage with spirits. This is the common characteristic of the wines discussed here (and we can really only refer to them as "wine" by courtesy, considering the lack of fermentation). *Hanepoot* can also appear alone on a label, but may be accompanied by a smaller-print "Jerepigo." Hanepoot is, of course, the local synonym for Muscat of Alexandria. Muscadel (or Muskadel) is the South African name for Muscat Blanc à Petits Grains; there is also an established red mutation, and both versions are used for (fortified) Muscadels.

Of course, other varieties can be and are used for Jerepigo, sometimes in nameless blends, but sometimes with more ambition: Laborie makes a comparatively expensive, smartly packaged version from Pinotage, fortified with Pinotage pot-still brandy. To get away from the associations of Jerepigo, they invoke a French tradition and call it Pineau de Laborie. But smart packaging and a fine product are not sufficient to attract much of a market at a decent price. When Monis came out with a notably elegant bottle of wood-matured Muscadel at the same price as a serious bottle of Cabernet, it was widely applauded by critics but lingered on the shelves for many years. Perhaps an even finer wine was the 1975 vintage Red Muscadel released in 1993 for KWV's seventy-fifth anniversary at a similar sort of price; it was dustily available at retail fifteen years later. An older KWV Muscadel that achieved some continuing fame, among cognoscenti at least, was the 1953 (bottled only in 1981). These older Jerepigos were generally heavily fortified, the KWV 1953 to 18.2 percent. The lower legal limit used to be 16.5 percent, but is now just 15 percent in order to try to appeal to a modern market. That, along with blandishments about serving it chilled, or with gin to make a "muscatini," might help sell a few bottles, but it appears that Jerepigo and Muscadel will remain a minority interest.

It is the warmer inland areas that remain the home of these *vins de liqueur,* with noteworthy examples coming from various cellars in the Breede River Valley. The region Boberg exists in the Wine of Origin system only for fortified wines from the Paarl and Tulbagh districts.

Sherry

There are some fascinating accounts in official 1890s reports from Groot Constantia of experiments in making sherry. Briefly, a Señor de Castro-Palomino proposed a treatment of wine by adding his mixture, "a colourless liquid product with a pungent odour, and known by the name of 'Mutagina'"; unfortunately, although results seemed promising over a few vintages, it was revealed that the "antiseptic" it contained was formaldehyde, and even in those relaxed days this was unacceptable. The real breakthrough in sherry-making came about in the 1930s when Dr. Charles Niehaus showed that good-quality sherries could be made here—although something of a myth has grown up suggesting that he discovered an indigenous *flor* yeast, whereas it was yeasts imported from Spain that proved crucial. Nonetheless, a thriving industry was created—including substantial exports, until a London court ruled in 1967 that the name *sherry* should be restricted to wines from the Spanish appellation. Maxwell's *Fairest Vineyards* of 1966 listed fifty-four different brands of Cape sherry available on the local market—many more than there were of red wines. Julian Jeffs, in his magisterial book *Sherry,* tells an amusing story of being offered in his youth something his host called sherry but which "certainly" was not—he later discovered it to have been South African. He remarks that "the astonishing thing nowadays is how closely the flavour of South African sherry approximates to that of the poorer Spanish wines; in fact many members of the wine trade have identified them wrongly in blind tastings."

In recent years, apart from some cheap stuff that was called sherry but was really a Jerepigo-type concoction, only a few decent but unexciting, and never bone-dry, sherry-style wines were made for the local market, still by the traditional solera system. It is uncertain how they will survive not being allowed to call themselves sherry even in the local market after January 2012. The real thing from Spain, one of the world's great wines, is internationally underappreciated. How much less chance will there be for South African sherry to stay fashionable, particularly now that it has been denied the name abroad and then at home, too?

4

WINE OF ORIGIN
Legislation, Labels, and Terroir

In 1966 one of South Africa's modern legendary wines was made (and repeated once, with equal success, in 1968), by or on behalf of George Spies, the manager at that time of the merchant Monis. Surprisingly little is known about it, but the wine seems to have been more or less experimental, and an important part of the experiment is suggested on the laconic label, which bears only the legend "GS Cabernet Sauvignon 1966" with, in tiny print at the bottom, "100%." This was before the Wine of Origin legislation was introduced to systematize and control claims regarding matters such as origin and grape variety, and the "100%" (an unprecedented inclusion on a label) indicated that no grape other than Cabernet was used in the wine. At the time, a reference to a grape variety on a label had no necessary relation to the truth. Later, in 1973, new regulations were to require that at least 30 percent of a varietal wine must be from the variety named on the label. It seemed a modest enough demand, and one that was progressively raised over subsequent years, but suddenly the number of bottles named "Cabernet Sauvignon" and suchlike markedly declined.

In 1970 the Minister of Agriculture had appointed commissions to inquire, first, into the marketing of estate wines, which had become a problem for smaller producers struggling against the power of the large merchants, and, second, into the feasibility of some sort of demarcation of areas of production. A system of control was becoming particularly important because Great Britain, the country's most important wine market, was soon to become a member of the European Economic Community. The resultant legislation of 1973 went much further than introducing a system of certification to regulate claims made on labels, and outlined an appellation system. This was perhaps the earliest such system outside Europe and, as it continues to develop, it is still among the most rigorous—although, like other non-European systems, it does not seek to control aspects such as grape varieties, yields, and planting densities on an appellation basis. The Wine of Origin (WO) scheme is administered by the Wine and Spirit Board (WSB).

Quality is controlled to a degree by the certification process, which must be undergone for any wine that will indicate vintage, origin, or varietal composition. Certified wines not only must have all their paperwork in order, they are analytically tested, and must also brave the palates of a board-nominated tasting committee to ensure a minimum quality standard. That process is inevitably criticized: arguably poor wines get certified, while some of the finest and most individual and interesting wines get rejected at least once and their claims must then be struggled for. (The problem has been particularly felt by those making white wines in a more oxidative, less overtly fruity manner than usual, and therefore vulnerable to accusations from unsympathetic judges of lacking sufficient typicity, or even of being oxidized.) The same tasting panels will also sample uncertified wines applying for an export license. The official seal of the WSB—locally known colloquially as the "bus ticket"—is affixed to the necks of all bottles of certified wine and carries information by which a wine can be traced back to the vineyard from which it originates. In conjunction with strict controls over all wine labels (front and back), which must be approved, the seal guarantees the veracity of any claims made on the label with regard to origin, variety, and vintage. As far as the required proportions of the claimed vintage and variety are concerned, the magic figure is 85 percent. If a single area of origin is given, the grapes must be a full 100 percent sourced from that area, although now multiple origins may be indicated.

From the 2010 vintage onward an alternative certification seal became available, and it appears likely to become extremely common on all certifiable wines—but, at least initially, not on wines exported in bulk for bottling in other countries. This new seal carries the same tracking number as the old one, but also indicates that the wine is "Integrity & Sustainability Certified"—referring to the producer's adherence to the requirements of the Integrated Production of Wine program (discussed in chapter 1). The "greenness" certified by the seal could, in fact, range from fully fledged organic and carbon-neutral production to essentially conventional production—as long as the producer is working with IPW, is committed to sustainable practices, and has achieved a certain percentage score (65 percent in 2012) in the audit.

One other industrywide seal became available starting in 2012 and looks likely to become important. This is the circular "Certified Fair Labour Practice" sticker from WIETA, the Wine and Agricultural Industry Ethical Trade Association. Largely prompted by the damning 2011 Human Rights Watch report into labor conditions in the Western Cape's wine and fruit industries, and fearful of the recurring damage threatened to exports, the most powerful forces in the wine industry decided to encourage all producers to submit to the WIETA auditing process (discussed in chapter 1). Those qualifying would be allowed to apply the seal to their bottles.

As to other requirements, a notice of the presence of sulfites was made mandatory early in the twentieth century, and a little later health warnings—to be selected from a range of possibilities provided by government—were introduced, to the irritation and occasional bemusement of most producers. These are for the local markets; of course, wines sold in other countries must conform to the relevant requirements there. Another significant bit of packaging legislation intended to serve a useful social purpose was the banning of the notorious *papsak* (Afrikaans for "soft bag"), the metallized container in which the lowest quality of wine was sold, usually in a five-liter size, usually from the back doors of cooperative wineries, and often to the victims of the Cape's endemic alcoholism. Now all packaging is required to be "self-supporting"—which means the devotees of tradition must rip away an enclosing cardboard holder to reveal the *papsak* nestled there.

The WO scheme contemplates large geographical units containing a number of smaller regions, which in turn contain any number of districts, which in turn contain wards—much as a set of Russian dolls works, although some of the dolls do not fit snugly, and some rattle around. The relationships are seen clearly in the table in this chapter. As these areas get progressively smaller, they are based more strictly on a distinctive unity of relevant features including climate and soil. (Detailed maps of regions, districts, and wards are available at www.sawis.co.za/cert/productionareas.php.)

The largest areas of origin within the scheme are the five geographical units, whose boundaries are those of the South African provinces in which wine is made. Northern Cape is primarily used for the largely bulk-wine-producing vineyards irrigated from the Orange River, but in 2011 a more southerly and potentially very interesting new district, Sutherland Karoo, was promulgated to contain the country's highest-altitude serious vineyards, with the most continental climate (see under DeWaal in the chapter on Stellenbosch for reference to the first wines commercially made from those grapes).

KwaZulu-Natal was promulgated as a geographical unit in 2005 for the minuscule wine industry that emerged mostly to cater to tourists in the Midlands area. Some Cape grapes have been imported for bottling there, but a few high-altitude vineyards have been planted and seem to cope with the lush climate. In the northerly Limpopo province geographical unit there are apparently some vineyards on a wildlife estate, but wines have not yet emerged to challenge the Western Cape's. As much can be said for reported vines in the ward of Saint Francis Bay in the Eastern Cape.

Western Cape covers everywhere else (see map 1)—the vast majority of South African wine, and virtually all of those mentioned in this book. With little meaning in terms of indicating significant origin, "Western Cape" is used on surprisingly many bottles, and not always and only for the large brands that source their grapes widely and blend them across regions. In fact, however, cross-regional blending, while there is a good deal of it carried out by the manufacturing wholesalers particularly, is less of a tradition in South Africa than it is in Australia, for example. This is probably because most of the cooperatives here, responsible for much of the bulk wine, are based within smaller demarcated areas and do not need to source grapes from elsewhere for their blends.

At the next level, there are five important regions (as well as Boberg, which is used only, and rarely, for fortified wines from selected districts). These have been undergoing some useful revision in the 2010s, making them more meaningful to consumers, and

Regions, Districts, and Wards within the Wine of Origin System

Region	District	Ward
Geographical Unit: Western Cape		
Breede River Valley	Robertson	Agterkliphoogte
		Bonnievale
		Boesmansrivier
		Eilandia
		Hoopsrivier
		Klaasvoogds
		Le Chasseur
		McGregor
		Vinkrivier
	Worcester	Aan-de-Doorns
		Hex River Valley
		Nuy
		Scherpenheuvel
	Breedekloof	Goudini
		Slanghoek
Klein Karoo	Calitzdorp	
	Langeberg-Garcia	
	No district	Montagu
		Outeniqua
		Tradouw
		Tradouw Highlands
		Upper Langkloof
Coastal Region	Cape Point	
	Darling	Groenekloof
	Franschhoek/Franschhoek Valley	
	Paarl	Simonsberg-Paarl
		Voor Paardeberg
	Stellenbosch	Banghoek
		Bottelary
		Devon Valley
		Jonkershoek Valley
		Papegaaiberg
		Polkadraai Hills
		Simonsberg-Stellenbosch
	Swartland	Malmesbury
		Riebeekberg
	Tulbagh	
	Tygerberg	Durbanville
		Philadelphia
	Wellington	
	No district	Constantia
		Hout Bay

(continued)

Regions, Districts, and Wards within the Wine of Origin System *(continued)*

Region	District	Ward
Olifants River	Citrusdal Mountain	Piekenierskloof
	Citrusdal Valley	
	Lutzville Valley	Koekenaap
	No district	Bamboes Bay
		Spruitdrift
		Vredendal
Cape South Coast	Cape Agulhas	Elim
	Elgin	
	Overberg	Elandskloof
		Greyton
		Klein River
		Theewater
	Plettenberg Bay	
	Walker Bay	Bot River
		Hemel-en-Aarde Valley
		Upper Hemel-en-Aarde Valley
		Hemel-en-Aarde Ridge
		Sunday's Glen
	Swellendam	Buffeljags
		Stormsvlei
	No district	Herbertsdale
		Napier
		Stilbaai East
No region	No district	Cederberg
		Ceres
		Lamberts Bay
		Prince Albert Valley
		Swartberg

Boberg (region) used for fortified wines from Paarl, Franschhoek, Wellington, and Tulbagh

Geographical Unit: Northern Cape

	District	Ward
	Douglas	
	Sutherland-Karoo	
	No district	Central Orange River
		Hartswater
		Rietrivier

MAP 1

Winegrowing Areas of the Western Cape

also now incorporate newer winegrowing areas that had not fallen within existing demarcations. Cape South Coast covers the wine lands with (mostly) some maritime influence from Elgin through Walker Bay to Agulhas and as far as the distant and isolated few vineyards at Plettenberg Bay.

The most significant of all the regions in terms of volume and usage on labels is Coastal Region—although, as it includes a number of areas that are certainly not characterized by any significant maritime influence, it cannot be said to indicate origin with much relevance. At the time of writing there were proposals to break this area into the West Coast and Cape Coastal regions. The former of these is easier to define than the latter, where the problem is how far inland it is possible to go without the same problem arising of giving implausible suggestions of maritime influence. Really, there needs to be an admission that not all of the Western Cape wine lands are coastal; areas like Tulbagh are undeniably inland and need a separate region to accommodate them.

Many of the districts that go to make up the demarcated regions are based on existing political-administrative areas (this is true particularly of the older districts). Generally, though, districts do tend to conform to larger geographical features like mountain ranges and rivers and so tend to express some consistent mesoclimatic patterns. The wards, however, generally show a higher degree of unity; they have proliferated since 1994 and continue to do so. New demarcations result from approaches being made to the WSB from producers who are interested in being able to distinguish the wines of their area, either because the plantings are new or because a group of producers is convinced that different conditions prevail for them than for the remainder of the district or region in which they are situated. A team of technical experts—viticulturists, enologists, and soil scientists—thoroughly examines the claims of the area in question. For example, when the board was asked to investigate the area commonly and casually known at the time as the Hemel-en-Aarde Valley, within the district of Walker Bay, as a possible ward, it recommended that three wards would better reflect the climatic, landscape, ecological, and soil distinctions in the area. It was a question, presumably, of either three wards or one new district being demarcated, and because the dominant producers in the area were all keen on reflecting terroir as meticulously as possible, they chose to accept three wards.

There is some debate about whether the use on labels of smaller areas like the wards is more harmful than helpful to producers, in a world in which most consumers are uninterested in details of origin—even of anything less than country, perhaps. So the increasingly meticulous delineation of appellations is scorned by many who focus on marketing. It is true (sadly so for those who are interested in terroir distinctions) that comparatively few wines that might indicate a ward as their origin do so when the traditional larger area is better known. Stellenbosch is a well-known and prestigious name and carries some cachet; Polkadraai Hills or Banghoek means little to the vast majority of wine lovers, even in South Africa.

The scheme does now allow labels to indicate more than one area as the origin—indicating a blend of, say, Stellenbosch and Paarl wines rather than having to resort to the larger and less usefully indicative Coastal Region. While this provision might have served to encourage producers to indicate origin more precisely, European legislation will not permit multiple origins for South African wine, which means that the provision is rarely invoked.

An unfortunate anomaly in the scheme must be mentioned, one dating back to its inception. To help large producers who had historically drawn grapes from widely dispersed areas, those producers were allowed to claim a single origin for their wines. In the forty years since then this systematic misrepresentation has continued to be permitted—so that, for example, a Riesling made from Durbanville grapes by the Perde-berg Winery in the Paarl district may be labeled as Wine of Origin Paarl, simply because this winery has been drawing grapes from the Durbanville farm continuously since before 1973, when it was given an exemption! On inquiry, I was told that forty-five Cape farms are involved in this travesty. In the 2010 harvest, more than 17 million kilograms of grapes were potentially allowed to have wine labels misrepresent their origins—that is, 1.38 percent of total production. The WSB, in response to some agitation on the issue, con-sidered the question and consulted all those producers qualifying for this use of "tradi-tional units of land." This is, of course, like consulting billionaires to see if they think there ought to be higher taxes on the superrich. Unsurprisingly, the WSB reported that "the vast majority of participants to the Wine of Origin Scheme have requested that their vested rights be protected and that the status quo with regard to traditional land be main-tained. The Board has therefore decided that the vested rights of producers be respected and maintained." It must be said that this is not the first time that the WSB, charged with maintaining the integrity of the WO scheme, has made this sort of choice.

The smallest production unit recognized by the Wine of Origin scheme is the single vineyard. Until 2004 the smallest area was the estate (a term strictly defined in law), and to protect the estate system no mention of a vineyard was allowed on a label (not even a back label). Now the concept of the single vineyard is recognized and supported, but any reference to this status is permitted only for vineyards registered as such with the WSB. The vineyard may be a maximum of 6 hectares, and must be planted with a single variety.

While there are no longer official estates, the idea of the estate, as a self-sufficient and homogeneous production unit from vine to bottle, is still to an extent protected by the regulated category of "estate wine." These are wines originating from any property reg-istered for their production, and must be grown, made, and bottled on a single and continuous property. It is not a category that most consumers in South Africa, let alone those in other countries, have understanding of or interest in, and it could fairly be said that even at the top level, comparatively few producers have registered their qualifying wines. For example, of the sixty-three wines attaining the highest ranking in the 2013 edition of the Platter *Guide,* only seven were "estate wines."

5

CONSTANTIA AND THE CAPE PENINSULA

BACKGROUND

"The cellar [at Buitenverwachting] is unused—and no wine has been made there since 1951; the fields are under cultivation (largely fruit) and the vineyards comprise table grapes. . . . The thatched roof supports enough vegetation for a garden." So wrote Jose Burman in *Wine of Constantia* in 1979. Burman could note a few wineries and wine farms still in existence—most notably Groot Constantia itself—but surburbanization threatened to triumph even where there was not indifference or neglect, as at Alphen, where "the pressures of the advancing city were so great that expropriations whittled it down to the stage of being unviable."

A generation later, with a revived and many times rethatched Buitenverwachting, the marvel of Constantia's having survived the growth of Cape Town (its city center just fifteen minutes' drive away) is enhanced by the fact that it has not only thrived as a wine area but has even expanded, and not just through being able to offer some of the Cape's finest wines, as it did in the past. It has grown partly by climbing the amphitheater of mountains on its border (with False Bay and suburban housing marking other limits), partly by investment justified by replacing some vineyards with a golf course and housing estates, and partly by Groot Constantia becoming a great tourist attraction. There can be little doubt, though, that a crucial element in the survival of Constantia as a winemaking area was state ownership of Groot Constantia. Without the continuation of this large estate at the center of the area, strengthened against demand for profitable returns or windfall gains, it would have been virtually impossible to prevent more land being swallowed up

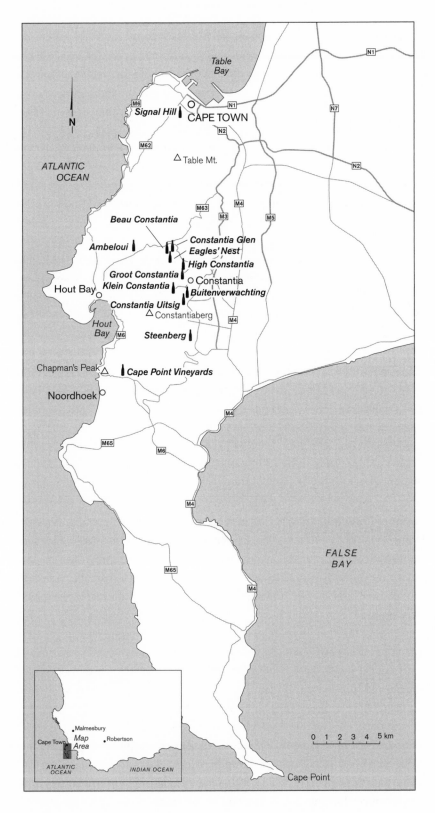

Table
Bay

N1

M6
Signal Hill
CAPE TOWN
N1
N7

N2

ATLANTIC
OCEAN

M62

△ Table Mt.

N2

M63
M3
M4
M5

Beau Constantia

Ambeloui

Constantia Glen
Eagles' Nest
High Constantia

Groot Constantia
Klein Constantia
○ Constantia
Buitenverwachting

Hout Bay ○

Constantia Uitsig
△ Constantiaberg
M4

Hout
Bay M6
Steenberg

Chapman's Peak △
Cape Point Vineyards

Noordhoek ○

M4

M65

M6

M4

FALSE
BAY

M65

M4

Malmesbury
Map
Area
Cape Town
Robertson

ATLANTIC
OCEAN
INDIAN OCEAN

0 1 2 3 4 5 km

Cape Point

MAP 2

Constantia and the Cape Peninsula

in difficult times by the luxurious suburb that presses hard against the vineyards. The threat is far from gone, however. It comes not just from the perennial wish of some to make more money through real estate deals than they could through winegrowing (and that is having an effect already), but from the possibility that the agricultural status of the land could be transformed by political fiat—rich, white-owned wine farms are not necessarily political favorites.

The first few centuries of winemaking at Constantia were integral to the story of winemaking at the Cape, and coterminous with its finest achievements, as discussed in chapter 2. As a winemaking area Constantia started collapsing in the last decades of the nineteenth century: weakening seems to be clear from the 1860s onward. It was far from only Groot Constantia that went insolvent, though only Groot Constantia was bought by the state and turned into an uneasy and expensive combination of model farm, training institution, and nursery of rootstocks for the phylloxera-struck industry. There has been no proper study of the causes of this collapse, which seems to have been more thoroughgoing than the grim endurance of many other winegrowing areas. Historians—such as there have been—have glossed over the question, vaguely adducing the arrival of oidium and of phylloxera, as well as the collapse of the export market for Cape wine in general and in particular reduced interest in the sweet wine that had been Constantia's great strength. Even the assiduous Jose Burman ascribes substantial cause of Constantia's "bleak future" to "a scourge which no local vine could withstand"—yet not only were these conditions general to the country, but phylloxera arrived in Constantia nearly a quarter of a century after Jacob Pieter Cloete died in 1875 leaving his estate insolvent.

Perhaps we are more aware of Constantia's decline because the area was, indeed, just more noticeable. The crucial element might have been the unfashionableness of sweet wine in an international market that was anyway much reduced; almost certainly the quality of Constantia wine had been achieved at a comparatively high financial cost (including more labor and lower yields) that was no longer supportable. Furthermore, the comparative coolness of the area rendered it rather more marginal and expensive to farm than more robustly sunny regions. And was the quality of Constantia wine declining by then, as some have alleged, making the spiral of cause and effect spin the region ever faster downward?

It is a strange fact that there are more people around today who have drunk Constantia wine from the late eighteenth and early nineteenth centuries than have drunk it from a century later! I myself have had a small, wonderful glassful of two-hundred-year-old Constantia, and some have had many more, but I know of no account of what the sweet Constantia of 1880 or 1900 or 1920 tasted like (there was still a little being produced throughout this period, and it was even noted in 1904 as the best Cape wine on offer at an export-drive event in London). Of course, the logical reason for this situation is that the earlier wines had been worthy of storage in ducal cellars and were therefore available for lucrative auction much later, and the later ones had not—but why did dukes no longer drink Constantia while they drank Sauternes and Tokay?

An interesting reference comes in George Saintsbury's famous *Notes on a Cellar-Book,* first published in 1920. There (page 98) he asks: "I wonder if there exists anywhere a bottle of the old original Constantia? I am happy to say that in my youth I once drank it. (I am sorry for anyone who has not, once at least, drunk both real Constantia and real Tokay.)" Then, in the Note to the third edition of his book (also 1920), he reveals that by "old original Constantia" he meant wine from "some years" before his father's death in 1860 (a year by which, as records show, exports of Constantia were still very strong). As Saintsbury delicately puts it, a firm of London wine merchants, in "kindly and complimentary fashion, informed me that they *did* possess some of the old original Constantia bottled in 1862, and requested my acceptance of a flask or two." He was not disappointed in the wine. "I think—and its great age in bottle would in any case make this likely—that my recovered Constantia was a little paler in colour and more delicate in body than her ancestress of the fifties. But the flavour was 'true', and I had neither mistaken it earlier nor forgotten it later." So any putative decline in quality would have come after the early 1860s.

Groot Constantia's story continues to have interest and significance beyond the boundaries of the estate itself. As explained earlier, the property was bought by the government in 1885, and (while some threats to its status had to be fought off) it experienced numerous vicissitudes as the Government Wine Farm, both producing wine and training a number of young "apprentices." By 1925 it had degenerated, concludes Burman, into "an expensive and useless project, but one which it would not have been possible to terminate without an outcry." The problem was solved—and some fresh impetus provided—by a disaster that year, when the manor house was destroyed by fire. The lack of a main building facilitated a decision to terminate the experimental wine farm. The house, incidentally, was rebuilt neither exactly as it had been when destroyed nor as van der Stel had known it, but in the form in which it was supposed to have been when "at its best" in its glory days.

Within a few years the farmland, with its rather lackluster, elderly, and not very extensive vineyards, was leased out to a private producer, reverting to the state only in 1957. When it did so, Minister of Agriculture Paul Sauer (the same man for whom the great Kanonkop wine is named) indicated that the government's intention was to turn Groot Constantia into a model farm producing high-quality wines. An advisory committee over the next years saw to the replanting of vineyards (concentrating on Pinotage, Cabernet, and Syrah), the remodeling of the cellar, and a strategy of bottling wine on the farm and selling it under the Groot Constantia label. The estate now proudly claims that it was "the first . . . to sell red wines which were both wood- and bottle-matured before marketing."

The rebuilding of the manor house had been an expensive project. Groot Constantia was proclaimed a historic monument in 1936 and grew in importance as a museum. But it was more than this, surely: winemaking in the Constantia valley was largely saved through government intervention, at least partly because the cluster of historic establishments there constituted a site of value to prevailing ideology. The National Party had come to power in 1948 and apartheid had become the state's official policy. Strengthening the image of the civilizing benefits of colonialization, of the superiority of the culture that Jan van Riebeeck had introduced to Africa, pointing to the heritage of Afrikanerdom in Dutch settlement—all these were elements of an increasingly conscious political project. The development of modern Groot Constantia was a valorization of past white settlement and part of the justification for present white power.

This was fortunate for the preservation of Constantia as a wine-producing area. During the 1970s, when local grape farms like Klaasenbosch, Alphen, Silverhurst, and High Constantia were being developed for expensive housing, Groot Constantia not only remained intact but grew: Hoop-op-Constantia was bought by the state and Nova Constantia by the Divisional Council, and both were incorporated into Groot Constantia in 1975; an adjoining property, Coleyn, was added in the early 1980s. In 1976 the Groot Constantia Control Board was established by the state, responsible for preserving the historic buildings and running the farm as a financially independent wine business.

As the national political changes of 1994 approached, amid some controversy and confusion a plan emerged to take Groot Constantia out of state structures. In 1993, ownership was transferred to the Groot Constantia Trust, a nonprofit company under a board representing "among others, the wine industry, the local residents of the Constantia Valley, the tourism trade, government and conservation organizations."

Through the 1970s and 1980s the wines of Groot Constantia improved greatly. But it was really Klein Constantia that rebuilt the area's reputation (this was a different estate, somewhat confusingly, from the section of van der Stel's divided property that first bore the name and later became known as Hoop-op-Constantia). In 1980 a dilapidated Klein Constantia started being developed, leading to a brilliantly auspicious maiden harvest in 1986 from newly planted vineyards—including Muscat de Frontignan, intended for a re-creation of the great sweet Constantia of the past. The other winery to confirm the restoration of the viticultural region was Buitenverwachting, bought by a German businessman in 1981.

And so there were three. By the end of the decade more big money made its way into Constantia, though significantly, it was not exclusively focused on wine production. In 1988 Constantia Uitsig was bought, and soon there was a fashionable restaurant, a cricket pitch, and a small luxury hotel. Even bigger money and more concentration on more widely sourced profits came into the valley when Steenberg, a farm older even than Constantia though without vineyards in those earliest days, was bought by Johannesburg Consolidated Investments in 1990. Planting vineyards and building a winery (inaugurated with the 1996 vintage) were straightforward. The problem for the investors was in getting permission for their other plans; but they somehow managed, and a lavish development was opened soon after the cellar: a luxury hotel and restaurant, a housing estate, and an eighteen-hole golf course with some rows of old Hanepoot originally to be reckoned among the hazards. Incidentally, further reflecting the "mixed" status of this part of greater Cape Town, on the other side of the road from Steenberg is Pollsmoor Maximum Security Prison, which had for some time sheltered Nelson Mandela.

Surprisingly, perhaps, golf courses and "vineyard estates" have not so far been the price demanded for further development of Constantia's viticulture, although there are likely to be more of them, even if Constantia Uitsig's owners do not manage to get planning permission for their project, as now looks likely.

The next notable wine-related development came about largely through flames—just as the impetus to do something about Groot Constantia had done seventy-five years previously. In 2000 an extensive fire on the mountain slopes destroyed areas of alien pine forest, as well as some fruit trees, making way for the vineyards of two new wineries, Eagles' Nest and Constantia Glen. The most exciting thing about some of the new high and steeply sloping vineyards is that certain aspects, with longer exposure to sunlight, are better suited to red-wine grapes than are some of the traditional lower or east-facing, mountain-shadowed vineyards.

The modern High Constantia came into being about the same time, recalling one of the early great names of the area: after the farm Witteboomen came into the hands of Sebastiaan Valentijn van Renen, he renamed it Sebastiaan's High Constantia. There's now little left except the name. David van Niekerk has produced some excellent wines, mostly reds—with something of a focus on Cabernet Franc—but also first-rate Sauvignon Blanc and the Clos André Méthode Cap Classique sparkling wine. Some cellar problems seemed to thwart progress after half a dozen years, however—hopefully only temporarily.

It appears that even now the story of Constantia wine has not ceased progressing—and certainly not the story of winegrowing in the Cape Peninsula, that mountainous, narrow arm thrust into the Atlantic. A Frenchman, Christophe Durand, has been using the Steenberg facilities since 2001 to make very good Syrah, Chardonnay, and Chenin Blanc under the Vins d'Orrance label from grapes sourced outside of the area. More responsive to Constantia's own strengths, a new, tiny producer of Sauvignon Blanc, Constantia Mist, in 2009 had the first wine off its 7-odd hectares of vines vinified by neighbor Constantia Glen. Beau Constantia, the highest and newest of the new properties, is three times the size and is planted with a range of red and white grapes; the first release was a 2010 Viognier named Cecily.

Across Constantia Nek, the saddle at the top of Constantia Mountain, where the road leaves Constantia and drops down toward Hout Bay on the other side of the peninsula from False Bay, a few new wineries have been established, too. One of them, Ambeloui, has in fact been making a very good MCC sparkling wine since 1998, from bought-in grapes as well as its own minute vineyard of Pinot Noir and Chardonnay. Hout Bay was declared a Wine of Origin area in 2009, though plantings remain minuscule.

The third Wine of Origin area in the peninsula is the Cape Point ward, established in the late 1990s to accommodate one winery, Cape Point Vineyards. This estate, which has established itself in the comparatively short time since 1996 as arguably the Cape's finest producer specializing in white wine, is at the extreme fringe of van der Stel's original grand property. And we must include in the chapter also the winery at the heart of Cape Town city, Signal Hill, and the tiny vineyard it leases scarcely any distance from where vines were first planted by the hopeful Dutch settlers at the foot of Table Mountain. So, from near one extreme of the Cape Peninsula to the other, grapes are now being grown and wine made again, a tribute to the land and the occasionally foolhardy determination of wine-loving proprietors.

Much of Constantia lies on the lower southeast slopes and at the foot of the mountainous amphitheater curving behind Table Mountain and facing False Bay—it's often called the Constantia valley, but it is not a valley in the traditional sense. All of the peninsula vineyards are cool by Cape standards, thanks to breezes (and sometimes vine-lashing salty winds in the most exposed areas) off False Bay; the mean temperature in February is little more than 20°C. The associated humidity does, however, bring fungal problems, and botrytis appears rather more often than is desired, though orienting vineyard rows to catch the prevailing southeasterly winds does help. Rainfall is fairly high, so little irrigation is needed once vines are established, but most of the vineyards are equipped to allow judicious irrigation. Soils are varied in origin as well as fertility, with a good deal of sandstone as well as decomposed granite with good water retention and draining capacity. They are acid, like most Cape soils, so they require careful preparation. In Cape Point there is a good deal more alkalinity. Topography is even more varied, with planting on the flatlands and the southern and southeastern slopes more or less in the afternoon shadow of the mountains, as well as—more latterly, at Constantia Glen and Eagles' Nest—on slopes getting more afternoon sun, which more than compensates for the greater coolness associated with higher altitudes.

It is the latter areas that perhaps show more promise for black grapes, although the other farms have frequently made successful, ripe red wines. By far the most planted variety in the peninsula is Sauvignon Blanc, with nearly 190 hectares (2011 figures). Cabernet Sauvignon and then Merlot follow, with 57 and 48 hectares, respectively, then Chardonnay, Cabernet Franc, and Syrah in that order. This must be one of very few established areas in the Cape with no Chenin Blanc, and only a tiny amount of Pinotage.

THE WINERIES

BUITENVERWACHTING

"Beyond expectation" is what the Dutch name means—and certainly most foreigners pronouncing it produce remarkable results. Fortunately, the wines, too, are mostly above the ordinary. The range is large but of high standard, from a decent MCC bubbly to a fine botrytised dessert wine, with some red and (mostly) white table wines at various quality levels.

The farm, on the lower eastern slopes of Constantiaberg, was originally part of Simon van der Stel's Constantia. The subdivision called Bergvliet was sold in 1793, following van der Stel's death, to Cornelius Brink; he kept a small portion (Nova Constantia), selling the remainder to his brother André Brink the following year, when it received its present name. An array of owners followed, as did temporary name changes and the deduction of what became Constantia Uitsig. By the mid 1950s, the vineyards had ceased producing wine. The modern revival began in 1981, when Buitenverwachting was bought by Richard and Christine Müller, who brought capital and energy. A new cellar was built and vineyards were replanted, including some blocks bought back from Uitsig. More recently, the cellar has been substantially upgraded, and there is continual reappraisal and reorganization of the vineyards, which have approximately doubled in size to some 110 hectares.

A rare advantage has been the continuous leadership since 1992 of just one cellar-master, the quiet but accomplished Hermann Kirschbaum—although the role of Lars Maack, Christine Müller's son, who is in charge of the property, is also important to the winery's unshowy success. Kirschbaum has been pulling back a little for some years, sharing more responsibility with Brad Paton.

Until recently, the Cabernet-led blend Christine was Buitenverwachting's (and perhaps even Constantia's) only unquestionably good red, with a record of improving for a decade in bottle. Still certainly the best wine in this farm's range, it remains excellent, now in modern-classic style: the alcohol level has crept up to about 14.5 percent, balanced by the concentration of fruit flavor, and the color is now more fashionably opaque (bled-off juice ends up in a delightful blanc de noir). Oaking is serious—up to 100 percent new—but not egregious, on this and other top reds, which include the varietal Cabernet Sauvignon and, more recently, Cabernet Franc. Those, too, are made for bottle maturation; they resist fruity obviousness and show less attractively in youth than does Meifort, the more exuberant, lighter-handled second-label red.

Buitenverwachting in 2006 joined the widening attempt to reestablish the area's reputation for sweet wines made from Muscat de Frontignan, with 1769, an excellent version to rival Klein Constantia's Vin de Constance. The leading dry whites are from Chardonnay and Sauvignon Blanc, the version of the latter called Husseys Vlei being one of the valley's best examples. A big seller is Buiten Blanc: a modestly priced, pleasant Chenin-based wine from mostly bought-in grapes and made in quantities (some 50,000 cases) rare in this area.

www.buitenverwachting.com

CAPE POINT VINEYARDS

It was perhaps something of a gamble when Sybrand van der Spuy in the mid 1990s eschewed the established grandeur and viticulture of Stellenbosch, where a Johannesburg-based tycoon might have been more expected to start a winery, and decided to go even farther down the Cape Peninsula than Constantia made likely. In fact, van der Spuy had already been (controversially) mining kaolin here. He had bought land and a homestead near the mine, and by 1997 Sauvignon Blanc was being planted on the south-ernmost, south-facing slopes of the Constantiaberg overlooking Noordhoek beach, with the chilly Atlantic just two kilometers away. But if viticulture here was a gamble even with van der Spuy's extensive soil and climatic analyses (there is evidence of some viticulture here in the early eighteenth century, but none much more recently), it paid off hand-somely, and from the maiden 2000 release, Cape Point Vineyards has been gathering plaudits.

The winery also has warmer vineyards on the other side of the peninsula, where Cabernet and Syrah grow, but the focus is now solely on the Noordhoek vineyards, as the range bearing the estate name narrows down to four white wines. There are 22.5 hectares of vineyard, 85 percent bearing Sauvignon Blanc and the remainder split between Chardonnay and Sémillon.

Duncan Savage, who arrived as (the second) winemaker in time for the 2003 harvest, also takes prime responsibility for viticulture. His markedly unromantic cellar—air-conditioned shipping containers resting on the concrete apron outside function as barrel cellars—was established in what had been a processing plant above the kaolin mine a little distance away; a relocation to another kaolin plant, near Noordhoek, is planned, together with a tasting room.

So the real focus is on Sauvignon Blanc, with the succulent, creamy Chardonnay always seeming like something of an afterthought despite its quality, and varietal Sémillon no longer being made, to the regret of many. The first-class flagship wine, Isliedh (named for a van der Spuy granddaughter rather than the whiskey), has generally included Sémillon, though overwhelmingly it is made from Sauvignon Blanc grown in the highest, most wind-lashed part of the Noordhoek vineyard. It has shown itself very capable of handling the wooding—barrel-fermented and -aged for ten months, with about 50 percent new oak. Invariably, however, the wine is tight and mineral in style, with citrus notes (lime to mandarin, depending on the ripeness of the vintage) as well as greenish hints and tropicality, and acquiring secondary characters as the wine ages—which it should beneficially do for ten or so years in the best vintages.

There are two varietal Sauvignon Blancs, usually with a small Sémillon admixture. The Reserve is one of the comparatively few local versions with full oak treatment, and its complexity is much enriched thereby—an intense, long, and vital wine with an ability to develop well over five to ten years without acquiring asparagus pungency. Savage has been working hard in his cool vineyards to overcome a tendency to greenness, and his efforts are clearly working, with the wines rather riper as of the late 2000s.

All the top Cape Point wines are more or less delicate, more or less powerful, depending on the vintage, but none so far has been less than compelling. It might be a touch absurd to ascribe anything like greatness to a terroir when we have tasted only fairly young wines from it, but there is some critical unanimity in doing so. There is clearly much more involved here than clever winemaking.

A range called Splattered Toad offers more cheerfully priced wines from mostly bought-in fruit, and there is also an export-only Sauvignon Blanc called Stonehaven.

Duncan Savage has also recently introduced a label under his own name, with a Bordeaux-style white blend and a Rhône-style red from mostly Swartland grapes. "I have to figure out how to make red wine!" he says, but those who've sampled wine from the barrel report it to be unsurprisingly excellent. Doubtless this is going to be a fine adventure.

www.capepointvineyards.co.za

CONSTANTIA GLEN

This is one of the newer wineries here, with some vineyards on steep slopes that had been covered by pines until the devastating fires of 2000. Previously the Allen family farmed cattle. Banker Gus Allen is now in charge of the property, though a few friends share in the wine business. There are 60 hectares, with 28 of dryland vineyard. The varieties planted cater to the four wines bearing the estate name: a fine, steely and mineral Sauvignon Blanc, now with a small but significant oaked Sémillon component, and two red Bordeaux-style blends. The one called Constantia Glen Five includes, obviously, all the main Bordeaux red grapes, while Three is dominated by Merlot, with the two Cabernets playing a smaller role. In 2012 an oaked Sauvignon-Sémillon blend called Two was added to the range.

For two years the Sauvignon was vinified by John Loubser at Steenberg. Karl Lambour was in charge of winemaking and viticulture starting in 2007, the inauguration date of the new cellar, designed to allow for as gentle as possible treatment of the grapes. From 2008 the red wines have been fermented without inoculation. Lambour is at his most vehement about brettanomyces and green flavors, but in relation to the latter he has been confident—and the early vintages have borne him out—that the vineyards' aspects usefully catch the afternoon sun spilling over Constantia Nek when the rest of the Constantia valley is in shadow, allowing for sufficient ripening. Lambour would permit no older barrels in his pristine cellar, so the first vintage of the red (not yet called Five) was matured entirely in new oak, which showed just a little too much. But a few years saw it fulfilling early promise, with a superbly smooth tannin structure. It is a cleanly modern wine—rich, round, and plush certainly, but not too ripely fruity and showing purity and finesse, along with a real density. This seems to be the settled style for the reds, made since Lambour left in 2012 by his former assistant, Justin van Wyk—who retains the great benefit of the sensitive winegrowing intelligence of Dominique Hebrard, formerly of Cheval Blanc, whose consultancy from the beginning should not be underestimated.

www.constantiaglen.com

CONSTANTIA UITSIG

Constantia View, as it was first named, was originally a part of Buitenverwachting, but it was barren veld when the subdivision was made in 1894. The new owner, Willem Lategan, "proved to be a most energetic and progressive farmer planting fruit and grapes," says Jose Burman, and was soon "exporting both wine and fruit to England." In 1941 the farm devolved on Willem's son, who changed the name by translation into Constantia Uitzig—now modernized to Uitsig. The farm was bought by businessman Dave McCay in 1988. There is still no cellar on the property, and the wines are now made at neighboring Steenberg, which is only marginally inhibitive, says André Rousseau, long the viticulturist here and for some years now responsible for winemaking too, though Steenberg's J. D. Pretorius shares the title.

Ownership has changed somewhat, too. In 2006 a consortium led by ANC-politician-turned-capitalist Tokyo Sexwale took 50 percent, almost certainly with plans involving the residential potential of this winery tucked among some of the country's richest suburbs (the luxury hotel on the property had long ago sneaked through planning restrictions). There is also commitment to developing the land for wine production, however, and a replanting program of the 32 hectares of vineyard began in 2009.

The land is not all necessarily the best in Constantia, being exclusively on the flatlands. Nonetheless, good wines are being made—it has been fascinating to see Rousseau over the years gaining confidence in translating his meticulously tended vineyards into wine, and the wines gaining hugely in stature. The focus is on white wine grapes. The Constantia Red is a fair Merlot-based Bordeaux blend in the international mold (ripely soft, oaky) with little real character, but useful for the three restaurants on the property. Similarly useful is the sparkling wine made from Chardonnay—impressive, but not quite up to its price, by far the highest in the country, for its maiden 2005 release.

The Chardonnay is unwooded and delicious (a wooded version is set to return to the range, after being abandoned some years back). The Sauvignon Blanc is as good as it should be, combining green fruit, tropicality, and a touch of minerality in satisfactory fashion. The Semillon is a serious, rather stately wine, one of the Cape's best. It's elegant, though not always bone-dry, with a fine acidity ensuring a good few years of satisfactory bottle-aging, and intelligently matured in only second- and third-fill oak. The problem—not unique to this wine—is the big alcohol consequent on the ripeness of the fruit: on occasion 14.5 percent and a touch obvious. Sometimes finest of all is the Constantia White (also modestly oaked), a varying blend of Sauvignon and Sémillon, the latter usually dominant, all tensioned by racy acidity. There is also an attractive and intense fortified dessert wine varietally named for the red Muscat of Alexandria, a local mutation. Incidentally, Uitsig was among the local leaders in an early switch to screw-cap closures; only the red is under cork.

www.constantia-uitsig.com

EAGLES' NEST

It was wildfires in 2000 that ushered vineyards into this part of Constantia, high on the Constantiaberg slopes. Until 1984 these were partly covered by indigenous vegetation, but mostly by pine forests. The Mylrea family bought 38-odd hectares of what became Eagles' Nest Farm and little changed, though they did some farming of fruit and flowers—only to be devastated (along with much of the pine) in 2000. After some deliberation it was decided to return to local farming traditions and plant 12 hectares of vines, mostly Syrah, Merlot, and Viognier. Some are on what are probably the steepest vineyards in South Africa, up to about 60 degrees, on which tractors must run on caterpillar tracks, so viticultural costs are high. This partly dictated the choice of growing primarily the fashionable Syrah and Merlot, together with Viognier, which was originally intended to be blended with the Syrah (Sauvignon doesn't command high enough prices to justify the farming expenses). The added hours of sunshine that these vineyards enjoy, compared to most of Constantia valley, makes later-ripening black grapes viable, while the coolness of the high altitudes ensures a degree of refinement. Vineyards face just about every direction except north. The soils are varied, but largely decomposed granite, with clay-rich subsoils giving good water-holding capacity; supplementary irrigation is available.

Results since the maiden 2005 vintage have been much more than encouraging. No other estate in Constantia has announced more ringingly the potential for red wines from certain parts of the area, and Eagles' Nest can surely prepare itself to be counted among the Cape's elite. The first few vintages were vinified at nearby wineries by Martin Meinert (of the eponymous Stellenbosch winery), who continues as consultant, but a new cellar was built in time for the 2008 harvest, with young Stuart Botha in charge. The Shiraz, particularly, has already shown itself to be in the top league of South African Syrah, despite the young vineyards; most impressively the first four or five vintages showed an improvement most years, and should only continue that trend. It is properly dry, modestly oaked (apart from the anomalous 2007) and on the elegant side of things, with a cooler-climate pepperiness in counterpoint to the deep red fruit. The Viognier too is made in an unshowy style and is very good, with a restrained expressiveness. Verreaux is a Merlot-based blend with Cabernets Sauvignon and Franc, though the proportions might change as the vineyards mature—Cab Franc looks particularly attractive on this site.

www.eaglesnestwines.com

GROOT CONSTANTIA

The story till modern times of this most historic of Cape wine farms has been told in chapter 2 and the introduction to this one. Being the property of a nonprofit but commercially oriented company and being located at the center of one of the country's most popular tourist attractions are factors with inevitable consequences. One is comparatively easy, substantial sales both in the estate's restaurants and to tourists; the other is a focus on producing wines that will give immediate pleasure to the visitors—not a bad thing, of course, but it does make for an inevitable "commercial" aspect to the wines. There's a fairly large range of them, and they are at the very least respectable. There are now just a Reserve Red (a Bordeaux-style blend) and a Reserve White (an oaky combo of Sémillon and Sauvignon) in the top Gouverneurs range, and they are better than respectable. In the standard lineup, the highlights are usually the Shiraz and the Chardonnay. Cellarmaster Boela Gerber's wines, especially the reds, are generally in a ripe-fruited, showily oaked style. Following in the footsteps of Klein Constantia in paying tribute to the great wines of old, there has been since 2003 an impressive dessert wine from Muscat de Frontignan, from partly desiccated and unbotrytised grapes, called Grand Constance. Much of the 90-odd hectares of vines is on the flat ground, with a dozen varieties planted including Constantia's only Pinotage block, though some vineyards creep up the lower slopes of the mountain. A continuous replanting program aims at reducing the proportion of virus-affected vines. If Groot Constantia is no longer the vinous focus of the area, it is at very least a good supportive player in a stellar team.

www.grootconstantia.co.za

KLEIN CONSTANTIA

As mentioned elsewhere, farm names can be confusing in Constantia's history, and this is not the same property that was called Klein Constantia after the breakup of Simon van der Stel's enormous domain on his death. The older Klein Constantia became known as Hoop-op-Constantia. The name was revived after 1823, for a deduction of land made from Groot Constantia by the widow of Hendrik Cloete and given to her youngest son, Johan Gerhard Cloete. It never attained the renown of the three established suppliers of "Constantia" wine—Groot Constantia, Hoop-op-Constantia, and High Constantia. Klein Constantia passed through the hands of a number of owners. Perhaps the most colorful of these were Abraham de Villiers, owner of a successful ladies' dress shop in Paarl, and the American heiress Clara Hussey, whom he met while investigating Paris fashions; the new Mrs. de Villiers bought Klein Constantia, and the couple took up residence and became sufficiently successful winegrowers. It's interesting to note that already the history of slavery was being sanitized in the Cape wine lands, and the slave bell at Klein Constantia was added during the 1920s as a decorative item to complement the manor house, which dated back to the early 1800s. De Villiers died in 1930 and his widow twenty-five years later, after allowing a cessation of winemaking on the property. Jan de Villiers, a nephew, inherited and later sold the farm.

In 1980, the run-down estate was bought by Duggie Jooste and reborn. The vineyards were replanted, after soil tests, according to the best understanding of the time, with the best planting material available, including a new virus-free clone of Cabernet Sauvignon. A sensitively designed production cellar was built, and cellarmaster Ross Gower took in the first vintage from the new vineyards in 1986. The Sauvignon Blanc from that maiden vintage was a triumph, and like the 1987—which was declassified because of a botrytis character and blended with some Chenin before being released as a blanc de blanc—proved for very many years the longevity of Sauvignon from this region. It also proved definitively that Constantia was once again a force to be reckoned with on the Cape wine scene. Many later vintages of the Sauvignon (a little Sémillon became an invariable addition) have also been first-rate and long-lived. It would be wrong to say, however, that there was not occasional inconsistency during Gower's tenure at Klein Constantia, which lasted until 2003. At that time a new broom replaced him and did some clean sweeping, which, as is so often the case, proved useful. (Gower started his own farm and winery in Elgin, but died from cancer in 2010.) Perdeblokke Sauvignon, from a higher-altitude vineyard, has also been made in recent years, often showing a little more concentration than the excellent standard version.

Gower was less successful with reds—never an easy proposition in the lower-lying vineyards of Constantia—and during the 1990s the wines were rather too hard and lean.

now some 63 hectares, and some grapes are bought in as well as sold) and is taking them increasingly in the direction of sustainability—they are now at least insecticide-free. Mechanical harvesting is used.

The range is smaller than when Loubser arrived, but still large, and likely to be trimmed a little further. Starting around 2009 there was also a good move to start delaying the release of the reds a year or two more than had previously obtained, when many were markedly far from showing very well. The reds include the flagship Catharina, an eclectic blend of Bordeaux varieties with Syrah and occasionally Nebbiolo; it is a good modern-style wine, ripe but fairly restrained, with firm tannic structure. The varietal Nebbiolo—a Cape pioneer of this variety—has improved enormously since its pallid early vintages in the late 1990s, and it is now an attractive and fairly interesting wine, though not quite a Barolo, even one of the modern oaky style. A reserve 2009 bottling called Garibaldi, sold at the 2012 Cape Winemakers Guild Auction, did show a previously unattained quality, however.

Undoubtedly it is the white wines that star. The estate's reputation was built on Sauvignon Blanc and Sémillon, and some years there are eight versions featuring the varieties either singly or blended, some in the entry-level Klein Steenberg range. The Sauvignon Blanc Reserve has sufficient character and structure to age well for a decade or more in the best vintages, as I have frequently observed. The house style and the climate make these obviously cool-climate wines, with a fairly green character (green pepper, asparagus, bean, blackcurrant leaf, etc.), though the standard version shows more engaging tropicality in youth; they all have a thrilling natural acidity and fine slaty minerality. The oaked Semillon, stern and bracing in its youth but often rich, even more demands aging. Inevitably, established as a producer of fine Sauvignon and Sémillon, Steenberg wanted to work with them together, and Magna Carta was introduced with the 2007 vintage, in a small and expensive bottling. This excellent wine, mixing oaked-Sémillon richness and racy, mineral finesse, shows every sign of likely maturity a decade hence; subsequent vintages have been equally impressive.

www.steenberg-vineyards.co.za

6

STELLENBOSCH

BACKGROUND

After Constantia, Stellenbosch is the oldest of the Cape's continuing winegrowing areas, and now perhaps its emotional and intellectual heartland. It is also in some ways the most important—particularly as the most internationally recognizable name in South African wine and as the source of a disproportionate number of its finest wines, though not the largest area in terms of production. Cape wine's iconic image of a whitewashed, gabled manor house among vineyards and oak trees at the foot of magnificent mountains is the iconic image of Stellenbosch.

In 1677 the Third Khoikhoi-Dutch War ended and the way was open for largely unhindered Dutch expansion into the lands of the indigenous inhabitants. Simon van der Stel was appointed commander of the settlement and mandated to continue the Dutch East India Company's expansion. On a visit of inspection to the Hottentots-Holland area in November 1679, he turned aside to explore the valley of the Eerste ("first") River and camped overnight on its banks. It seemed a promising location for a new settlement. By 1683 there were thirty families living in the area that van der Stel had named after himself. By 1692, records reveal, 233,200 vines had been planted, and the Cape's history of wine production had taken a vital new turn.

Expansion happened elsewhere, too, of course, and even more successfully in terms of quantity, particularly along the Berg River in the Drakenstein Valley (the larger Paarl area, essentially). In 1753, a century and a year after the landing of van Riebeeck, Stellenbosch had more than a million vines planted, about a quarter of the colony's total, though it was still outranked by the peninsula area ("the Cape") and increasingly by Drakenstein. By the end of the eighteenth century, just before the major expansion of the Cape wine lands was initiated by the coming of the British, the number of vines in Stellenbosch was closer to four million, more than a third of the total (with Drakenstein forging ahead and the Cape and the rest of the colony proportionately and actually falling behind).

Many of those grand gables in the vineyards and in Stellenbosch town itself date from the period of prosperity in the late eighteenth and early nineteenth centuries. A century later, Stellenbosch's viticulture was in the same parlous state that characterized the whole colony. Even famous properties like Rustenberg and Vergelegen had declined sharply. No doubt it was the presence of grand manor houses on many of the farms that made them attractive to new owners who were rich enough not to require an income from the produce of the vineyards. Rustenberg was bought toward the end of the century by Sir Jacob Barry, and in 1892 a run-down, phylloxera-ridden Schoongezicht was bought by John X. Merriman, the future Cape prime minister; the two properties were to be united in the middle of the twentieth century by another family of rich industrialists, the Barlows. Vergelegen was acquired by mining magnate Sir Lionel Phillips in 1917 in a state of decay, and although much money was spent on the estate, vines were replaced by mixed agriculture; it was only after 1987, when the estate became a tiny part of a huge international company, that winemaking began to flourish once more. "Outside" money played a not insignificant part in the reestablishment of ambitious winemaking in the second half of the twentieth century, particularly in this, its most prestigious region.

Of course, by far the largest part of Stellenbosch is not claimed by magnificence or owned by rich individuals or corporations—any more than, say, Bordeaux is all Yquem and Margaux—and much is occupied by small and modest properties, or by grape farmers selling to the commercialized cooperatives or the big merchants. While there are more private cellars concentrated in Stellenbosch than in any other area, the largest of the country's wine and spirits producers, Distell, is also based here. But this is generally the most expensive vineyard land in the country (apart from Constantia, perhaps) and still tends to be the area that most attracts rich capitalists, golfer-millionaires, IT moguls, and the like, seeking a grand wine-lands lifestyle and what one of them, banker G.T. Ferreira, who founded Tokara, referred to as "greater ROE"—return on ego rather than return on equity.

At the center of this large district, which now has little farming activity other than viticulture, is the town from which the district takes its name. With its mature oaks (the descendants of those planted at van der Stel's behest) and some lovely old buildings in the center, it has a good deal of charm and beauty, but it is now bustling and car-thronged. The University of Stellenbosch houses the important Department of Viticulture and Enology, which was formally started in 1917 (with viticulturist A.I. Perold as its director) though there had been teaching in these subjects here since 1889. The internationally reputed Institute for Wine Biotechnology at the university was founded in 1995. North of the town is the country's other important viticultural and winemaking educational establishment, the Cape Institute for Agricultural Training,

N

INDIAN OCEAN

R45

Malmesbury
Robertson
Cape Town
Map Area
ATLANTIC
OCEAN

R310

△ Simonsberg

BANGHOEK
VALLEY

Oldenburg

Bartinney

Zorgvliet

Delaire Graff

Thelema

Tokara

Le Riche

Stark-Condé

JONKERSHOEK
VALLEY

Neil Ellis

R310

Rustenberg

Delheim

Muratie

Quoin Rock

Morgenhof

Glenelly

○ Stellenbosch

Remhoogte

Kanonkop

R44

Dalla Cia
Vilafonté
Stellekaya

Flagstone

Le Bonheur

Warwick

Laibach

Klapmutskop △

De Meye

L'Avenir

Edgebaston

Botanica

Fleur du Cap/Bergkelder

Simonsig

M23

Kanu

Beyerskloof

Meinert

DEVON VALLEY

Neethlingshof

Overgaauw

R304

Hartenberg

Sterhuis

BOTTELARY HILLS

STELLENBOSCHKLOOF

DeWaal

Mulderbosch

M12

Villiera

R101

DeMorgenzon

Jordan/Jardin

Reyneke

De Toren

Kaapzicht

Mooiplaas

POLKADRAAI HILLS

Saxenburg

Bein

M15

M23

Nico van
der Merwe

Kleine Zalze

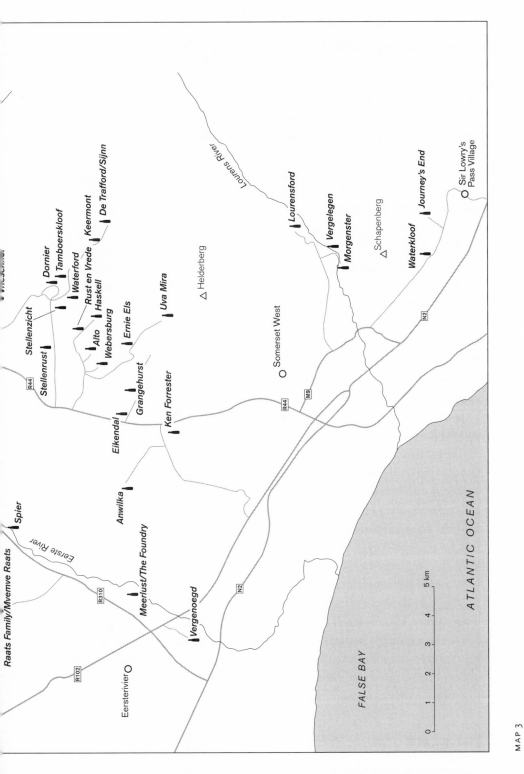

MAP 3
Stellenbosch

Raats Family/Mvemve Raats

Spier

Eerste River

R310

R102

Eersterivier ○

Meerlust/The Foundry

Vergenoegd

N2

Anwilka

Eikendal

Grangehurst

Ken Forrester

Stellenrust

R44

Stellenzicht

Dornier

Tamboerskloof

Waterford

Keermont

Rust en Vrede

De Trafford/Sijnn

Alto

Haskell

Webersburg

Ernie Els

Uva Mira

△ Helderberg

Somerset West ○

R44

M9

Lourens River

Lourensford

Vergelegen

Morgenster

△ Schapenberg

Waterkloof

Journey's End

Sir Lowry's
Pass Village ○

N2

ATLANTIC OCEAN

FALSE BAY

0   1   2   3   4   5 km

better known simply as Elsenburg, which offers qualifications in association with the university. ARC Infruitec-Nietvoorbij, a major parastatal research facility, incorporating since 1997 the Nietvoorbij Institute for Viticulture and Enology, is also located on the outskirts of Stellenbosch, and the town is also the home of many other industry-related bodies and institutions.

Urban development has necessarily encroached on the surrounding vineyards, but the effect has not yet been crucial—and in one way it has been beneficial to wine quality, by prompting a vineyard move farther up the mountainsides, leaving the flatter lands to human activities less important than winegrowing. This move up the slopes is very apparent in any of the many mountainous vistas offered the observer. Viticulturally, the Stellenbosch district is necessarily diverse owing to the range of soil types, the manifold slope aspects offered by the mountains and hills, the different elevations, and the different degrees of exposure to and protection from the cooling sea breezes off False Bay—which make the area as a whole effectively much cooler than its latitude would suggest. In recognition of this diversity, increasing numbers of wards have been defined in recent years, though as yet not many find their way onto bottles: as long as Stellenbosch is the most recognizable Cape area of origin, it requires some reflection before even the most terroir-conscious abandon the district name for one more specific. In fact, of course, here as elsewhere in the Cape, it is still too early to be confident about the effects of terroir on winegrowing—specific effects, that is, beyond the manifestation of good quality. Some associations are emerging between different areas and grape varieties and styles of wine, and these are mentioned below, but they remain general, and tentative in many cases.

The most notable area that is not yet established as a ward is the one generally on the slopes of the Helderberg. Paradoxically, it is precisely because this is such a comparatively well known and prestigious association that a ward has been slow in coming: exclusion and inclusion could be significant for producers, and politics and the prospect of squabbles over boundaries are likely to maintain the status quo. Another important area with perhaps a character of its own is around the Schapenberg, a mountain between Somerset West and Sir Lowry's Pass village. Investigations are already under way to establish the basis for further wards; they should emerge, politics permitting, in the near future.

Vineyard plantings are mentioned in more detail in the brief characterizations of wards offered below, but it is worth noting how dominant Cabernet Sauvignon is in the district as a whole, with 2,873 hectares. Sauvignon Blanc follows with 2,011 hectares, Syrah with 1,939, and Merlot with 1,725. Chenin Blanc (1,339) still beats Chardonnay, which has just under 1,000 hectares, while Pinotage has just over 1,000. The figures refer, as do all those that follow, to the status of plantings at the close of 2011.

THE WARDS

The Simonsberg-Stellenbosch ward, mostly on the southwestern foothills of the great Simonsberg but also on the slopes of Klapmutskop in the north, is so named to distinguish it from the mountain's northwesterly slopes, which constitute the Simonsberg-Paarl ward. This is the largest of the Stellenbosch wards, and the one that reaches farthest north, although there are a few wineries farther north still, in the generic Stellenbosch area to the west and northwest of Simonsberg. The ward is home to some famous and well-established estates, including Kanonkop and Rustenberg. Aspects necessarily vary here, as does exposure to the strong southeasterly winds, which restrict growth—for the most part beneficially, as the yellow to reddish-brown soils are fairly fertile with high-yielding potential, mostly derived from granite, but well structured and able to retain water well. This is widely regarded as prime red-wine country, and Cabernet Sauvignon is by far the most-planted variety (333 hectares), with Merlot in third place behind the inevitable Sauvignon Blanc (213 hectares), followed by Syrah, Chardonnay, and then Pinotage.

Stretching from the southern slopes of the Simonsberg, between its mountainous southern extension and the great amphitheater of mountains above the village of Pniel, which then descends via the Helshoogte Pass back to Stellenbosch town, is a magnificent valley that encompasses the small ward of Banghoek (sometimes called Banhoek). Banghoek literally means "scary corner/place," and was apparently so called because of the wild animals (most frightening were the leopards, it seems) encountered by under-standably trepid Dutch settlers. Most of the viticulture in Banghoek is comparatively recent; the area was really opened up by the success of Thelema and Delaire on the mountainsides to the west of the valley (with Tokara just on the Simonsberg-Stellenbosch side of the divide). Rainfall is higher here than in most parts of Stellenbosch, and it is a little cooler on the higher slopes. Soils are granite-derived, with some sandstone admixture at higher altitudes. Cabernet Sauvignon (76 hectares), Syrah, and Merlot dominate the vineyards, with Sauvignon Blanc and Chardonnay some way behind. Newish Banghoek estates not discussed in more detail below, but starting to offer serious and interesting wines, include Bartinney and Oldenburg. Oldenburg was in fact established in the 1960s, among the first in the area, but sadly neglected more recently until the vineyards were completely replanted by an ambitious new owner, Adrian Vander-spuy; they are now starting to mature, with gratifying results in the wines.

Continuing to move in an anticlockwise direction around the town, running southeast of Stellenbosch, is the Jonkershoek Valley. The historic Lanzerac estate is almost in the town itself—the famous name and property sold by business magnate Christo Wiese in 2012 to an undisclosed foreign buyer and still spotted on bottles of ultraripe, ultraex-tracted, and high-alcohol wine. Otherwise, the small handful of wineries here are very good—though it's uncertain exactly what is happening at Klein Gustrouw, where just a few parcels of vines are being maintained to keep the label alive (the wines made elsewhere) while a major replant happens. Rainfall is relatively high here (about 1,000 millimeters annually); soils are varied, but the vineyards are mostly planted on stony decomposed granite, giving moderate vigor. Some are planted high on the slopes, up to 600 meters above sea level, but most are between 200 and 300, on steep southeast-facing slopes. The narrowness and steepness of the valley mean fewer than usual hours of full sunlight. Plantings follow the pattern already observed elsewhere, with Cabernet Sauvignon's 63 hectares at the fore.

South of Stellenbosch, its apex pointing to the town, lies the so-called Golden Triangle, with the Stellenbosch Mountains on the western boundary, the Helderberg to the south, and the busy R44 road usefully supplying an approximate third side that nature neglected to mark sufficiently. The area, not demarcated into wards, is generally famous for its red wines and hosts some of the district's grand old estates (Stellenzicht, Rust en Vrede, Alto) and many of the smartest younger ones, including Waterford and De Trafford. Aggressively marketed Bilton is also here, making big, lush, ultraripe wines (one ludicrously expensive) and the occasional more elegant one, just to confuse the critics. The west-facing foothills of the Stellenboschberg are derived from shale, while the northern slopes of the Helderberg have the more usual granitic infrastructure, but with some sandstone admixture reducing the acidity of the granite. We are getting close to the ocean here, with False Bay just ten kilometers or so from the Helderberg, and the southeasterly winds can be fierce as well as cool, especially at higher altitudes on the more exposed slopes. Vineyards are planted from the valley floor to high up the mountainside—Uva Mira has vineyards between 420 and 620 meters above the level of False Bay so close by. As in so many parts of Stellenbosch, the folds and slopes of the mountains allow for more diversity than is useful for making generalizations. Certainly Chardonnay can do extremely well here, especially at higher altitudes, but there is a good basis for the tradition of Cabernet planting—although the success of Syrah has led to something of a local tradition of blending it with the Bordeaux varieties, and Cabernet Franc has established a name for itself in the Helderberg area.

Farther south, and to the west and southwest of the town of Somerset West, is an isolated but important group of wineries gathered around the Schapenberg, just four kilometers from the coast and its cooling (sometimes battering) winds. This was the hill where the sheep of Willem Adriaan van der Stel used to graze, and where he had a lookout post to spot visiting ships before anyone else could, allowing him a competitive edge in selling his produce. His great estate, Vergelegen, was on Schapenberg's shale-based northern slopes, going down to the valley of the Lourens River, and there, in the various parts of that now-divided property, some of Stellenbosch's finest wines are made—as they are promising to be on the southern side, at Waterkloof.

To the immediate east of Stellenbosch town are two small wards of lesser note. Papegaaiberg is comparatively negligible in terms of wine production (curiously, the only Stellenbosch ward where white grapes predominate, with Chardonnay, Chenin Blanc, and Sauvignon Blanc the most-planted varieties). Devon Valley has a rather more usual pattern of plantings, but although it has something of a reputation for red wines, and grapes are exported to other wineries, there are few producing wineries of significance here.

Much more significant, though in an area that is as yet undemarcated as a ward, is the Stellenboschkloof, on the south-facing side of the Bottelary Hills—the valley through which the first road from Cape Town to Stellenbosch ran. South-facing slopes open directly onto False Bay, while north-facing ones and the valley floor are more sheltered.

The yellow to reddish-brown soils are well structured, like other granite-derived soils in the larger area, but vary in detail—as do the aspects and altitudes on which vines are planted. White grapes do particularly well here, and there are many fine Chardonnays and Chenins in particular; reds tend to be more robust.

The Polkadraai Hills close off the Stellenboschkloof. The fairly new ward that takes its name from them, and which like the kloof includes both well-established and younger wineries, has vineyards planted on varying elevations and aspects, but mostly facing south and southwest, open to the cooling effect of False Bay and even early morning mists. Layered soils are granite-based higher up, shallower and sandy lower down. Cabernet Sauvignon, with 158 hectares, now covers a little less of the vineyards than does Sauvignon Blanc; Syrah covers nearly 130 hectares, and Merlot more than 90.

On the granitic northern slopes of the Bottelary Hills is the large ward of that name. There is plenty of soil variation here, though, with spreading pockets of shale, and clay beneath the shale-based soils in the Koelenhof Valley within the ward. Again, variations in soils and in aspects of this hilly area make generalization difficult. Pinotage seems to have found something of a home here—Bellevue is a historic site for it, and in more modern times Kaapzicht has been a notable producer, as has Beyerskloof—although, in fact, this winery is just to the west of Bottelary ward, in undemarcated Stellenbosch land. There are still many vineyards of bushvines here, of Pinotage and older Chenin Blanc, and many unirrigated ones. Unusually, in fact, white grapes are particularly important in this ward, with Chenin Blanc the most planted variety at 459 hectares, followed by Cabernet Sauvignon with 364 and Sauvignon Blanc with 335. Syrah, Pinotage, and Merlot follow.

THE WINERIES

ADORO

Frankly, I'm locating this stylish little négociant winery in Stellenbosch just as a nod to the actual cellar (though even that is equally close to Paarl). Precise expression of little parcels of terroir is not what the three Adoro wines are about: Ian Naudé is both a stylist and a believer in the virtues of blending, and the larger the palette he works from, the happier he is in constructing his elegant wines. That said, the palette is prepared in the diverse vineyards rather than in the cellar: this is very much a partnership between the winemaker and viticulturist Lucas de Kock. They search out vineyards that suit them, make contracts with the owners, and prescribe management, yields, and the like; the wines are made in a rented cellar in the Joostenberg area (not open to the public). The business is owned by the Aspen Freight group, which also owns Benriach Distillery in Speyside.

Naudé has a good deal of experience internationally and in South Africa, enough experience to be able to carry through his aim of combining the traditional virtues of restraint with more modern, assertively fruit-driven structure. There are three important wines in the portfolio. The Sauvignon Blanc can come from any or all of five areas depending on the vintage, usually with modest alcohol levels even though the wine does not insist on "green" flavors (there's always a contribution, anyway, from warmer Stellenbosch, which gives it hints of tropical fruit); the balance comes from cooler vineyards in Darling, Durbanville, Elgin, and Elim. Overall, though, a gently rounded, elegant minerality controls the wine.

This Sauvignon is also a component in the Naudé White blend—an interesting compromise between the two main emerging styles of such wines, the warmer-country autochthonous blend and the Graves style. This one is invariably based on Chenin from the Swartland and Durbanville, though again, the proportion can vary substantially with the vintage. The other two components are Sémillon and Sauvignon. It's a subtle, charming wine, flavorful despite the very modest alcohol (just 11.5 percent in 2008); some will find it altogether too restrained, too polished, and insufficiently characterful—but that's what Naudé is aiming for.

In its warm generosity, the Adoro Red is a more typical Cape wine. It is Syrah-based (grapes from Stellenbosch and Swartland), with a minority of Cabernet Sauvignon and Merlot (both from diverse Stellenbosch vineyards), and sometimes Swartland Grenache and Mourvèdre. Judiciously oaked, and best after five years in bottle, it's a fairly serious, sweet-fruited, richly elegant wine—and, like the others, a good food companion.

www.adorowines.co.za

ALTO

So central is the wine named Alto Rouge to Stellenbosch's wine history and indeed to South African wine culture that it is almost shocking for locals to realize that elsewhere it is labeled Alto Estate. The wine goes back to the early 1930s, although then it was not the blend of Bordeaux varieties plus Syrah that it is now. The farm name itself dates to 1919, when the original property founded in 1693 was subdivided. Partly still wilderness, Alto was planted exclusively to red varieties, among the first in the Cape with such a focus. There are now some 93 hectares of essentially north-facing, granitic vineyards trellised on the slopes of the Helderberg (some rising to an altitude of 500 meters), usefully open to afternoon breezes from False Bay.

Now owned by Lusan Premium Wines (a joint venture between German financier Hans Schreiber and Distell), Alto still produces only red wines: in addition to the Rouge, there's Cabernet Sauvignon and Syrah and, intermittently, a port made from Syrah. Generally, winemaker Schalk van der Westhuizen's orientation is classic, insofar as the wines are made for aging, with a moderately serious tannin-acid structure. All have pretty hefty alcohol levels, though they carry them well. The Shiraz is more modern, in that it tends to ultraripeness, and in its comparative lack of success one perhaps senses the winemaker's unease with this approach. The wines are competitively priced. Partly because of pressure to produce greater volumes, Alto no longer shares the heights of Cape red wine reputations, and is mentioned here for sentimental and historical reasons more than anything else, for Stellenbosch without Alto would be a lesser place.

www.alto.co.za

AMANI

Amani—the name means "peace" in Swahili—was established in 1995, and was acquired by Oklahoma-based Jim Atkinson in 2002. He, with his daughter and son-in-law, Lynde and Rusty Myers, came to live in South Africa and run the farm. The Myerses took over ownership in 2008. Architecturally, the winery style is more urban African contemporary than Cape Dutch, but the views across to False Bay from its high position on the Polkadraai Hills are quintessentially Stellenbosch. There are 32 hectares of Cabernets Sauvignon and Franc, Merlot, Mourvèdre, Syrah, Chardonnay, Sauvignon, and Viognier. They are moving toward organic farming here, but on a basis of modern technology: a "pressure bomb," for example, is used to measure leaf moisture potential, so the vines are not under- or overirrigated, and aerial infrared photography identifies different levels of vigor around harvesttime, so that each block may be harvested three times, according to vigor levels. In 2005, after a succession of consultants and winemakers, Carmen Stevens, the country's first black female winemaker (who has had a successful career since leaving Elsenburg in 1995), arrived in the cellar. She makes a range of well-crafted wines with a clear "commercial" aesthetic: rich, powerful, and fruity, subtly oaked; they have enough structure to age a few years, but not enough to disturb anyone.

www.amani.co.za

ANWILKA

It did Anwilka little harm when the maiden 2005 vintage was tasted by Robert Parker and he decided that it was "fabulous . . . the finest red wine I have ever had from South Africa." One can surely be confident that Parker was not unduly influenced by tasting the wine in Bordeaux (after sampling two hundred local reds of the same vintage earlier that morning), where 90 percent of the wine is released to the international market through the Bordeaux trade, and being offered it under the auspices of two Bordelais partners in this joint venture—Bruno Prats, former owner of Château Cos-d'Estournel, and Hubert de Boüard de Laforest, coproprietor of Château Angélus. The third partner in Anwilka was Lowell Jooste, at the time an owner of Klein Constantia Estate.

They bought the 40 hectares of gently sloping vineyards in the Helderberg area in 1997. The vines had been neglected and an extensive, carefully planned replanting program was begun, to just Cabernet Sauvignon, Merlot, Petit Verdot, and Syrah. Only the best vineyards—vigorously pruned and green-harvested—produce grapes for the top wine. Some grapes are sold off; some go into a second label, Ugaba. Jean du Plessis took over winemaking from Trizanne Pansegrouw in 2009—and no doubt gets useful advice from his eminent employers.

There is no attempt to push the wine into the Bordeaux mold—the addition of Syrah to the predominantly Cabernet Sauvignon base would anyway militate against that. But in the most modern tradition of Bordeaux it is designed to give early pleasure, which it undoubtedly does. Until 2009, in fact, the wine was among the earliest released of serious Cape reds, after spending less than a year in oak (of which typically half is new), and if anything it was rather too easygoing for serious claims to be made for it. But the 2009 (a great vintage anyway in the Cape) was a breakthrough for the wine, adding more depth and structure to the intense fruit. If it was indeed a taste of things to come, then more critics might be moved to echo Parker's enthusiasm.

In 2012 a merger was announced between Anwilka Vineyards and Klein Constantia, with just the two French owners taking a small stake in the new company. The intention is to keep the two brands entirely independent and functioning separately, at least at the level of production.

www.anwilka.com

BEIN

If their setup is probably the smallest professional winegrowing establishment in the Cape, Luca and Ingrid Bein must number among the most engaging. Some decades ago, as veterinary surgeons in Switzerland, they "fell in love with South Africa in general and Stellenbosch in particular." With the democratic transition under way, in 1993 they bought these 3 hectares in the Polkadraai Hills (in what was to become the Polkadraai ward) just outside the town of Stellenbosch, and it became their home and their passion. This was no executive lifestyle choice: they both acquired degrees in viticulture and enology from Stellenbosch University and set about making wine from their 2.2 hectares of Merlot in the small, well-equipped cellar they built. The southern slopes, with deep and highly weathered granite soils, receive some coolness and humidity with breezes from False Bay, clearly visible in the not-too-far distance. While there is no organic accreditation, the Beins follow a careful environmentally friendly approach: manure from their donkeys is the fertilizer, no insecticide is used, and nets protect the ripe grapes from avian depredation. High-tech stuff is not ignored, however, and infrared imaging allows them to stagger picking based on vigor. The first bottling of the unshowy Bein Merlot (as modest, charming, and unpretentiously serious as the owners) was in 2002. It seems to have improved continually with the age of their vines. Now there is also a Little Merlot (a second label, made from younger vines) and a Pink Merlot from saignée juice. A rather too enthusiastically oaked Reserve version has also appeared.

www.beinwine.com

BEYERSKLOOF

Oddly, for some years a Cabernet Sauvignon was the only wine that Kanonkop's then winemaker, Beyers Truter, made at Beyerskloof, his tiny joint-venture farm in the Koelenhof area. Now, although there is one attractive Bordeaux-style blend, it is Pinotage in virtually all possible guises that rules here. When Truter arrived in 1988, he found "nothing" except "some grass and a donkey. Oh, *ja,* and some ducks." The little parcel of land, with shallow, gravelly soil that appealed to Truter because it reminded him of the Médoc, had been part of a larger farm, Nooitgedacht, which centuries before had belonged to the Beyers family from which Beyers Truter is descended. The new name must have been pretty inevitable. So Cabernet and Merlot were planted and a small cellar was built where today the senior wines in the range are made; others are vinified elsewhere. In 1997 a nearby farm with some 50 hectares of vines was bought, mostly planted with Pinotage (some trelllised, some bushvine). Approaching 100 hectares of vines are now farmed.

Expansion of range and ambition was heralded by the success of the varietal Pinotage, first made in 1995, when Truter sourced grapes from old bushvines throughout Stellenbosch. The 2000 edition of the Platter wine guide noted that the 1999 vintage was made "in outsize quantities," about 30,000 cases. Production was to rise fivefold of this easygoing but not frivolous wine, juicy, fruit-filled, and fresh. Truter left Kanonkop in 2004 and the Kriges of Kanonkop sold out their share in Beyerskloof, which is now jointly owned by Truter and Simon Halliday, of the English wine company Raisin Social.

Pinotage owes a good deal of its progress and prestige (however challenged this might be) to Beyers Truter, and the grape is central to Beyerskloof. There is a Pinotage Reserve that is much more serious than the standard version. In the Kanonkop tradition, it is made after the model of Bordeaux, with a good deal of new French oak; in fact, despite the mighty tannins of its grape, there is a good, fresh acidity offsetting the sweet red berry fruit, and it is not a million miles from elegance. With the 2006 vintage an even more restricted version was introduced, based on the best barrels—its name, Diesel, will seem strange to those who don't know that this was the name of a beloved dog, featured on the label.

There is also a Cape blend called Synergy, and a senior version of it called Faith (replacing what used to be called Synergy Reserve). Cabernet Sauvignon and Pinotage usually dominate, with Merlot playing a softening role; it is grandly oaked and tends to be both richly savory and sweet-fruited, designed for impressiveness rather than subtlety.

The wine called originally Beyerskloof and now Field Blend (alluding to the original 5 hectares of Cabernet Sauvignon and Merlot interplanted at the home farm) does have a good track record. Again, despite a lot of power, Truter manages to achieve an element of refinement. The indications given by the fruit intensity, balance, and structure of all the top-end Beyerskloof wines, together with limited track record thus far, suggest that they should age beneficially for a decade or more.

It must be noted that there is a delightfully fresh rosé, with a Charmat-method sparkling version a little less convincing, and there is a moderately pleasant port-style wine partly made from Pinotage. Even white wine is not beyond Truter's ambitions for his beloved grape: 2008 saw the introduction of a Chenin Blanc–Pinotage blend, where the Pinotage had been removed from the skins directly after pressing to produce an effectively white wine.

Beyers Truter's son Anri has numbered among the winemakers here since 2004.
www.beyerskloof.co.za

BOTANICA

Virginia Povall is one of, rather remarkably, a handful of American female winemakers in South Africa (others being Andrea Mullineux of Mullineux Family, Mary-Lou Nash of Black Pearl, Samantha O'Keefe of Lismore, and Zelma Long of Vilafonté). She bought a flower farm and guesthouse in the Devon Valley in 2008 and started planting vineyards, but has been making wine, in the hospitable Zorgvliet cellar, from bought-in grapes. Finest of these wines is a delicately rich, very lightly oaked Chenin Blanc from very old (about 50 years) bushvines on the arid Skurfberg, near Clanwilliam in the Olifants River region. Also showing delicacy and finesse, though as yet not the same quality, is a more recent addition, a Pinot Noir from Walker Bay fruit. These two wines are beautifully packaged, bearing striking botanical paintings. A larger-volume, less-expensive range is called Big Flower, with a very acceptable Cabernet Sauvignon and a Merlot. Corporate New York's loss (not entirely, as she still does a little consulting there, despite having definitively moved here) is undoubtedly Cape wine's gain.
www.botanicawines.com

DALLA CIA

Giorgio and Simonetta Dalla Cia, both qualified enologists, arrived in South Africa from Italy's Friuli region when Giorgio took up the position of winemaker at Meerlust in 1978. Twenty-five years later, Giorgio "retired" to fully develop his family's wine and grappa business. Dalla Cia and son George had started distilling grappa in 1996 while he was still at Meerlust; today they have their own distillery and winery in the Bosman's Crossing complex in Stellenbosch, where they make some 9,000 cases of wine annually. While Dalla Cia was known primarily for his red wines at Meerlust, the first two wines under his own label were a Sauvignon Blanc and a Chardonnay, from 2003. Since then he has added a Cabernet Sauvignon as well as a Bordeaux-style blend, modestly named Giorgio. Fruit for all wines is bought in—as well as, reportedly, some of the unblended wine itself. As good Italians, the Dalla Cias believe wines are made to go with food, and their wines resist excess in either structure or flavor. The reds have a balance and build that should allow a good few years' development, though they are very drinkable in youth.

Giorgio Dalla Cia has also put his name behind a new internationally funded winery called 4G, which is producing just one wine, called G. The wine started being heavily marketed locally and internationally in 2012, trying to achieve an unprecedented price for a South African wine (four times the price of, for example, Sadie Family Columella). It is a very good wine of its type—which means that it well fits the model of rich, powerful, cashmere-tannined cult California Cabernet.
www.dallacia.com

DELAIRE GRAFF

Situated spectacularly at the top of the Helshoogte Pass outside Stellenbosch, Delaire was established in the early 1980s by John and Erica Platter, founder-editors of the annual wine guide that still bears their name. There have been numerous changes since they left in 1988—four owners, for a start. The current one, Laurence Graff, of Laurence Graff Diamonds International, came in 2003 and has been spending money on a scale (mostly on grand lodgings and a restaurant, but also on vineyards and cellar) that can be hopefully interpreted as a commitment to stay. The number of winemakers has been rather more significant: since 1988 there have been nine—at least a local record. The latest, Morné Vrey, took charge in 2009, having been an assistant here for a couple of years. Changes of owner and winemaker over the years have meant some very different approaches to the task of transforming the fruit from cool, high vineyards into bottle, even though the quality of the shifting range has been consistently good. It does look now, however, that Delaire might be achieving stability. Wines made by Vrey with his predecessor as cellarmaster, Chris Kelly, were showing a fine purity of fruit and an elegant harmony that has not always been the case here, and Vrey is maintaining this approach. The rather good port is his own idea, reflecting his origins in Calitzdorp. Among the dozen wines on offer, the best are probably the reds, notably one of the Cape's best Merlots, the Cabernet Sauvignon Reserve, and the Botmaskop, a Cabernet-led Bordeaux blend with Syrah. In 2012 the estate released Laurence Graff Reserve 2009, a label it will use for a barrel selection of Cabernet Sauvignon in the best vintages; while it is extremely expensive by South African standards it is certainly impressive, with tight fruit and both concentration and finesse. There has been extensive replanting of the vineyards in recent years, and about 20 hectares are under cultivation, with the accent on the Bordeaux reds as well as Chardonnay. Just one block of Sauvignon will remain, as there are too many north-facing slopes, and there will always be some need to buy in grapes.

www.delaire.co.za

DELHEIM

Delheim was one of the smarter names among wine estates in the 1980s (when good ones were admittedly in rather short supply) but would now be generally recognized as the producer of sound rather than exciting wines. The history of the farm on the south-western slopes of the Simonsberg dates back to 1699, when Willem Adriaan van der Stel granted 25 hectares of freehold land here to German Lourenz Kamfer, who named the farm De Driesprongh, believed to mean "where three roads meet." Jumping three centuries (during which the boundaries changed somewhat; the present estate was registered in 1903), in 1938 the farm was bought by Hans Hoheisen, who planned to use it as a retirement home for himself and his wife, Deli. Hoheisen was responsible for introducing vines onto Driesprong, and in 1949 Delheim—"Deli's home"—was born. Deli's nephew, Michael "Spatz" Sperling, arrived in South Africa from Germany in 1951 to help; it is he and his family who have built Delheim into the popular property it is today.

In 1975 the farm Vera Cruz, three kilometers away at the foot of Klapmutskop, was bought. There are 148 hectares in total planted now, with fifteen varieties in the climatically different parts of the area. The majority of the reds are planted on the loamy-sand soils stretching down the warmer, drier area in the Klapmuts vineyards, while the whites are in the red granite and rocky black turf on the cooler, windswept slopes of the Simonsberg, where the aspects reduce the amount of available sunshine. Most of the remainder of the 354 hectares that make up the two properties is given over to fynbos—the Sperlings have a deep concern for the environment, felt throughout the farm.

Victor Sperling is viticulturist and cellarmaster; he and his winemaker (a new one since 2012) oversee the large range of wines (seventeen labels in 2013), divided equitably between reds and whites. Styles vary from the deliberately commercial, as in the Pinotage Rosé, through to the more serious flagship Grand Reserve, a Cabernet Sauvignon–based red first made in 1981 (by a young Kevin Arnold). The other top wine in the range is the Vera Cruz Shiraz, a small bottling from a single vineyard. The wines are mostly in restrained, unshowy style, with new oak well and sparingly used.

www.delheim.com

DE MEYE

This farm is in a quietish, northern corner of Stellenbosch, and its wines are also a little out of the mainstream—unfortunately so, as they are consistently sound and made in a gratifyingly restrained, well-balanced way. The farm, named after a river in the area in Holland from which the first Myburgh came to the Cape in 1655, has been in the same family for several generations: the current owners, Jan and Philip Myburgh, are the fifth and sixth. The 65 hectares of mainly rich, fertile soils with generally southeasterly aspects are planted to Syrah, Cabernets Sauvignon and Franc, Merlot, Chardonnay, and Chenin. Until 1998, the first vintage to appear under the family's own label, the crop was sold to the merchants. Now some 18,000 cases of their range are bottled annually, and the remaining grapes sold off. The range, made by Marcus Milner since 2000, is headed by Trutina, a Cabernet-led blend with Syrah, a compatible mix with character but not at all showy. Accessible on release, it has the balance of fruit, structure, and oak to age well. The other wines, all single-varietals, are similarly eminently drinkable and decent, and the less ambitious Little River range offers good value.

www.demeye.co.za

DEMORGENZON

This farm, on the highest southern and eastern slopes of the Ribbokkop in the Stellenboschkloof, was originally part of the old Uiterwyk farm (see DeWaal), and for some time was home to L'Emigré wines. It was bought in 2003 by Wendy and Hylton

Appelbaum, with backgrounds in big business. The name, Dutch for "morning sun," was inspired by the high-lying land being the first in the valley to see the sun. The Appelbaums inaugurated a thorough overhaul of the vineyards after a detailed analysis of their land, carefully replanting 50 or so hectares, though leaving some 5 hectares of old Chenin vines. The focus is increasingly on Rhône varieties, with Syrah, Grenache, Mourvèdre, Viognier, and Roussanne, but in the usual eclectic Cape fashion there is also Sauvignon Blanc, Chardonnay, and Pinot Noir, with trial blocks of Barbera, Primitivo, and Petite Sirah. No doubt the most unusual aspect of viticulture here (an attractive counterpoint to the move to fully sustainable, "natural" farming) is the piping of music nonstop throughout the vineyards in accordance with certain arcane theories—the music is mostly, it seems, of the German Baroque, in defiance of the terroir and the origins of the grapes! The area of the estate set aside for the restoration of indigenous vegetation is, however, left to the music of the spheres.

In the early years the DeMorgenzon wines were made by diverse eminent winemakers in their own cellars—most notably the handsome Chenin Blanc of Teddy Hall. A full-time winemaker was appointed in 2009, however, and in 2010 Carl van der Merwe moved here from troubled Quoin Rock. Some grapes continue to be brought in, and a new range was established, called DMZ. Thus far, only the fine, seductively opulent Chenin Blanc appears under the DeMorgenzon label. Things are very much at an early stage here, but on the basis of what has been glimpsed so far, of the terroir, and of the owners' clear and well-funded intentions to make serious, ambitious wines, this is undoubtedly a winery to be welcomed, and closely watched.

www.demorgenzon.co.za

DE TOREN

This winery shows one expression of modern Cape winemaking at its best: a perfectly thought-through project (from its founding in the mid 1990s), marketed with flair, attention to detail, and hard work—and with two wines that superbly meet their aim: easily approachable young, with forward fruit, and an element of seriousness that is neither intimidating nor imposing, all with a rather Californian polish. The farm is on the southern slopes of the Polkadraai Hills with a view to False Bay, which obligingly sends its cooling breezes to the well-drained vineyards. Cabernet Sauvignon was there from the start of the project, but the idea was to make a blend using all the main red Bordeaux varieties (hence the rather flash name Fusion V for the flagship). The 26 hectares are planted with due regard to soil variations, and eighteen different clones are proudly claimed: seven Merlots, five Cabernet Sauvignons, and two each for Cabernet Franc, Petit Verdot, and Malbec. Infrared aerial imaging monitors the grapes for ripeness, meaning the grapes can be harvested and vinified by batch.

De Toren (Dutch for "the tower") gets its name from the elevator shaft that contains a 4,000-liter pressure tank to transport wine between levels—the winery is designed around gravity flow, another instance of meticulous planning. With all this suggestion of perfection, with enthusiasm from Robert Parker for the maiden 2000 vintage of Fusion V, is there space for less than total praise? Only, perhaps, if one wants a little somberness, a little bite, a touch of elegant austerity. The wine is not usually a blockbuster: despite the 14.5 percent alcohol it balances happily with the fruit, ripe tannin, and fresh acidity, and only half of the oak is new. Of all the good modern Cape wines, perhaps Fusion V is most attuned to a world in which bottle maturation is scarcely a question for most wine drinkers. The wines do keep, perhaps even gain a little complexity, but when tasting them on their release, there is nothing to suggest anything other than gratification from early consumption. Albie Koch has been winemaker here from the start, a not altogether common asset in nonfamily wineries in the Cape.

The second wine is called Z (pronounced in the American way, which perhaps confirms De Toren's orientation). Though less expensive, it is more an alternative than a junior wine. Slightly less oaked, it has a predominance of Merlot in the five-variety blend; a little lighter than Fusion V, it also is charming and drinkable.

www.de-toren.com

DE TRAFFORD

The Traffords' farm and winery is one of the Cape's most tucked away, high in the fold between the Helderberg and Stellenbosch Mountain. (The "De" in the winery name is not pretension, merely the closest they could get to registering their own name as a brand.) It was wild grazing land when the family bought it in 1976, and remained without vines (apart from a tiny noncommercial vineyard) until after quota restrictions were lifted. The winery was registered in time for the 1992 harvest, and new vines were planted a few years later. David Trafford, an architect, was realizing that, as he says, whatever profession he might have chosen, "winemaking was thrust upon me." He has borne up well. Not that the operation is anything other than tiny—just 3,500 cases annually—but they sell extremely quickly and at the very good price his international reputation allows. There are just 5 hectares of low-yielding vines on the high slopes of the home farm, Mont Fleur, at an altitude of 350 to 410 meters: Syrah, Merlot, Cabernets Sauvignon and Franc, and Pinot Noir. David also buys in Cabernet, Merlot, Syrah, and Chenin Blanc from three other farms in the area. There are five single-varietals and two blends in the range, as well as the sumptuous straw wine made from Chenin—the 1997 was the pioneer of this style in the Cape. The wines are subject to minimal handling, not inoculated and not filtered (though lightly fined). And all are high in alcohol—the mystery being how they manage to carry the load of about 15 percent with grace. They have, of course, a touch of lush ripeness, but also a tightly wound concentration, with firm structures and well-judged oaking. David thrusts aside any suggestion of criticism about the alcohol levels—"it is what the vineyards deliver," he insists. Well, the vineyard that delivered 12.9 percent on the 1994 Cabernet Sauvignon was delivering 15 percent by 2000, so it is not quite as simple a matter as terroir. But certainly Elevation 393, made from the three varieties in the Mont Fleur vineyard (no Pinot) and named for its height above sea level, aims to show the character of this vineyard as a whole rather than express varietalism. Both the Cabernet Sauvignon and the Syrah 393 similarly show some finesse despite their ripeness and are lithe and firm as well as evidencing clean, bright fruit, and the Chenin Blanc is a good white match for them. De Trafford wines develop well and keep for many years. In a series of vertical tastings in 2008, noted British connoisseur Remington Norman suggested good drinking for at least fifteen years for the top wines from better vintages.

A new Trafford diversification came as a surprise in 2009, with the release of maiden 2007 wines from vineyards in the Swellendam district under the Sijnn label. The wines are at present made in the Stellenbosch winery, but the brand is entirely distinct. At the mouth of the Breede River (Sijnn being its indigenous name, pronounced more or less as "sane," apparently) that sustains so much intensive viticulture, David Trafford established a remarkable, isolated vineyard, based on a "gut-feel" that the conditions were propitious: the soils are poor and stony, there's wind, and there's low and sporadic rainfalls throughout the year. Low yields are wanted and expected from the widely spaced bushvines. Initially 12 hectares were planted, mostly of Mediterranean varieties: Syrah, Mourvèdre, Touriga Nacional, and what was thought to be Tempranillo but is the minor port variety Tinta Amarela (Trincadeira). The latter disappointed David at first, but he has found it a very interesting, though difficult, grape. "We also planted a little Cabernet Sauvignon as it just seemed silly not to. It doesn't really fit into the concept and interestingly, doesn't really blend into the blend!" The maiden vintage from the young vines was 2007, and it was immediately apparent that this project—this terroir in these hands—could be exciting. The moderately oaked blend, called simply Sijnn, is Syrah-based, with contributions from the other reds, especially Mourvèdre, and it improved with each vintage for the next few years. The very satisfactory oaked White blend was at least initially from just Chenin and Viognier. The Rosé has been admired by some and thought by others, including me, to be decidedly odd and unappealing. As one might expect from this team, the wines are ripe, mostly with high alcohols that are somehow balanced and integrated, and they are full of flavor and character. What will this terroir produce when the vines mature? It should be well worth finding out.

www.detrafford.co.za
www.sijnn.co.za

DEWAAL

It's a pity when marketing demands do away with a good historical name—as happened when the name of this farm, Uiterwyk, disappeared from the label. The original, larger property was granted to Dirk Coetzee among the second group of settlers given farms in the Stellenbosch area. The name, meaning "outer ward," referred to the common grazing land outside his native Kampen in the Netherlands. Fortunately for sentimentalists, the de Waal name is pretty historic in these parts, too. The current generation is the sixth on

Uiterwyk (and the ninth generation of winemakers in the family). When a de Waal bought the farm in 1824, 100,000 vines were already planted. Today there are 120 hectares of vineyard, mostly facing south and southeast, running from the valley floor up the slopes of the Stellenboschkloof and planted with Pinotage, Merlot, Syrah, Sauvignon Blanc, and Viognier. The crowning glory of the vineyards—as reflected in the wine—is the blocks of fifty- to sixty-year-old Pinotage. In fact, the oldest block is one of the oldest Pinotage vineyards anywhere. It was C. T. de Waal, a lecturer at Elsenburg Agricultural College, who made the first wine from the pioneering Pinotage here, in 1941.

Things went into flux in 2011, with the three de Waal brothers each having their own brands but still all associated with the jointly owned estate. Pieter de Waal retains the original label and sources wines from his brothers Chris and Daniël (it was the latter who was responsible for the red wines on which the estate's reputation depended). There are three Pinotage wines in this brand. Top of the Hill, from those oldest bushvines, is the most ambitious—if one gauges ambition by the amount of expensive new oak used: this one now gets twenty-seven months of oaking in all-new French barriques, and the richness and depth of fruit to cope with it fairly admirably (I think that, as usual, a little less would be more). It is undoubtedly one of the top examples of the variety in this Bordeaux-inspired style, with more elegance than rusticity, and the gorgeously sweet, ripe fruit is not jammy. Less oaky, and sometimes a touch more refined and less assertive, is the CT de Waal, from the second-oldest vineyard block. These top wines have the ability to mature well for five to ten years at least. The standard Pinotage is a well-made wine from younger vines, intended to be less wooded, less intense, with less tannic power. The alcohol levels of DeWaal wines rarely exceed 13.5 percent, which is a bonus. There is also a decent-enough Merlot. Now defunct is the Cape Blend—the first wine to proudly bear this name on its label, and in fact the first such blend to assert Pinotage as a component since the "invention" of the style by Welgemeend a generation earlier. This is primarily a red wine farm, but it also produces a Sauvignon Blanc and a Viognier—neither of which is impressive.

Chris de Waal's brand is Cape Gable. Danie and Ingrid de Waal's own wines come under the umbrella of Super Single Vineyards, but their Pella brand has been around since 2004 with a sound and rather luscious Cabernet Sauvignon; other bottlings have been made more recently, including Thomas Se Dolland Pinotage from a very old Pinotage block on their own Stellenbosch farm, Canettevlei. Another range is set to develop greatly over this decade, with the maturing of vineyards on the de Waals' pioneering property in cool, high-lying, continental Sutherland-Karoo. Mount Sutherland Syrah 2009 was the first of these wines to appear. It suffered somewhat from late picking, and it was tempting to dismiss it as yet another powerful and rich Syrah made in the cellar rather than the vineyards—but a certain purity of fruit and freshness support my instinct that, if the origins are allowed more sway in the wines, this new winegrowing area could be an invaluable asset to the Cape.

www.dewaal.co.za

www.supersinglevineyards.co.za

DORNIER

Dornier has one of the Cape's most striking modern wineries: industrial-chic but relating interestingly to the mountain setting of the farm in the Blaauwklippen valley. It was the work of Swiss artist Cristoph Dornier, who bought his first farm here in 1995, later adding two adjacent ones; the first vintage was 2002. Cristoph died in 2008, but his son Raphael continues to manage Dornier. It is a large farm of some 170 hectares, with a good deal of that devoted to indigenous vegetation and just 65 hectares to vineyards. In the cellar J. C. Steyn aimed at quiet elegance in his wines, usually with success (he was here from 2005, but a new winemaker arrived in 2012). Things took a while to settle down, and blends have changed in the two flagship Donatus wines—one red, one white—and might well change further, as the shape of the vineyards (partly taken over from previous owners) is modulated: high-density plantings of Cabernet Franc, for example, are likely to be significant. Some grapes are also bought in as necessary.

Donatus Red has been made largely of single-vineyard Cabernet Sauvignon, showing fresh elegance, sometimes forward fruitiness, and sometimes the promise of complexity. The White has shifted to an interesting blend of mostly Chenin with Sémillon, and the oak regime has been reduced, but in fact the wine sometimes shows a little too much austere restraint. There is a smallish range of decent varietal wines—Merlot, Cabernet, and Pinotage, with a Chenin from Swartland grapes joining the lineup in 2009. The Cocoa Hill wines are entry-level offerings. But again it must be said that this winery has not yet achieved focus, even apart from the latest winemaker change, and experiments continue: Swartland Syrah has also been brought in, for example, and some Cabernet vineyards have been grafted over to Tempranillo. Malbec is the latest addition to the fairly standard array of varieties.

www.dornier.co.za

EDGEBASTON

In 2009 David Finlayson, the third generation of winemaking Finlaysons in the Cape, left Glen Carlou where he had worked and lived for two decades (though it had been for some time out of his family's ownership) and started devoting himself full-time to a new family property now in his name. Father Walter had taken care of the first vintages since the winery was established in the Simonsberg foothills in 2004. The 24 hectares of vineyards are planted to Cabernet, Syrah, Chardonnay, and Sauvignon Blanc, and some grapes are also bought in—this looks likely to happen increasingly, as Finlayson experiments with varieties not grown on the home farm. A new winery has been built, one a little more elaborate than the "shed" at first contemplated, and early promise is being fulfilled. As might be expected from David Finlayson, judging by his work at Glen Carlou, the wines are fairly bold and modern, but not aggressively so, and expertly crafted. He has clearly also moved in a more "holistic" direction in the vineyards, using aspects of biodynamic viticulture as well as more scientific methods; in the cellar there is a parallel movement toward more natural winemaking, with some spontaneous fermentation, large wooden vats for maturation, and manual punchdowns of the fermenting must rather than mechanical pumpovers. Two Cabernet Sauvignons, one of them a reserve version named GS in homage to George Spies's fine GS Cabernets of the 1960s, have been perhaps the most impressive of the wines, as well as good Syrah and Chardonnay. Very possibly, however, things will be looking even more impressive over the next years, as the winemaker settles down with his maturing vineyards.

www.edgebaston.co.za

EIKENDAL

There has always been remarkably little to say about Eikendal since the modern Helderberg property was established (on land first granted in 1793) by the Swiss Saager family in 1981. It was always truly said, however, that it kept on in its quiet way producing very acceptable wines with little flash, and thriving less on marketing than on a reputation for good value. Eikendal's stability was helped by having Josef Krammer remain as winemaker for fifteen years before his retirement. Since then there have been a few, with Nico Grobler rising from assistant to chief winemaker (and, in a positive move, also responsible for the vineyards) in 2009. And here a welcome change does seem to have been inaugurated. Alcohol and ripeness levels, which had been rising, are now getting lower again, and elegance is once more a focus. The best of the whites was always the Chardonnay, and from 2010 it evidenced this new more restrained, taut approach. The leading red, Classique, has been a sleek and supple but often too-powerful blend based on Cabernets Sauvignon and Franc, but cellar sampling shows that this too is toning down for the better (and gaining an increased Merlot component). The 50-odd hectares of mainstream varieties produce some 40,000 cases annually (some grapes are also bought in), mostly in the large range of less-ambitious wines, with about 70 percent of production being red.

www.eikendal.com

EPICUREAN

Just one wine is produced here, and generally only some 250 cases of it are made: a luxuriously priced blend, usually based on Cabernet Sauvignon and Merlot, sourced fairly widely and made at the Rupert and Rothschild cellars in Paarl by Schalk-Willem Joubert—supposedly taking into account the advice of the brand's owners. Those owners include four rich and successful businessmen, one of whom is former Gauteng premier Mbhazima Shilowa; the others are Ron Gault, Mutle Mogase, and Moss Ngoasheng. As might be expected, the wine is a touch showy and powerful, with plenty of oak (80 percent new, pretty well absorbed) but beautifully made and well balanced. The back label nicely puts wine drinking in perspective with a quote from the Greek philosopher for whom the wine is named: "We should look for someone to eat and drink with before looking for something to eat and drink, for dining alone is leading the life of a lion or wolf."

www.epicureanwine.co.za

ERNIE ELS

Conveniently for Ernie Els, an international golfing star with ambitions in wine, he had a good friend in Jean Engelbrecht, owner of Rust en Vrede, and in 1999 they started their own red-only wine venture. It is now entirely owned by Els. The maiden vintage of Ernie Els, as the flagship is named, was 2000; it was destined to be sold, Engelbrecht warned in advance, at a price "commensurate with Ernie's international standing"—which is indeed one way of deciding wine value, and it was briefly the most expensive South African wine. This and a few subsequent vintages were made from bought-in grapes and vinified by Louis Strydom at Rust en Vrede. A few years later they bought a portion of Webersburg, not far distant, on the higher north- and west-facing slopes of the Helderberg, and from whose vineyards fruit for their venture had been sourced. There are 72 hectares of vines, with the five red Bordeaux grapes as well as Syrah and a little Mourvèdre. A cellar was built in time for the 2005 harvest; Strydom moved there full-time and is now also managing director.

In the cellar, all varieties are vinified and barrel-matured separately. Ernie Els Signature spends twenty months in new French oak barriques, followed by eighteen months in bottle before release. The blend is Cabernet-led, with the other four Bordeaux varieties. To add freshness to the power of the Cab, the Franc, Petit Verdot, and Malbec (up to a maximum of 15 percent of the blend) are unwooded and from the subsequent vintage. The same method and grapes are used for the Proprietor's Blend, along with Syrah, which is the major component—this mix, they believe, best represents the area's terroir and started off as essentially another interpretation of the Rust en Vrede Estate wine. It spends less time in oak than the Ernie Els; both French and American oak are used, with around 80 percent new. An addition to the range was made in 2007, appropriately called Big Easy (Els's nickname), a less-grand version of the Proprietor's Blend; and a few other more moderately priced wines have been added since then, including a few whites. The wines are emphatically new-world in style, and really designed for the palates to which Californian blockbusters appeal: they are very ripe, often with alcohols of at least 15 percent, and can have more residual sugar than classicists approve of. But they are undoubtedly very well made, sleek, well structured, and well balanced, with neither oak nor sweetness too obvious. Strydom was quoted in the 2013 Platter *Guide* as saying that he is moving in pursuit of elegance: "It used to be the bigger, the better, and we in the Helderberg were well positioned to deliver on that. Now there's a shift to greater refinement and the trick is to step back a little in the winemaking process without losing the essence of place." That sounds good.

www.ernieelswines.com

FLAGSTONE

Bruce Jack burst onto the local wine scene with a bunch of 1999 wines, a lot of joie de vivre, and a winery amid the history and the rapidly developing commercialism of Cape Town's Waterfront. The last of these provided vital cold-storage space (originally intended for the fishing industry) for the grapes he brought in from vineyards scattered around the Cape—not yet from the family farm near Napier, where he was planning to plant 40 hectares, but from interesting sites he had found. After a few years it proved more sensible to establish a larger winery in an unromantic setting in old buildings in a light-industrial park in Somerset West. Jack acquired a well-deserved reputation over the years not only for the odd names he gave many of his wines but, more important, for his dynamism and his passionate searching out of interesting and unusual terroirs. No doubt the breadth and depth of his knowledge of the Cape wine lands were among the attractions he held for Constellation, then the world's largest wine company. It was an apparently unlikely match between quirky individualism and corporate global gigantism, but one that resulted in Constellation (now Accolade) appointing him as its chief winemaker in South Africa, and taking ownership of Flagstone.

Bruce Jack remains in creative control (the winemakers are Gerhard Swart and Gerald Cakijana), and it seems that the Flagstone recipe, if that is how it can be described, has not been tampered with. Quantities have become large, and there are a lot of wines in various ranges—the Flagstone ones all bearing more or less whimsical names (poetic ones, if you prefer, as Bruce undoubtedly would—and his prose style is as flamboyant and deft as his winemaking). Among the best are a handful from Elim, including the elegant Fiona Pinot Noir, a more powerful Cabernet called Music Room, Free Run Sauvignon Blanc, and the newer Word of Mouth Viognier, which also uses Elgin fruit. Dragon Tree is one of the oldest of the Flagstone labels, a rich and fruity blend of Cabernet, Syrah, and Pinotage. Writer's Block Pinotage, from high-lying Breedekloof vines, is a polished and restrained version of the variety taken seriously, and an expensive but even finer reserve bottling of this wine, called Time Manner Place, was introduced in 2010. They are all modern, bright wines, displaying Jack's exuberance but also his cool, intelligent control, traits he has apparently transferred to his team. All bottles, incidentally, are under screw cap—Flagstone was one of the first local wineries to adopt this closure wholeheartedly, a useful measure of Jack's willingness to embrace new trends and of his devotion to pure-fruited wines.

The Flagstone home is now with megabrand Kumala, closer to Stellenbosch town. *www.flagstonewines.com*

FLEUR DU CAP

This range was inaugurated in 1968 with a Cabernet Sauvignon 1966. Then as now made at the Bergkelder ("mountain cellar") in Stellenbosch, it was a label for the Distillers Corporation and now vies with Nederburg as the most prestigious of Distell's brands.

The name comes from that of a Herbert Baker–designed villa owned by the huge corporation on the banks of the Lourens River in Somerset West. Though a fraction of the size of Nederburg's production, some 145,000 bottles are produced annually for the two ranges under the Fleur du Cap name. The standard range runs the gamut from a modest Natural Light up to a first-rate Noble Late Harvest from Riesling and the plush, usually Merlot-based Bordeaux-style blend Laszlo, honoring Bergkelder's onetime cellarmaster Julius Laszlo. These wines have always been reliable if unexciting, but have made great advances in recent years.

Even more interesting, however, is the Unfiltered Collection, which has expanded since the first three were introduced in 1996. There have occasionally been questions asked about whether the name of the range belongs more to the realm of publicity than to actual cellar practices, considering that the wines have such a polished appearance, with no trace of turbidity. I raised the matter some years back with Linley Schultz, then Distell's general manager for wines, and he convinced me that the "unfiltered" claim was valid, enabled by a meticulous set of practices in the cellar. The wines, anyway, speak of quality. In this they have been led by the whites, which, in something of a revolution around the turn of the century, raised their levels hugely. Now the Sauvignon Blancs in particular (there is a Limited Release version too) are excellent, with the Chardonnay and the white blend not far behind. The reds are also now improving—they retained for some years the characteristic old Bergkelder hardness, resulting partly from excessive acidification—and the Cabernet Sauvignon is now particularly good. This wine is (at least sometimes) made from a single vineyard in Bottelary, but sadly, all the wines in all ranges blandly declare their origin as Coastal or Western Cape. Although Fleur du Cap does source its grapes from fifty growers, some far distant from the Stellenbosch home cellar, and the primary declared interest is quality and varietal expression rather than terroir, it is surely time that Distell started providing more precise indications of origin for its most interesting wines. Nonetheless, as far as quality goes, the young winemakers under Andrea Freeborough are working very well with their viticulturists. Too often restaurant-goers in South Africa are confronted with a wine list that has very obviously been designed by Distell; while such practices are always to be regretted, at least now, with the wines of Fleur du Cap and Nederburg available, the diner can get good-quality wine.

www.fleurducap.co.za

THE FOUNDRY

The Foundry is a joint venture established in 2000 between Chris Williams, cellarmaster at Meerlust (and set to become a Master of Wine), and James Reid, South Africa's operations director of the mighty international Accolade Wines. Since he took the senior position at Meerlust in 2004, Williams has made the wines there, but by 2010 a potential new home was emerging for the brand on a historic farm bought by Reid in the Paardeberg area, where the charming old buildings include a small winery that will be rented to the joint company when the time seems right to move. There were also

10 hectares of Syrah and Cabernet planted, which will find their way into a range that was set for expansion (just awaiting better market conditions); in fact, 2010 saw the release of a new Grenache Blanc made from southern Swartland grapes, followed by a Roussanne in 2011. These wines will form the nucleus of a Paardeberg range, and both are very good: pure-fruited and probably more focused, less richly broad than is the dominant emerging tradition with Rhône-style whites in the Cape, especially the Swartland. The Syrah and Viognier for which the Foundry had already acquired a substantial reputation—both are among the most restrained and classically made of local versions, and certainly to be numbered among the leaders—will still be sourced from Stellenbosch vines. Reflecting on his concentration on single-varietal wines, Williams acknowledges the possibility of blends in the future, but says he feels the "need to understand them as varieties first and wait for the vines to mature to get a real sense of character and quality before blending."
www.thefoundry.co.za

GLENELLY

Of all signs of Bordelais interest in the Cape, May-Eliane de Lencquesaing's has been evidenced most eloquently—and with remarkable enthusiasm and energy for anyone, let alone an octogenarian. The former owner of Château Pichon-Longueville Comtesse de Lalande bought the property, then largely planted to fruit trees, in 2003. A few early vintages from bought-in grapes were made in nearby cellars while renovations to the buildings were carried out, a start made on planting 60 hectares (out of the estate's 123) of vineyards, and a six-hundred-ton-capacity winery built. By 2009 all the wines derived from her own vineyards and rested in barrel in this remarkable building. It is a huge, austere concrete block, yet one designed to be eventually sympathetic to the environment, and showing great innovation within, even beyond the careful design to ensure that gravity is responsible for most of the vinous flow (through a system of mostly hidden pipes)— at least until the bottling is done, many floors down. As for other innovations, there is, for example, the largest cast-concrete roof in southern Africa, the barrels rest on beams made from recycled plastic, and ambient temperature control is done in an energy-efficient manner via cooled concrete rather than air-conditioning. Winemaker Luke O'Cuinneagain has imported from Château Angélus in St.-Émilion, where he spent some time, an intricate system of grape sorting that includes a "Mistral" machine, which literally blows away any raisined fruit or anything lighter than a lusciously filled berry. So far no yeast inoculation has been used, and natural winemaking is to be expected through the process. The care and attention to detail are obvious in the vineyards, too, where each block (defined by variety and soil type) has probes reading all sorts of information to govern decisions about irrigation.

With this sort of commitment, investment, and intelligence in an area with proven capacity to produce good red wine (Rustenberg is a neighbor) it is reasonable to have high expectations, and the earliest estate wines are not disappointing. The Grand Vin de Glenelly blends about 50 percent Syrah with Cabernet Sauvignon, Merlot, and

Petit Verdot. By contrast, Lady May, the flagship, has been essentially a Cabernet wine, with an admixture of Petit Verdot, since the maiden 2008 release. Despite having the same high alcohol (about 14.5 percent) as the Grand Vin, the Lady May presented itself as more elegant than might have seemed likely from the analysis, with no sign of overripeness and with a drier finish than is often the case with Cape reds. The subsequent few vintages confirmed Lady May as ranking among the finest such blends in the Cape.

The Chardonnay, which debuted with the 2010 vintage, is also called Grand Vin, with the variety name attached. It, too, seems consecrated to finesse. There is also a second range, called the Glass Collection (Mme. de Lencquesaing is a notable collector of glass), which consists of single-varietal wines, unsurprisingly also good, albeit less serious and designed for earlier drinking. This is undoubtedly a winery that will make a substantial contribution to Stellenbosch wine.

www.glenellyestate.com

GRANGEHURST

Jeremy Walker—a former oil company executive who also had winemaking experience and an enology degree—turned a squash court into a cellar on his family smallholding on the slopes of the Helderberg, and set about his maiden bottling, from bought-in grapes, in 1992. Innovatively, he obtained some financing for expansion from debentures, later converted to "futures." A guest cottage became a barrel cellar, but by the turn of the century acclaim and growth had made it possible and necessary to build a new maturation cellar and winery. All the grapes had been bought in, but in 2000 a 13-hectare farm was bought in the greater Simonsberg area, in partnership with John Hill, who had also become a partner in the winery. Six grape varieties were planted in 2002 and 2003: Cabernet Sauvignon, Pinotage, Merlot, Syrah, Mourvèdre, and Petit Verdot. Other grapes are bought in to supplement those as needed. Production is still small, however, with some 5,600 cases annually—all red wine, except for one rosé.

This is one of the more serious-minded, though insufficiently appreciated, ranges in the Cape, made in a traditional manner in large open fermentation tanks, with the must punched down. Walker was one of the earliest local winemakers to abandon the automatic acidification taught at the academies, and has not added acid since 1992. A sorting table was added to the production line in 2004, but the grapes are still pressed in wooden basket presses. The wines are not always easily gratifying in youth—and anyway tend to be released much later than most, often with four or five years in bottle. A few do show dry tannins, perhaps from overlengthy oaking—some of them may spend thirty months in barrel—but the best are harmonious, elegant, classic (though not without concession to new-world evidence of pure fruit), and among the most ageworthy of Cape reds. Virtually all of them are highly recommendable. The Cabernet Sauvignon Reserve is perhaps not usually quite as good as the Cabernet Sauvignon–Merlot, which tends to have some Petit Verdot in it too; Nikela is one of the most elegant and polished of the Cape blends, with Pinotage as the largest component, along with Cabernet, Merlot, and Syrah.

www.grangehurst.co.za

HARTENBERG

This substantial and popular Bottelary Hills property is one of the more serene wine farms, with the nineteenth-century manor house and cellar well off the road and shaded by well-established trees. A natural water source flows through the property into a wetland system, never cultivated, that occupies 65 of the farm's 170 hectares. Vineyards, though, were here more than three centuries ago, when land was cleared and two thousand vines were planted even before Christoffel Estreux (or L'Estreux; he quickly changed his name to Esterhuizen) was granted title in 1704. A later owner added a neighboring property, Weltevrede, in 1726. A succession of owners followed, all farming grapes as well as grain and cattle. In 1948, the farm was sold to Dr. Maurice Finlayson and his wife, Eleanor, whose sons, Walter and Peter, and grandchildren have engraved the Finlayson name in the South African wine industry. Their wines were marketed under the Montagne label. Then, after a brief period in which Gilbeys owned the property (marketing wines under both Montagne and Hartenberg labels), it was bought in 1987 by Ken Mackenzie (with, briefly, a partner), and since his death has been owned by a family trust.

Of inestimable value to the development of the modern property and its wines is the stable tenure as cellarmaster since 1993 of the widely respected Carl Schultz. There's a range of soils here, varying from decomposed granite to Malmesbury shale, allowing for a plausibly large number of grape varieties—and few wineries in the Cape make so broad a range at such a high level of quality. The 94 hectares of vineyard are made up of Cabernet Sauvignon, Merlot, Pinotage, Syrah, Chardonnay, Riesling, and Sauvignon Blanc. To take advantage of morning or afternoon sun, vineyards face north, west, or east and vary some 250 meters in altitude. Irrigation is available as required.

Syrah is recognized as Hartenberg estate's strength, with the single-vineyard Gravel Hill the flagship. As its name suggests, the vines grow in poor, dry, gravelly soil; the block was first bottled in 1978, but its fame arrived over the fourteen years it was a special bottling for the Cape Winemakers Guild's annual auction. From 2005 the wine has headed the regular range. The tight, dry profile of Gravel Hill Shiraz suggests a classic European style that requires time to open and reveal its core complexity. In 2006 Hartenberg released a trio of more expensive wines made in ripe, "international," smartly oaked style: the Stork Shiraz (from clay soils), the Mackenzie Cabernet Sauvignon–Merlot, and the Eleanor Chardonnay. These big, rich wines are serious enough, very good of their type, and structured to benefit from several years' maturation.

After a small dip during the later part of the 1990s caused by cellar hygiene problems (which were solved with sufficient despatch), Hartenberg's reputation has only increased. The wines are modern, mostly unshowy, and interesting as well as deftly made.

www.hartenbergestate.com

HASKELL

American Preston Haskell, a leading property developer in Russia and a longtime visitor to the Cape, bought a farm in the Simonsberg foothills in 2002 with a mission to make high-quality wines. The fine modern cellar was built in time for Rianie Strydom (married to another winemaker, Louis Strydom of Ernie Els, not far down the road in this particularly lovely part of the Stellenbosch district) to take in the maiden 2005 harvest. Until 2009, however, with the 2007 vintage, the only wines to appear came under the Dombeya label, which has in fact consolidated into being less of a second label than a separate brand—one that is sufficiently successful for it probably to acquire its own premises sooner rather than later.

The wait proved to be worth it, with the maiden wine under the Haskell label, the Pillars Syrah 2007, winning some very important awards before it was even released, including being named Red Wine of Show at the Tri-Nations competition with Australia and New Zealand. It is undoubtedly a modern wine, ripe and quite showy and sweet-fruited, with a lovely perfumed quality; fresh, too, with a subtly forceful and very fine tannin base. This was the first of a trio of single-vineyard Syrahs: Aeon (with a dollop of Mourvèdre) followed soon thereafter, and a first vintage from the Hades block was picked in 2013. As promising as these, however, is Haskell IV, a terrific Bordeaux-style blend based on that more traditional Helderberg star, Cabernet Sauvignon. Cabernet also makes its way into Haskell II, with Syrah and Mourvèdre. Just when it looked as if this was going to be a red-only label, a single-vineyard Chardonnay appeared with the rich, powerful, but certainly not inelegant 2010 Anvil—Chardonnay had, in fact, been the star variety in the Dombeya range, so this was not entirely surprising.

Rianie Strydom has stepped back marginally to become something between a consultant and a cellarmaster, with viticulturist Wikus Pretorius now also acting as winemaker. Winemaking is meticulous and even interesting, involving some early experimentation with different techniques: carbonic maceration and native yeasts both featured in the maiden Pillars. There is every reason to expect that the members of this team will continue to achieve excellent results for their American boss, while the determination to combat virus in the vineyards will bring its own reward. An interesting viticultural experiment was announced in 2012, whereby the whole Pillars vineyard will be farmed organically but half of it also according to biodynamic principles, with the results of the differing treatments being carefully monitored. At the present rate of progress, Haskell could rapidly gain recognition as being among the top few dozen Cape wineries.

The Dombeya range, made by the same team but now marketed separately, is fair to good and reflects the plantings on the 13.5 hectares of vineyards—Cabernets Sauvignon and Franc, Syrah, Chardonnay, and Merlot—though it is likely that imported grapes will increasingly be needed.

www.haskellvineyards.com
www.dombeyawines.com

JORDAN (KNOWN AS JARDIN IN USA)

Few Cape wineries have quite the image of consistent sheer professionalism that winemaking couple Gary and Kathy Jordan bring to this family-owned property in the Stellenboschkloof area. The farm dates back to the 1700s, and was pretty neglected when bought by Ted and Sheelagh Jordan in 1982. Vineyard planting began in 1983 on 85 of the farm's 134 hectares. A later purchase of neighboring land increased the size to 146 hectares, and subsequent development has brought the vineyards to 105 hectares devoted to a wide range of classic varieties: Chardonnay, Chenin Blanc, Riesling, Sauvignon Blanc, Cabernet Franc, Cabernet Sauvignon, Merlot, and Syrah, most of which are used in varietal wines as well as the red blend Cobblers Hill.

The large range is perhaps more justified here than on many estates by a splendidly varied landscape: the property has slopes facing all directions, at altitudes from 160 to 410 meters. Soils, too, are varied, ranging from deep, well-drained clay-loam to gravelly and sandy duplex with clay underbase. Good exposure to the maritime influence of the southeasterly wind off False Bay adds to the mix of conditions suitable for a diversity of varieties. White varieties are generally grown on the south- and southeast-facing slopes, reds on those facing north and northwest. Most of the vineyards are mechanically harvested.

Until 1993, the crop was sold off. In preparation for producing wine under their own label, Gary Jordan and his wife, Kathy (his tertiary education in geology, hers in economics), spent a year at the University of California, Davis, studying viticulture, and then worked a vintage at Iron Horse, an experience that informed the approach to their own wines. They describe their goal as "individual wines that combine the concentrated fruity accessibility of the New World with the classic elegance of the Old World," which is as fair a summary as is possible, as long as one puts a little more stress on the New World side of things.

Production has grown to some 60,000 cases annually (the cellar, run as far as possible on gravity, has been extended a number of times over the years to cope with this increase, and other winemakers have been brought in to assist Gary and Kathy); along with the Estate range (marketed in the USA as Jardin, to avoid conflict with the existing Jordan Winery there) there are two other ranges offering very good value, Bradgate and Chameleon.

Jordan is perhaps best known for its Bordeaux-style blends, the top two versions of which are called Cobblers Hill and Sophia (the latter a barrel selection), and its Chardonnays, which also come in a range of guises. The reds are smart, modern, and very good, the new oaking seldom overdone, rich and fruit-filled, but firmly structured and able to age well for ten years at least in the best vintages. The barrel-fermented Chardonnays are typified by a limy zest with underlying leesy richness; partly spontaneous fermentation infuses greater complexity, with a little tank-fermented wine to lift the fruit. The Nine Yards Chardonnay, from a section of the best vineyard, is the flagship white—made in a bright, bold style with good depth and proven potential to develop with age; consistently one of the top ten Chardonnays of the Cape. A fine dessert wine from Riesling, called Mellifera, is also a highlight of the range.

If there's seldom anything to provoke gasps of astonishment or wonder from Jordan, one must applaud the making of so many wines at such a high level of achievement, and the marketing of them with equal professionalism and firm charm.

www.jordanwines.com

JOURNEY'S END

Western Wines was responsible for the development of Kumala as the Cape's leading export brand and its managing director at the time, Englishman Roger Gabb, was tempted in 1996 into buying a small, derelict estate on the lower, southwest-facing slopes of the Schapenberg outside Somerset West, with splendid views across False Bay to the end of the peninsula. In the first few years 20 hectares were planted to Chardonnay, Syrah, Cabernet Sauvignon, and Merlot grapes, and by 2008 the vineyards had grown to 30 hectares, with Cabernet Franc now included. Gabb also bought 6 hectares of Sauvignon Blanc from neighboring Mount Rozier. The wines were made at Stellenbosch University's Welgevallen cellar until a new cellar and tasting center were built among the home vineyards, ready in time for Leon Esterhuizen, full-time winemaker since 2005, to take in the 2010 harvest. This decisive step seems to have crystallized a growing focus and deter-mination, after a rather lackluster few years following the maiden 2002 vintage—although the Chardonnay had been promising right from that damply inauspicious year, despite being somewhat compromised by a rather too generous dollop of residual sugar. By the end of the century's first decade, an improvement was obvious, as vineyard manager Paul Fourie learned to get the best out of maturing vineyards on what should be an excellent site while Esterhuizen more adroitly handled the fruit. The Chardonnays are now good, from the screw-capped Haystack, the entry-level offering, to the standard version, and up to the new-oaked, tiny-quantity Destination Chardonnay in the Reserve range, intended to be made only in the best years. The reds, led by an elegant Cape Doctor Shiraz, are as yet not quite as interesting, but now that all is in place here, they too should pull themselves together and help Journey's End on its way—to use an entirely inappropriate image.

www.journeysend.co.za

KAAPZICHT

The first wine made under their own label by the Steytlers off their Bottelary farm was a Weisser Riesling 1984. It is no longer in their extensive range, and was a far cry from the big, powerful red wines for which they are now best known. The family had owned Rozendal since 1946, but it was only after Danie Steytler, grandson of the founder, became farm manager in 1976, after completing his agricultural studies, that ambitions emerged to divert a little of the grape production from supplying a large merchant house. Danie counts his tenure as cellarmaster from 1979. The name of the farm was too similar to some other brands to be used for a registered wine estate, however, and the splendid views of Cape Town and Table Mountain prompted the choice of Kaapzicht ("Cape view"). Home production remained minuscule for many years, but then grew steadily and dramatically—now, from the 162 hectares of vineyards at Kaapzicht they make some 40,000 cases of wine annually, with nearly twenty different wines. While Danie Steytler remains cellarmaster, the next-generation Danie formally took over substantial winemaking duties with the 2009 harvest. A young man as solidly built as his wines, he oversaw the introduction of a new flagship Bordeaux-style blend—initially just Cabernet Sauvignon and Merlot, with plantings of the other main varieties needing to mature before helping to justify the name Pentagon. The unsubtle, massive blockbuster style of the top Kaapzicht wines—particularly of the Steytler Pinotage and Steytler Vision (Bordeaux varieties with Pinotage)—has no doubt played a part in the numerous local and international awards they have won, and they are certainly very well made examples of that conqueror style.

www.kaapzicht.co.za

KANONKOP

Of the few generally unquestioned "first growths" of the Cape (in recurrent idle analysis), Kanonkop is the least grand in outward appearance and presentation and probably held in the greatest affection by many who have long known its fine red wines and heard of their earlier reputation. It retains the idea of being a Cape farm rather than a gentleman's estate or the luxurious acquisition of a newly rich man or large company. Not irrelevantly, this is one of the few indisputably top large properties that is owned and run not only by a family, but by an Afrikaans family.

The name is not old, though it alludes to the antiquity of the original farm: from the hill *(kop)* to the back of the farm a cannon would signal the arrival in Table Bay of Dutch East India ships seeking victualing. There is no fine mansion—that is on Uitkyk, the property from which Kanonkop was abstracted (the remnant sold by Senator J. W. Sauer in 1930). Uitkyk, incidentally, is owned by Lusan Holdings, and although its Carlonet Cabernet can be good, the property should be making better wines than it has for a few decades now, and is perhaps showing signs of starting to do so.

J. W. Sauer's son was another National Party politician, Paul Sauer (minister of transport for some time), and it was he who ran Kanonkop's grape farming in those early days—when already the farm had a reputation for quality among wholesale merchants. With the passing of Wine of Origin legislation in 1973 and the recognition of estates, two years before Paul Sauer's death, the first wine was bottled under the Kanonkop name, a Cabernet Sauvignon. Sauer's son-in-law, Jannie Krige, took over the farm, and it then passed to Johann and Paul Krige, the present owners.

Jan Coetzee, the first winemaker, left in 1980 and for nearly twenty-five years Beyers Truter made the wines and, with his extroverted personality nearly as much as with his skills in the cellar, helped bring Kanonkop to eminence. When Truter's departure for

Beyerskloof was imminent in 2002, Abrie Beeslaar started taking over the winemaking at Kanonkop (the first vintage that was properly his was 2004), while viticulturist Koos du Toit has a superb understanding of the Kanonkop vineyards. Some changes were introduced—there are triage tables, for example, though the wines are still fermented in large open cement tanks.

The pebbly, granitic soils that predominate on the lower, western slopes of the Simonsberg seem particularly suited to red wine (one of Truter's first stands in the early 1980s was his insistence that the white grapes be removed), and the 100 hectares of vineyards are all planted to red varieties: half to Pinotage, 35 percent to Cabernet Sauvignon, and the remainder to Merlot and Cabernet Franc. The Pinotage vines are grown traditionally, *en gobelet*, some dating from near the middle of the twentieth century. There is one small portion of the estate that has particularly sandy soils; apart from this section irrigation is limited.

Truter's contribution to South African winemaking will long be regarded, but undoubtedly one of his most distinctive legacies was his long struggle at Kanonkop to bring recognition of the seriousness of Pinotage as a variety. He did indeed show that it was a wine that could benefit from being made in essentially the Bordeaux pattern, and that it could mature into something like excellence over a decade or longer. It must have been a particular satisfaction when his 1989 Pinotage Reserve won a trophy at the International Wine and Spirit Competition in London, playing the major role in bringing him the trophy for International Winemaker of the Year. Although many other producers are now treating the grape with expensive respect in the cellar, and Kanonkop's is not alone on the top rung, the cellar's Pinotage remains very good. With 80 percent new oak and 14.5 percent alcohol, it is a very substantial (sometimes arguably overoaked) wine; the tannins are big but ripe and well disciplined, and the aromas and flavors are pure. Some vintages going back into the 1970s are still eminently drinkable, though showing much more rusticity than the suave modern wines do—in some years the Burgundian origin of one of Pinotage's parents is very apparent. In 2010 Kanonkop's first new label in forty years was announced: a mere one thousand (very expensive) bottles of 2006 Pinotage made solely from the low-yielding oldest vineyard, planted in 1953. Succeeding vintages have been sold in fairly rapid succession, to the point that the wine is now being sold *en primeur* (i.e., while still maturing in the Kanonkop cellar). The all-new-oaked wines are rather richer and perhaps deeper than the standard bottling, and beautifully structured.

The estate's second wine, Kadette, is usually made with about half Pinotage (plus Merlot and the Cabernets), and is a sophisticatedly rustic, chunkily tasty wine. It's made in large quantities, too: usually more than one hundred thousand six-bottle cases; there are about eight thousand of the Pinotage, which is more than Paul Sauer and the Cabernet Sauvignon.

There is no doubt that, like all other older Cape wines, Paul Sauer (usually about 70 percent Cabernet Sauvignon, with Franc and Merlot) has changed over the past decade or two. It remains just on the classic side of things, but, like much good Bordeaux today, it is riper and bigger and more substantially oaked (two years in new French barriques). Abrie Beeslaar has chosen not to do anything other than continue the (modernized) practices of Beyers Truter. This was one of the earliest of the Bordeaux-style reds in the Cape, and fairly frequent vertical tastings (the Kriges have always kept back good quantities of each vintage and are characteristically generous with them) have demonstrated a fine continuity of finesse and ability to mature for ten, sometimes twenty, years with grace and enough fruit for balance. Paul Sauer is undoubtedly among the most reputed Cape reds, both locally and internationally (in Europe at least): in 2008 it won the Pichon-Longueville Trophy for best international red blend for the third time, with the 2003 vintage. The wine remains less expensive than many wines that would envy its quality and even more its reputation.

The Cabernet Sauvignon has not quite the same cachet as Paul Sauer, but is in many vintages as fine, as richly elegant a wine; in some vintages it might well even be thought the better of the two, at least by those who appreciate it being often a touch lighter. All in all, Kanonkop's reputation has never stood higher than it does now, and it has been the most consistent, and probably the best, of the pre-1994 producers.

www.kanonkop.co.za

KEERMONT

This is one of the bright new hopes of Stellenbosch. Neighboring De Trafford in the lovely Blaauwklippen Valley, the 155-hectare farm has 27 hectares of vineyard planted at altitudes ranging from 250 to 400 meters above sea level, on both warmer north-facing Helderberg slopes and cooler west-facing Stellenbosch Mountain ones. Two-thirds of these were planted on fallow land between 2005, after Mark and Monica Wraith bought two properties here and amalgamated them, and 2009; some 8 hectares are of well-established vines, including Chenin Blanc planted in 1971 and some Syrah from which De Trafford has for many years made a wine under its own label. Apart from Chenin, the main focus is on Syrah and Cabernet Sauvignon. With young Alex Starey responsible for vineyard and cellar, there's a genuine attempt to express terroir and, to that end, to do things with the minimum of chemical farming, irrigation, and winemaking intervention.

The wines are almost elegant, though ripe and with high alcohols; they are properly dry, refined and understated, and look likely to get better and better, judging by the trajectory of the first few releases. The Keermont blend, which first appeared with a 2007, combines Cabernet and Merlot with Syrah. The (similarly unfiltered and unfined) Syrah's first vintage was 2008 and looks perhaps even more promising. The first white wine came two years later: Terrasse, a lightly oaked and well-focused blend of Chenin with a little Chardonnay and Viognier. For the maiden dessert wine, Fleurfontein, in the same year, Chenin and Sauvignon Blanc were desiccated on the vine. This is undoubtedly a winery to watch closely as the vines mature.

www.keermont.co.za

KEETS

Chris Keet was responsible for wines and vineyards at the much-lamented Cordoba winery on the Helderberg (it has been for sale for ages, with the vineyards still producing grapes that are sold off, but it's now many years since the label was used). He established a fine reputation there for lighter, more elegant Bordeaux blends, and the single wine he now makes under his own name—maiden vintage 2009—is in that understated tradition, although he's allowing himself a little more alcohol than he did at Cordoba. It's called First Verse, a five-way blend, with the leafy fragrance of Cabernet Franc one of the enticements, untrammeled by the scents and flavors of new oak as none is used, with no apparent loss of structure. The wine is made in rented space in Stellenbosch, from which Keet also works as a consultant, something that gives him plenty of chance to find choice vineyards for his wine; the early vintages at least were widely sourced within Stellenbosch.

www.keetswines.co.za

KEN FORRESTER

Ken Forrester is a dominant personality on the Cape wine scene, his passion, energy, and commitment leading to many having no doubt about his views on matters of social concern (he's a prominent supporter of the Pebbles charity, which focuses on children suffering from fetal alcohol syndrome) as well as matters vinous (he waxes very angry about the industry's insufficient concern for the blight of leafroll virus). The Forresters (Ken, wife Teresa, and two daughters) abandoned Ken's life as a successful and eminent Johannesburg restaurateur for the farm called Scholtzenhof at the foot of the Helderberg (though he has a wine-lands restaurant, too) in 1993. It is an old farm, originally granted to Frederich Boot of Gotha in 1689 as Zandberg; the Cape Dutch homestead built in 1694 was derelict when the Forresters arrived, but has now been restored.

There are 33 hectares of vineyard, mostly comparatively youthful and terraced, but also some bushvine Chenin, which goes into the splendid, oaked Noble Late Harvest called simply T (for Teresa) as well as the FMC, an opulent, off-dry, and obviously oaked wine that has become something of a benchmark for this style of wine in the Chenin renaissance of which Forrester is a major proponent. He also makes two other versions, an ambitious partly oaked version and a delightful simple one in his entry-level range under the Petit label.

The *M* in the FMC Chenin Blanc name refers to Martin Meinert, a longtime friend, collaborator, and consultant here, who complements Forrester's untrained but fine winemaking skills and instincts with his own measured, elegant approach. While the focus is on Chenin, there are a few other Forrester wines, as well as a number made for clients. The standout red is a big, flamboyant, and attractive Rhône-style red called the Gypsy.

www.kenforresterwines.com

KLEINE ZALZE

The history of this farm, on the southern outskirts of Stellenbosch, began when a German settler named Nicolaas Cleef planted the first vines in 1683. He named the farm De Zalze after his home village, Gross Salze. The first wine was made in 1695—as was the official grant to him of the two-part farm. In more modern times, with a great many owners in between, the portion known as Kleine ("small") Zalze was bought in 1968 by Gilbeys Distillers and Vintners and used primarily for bottling wines under the famous Alphen label. In 1996 Kleine Zalze was sold to Jan Malan and his attorney brother-in-law, Kobus Basson; Malan subsequently sold his interest to Rolf Schulz. On the home farm itself there were 30 hectares under vine, but 55 more were bought from neighboring Groote Zalze in 2002, thus effecting something of a reunification. The vineyards are fairly evenly split between white and red, but the annual production of some 200,000 cases also demands that grapes be bought in from as far afield as Koekenaap, Darling, Durbanville, and Walker Bay. But vines and wine are far from the only concerns of Kleine Zalze, where there is also a golf course, hotel, guesthouse, restaurant, and upmarket residential complex.

The old cellar was substantially refurbished after 1966, including adding a large maturation cellar cut into the granite beneath. After some early winemaker turnover, Johan Joubert joined as winemaker in November 2002; he is now cellarmaster, with a substantial team in support.

There are five ranges of Kleine Zalze wines, headed by the Family Reserve, from single vineyards on the estate except for bought-in Sauvignon Blanc; together with the Vineyard Selection from home or other Stellenbosch grapes, they make up the elite of Kleine Zalze's production. The Cellar Selection, Foot of Africa, and Zalze ranges are for different markets at a less ambitious level.

Kleine Zalze's varietal wines have done extremely well in competitions, particularly in South Africa but also internationally, which is not entirely surprising in view of the skill with which they are made and their style. They are generally picked ripe, but not excessively so, and show plenty of fruit as well as the evidence of generous and expensive oaking, over a structure that is not too challenging in terms of acid or tannin. They not infrequently have high alcohol levels and a little more residual sugar than classicists would approve of, though the wines also show some refinement. In short, they are in all ways very winning wines, expertly and internationally styled, consistently of high technical quality. Perhaps the star variety is Chenin Blanc, with versions at most levels from Vineyard Selection down, made from bushvines (some old), the Vineyard Selection one in the modern blockbusterish style, with new oak, some sweetness, and plenty of power.

www.kleinezalze.co.za

LAIBACH

In its latest guise the farm dates to 1994 when it was bought by entrepreneur Friedrich Laibach, but it goes back to the early nineteenth century, when it was part of a vast holding in the valley between Stellenbosch and Paarl. Some 40 hectares of the lean, deep red soils on the northeast-facing Simonsberg slopes have been replanted with red and white varieties. There's a real commitment here to "natural" winemaking: the vineyards are unirrigated and grown with as little help from the agrochemical industry as possible—most of the farm is certified organic and lovingly tended by Michael Malherbe. "It's his garden," says Francois van Zyl, who has been in charge of the cellar since 2000. The ladybird beetles that help control mealybugs have given their name to two of the wines (which together account for more than half of the farm's production)—a blend of Merlot and Cabernets Franc and Sauvignon, and a white version from Chardonnay, Chenin, and Viognier. The latter is characterful and good but can be a touch too oaky and sweet, but the red is probably the most graceful of the Laibach wines. Overoaking (though not excessive) and consequent big dry tannins (exacerbated by powerful alcohol) on many of the Laibach reds have also been something of a problem. Nonetheless the wines are serious and well-fruited, including the flagship Bordeaux-style blend, Friedrich Laibach, and perhaps the style will settle down with more restraint. Part of Laibach's commitment to expressing terroir is the introduction of some single-vineyard wines: there's a Cabernet from a mature vineyard, the Widow's Block, and the Claypot Merlot (the standard version is also one of the Cape's better Merlots).

www.laibachwines.com

L'AVENIR

The farm had long supplied grapes to Nederburg before it was bought by Mauritius-born Marc Wiehe. He met his winemaker, François Naudé, when the latter (an upcountry pharmacist-turned-handyman who'd come to the Cape to see if he could do more with his love of wine) came to discuss a new fireplace. They bottled the first wine under the new label in 1992, and the ebullient amateur proved a singularly adept winemaker, soon establishing a reputation for, particularly, Chenin Blanc (this was one of the first wineries to take the Cape workhorse seriously) and Pinotage, the variety with which Naudé became most associated. Significant change came in 2005 when the property was bought by Chablis-based Michel Laroche (Laroche later merged into Jeanjean, one of France's largest wine companies, the merged company known as AdVini, which now owns L'Avenir). Naudé, with some health problems, went into semiretirement, and "flying winemaker" Tinus Els came in as cellarmaster. The wines (in addition to nearly all going under screw cap) became a little more subtle and elegant with the change, and it's not hard to imagine M. Laroche's influence on the Chardonnay, for example, which became much less oaky and more refined and steely—more *chablisien*, in fact. Pinotage and Chenin remain the signature varieties, however, and make the two varietal wines in the top Grand Vin range. The Grand Vin Chenin came in with the 2007 vintage, from a vineyard planted in 1976. It's a beautifully balanced wine, with a little residual sugar invisibly enriching some stony minerality, and untrammeled by oak—it spends just six months in older barrels. The Pinotage continues the tradition of being much oakier, and is a big, serious wine. The best of the others, in a range beneficially reduced in recent years, is the Stellenbosch Classic, an elegant Bordeaux-style blend; there is also a very acceptable Sauvignon Blanc along with a decent Cab and a Merlot, and a second-tier range of varietal wines "by L'Avenir." It is a fairly large farm, with more than 70 hectares of vineyard.

www.larochewines.com

LE BONHEUR

Le Bonheur's French name reflects the origins of its first owner, Jacob Isak de Villiers, one of the first Huguenots to arrive at the Cape, in 1689. It is now owned by Lusan Holdings. There's a lovely Cape Dutch–style manor house, beautifully maintained and used for tastings and ceremonial functions. The estate has about 70 of its 163 hectares planted to vines, mostly on the slopes of the Klapmuts Hill in the Simonsberg ward. In the 1980s, when the winery was partly owned by Mike Woodhead, it was not only one of the early places to demonstrate the real potential of Sauvignon Blanc in the Cape, but the Cabernet Sauvignon and the Merlot-based Prima were exciting wines, among the best. I remember long discussions, over many referential glassfuls, about whether the 1986 was maybe even better than the 1984. Replantings with higher-yielding vines and the loss of Woodhead's personalized viticultural and winemaking passion are among the reasons why, although the wines today are sound, they are no longer particularly exciting. The Cabernet and Prima, the best wines, are firmly structured, with substantial tannins, and deserve a few years in bottle, but then will give pleasure and usually develop for a few more. The Chardonnay and Sauvignon Blanc are very decent examples.

www.lebonheur.co.za

LE RICHE

During the shake-up in Cape wine in the mid 1990s, Etienne le Riche left the grandeur of Rustenberg to do his own thing in vastly more modest circumstances, but with the luxury of independence. It was a good move for Rustenberg, wanting to reinvent itself in a more modern image, and a chance for le Riche, after twenty years there, to reexamine his own classic leanings and apply them anew. So he settled on a small farm in the Jonkershoek Valley (with occasional forays to the southwest of France, where he makes a wine in Bergerac). The home farm is called Leef op Hoop—the Afrikaans meaning, poignantly and perhaps appropriately, "live on hope." No less appropriately, perhaps, for the estate-winemaker-turned-garagiste, there was a somewhat dilapidated old cellar there that had for decades been used as a shed for tractor and tools. Le Riche, always willing to see the virtues of tradition, was happy to use the old open concrete tanks for fermentation. Not all the grapes for this wine come from the Jonkershoek slopes of the home farm, however: a third or so are bought in from elsewhere in the Stellenbosch area.

It is slightly uncommon in South Africa for varietal Cabernet to be the focus of a winemaker's ambitions rather than a blend, but nine-tenths of the sixty tons of grapes le Riche crushes in his open concrete *kuipe* is Cabernet—there is some Merlot for blending into a second-level wine, and latterly he has also made a characteristically understated and elegant Chardonnay. But the flagship wine is the Cabernet Sauvignon Reserve (usually about 4,500 cases of it are produced), and it has a completeness that sometimes eludes a straight varietal. While restraint and harmony are the main characteristics, this does not imply a lack of fruit—just that it is well contained and serves the fresh, vinous whole, governed by a firm structure of tannin and acidity and supported by judicious oaking (less than half the barriques are new). Alcohol levels do not generally go above 14 percent. They did in an uncharacteristically very ripe and plush 2008, which had some admirers worried, but it was claimed to have been a vintage-influenced anomaly. However, it might well be significant that Etienne's son Christo has joined the winemaking team (while his daughter Yvonne now handles the public relations), and it will be interesting to watch the evolution of the wine and whether it moves to a more blockbusterish style.

This small family winery, however, still produces one of the best, most reliable of the Cape's classically styled wines, whose quiet, gentle firmness and good humor reflect the vigneron. There is also a standard Cabernet and a Cabernet-Merlot blend, both good, serious wines in the same mold.

www.leriche.co.za

LOURENSFORD

This huge, 4,000-hectare Somerset West property was part of Willem Adriaan van der Stel's great Vergelegen estate, and includes some of its finest terroir. The modern estate was founded in 1999 under the ownership of the hugely rich businessman Christo Wiese. All that money did not bring early success, however. It seems that many of the viticultural decisions were unfortunate (some of them were later reversed), and the winemaking in the magnificently appointed cellar was for many years somewhat less than triumphant. This bad start was finally admitted by 2007, when a new cellarmaster, Chris Joubert, was appointed. He started wielding his new broom with great vigor. Already there are some good wines being made—although the large range does not necessarily argue a sufficiently focused approach and suggests that a commitment to commercial success is a priority. Things have certainly improved markedly, however, and there is every reason to hope that the 300-plus hectares of increasingly virus-free vines (producing 120,000 cases under the Lourensford labels) is starting to give us wines worthy of the splendor of their origin.

www.lourensford.co.za

MEERLUST

Few Cape wineries have Meerlust's enduring aura of history, continuity, and fine winemaking, yet by the end of the twentieth century there were some murmurs that while the history was fine, they'd better do something about the wine before its popular reputation caught up with its unexciting reality. Perhaps veteran winemaker Giorgio Dalla Cia, just bowing out, had become a little stale in the job. Fortunately, in more recent years there has been something of a reenergization at the Meerlust cellar (reflected in a total physical overhaul in 2008), with new winemaker Chris Williams arriving in time for the 2004 vintage. Williams had formerly been assistant to Dalla Cia before accepting appointments elsewhere, and had no doubt learned much from the older man's classic approach, but he has imbued that spirit with an edge of modernism, mostly expressed through brighter, often riper fruit.

History is indeed a vital part of Meerlust's enviable image. The lovely Cape Dutch homestead dates to the turn of the eighteenth century, when rich free burgher Henning Huysing took possession of the land. The name means "longing for the sea"—reflecting the accomplishment of this desire, no doubt, as the property is on the edge of the Stellenbosch district, only some five kilometers from False Bay. After Huysing's death there were a number of owners until Meerlust was bought in 1757 by Johannes Myburgh, who not only expanded the farm and developed the complex of buildings (cellar, slave workshops, etc.), but inaugurated the Meerlust dynasty that continues to this day. Hannes Myburgh is the present owner, and this must be one of the few grand old houses in the wine lands that shows itself as a loved and lived-in home.

But there had been much decay and little real interest in wine for much of the time before seventh-generation Nico Myburgh took over the estate in 1950 and energetically set about repairing the fabric, replanting vineyards and establishing new ones. In 1975 Meerlust Cabernet Sauvignon was produced for the first time by Nico and Giorgio Dalla Cia, and five years later Rubicon and Pinot Noir; Merlot and Chardonnay followed later in the decade.

Rubicon, one of the pioneering Bordeaux blends, is often very good, and particularly impressive in that it is made in fairly substantial quantities compared with some of its prestigious competitors. Cabernet is always the majority component, with Merlot and Cabernet Franc. Chris Williams's wine is generally more approachable in youth than it sometimes was in earlier years, with forward ripe fruit (accompanied by higher alcohol levels and lower acidity) and the charms of more new oak. That said, it is far from a blockbuster: rather, it shows an excellent balance between modern winemaking and classic ideals. In lesser vintages (such as 1996 and 2002), Rubicon is released as Meerlust Red—inevitably a good bargain.

Something of a triumph for Chris Williams was the first red wine he released that had been entirely his doing: the first varietal Cabernet Sauvignon since 1993 (2004 vintage, and looking set to become a fixture). It proved to be another wine happily balancing classicism and modernity; tight in youth, with firm, ripe tannins, and a fine vinosity more apparent than fruitiness. The Merlot is quite a serious example in a similar style, though not quite as good a wine. Pinot Noir was never a strength of Meerlust, but here too Williams has worked hard in vineyard and cellar to make a purer-fruited, fresher wine, and his Pinot is among the top handful of Cape examples— almost certainly the best from Stellenbosch. The Chardonnay used to be notably oaky, but is now restrained and elegant; a portion of the wine is from uninoculated fermentation.

A good deal of the credit for Meerlust's quiet renaissance must go to Roelie Joubert, whose work in the 110 hectares of vines gives Williams the fruit he needs. Williams has summarized, when asked to account for Meerlust's success: "Gravel soils, mature vines, Roelie Joubert's green fingers (ask his wife who he loves more, the kids or the vines), low yields, very good quality, properly seasoned oak, not stuffed up at bottling." Meerlust now firmly occupies a position among the leadership of Stellenbosch wineries; the concern for the social fabric of the community on the farm is also laudable and noteworthy. See the Foundry in this chapter for Chris Williams's own wine range.

www.meerlust.co.za

MEINERT

Martin Meinert is handsome and charming and, in his quiet way, one of the more important and respected winemakers of his generation. He was the cellarmaster who managed the relaunch of Vergelegen, but in 1997 he left to concentrate (apart from a few consultancies) on Devon Crest, a small farm in the Devon Valley that he had bought in the late 1980s. The winery was built in 1990 and the vineyards were gradually replaced, but although some wines were made, none was released under the Meinert label until a few 1997s. That year also saw some adjacent vineyards added, giving a total of nearly 14 hectares of vines on slopes with a southerly aspect.

There is just one white wine (and that only since 2008—a good Sauvignon Blanc from Elgin grapes, made in honor, Meinert says, of a white-wine-loving new wife), and Meinert's reputation for elegant, classically styled wines rests on his mostly Bordeaux-oriented reds. The varietal Cabernet and Merlot are serious but early-approachable, cleanly fresh and modest, well-structured wines designed to partner with food. The blend of those two varieties, Devon Crest, is more ambitious, using the better vineyard offerings. It is generally rather riper, rounder, and more concentrated, but still marked by restraint (typically just 25 percent new oak) and elegance. Continuing the progress toward expressive power, the flagship, Synchronicity, blends the best of all the reds grown on the farm, which means that it includes Pinotage as well as Merlot, with Cabernet substantially in the majority. The 2008, released in 2012, was a very good, harmonious wine, eminently drinkable and yet with ten years of life ahead of it. The FCM (Family Collection Meinert) range is the expanding place for experimental wines.

If Martin Meinert's wines can seem a trifle old-fashioned, they have the virtues rather than the vices of the Cape's past; the main concession to modernity is that they do not require more than a few years in bottle before drinking very pleasingly. With an established reputation and a small production, Meinert has no need to compete with louder wines, and we must be grateful (as a loyal customer base certainly is) that the standards of understatement have this eloquent champion.

www.meinertwines.com

MILES MOSSOP

Miles Mossop's day job is cellarmaster at Tokara, but he is allowed to do what many ambitious young winemakers want to do and make a few wines on his own account—and he does it very well. As the son of the late Tony Mossop, wine critic and maker of fine port, Miles had the advantage of being exposed early on to a wide range of international wines as well as to a passion for the stuff. The first vintage of his own was 2004, with the release of Max, a blend generally of half Cabernet with Petit Verdot and Merlot, from different Stellenbosch vineyards. It is a smart, ripe, plush, modern wine—unexceptionally good and correct. Saskia is a big, sumptuous wine, one of the new-wave blends, based on Chenin Blanc from Stellenbosch, with Viognier from the Voor-Paardeberg, vinified separately in oak with native yeasts. As with the Max, oaking is seamless and subtle. All the Mossop wines to date show admirable consistency of quality, if not great individualism. Production is still small—some 1,000 cases. A third wine, a botrytised Chenin Blanc, was produced in 2009, to be named Kika, after Miles and Samantha Mossop's third child—continuing their accord with the slightly twee and widespread South African practice of invoking family names on wine labels; whether the idea for the third child or that for the third wine came first, requiring the other, I can't say.

www.milesmossopwines.com

MOOIPLAAS

The name means "beautiful farm," not inappropriately for this large property (240 hectares, including a 50-hectare private nature reserve) high in the Bottelary Hills. The establishment of the farm dates back to 1806, according to the current owners, the Roos family, who have been here since 1963, and it has a handsome old Cape Dutch homestead. Since 1995 wine has been made under their own label, though just 8,000-odd cases of it come off the 120 hectares of vine. The unwooded Chenin Blanc Bush Vines, rich and lovely but not too powerful (freshened by a dash of Sémillon), is perhaps the most pleasing of the range of mostly varietal wines, which are ripe but fairly restrained. Rosalind has been the flagship red since 2003, a slightly old-fashioned Cabernet Franc–based blend; it is matured for two years in barriques, half new, and aims at elegance.

www.mooiplaas.co.za

MORGENHOF

Morgenhof is a charming cluster of buildings, woods, and vineyards in the foothills of the prime western slopes of the Simonsberg. It has had many and disparate names over the years: when it was granted in the late seventeenth century it was known as Harmony, but some later problems led to the name Onrus ("unrest"). At some stage it became Morgenhof, and this is how it was known when it was bought by a consortium of German businessmen in 1982. They committed themselves to restoring not only the farm in general and the vineyards in particular, but also the dilapidated buildings—starting, of course, with the original cellar. The first wine bottled under the Morgenhof label was a Cabernet Sauvignon 1984. In 1993 the estate was sold to Alain and Anne Huchon from France, who came to live in the Cape in that year; this was one of the first significant international investments in the local wine industry and the most French note struck since the arrival of the Huguenots. The Huchons did even more to overhaul the 212-hectare property and buildings but also infused a bit of their heritage with a formal French garden to top off the new underground barrel cellar. More recently the homestead has been converted into visitor accommodations. Anne Cointreau (the former Mme. Huchon, who reverted to her famous maiden name on her divorce) is now the sole owner.

Under the French regime new hillside vineyards, with their various though generally southerly aspects and maximum altitude of 410 meters, were plotted by satellite. Soils on the farm range from sand-clay loam to Hutton and Clovelly. The 74 hectares of vineyard are planted to Cabernets Sauvignon and Franc, Merlot, Petit Verdot, Pinotage, Touriga Nacional, Chardonnay, Chenin, and Sauvignon. After something of a dip, the wines have improved since Jacques Cilliers took over in the cellar in 2004. The reds in the Estate range are led by a handsome, firmly tannic Cabernet-based Bordeaux blend, the Morgenhof Estate (the 2004 still selling in 2010, and the last I have tasted). The Chardonnay, Brut Reserve, and Chenin Blanc are good too—the last of these, from forty-year-old vines, well structured, with intense ripe flavors, but fresh rather than overpowering. There is also a range of cheaper wines under the Fantail label.

www.morgenhof.com

MORGENSTER

Morgenster was, until a division in 1708, part of Vergelegen, the estate of Cape governor Willem Adriaan van der Stel. A refugee Huguenot bought the section now called Morgenster—"morning star" in Dutch—and built one of the finest examples of Cape Dutch architecture. On the ornate gable a scallop shell frames a star, providing the logo of the modern estate. In 1992 the property was bought by Italian magnate Giulio Bertrand, who had new vineyards planted in line with his central aim to produce a wine inspired by St.-Émilion. He also persuaded Pierre Lurton of Cheval Blanc (later of Yquem too) to consult, supporting a first-rate local team.

There are 30 hillside hectares of vineyards, cooled by breezes from False Bay. The range of wines is small. While the later years of the century's first decade saw the emergence of tiny bottlings based on Sangiovese and Nebbiolo, the flagship is the Morgenster itself, a varying blend of Cabernet Franc, Cabernet Sauvignon, and Merlot. Lourens River Valley red, the "second" wine, has been produced since 1998 and is often a very good and hardly cheap alternative, with a track record of aging beneficially for up to a decade.

The Morgenster is the superior wine, however, though it has been a little confusing. It emerged with a Cab Franc–dominated 2000 that was immediately hailed for its elegant classicism; then 2001 was to disappoint some and delight others, with a richer and sweeter wine based on Merlot, the variety that has tended to dominate many subsequent vintages. (To hear Lurton speak—justifiably—of "cashmere tannins" is a pleasure in itself.) Those later vintages, while usually extremely good, have not indicated that the estate's stylistic approach is settled (the style of the Italian-oriented wines is at least as wavering—recently they have suffered from ultraripeness). To some extent the vagaries may be a matter of responding to the vintage, to some extent of uneven vineyard development, but although there is no doubt that the flagship is one of the better Cape Bordeaux blends in all its guises, more sense of direction would be comforting. But it is not certain that stability will be enhanced by the resignation of resident winemaker Marius Lategan in 2009; he was replaced by Henry Kotzé, formerly of the less prestigious but well-reputed Eikendal and before then the redoubtable Neil Ellis. Those who hailed the 2000 Morgenster still have great hopes, however. In searching for consistency somewhere, it can be said that one of the Cape's finest olive oils also comes from this estate.

www.morgenster.co.za

MULDERBOSCH

Mulderbosch is not what it was—it's not even *where* it was. The original Mulderbosch was on 47 hectares in the Bottelary Hills, with maiden vintages in the early 1990s. Winemaker Mike Dobrovic won a degree of acclaim for his wines—which generally catered to that established category of people who say they like dry wine but appreciate a subtle dollop of residual sugar. Property and name were bought in late 2010 by Terroir Capital, the company of Charles Banks, former co-owner of cult California winery Screaming Eagle. Mulderbosch was fairly well established in the United States, which was important to Banks, and its definitive transformation from place into brand was underlined when the farm was promptly swapped with Kanu (whose Polkadraai Hills vineyards were more extensive and in better condition—no doubt money was involved, too), and the latter's winemaking facilities were substantially upgraded and enlarged. Grapes from the new property will be used for the Mulderbosch range, but fruit is also brought in—in large quantities. It will take a little while to see how the wines are styled under cellarmaster Adam Mason (who was seduced here from Klein Constantia), but the early intention is clearly to aim at the substantial upper-middle ground, and leave high terroir-related ambitions to Fable, the property in Tulbagh that Banks bought about the same time. Banks has been notably impressed by local Chenin Blanc and is confident that generally, but with Chenin in particular, South African wine can offer an unmatchable quality-to-price ratio. Chardonnay, rosé (already made in huge volumes and the biggest-selling rosé in Sweden), and Sauvignon Blanc are sure to feature in the range. Faithful Hound, the Bordeaux-style blend, should become a range in its own right.

Incidentally, in a move that is so far unique in South Africa, Banks not only allows his winemaker to produce his own range of wines—called Yardstick, and developed in partnership with leading chef Peter Tempelhoff—but has provided separate facilities for it, and has invested financially in the project. The maiden releases at the top level made it clear, in fact, that it would be worth investing in: a Pinot Noir and a Chardonnay, both from 2011 Elgin grapes, both fresh, elegant, and restrained, with modest alcohol levels.

www.mulderbosch.co.za

yardstickwines.com

MURATIE

Muratie is wonderfully redolent of Cape history (with even the thick cobwebs in the old cellar surely dating back a century or two). Still there is the little house built by Lourens Campher, a German soldier who in 1685 was allocated a "certain piece of land": in his first year Campher planted one bag of wheat and harvested eight bags on this, one of the earliest mountainside farms. Still there is the tree planted by Campher and Ansela, the slave daughter of an Angolan slave and a local soldier, whom Campher used to visit regularly in Cape Town over some fourteen years (during which time they had three children) before she was freed in 1699 and came to live with him on the farm.

From the current perspective, the next significant date was 1763, when rich Martin Melck bought Muratie, which stayed in the Melck-Beyers family for about a century before being sold off (it was later to return to Melck ownership). But in 1926 a German artist, George Canitz, fell in love with the old manor house and bought the neglected property. With the valuable friendship and advice of I. A. Perold he introduced a number of red varieties, notably Pinot Noir; for a long time this was the only varietal Pinot in the country. Canitz died in 1958, and for a generation the farm was owned by his daughter Annemarie and run by her teetotaler winemaker Ben Prins. (One of my own early memories of vinous pleasure is the Muratie port I used to buy, after long chats with Mr. Prins, in the late 1970s.)

There were some changes as well as some benign neglect after Ronnie Melck, then managing director of Stellenbosch Farmers' Winery, bought Muratie in 1987. In 1988 a replanting program was begun and some minor alterations were made to the cellar, but there was little exciting happening in the way of wine. In the mid 1990s the Pinot was well rated (appreciation for it was probably ascribable in part to ignorance; it is now a pleasant wine but seldom more than that), and a Bordeaux blend was introduced named Ansela van de Caab after the slave who became an owner. It now often includes a little Syrah. Things started brightening more in the twenty-first century, and continue to do so. Ansela continues as one of the more classically oriented and serious reds in the Cape, dry and elegant, while modernism is better expressed in the powerful, new-oaked Ronnie Melck Shiraz. Laurens Campher was introduced with the 2010 vintage as an interesting combination of Chenin, Sauvignon, Verdelho, and Chardonnay—a little sweet and oaky, but perhaps this was a teething problem. The Isabella Chardonnay is among the best of the other wines. Generally, with Francois Conradie in charge of the cellar and vineyards since 2005, the wines have become rather cleaner and fresher. The majority of them are red, reflecting plantings in the 42 hectares of vineyard.

www.muratie.co.za

MVEMVE RAATS

Bruwer Raats of Raats Family in 2004 teamed up with friend Mzokhona Mvemve (the Cape's first qualified black enologist, who gained early cellar experience assisting Raats at Delaire) to make a single wine under this label, called De Compostella. It has generally been something of an elegant blockbuster, a powerful but not too flashy Bordeaux-style blend, led by Cabernet Franc and showing a little more alcohol strength and a little more new wood than the Raats Cab Franc. It has performed even better, though, than that wine for *Wine Spectator* and *Wine Advocate,* which evidences a clever orientation to its chosen focus market. For the 2009, however, the blend changed, with Malbec now an equal partner with the Cabernets, plus a little Merlot and Petit Verdot—still all variously sourced Stellenbosch fruit. It might have been the general excellence of that vintage, but the wine showed in its youth a new complexity, elegance, and completeness, and signaled its unquestionable position at the top level of such blends in the Cape.

www.raats.co.za

NEETHLINGSHOF

It's not uncommon with longtime producers to find that it's easier to talk of the history than of the character of the wines, owing to a lack of continuity in direction. The issue is often a change in winemaker (which we had at Neethlingshof when De Wet Viljoen took over for the 2004 vintage from Philip Costandius, who'd been here just two years himself) and sometimes, as also here, an intention to make "softer, more accessible" wines. That strategy is more reflected in the larger-volume wines than those in the Short Story Collection (which replaced the Lord Neethling wines—the new name of the range and the wines in it loudly announce the marketers and their strategies!). These are perhaps more modern and fruity than they used to be (they were always rather oaky and powerful), but the Owl Post (a Pinotage) and the Caracal (a Bordeaux blend with a dollop of Pinotage) are still impressive. Maria, a Riesling Noble Late Harvest, is sometimes very good. The large range of less-ambitious wines, red and white, sold simply under the Neethlingshof label, have been of varying quality—and style. The label itself was redesigned in 2009; it still shows the famous long avenue of stone pines leading up to the manor house, but the new look makes them "appear less imposing and more welcoming"—which is the apparent intention with the wines, and perhaps appropriate for a winery that is a substantial tourist destination.

As to the history: the farm, lying between the Bottelary Hills and the Papegaaiberg, was originally granted in 1692 and given the splendid if inaccurate name De Wolvendans— "dance of the wolves," probably referring to jackals. After passing through many hands, the farm was bought by Johannes Neethling ("Lord" was a tribute to his flamboyance) in 1861 and acquired its present name, as well as 200 additional hectares. His descendants (the Louw family) owned the farm until 1963, when it was bought by the Mombergs (one of them a National Party MP). Jan Momberg in 1971 bottled the first wines under the

Neethlingshof label—a Clairette and a Chenin Blanc. In 1985 he sold the estate to international banker and financier Hans-Joachim Schreiber, and it is now part of the Lusan group of wine farms he formed in partnership with Distillers Corporation (now Distell) in 1999. There are 95 hectares of vineyards, split roughly equally between red and white varieties, with the eminent professor Eben Archer in charge of them. A large chunk of the estate—more than 100 hectares—has been set aside for conservation.

www.neethlingshof.co.za

NEIL ELLIS

Neil Ellis is one of the most widely respected of the Cape's senior winemakers. With qualifications in enology, chemistry, and microbiology, he spent a few years with the KWV starting in 1973 before moving to Groot Constantia and then Zevenwacht. In the mid 1980s, however, he took a step that was virtually unprecedented for an individual in South Africa, seeking out vineyards from which he could purchase grapes for his own wines. A few employed winemakers had started making their own wines, but Ellis was the first to work as a serious négociant. Neil Ellis Vineyard Selection was launched in 1986 with a Rhine Riesling, a Sauvignon Blanc, and a 1984 Cabernet. Initially he rented winemaking space, but then he teamed up with Hans Peter Schröder, a Stellenbosch-born businessman who'd long lived in Japan. In 1989 Schröder had bought the farm Oude Nektar in the Jonkershoek Valley (with a farming history going back to 1692 but releasing wines from its own cellar and under its own label only in 1983). He immediately started replanting vineyards—while being one of the earliest to pay great attention to the protection of the environment and the restoration of the indigenous flora—and reconstructing vinification and barrel-maturation facilities. Eben Archer came to advise in the vineyards, and Neil Ellis in the cellar. In 1993 Ellis and Schröder formed the partnership Neil Ellis Wines, based at Oude Nektar, where new vinification and maturation cellars were completed in 1999. Little more than a decade later, however, the first stages were made of a move to new facilities on the Helshoogte road. Sales, marketing, and administration moved there in 2010, and production facilities were planned.

Grapes are still sourced widely, but the majority for the two ranges—Vineyard Selection and Premium—come from the 40 hectares of vine on Oude Nektar; the larger Contreberg in Groenekloof, which is farmed by Neil Ellis Wines in partnership with its owner; and the Whitehall farm in Elgin. Ellis was a great pioneer in seeing the winegrowing potential of different areas. In 1990 he had produced the first certified Sauvignon from Elgin, and in 1997 the first Chardonnay including Elgin fruit. Today the Whitehall vineyards there supply both Sauvignon Blanc and Chardonnay, varieties for which this cool, high-lying area has proved ideal. Groenekloof Sauvignon Blanc was introduced in 1993, showing for the first time the great potential of the high, Atlantic-cooled Darling hills; the wine remains deservedly one of the best known of the Ellis range. The home farm of Oude Nektar is the primary source of fruit for the red wines. High rainfall, mostly deep red clay soils, and generally south- and west-facing vineyards provide conditions to produce high-quality Cabernet Sauvignon, Merlot, and Syrah. Ellis's son Warren, with a master's degree in viticulture, is responsible for the vines.

Apart from an occasional use of the experimental Aenigma label, the Neil Ellis wines are all varietal, mostly single-varietal. Annual production is more than 50,000 cases. The Vineyard Selection regularly includes Cabernet Sauvignon, Syrah, and Sauvignon Blanc, to which a Stellenbosch-sourced Pinotage and a very good Grenache from Piekenierskloof were added in 2007. They are all modern, clean, well-fruited wines that are always very soundly made and—apart, perhaps, from a little too much generosity with new oak sometimes—well balanced; they are not overripe, and always fermented properly dry, which is not the invariable rule in the Cape. The reds and Chardonnays from the better vintages can keep beneficially for a decade. The Premium Range, which includes the Sauvignon Blancs from Elgin and Groenekloof as well as a pair of Chardonnays from Elgin and Stellenbosch, is also serious and good. Overall, if there is nothing truly out-standing, not many producers manage this breadth of range with as much distinction and an absence of duds.

www.neilellis.com

NICO VAN DER MERWE

This is one of the larger ranges of wines made by a "moonlighting" winemaker. Nico van der Merwe has been Saxenburg's cellarmaster since 1990. In 1999 he started his own venture under the name Wilhelmshof, with the help of wife Petra and brother Robert Alexander, winemaker at the Trawal co-op, with wines made in his and his brother's cellars, from both Stellenbosch and Olifants River. In the mid 1990s, the name changed to Nico van der Merwe Wines, Nico became sole winemaker, and work started on a small cellar on his new property in the Polkadraai Hills, not far from Saxenburg where the wines were made until his own place was ready in 2011. But grapes continue to be bought in, with the emphasis on reds and particularly on Syrah. The flagship Mas Nicolas is a blend of Cab and Syrah, big, dark, and succulently serious, and the Nicolas van der Merwe range (the ringing of changes on the name can be confusing) includes a massive, showy, oaky, and ripe Syrah, uncompromisingly matured in new American oak. There's a delicious Cape Elements Shiraz-Cinsaut-Grenache, recalling Nico's serious involvement in the south of France, and an entry-level range of varietal wines called Robert Alexander.

OVERGAAUW

For much of the first decade of this century, this property in the Stellenboschkloof area did not keep up with developments in the Cape or even in its own past. It relied too much on the memory of its contributions during the 1980s, when it produced the Cape's first varietal Merlot (1982) and its Tria Corda was one of the earliest of the Cape Bordeaux-style reds (the first vintage included Cinsaut). It has also long been the only local estate to make a Sylvaner. David van Velden, winemaker since 2003 though father Braam remains owner, is the fourth generation of van Veldens here. The estate was originally part of a larger property, By-den-Weg, granted in 1704; the split was made in 1906 when Abraham van Velden bought a portion of it and named it Overgaauw (the maiden name of the wife of the first van Velden in the Cape). Four years later the first grapes were pressed in his new cellar. The first bottlings under the Overgaauw label were from the 1971 vintage. They included a port, for another contribution of Overgaauw was to be a pioneer of classic port styling and Portuguese varieties. At their low ebb, the wines were not exactly bad (dull, a touch rustic and earthy, one could say, prompting the thought that a good deal of replanting of virused wines was needed, as well as a thorough examination of the cellar). But David van Velden, now fully in charge, seems to have sorted things out. Some vintages appear to have gone unbottled, or at least unsold, and with the 2009 vintage the Tria Corda, for example, seemed back on track, and various varietal offerings in the Estate range are also much improved. So happily, things are looking promising here again. There's also a screw-capped entry-level range called Shepherd's Cottage.

www.overgaauw.co.za

QUOIN ROCK

There was more than a nomenclatural frisson when the 158 hectares of Quoin Rock were part of the farm called Knorhoek—*de plaats waar de leeuwen knorren,* the place where lions growl. Martin Melck had acquired most of this part of the Simonsberg slopes by the end of the seventeenth century, and it was probably he who gave it the name. Knorhoek itself has been bottling wines under its own label since 1997, and the subdivision came in 1998, when the Quoin Rock part was bought by Scottish-born Gauteng entrepreneur and wine lover Dave King (widely known for his very public battles with the Receiver of Revenue, which led to the estate's attachment and sale in 2012). The winery's name refers, however, to a geographical feature near far-off Cape Agulhas, where King also acquired a farm—providing grapes that are brought by refrigerated truck to the Stellenbosch cellar.

The property was established under the eye of New Zealand consultant Rod Easthope, who had overseen the renaissance at Rustenberg. A fine, large cellar was built and a major vineyard program inaugurated in 2000, replacing virus-infected vines (and a lot of pear trees) with 30 hectares of Cabernet Sauvignon, Syrah, Viognier, Merlot, Cabernet Franc, Mourvèdre, and Sauvignon Blanc planted over the next two years. In cooler, more humid Agulhas, Chardonnay and Sauvignon Blanc were the main varieties planted in 1998, with smaller plantings of Merlot and Pinot Noir. Carl van der Merwe arrived as full-time winemaker in time for the 2001 harvest. He left for DeMorgenzon in 2010 and his assistant, Narina Cloete, took over.

Irrigation at Quoin Rock is genuinely kept to a minimum. So too is chemical intervention at both properties, where farming is close to organic: if a herbicide or pesticide is needed, it is manually applied on a vine-by-vine basis. Composts, mulch, and cover crops, as well as canopy management allowing air movement through the vines, all play their role in keeping things as natural as possible. Biodiversity is encouraged, and there's a continuing project to reestablish the indigenous fynbos—which often finds its (controlled) way among the vines. The approach in the cellar has also been noninterventionist, with no yeast inoculation, no acidification, no enzyme addition.

The Simonsberg Syrah, ever more serious with each vintage it seems, is one of the best of the Stellenbosch wines from this variety (it includes a splash of Mourvèdre), aimed at a modestly oaked northern Rhône style, with lightly perfumed lily and red-fruit aromas, a harmonious palate with fresh acidity, and tannins that inform but do not obtrude, as well as an overall sense of delicacy despite the ripe 14.3 percent alcohol. The top white from the Stellenbosch vineyards is a wooded wine called Oculus, downplaying the varieties: it has sometimes been pure Sauvignon Blanc, but the 2006 introduced (with great subtlety) 15 percent Viognier. It is, fittingly, released only after a few years in bottle. The Cape Agulhas Sauvignon Blanc is very different, with a more piercing acidity, fresh, vibrant, and somewhat austere in youth. An occasionally released version called the Nicobar sometimes has a little undetectable residual sugar and is matured in older oak. The Agulhas Chardonnay and Cap Classique are also good.

It must be said that Dave King's financial battles have meant that what was emerging as one of the Cape's leading wineries has been starved of investment, with inevitable consequences. We are going to have to see what happens—and what has already happened, as yet unrevealed in the wine. By 2012, when an initial attempt by the Revenue Services to auction the property failed, the vineyards seemed to be suffering. The Agulhas farm was in a worse position for a while, it seems. Both properties were later that year purchased by a Ukrainian businessman, Denys Aloshyn, despite a warning from Mr. King that legal challenges (presumably from him) might even see a new owner eventually losing the estate.

www.quoinrock.com

RAATS FAMILY

Bruwer (pronounced "Brewvair") Raats is a man built on a large scale, and the wines he made for other wineries generally tended to match those proportions; they were massive, alcoholic, and very ripe. Nothing could contrast more with what he has been doing under his own label since he set it up in 2000 (in those days with brother Jasper and father Jasper Sr., now he owns the company himself; his wife, Janice, is general manager). For some years the wines were made by Bruwer as a sideshow at Zorgvliet, where he was cellarmaster, but then facilities were established in the Polkadraai Hills on the other side of Stellenbosch, and Bruwer started working full-time at his family business—including regular but rewarding marketing trips, notably aiming at the elusive serious wine-lover in the United States; the wines have rated very well there. Along with a pair of good entry-level wines under the Original label, there are two top-level varietals: Chenin Blanc and Cabernet Franc, the latter one of the earlier such bottlings in the Cape, and now possibly the finest. Raats owns no vines and sources grapes fairly widely. The Chenin Blanc comes from three old (forty-plus-year) vineyards in Stellenbosch. It is partly oaked (mostly older wood), which lends creamy breadth and is subtly integrated with the vibrant and fresh fruit, and has a lovely tangy knot of peach and tangerine in the finish. The Cab Franc is also sensitively oaked—about a quarter new, and generally understated and elegant with perfumed fruit, though the firm structure can mean a touch of leanness and dry severity in some lesser, fortunately rare, vintages. Raats is also a partner in the Mvemve Raats label.

www.raats.co.za

REMHOOGTE

In 1994 Murray Boustred was one of the first local business tycoons in the modern era to show a yen for a Cape wine-lands lifestyle when he and his wife, Juliet, bought this run-down property among some classy neighbors on the Simonsberg slopes. The farm has title deeds dating from 1812, and the name, meaning "braking heights," harks back to the days when ox-drawn wagons descending the steep hill into Stellenbosch would need to apply their brakes around this point. The rehabilitation of the property involved restoring old buildings and constructing a new cellar, as well as a good deal of replanting; but some mature Pinotage, Merlot, Cabernet, and Chenin Blanc survived, with Syrah added to the tally of varieties. There are now 30 hectares of vines on the clay soils.

Murray himself initially took on the bulk of the winemaking responsibility, with the advice of Michel Rolland, the famous Bordelais winemaker and consultant. His well-qualified son Chris became cellarmaster in 2007, a few years before Rolland started cutting back on all his overseas commitments. Rolland's Bonne Nouvelle, discontinued when he pulled out, for some years led the Cape blends for which the property was best known. In fact, it included less and less Pinotage over the years, finally getting down to 6 percent. The Estate Blend, with Merlot as the majority component along with Cabernet Sauvignon, generally has rather more Pinotage—up to 30 percent. After Chris Boustred took over in the cellar there was a return to producing varietal bottlings of Merlot, Cabernet, and Pinotage, with the Merlot Reserve being the most impressive. A good and serious oaked Chenin Blanc, named Honeybunch, from a venerable single vineyard was introduced with the 2010 vintage. As for the reds, since they have been released comparatively late (in late 2012 the available top reds were from 2007), it is not yet clear if the withdrawal of Rolland will significantly affect the Remhoogte style. The wines had been marked by a typical Rolland lushness derived from very ripe grapes, with consequent alcoholic power accompanying the solid fruit, making for impressive and pleasing, if not especially graceful or interesting, wines in this mold.

www.remhoogte.co.za

REYNEKE

The Reyneke family bought the farm Uitzicht in the Polkadraai Hills in 1988. From making unprofitable and dull deliveries of grapes to a co-op to the biodynamic success of today has been a difficult journey, but one now revealed as very worthwhile (though winemaker changes have also been significant). In the early days, Johan Reyneke Jr. was struck by the contradiction between his studies in environmental philosophy and his work helping his mother to spray the vines with pesticides. But to change things was not easy: the all-powerful bank was doubtful about a turn to organic farming. Initial organic experiments were not successful, but Reyneke's exposure to the wines and teachings of Nicolas Joly in Europe encouraged him. A local well-respected viticulturist also encouraged him to make his own wine, which would offer better returns than selling to the cooperative. In 2001 Reyneke's first organic Pinotage was produced. Two years later, the farm was put under biodynamic conversion, which took three years, with organic certification an obligatory interim stage. All his wines are now certified as biodynamic by Demeter (in late 2012 this was the only registered biodynamic producer in South Africa).

Though one of the few farmers fully committed to biodynamics, Reyneke is not without pragmatism—knowing that if he fails the farm would revert to conventional viticulture under new owners. He acknowledges being pulled between science and "the magic of nature," but believes in the value of this "creative tension." He is also not averse to irrigating, something that European biodynamicists frown upon. In fact, this charming and intelligent man is far from a zealot, and it is clear that his real commitment is to the land rather than to any mystical dogma. He displays a framed quotation from American environmentalist Aldo Leopold suggesting that true conservation can happen only when "Abrahamic" concepts of overlordship are jettisoned. "We abuse land because we regard it as a commodity belonging to us. When we see land as a commodity to which we belong, we may begin to use it with love and respect," says Leopold. There is also, incidentally, much to suggest that Johan Reyneke treats his workers with some decency and respect too—not always part of a "holistic" approach.

The 35 hectares under vine consist of Cabernet Sauvignon, Merlot, Pinotage, Syrah, Chenin Blanc, and Sauvignon Blanc. These are vinified as naturally as possible, with no inoculation for either alcoholic or malolactic fermentation. The range is mostly of varietal wines, except for a prestige Reserve Red from Syrah and 35 percent Cabernet, and Cornerstone, which adds a few more varieties to that blend. The wines have been made by various people over the years—including Reyneke himself for a few of them—but his strengths and passions are really in the vineyards. From the 2010 vintage on, the wines have been made by Rudiger Gretschel, formerly of Boekenhoutskloof and now responsible for the production of all Vinimark's wine interests (Vinimark shares ownership of the Reyneke brand, but not of the farm). The few vintages before 2010 had really at last proved what Reyneke's vineyards are capable of, when Chris and Andrea Mullineux (now based in the Swartland) made, inter alia, the first superb Reserve White from oaked Sauvignon Blanc. But all the Reyneke wines contine to show a purity and restraint, with an earthy sort of tug from the natural ferment, charm and some complexity, and a mineral vibrancy that is not easily to be ascribed merely to acidity. In addition to the range of biodynamic wines off the farm, a small Organic Range was introduced in 2011, made from outsourced fruit.

www.reynekewines.co.za

RUDERA

Rudera (which appears on the Paarl map in chapter 7) was founded by Teddy and Riana Hall, while Teddy was at Kanu, in 1999—one of the earlier "moonlighting" establishments by full-time winemakers. He'd already built up a reputation at Kanu for his particular love of Chenin Blanc and skillful way with it, so it was not surprising that an intense, powerful, and off-dry Chenin was the first offering here. It actually appeared under the Robusto label, but some bureaucratic snarls obliged them to change the winery name a year later. The new name apparently comes from the Latin *rudus*, meaning "broken fragment of stone." Robusto became the name of just one of the three regular Chenins produced within a few years—one a Noble Late Harvest, another a less flamboyant, fresher version of Robusto. A Cabernet Sauvignon 2000 and a Syrah 2001, both rather elegant and restrained, marked the extension of the range. These wines all continue, although Teddy Hall moved on to his eponymous winery after his marriage failed and Rudera went to Riana in 2008. Rudera is now a partnership between her and Johan and Elbie Janse van Vuuren, and the winery has acquired the old D'Olyfboom [olive tree] estate in Paarl, where the wines have been made by Adele Swart since 2011. Most of the grapes are from Stellenbosch, however, where they own 10 hectares of vines, from which they take fruit for the Cabernet and Syrah, selling off the remainder. The Chenin is bought in from the same Stellenbosch vineyards used since 1999. The wines have continued—at least up to the latest wine-maker change—in the tradition established by Teddy Hall: rich, concentrated, forceful, and stylish.

www.rudera.co.za

RUSTENBERG

Driving up the long, winding road of this historic estate, I'm surely not the only one who doubts if there can be a lovelier wine farm anywhere. And then you arrive at the old Schoongezicht manor house—set against the splendors of the Simonsberg—which just confirms the notion. After that there's the fine modern winery and tasting room to remind you that more is involved here than history and landscape. The property dates back to 1682, when some 80 hectares of land were granted to Roelof Pasman. A century later Rustenberg passed into the ownership of Jacob Eksteen, who in 1810 gave a large section of the farm, to be called Schoongezicht ("lovely view"), to his son-in-law, Arend Brink. Just three years later Schoongezicht was acquired by one of the Constantia Cloetes, who added the present Cape Dutch façade to the homestead—although it is not this house, but that of Rustenberg itself, which features on the winery labels. The mid-nineteenth century saw both farms decay, amid recession and vine disease. Toward the end of the century Rustenberg was bought by Sir Jacob Barry, and in 1892 a run-down, phylloxera-ridden Schoongezicht was bought by John X. Merriman, the Cape Colony's minister of agriculture and later its last prime minister. It is claimed that from that year wine has been continuously bottled here—presumably the longest run of any winery in the Cape. Both farms were rehabilitated and revitalized. Rustenberg passed, on Merriman's death, to his son-in-law, Alfred Nicholson, who had been involved with it since 1892. It was bought by Peter Barlow, a member of a rich industrialist family, in 1941; he also acquired Schoongezicht in 1945, meaning that the great estate could once more be reunited. Barlow died in 1975, but his oenophile wife, Pamela, lived in the Rustenberg house till her death in 2008. Their son Simon took over management of the estate in 1987.

In the 1970s and 1980s, with Etienne le Riche as cellarmaster starting in 1974, Rustenberg was a leading producer, especially of red wines, specializing in a Cabernet Sauvignon and a Cabernet-Cinsaut blend first called Dry Red and then just Rustenberg. The Cabernet from 1982 is, for example, one of the few legendary Cape reds of that decade. Almost uniquely at the time, le Riche did not inoculate with commercial yeast (the Jacobsdal estate in Stellenbosch also claims never to have made use of commerical yeast since its first own-label bottling in 1974). The few white wines appeared under the Schoongezicht label. By the mid 1990s, under a new sort of scrutiny, it was becoming obvious that not all was well in the old cellar, and Simon Barlow started taking the first steps in a major and very expensive program of reconstruction and development. Some historic buildings were gutted to take in a superbly equipped new winery (with suddenly lots of money for new barrels to replace the old ones that had certainly been causing some of the problems), and the vineyards too were replaced or upgraded in the light of up-to-date viticultural understanding. There were now to be 100 hectares planted on the red granitic soils of the lower slopes of the Simonsberg. Vineyard material was imported directly from France (via a few years of quarantine in remote, less-exalted terroir). "Water deficit management"—as distinct from irrigation, insisted viticulturist Kevin Watt—was introduced, along with complex systems to monitor temperatures and soil moisture levels. Marketing too was vitalized; part of the image rebuilding was the reintegration of the white wines under the Rustenberg label, and an initially small new range of second-level wines was established under the Brampton label. The latter proved almost too successful for comfort: it grew and grew and was eventually sold to DGB in 2009.

Le Riche left the cellar (any recriminations well hidden), embarking on an independent course that has proved to be a great one. In his place Barlow appointed New Zealander Rod Easthope, reflecting the infatuation with Antipodean winemaking that some forces in South Africa were encouraging as an antidote to the staleness (as well as perhaps good old-fashionedness) of Cape wine in the light of sudden international exposure. This change—reinforced by Australian consultant Kym Milne—was a good move for a winery determined to modernize and aiming to match an international elite, though not everyone liked the new style of red wine that appeared—brighter, fruitier, more modern. Two new fashionably single-vineyard (and for the time very expensive) flagships were introduced: Peter Barlow, a ripe, showy, oaky Cabernet; and Five Soldiers, a Chardonnay equally lavished with new oak and plenty of attention.

Easthope soon reduced his role to that of consultant, and Adi Badenhorst became cellarmaster in late 1999. He moved on after just less than ten years, leaving something of a mixed message about Rustenberg, with some wines in a fairly classic mold, but the Peter Barlow, for example, pushing the bounds of ripeness fairly hard on occasions; it is not certain that relations between the cellar and the vineyard (with Nico Walters now in charge there) were always harmonious. Badenhorst's successor was his assistant since 2003, Randolph Christians, which, together with substantial input from Simon Barlow and the renewed consultancy of Kym Milne, has ensured a modicum of continuity—as, indeed, has the land.

A longer-term continuity is much needed, and should be helped by the integration into the team of Simon's son Murray, after his return from postgraduate winemaking studies in Australia. But we shall have to wait and see if a solid sense of stability will come to Rustenberg, which as recently as 2012 was still reworking its range (partly in light of the disposal of the Brampton label).

The wines are mostly very good, if not outstanding. The Peter Barlow 2006 was more restrained than the 2005, making an excellent modern Cabernet, but one with a good, firm structure and some freshness. Five Soldiers is among the Cape's better Chardonnays, concentrated but refined and not evidencing its now 70 percent new oak, and repaying a good few years in bottle. In the main Stellenbosch Regional (not single-vineyard) range, John X. Merriman is more understated, a moderately distinguished Bordeaux-style blend. The Syrah can be excellent, and the Chardonnay—once a reduction in oakiness and sweetness is consolidated—should be good. There's a most attractive and interesting Roussanne (it was the Cape's first varietal Rousanne).

Rustenberg may be on its way to recovering some of the reputation that it lost in the first decade or so of this century. It must perhaps resolve on an aesthetic—deciding primarily where it wants to be on the classic-modern continuum. As a well-capitalized family-owned winery with the next generation's commitment and enological knowledge assured, there is reason to hope that it will attain real stability, consolidating Simon Barlow's 1990s modernizing revolution and allowing the estate to assume its full dignity as one of the Cape's "first growths."

www.rustenberg.co.za

RUST EN VREDE

By the 1920s a tradition of more than a few centuries of winemaking here at the foot of the Helderberg had ended, though grapes were still grown. By the time it was bought by former rugby Springbok Jannie Engelbrecht in 1978, the farm—including the fine old homestead of 1825—was virtually derelict. The original property, Bonte Rivier, was granted to the wonderfully named Willem van der Wêreld ("William of the world") in 1694, though he had moved onto the property in 1685, and the 1692 census stated that he had 7,500 vines. After a testamentary division of 1832, the upper section, with its cellar built in 1780, was renamed Rust en Vrede ("rest and peace").

Engelbrecht followed the example of his neighbor Alto in making this a red-wine-only estate, and his first wines were varietal Cabernet Sauvignon, Syrah, and Tinta Barroca from 1979, made in the renovated old cellar. Now there are 45 hectares of Cabernet, Merlot, and Syrah on the variously oriented slopes, with many of the vines dating from a replanting program begun in the early 1990s. Supplementary drip irrigation was introduced only in 1999, after Jannie's son, Jean, took over running the property.

The estate built up a good reputation, particularly for the near-decade from 1988 when Kevin Arnold was winemaker. After a short hiatus Louis Strydom arrived as cellarmaster, before moving full-time to Ernie Els Wines (in which at that stage Jean Engelbrecht had an interest). Coenie Snyman has been winemaker since 2006. In the early years of the century it became clear that there were cellar hygiene problems—subsequently solved, largely by turning the old barrel cellar into a (highly reputed) restaurant! About 2004, family squabbles led to Jean moving out until 2007, at which time rest and peace were restored and he was installed as the owner of the estate.

Until recently, Rust en Vrede's reputation rested on a Cabernet Sauvignon, which could be very good, and the Estate Wine, which made its 1986 debut as a Cabernet-Merlot but took on Syrah in 1988 to make the blend that is now standard. Two new wines emerged in 2007: a single-vineyard Syrah, and the 1694 Classification—a Syrah–Cabernet Sauvignon blend; the former is very expensive, the latter remarkably so by local standards. Though made in tiny quantities, they set the seal on Rust en Vrede's commitment to wines designed to appeal to a predominant section of the United States market, where, in fact, Jean Engelbrecht has been successful in marketing his wines. In their heavy bottles, with up to 16 percent alcohol and a dollop of residual sugar, they are ultraripe, opulent, and oaky, and clearly the models for the less-grand wines in the range (few of which ever have less than 15 percent alcohol). They are undoubtedly good wines of their type—balanced in their lush generosity, beautifully smooth, and accessible early. There was a brief period in which Rust en Vrede made rather elegant and interesting, albeit powerful wines, in the late 1990s (when the earlier overly generous acidification and oaking were tempered), but that is a matter for nostalgia.

Jean Engelbrecht also owns another winery in Stellenbosch, Guardian Peak, which does not have vineyards of its own. Lapa Cabernet Sauvignon is the best known of its half-dozen red wines, which tend to be a bit less grand than those of Rust en Vrede, but also tending to tasty blockbusterism: ripe, powerful, and often with a definite sweetness. A further wine, also in a rather extreme Californian style, is made by Philip van Staden at this cellar: Cirrus, from Syrah with a dash of Viognier, is a partnership between Engelbrecht and Ray Duncan of Silver Oak Vineyards in California. The maiden vintage was 2004. Very different concerns are evident in the white wine made under the Engelbrechts' Donkiesbaai label by the Rust en Vrede team. It is called Steen, the now seldom-used but traditional local name for Chenin Blanc, and it does indeed come from older Chenin vines, high on the Piekenierskloof in the Olifants River region. This rare entry of Jean Engelbrecht and his winemaker into white-grape territory only makes one wish that it might be start of some rethinking, so good is the wine!

www.rustenvrede.co.za

www.guardianpeak.com

www.cirruswines.com

www.donkiesbaai.com

SAXENBURG

This 200-hectare farm on the Polkadraai Hills was granted in 1693 to Joachim Sax, from whom its name derives. Sax introduced vines and built a homestead in 1701—but the current house, in similar style, dates from 1945, when fire destroyed the original. Saxenburg's modern wine-producing era began in 1980, when industrial giant Anglo-Alpha bought it and marketed wines as Saxenheim, the Saxenburg name being already registered. In 1989 Adrian and Birgit Bührer of Switzerland acquired Saxenburg (originally with partners) and also bought back the name from the large merchant Gilbeys. At that time, some grapes for the wines were sourced elswhere, but Saxenburg now has an adequate 85 hectares of hillside vineyards. Red varieties account for 80 percent of plantings: Cabernets Sauvignon and Franc, Malbec, Merlot, Pinotage, and Syrah, with the remainder planted to Chardonnay, Chenin Blanc, Sauvignon Blanc, and Viognier.

A major influence on Saxenburg's success must be the long tenure of Nico van der Merwe, winemaker since 1990. Certainly he must be one of the hardest-working wine-makers around: not only did he also work the harvest at the Bührers' property in the south of France, Château Capion, from 1996 through 2004, giving him invaluable experience, but has has also since 1999 had his own eponymous label (discussed elsewhere). Saxenburg and Nico are best known for Syrah. The 1998 Shiraz Select was introduced as one of the most expensive local wines in its day. It has always been unabashedly big—a block selection, picked ripe to give a powerful sweet-fruited wine, flourishing its two years in new oak, equally shared between French and American. All the varietal reds in the Private Collection range are ripe and burly, carefully oaked and with a balance and structure allowing for several years' beneficial maturation. The Chardonnay and Sauvignon Blanc are also good, the former generally more restrained than the latter opulently styled wine. There is also the easy-drinking Guinea Fowl range, and a white and a red under the Concept range, which blends home wines with juice from Château Capion.

Saxenburg certainly has a less commanding image than was the case a decade back. Perhaps the influence of the next generation of the owning family, Fiona and Vincent Bührer, was being felt when something of a renaissance seemed to be in the air from about 2011, when the white-wine cellar was expanded, and the vineyards started undergo-ing what seems to be a major makeover, with Pinot Noir and Sémillon, for example, being newly planted.

www.saxenburg.co.za

SIMONSIG

Frans Malan, father of the three Malan men who now own and run this large and very successful family estate in the foothills of the Simonsberg, was one of the great figures of twentieth-century Cape wine. A prime mover in the establishment of the Wine of Origin legislation in the early 1970s and of the pioneering Stellenbosch Wine Route, he also made the Cape's first modern Champagne-method sparkling wine, Kaapse Vonkel, in 1971, and in 1978 probably the first seriously oaked white wine, the blend of Sauvignon Blanc and Chenin initially called Blanc Fumé. He was also prescient in many other ways: quoted in Graham Knox's *Estate Wines of South Africa* (1976), he held out great hopes for both Syrah and Chardonnay, both then little known here and recently planted on his property.

Frans, with a master's degree in enology, took over the management of the farm called De Hoop from his father-in-law in 1953, when it was still engaged in mixed farming but produced wine for the merchant houses. He improved both cellar facilities and vineyards. Then in 1964 he bought a largely undeveloped farm a few kilometers distant and renamed it Simonsig, referring to its direct view of the Simonsberg. That farm originally formed part of the Nooitgedacht farm, which was granted back in 1682; De Hoop had been part of Koelenhof, also granted at that time. The name De Hoop was not available for registration for the joint property, so Simonsig was used. The first wines to appear under this label were three from the 1968 vintage: Clairette, Steen, and Riesling. Another farm, Morgenster, is also included in the domain.

There are now 210 hectares of vineyards: Cabernet Sauvignon, Syrah, Sauvignon Blanc, Chardonnay, Pinotage, Chenin Blanc, Pinot Noir, Merlot, and a few others in a very minor way. The soils are of the sandstone, decomposed granite, and shale typical of the area. Johan Malan has been cellarmaster here since, remarkably, 1981—few in the Cape have that sort of tenure, though he now has three winemakers working with him. Brother François has been in charge of the vineyards for about the same length of time; Pieter, the oldest brother, is the business development director.

As might be expected, the range of wines made is large. The owning trio are well aware of the dangers of slipping into dullness as a successful family farm and have tried to make sure that this has not happened, being alert with their marketing, with the property a goal for visitors, and above all with the range of wines on offer, which is continually tweaked where necessary. Perhaps with some of the wines they do suffer from the unsexy image associated with a family farm known for its good value, although they have a substantial reputation for at least a couple of their wines, which achieve good prices. The Redhill Pinotage is imposing and sleekly powerful, with dense fruit in genuine harmony with the high alcohol (often approaching 15 percent) and making lavish use of new French and American oak. It is generally a more successful wine than the nonetheless good Frans Malan Cape blend, which adds Cabernet and Merlot to the majority Pinotage component. Merindol Syrah is in the same sort of mold—brightly modern, big, intense, ripe but not overripe, and certainly well made. The Cabernet-based Bordeaux blend called Tiara used to be in rather more restrained mode but, sadly, was the one least easy to sell, and in more recent years it has tended to follow the showier trajectory of the others. All of these reds benefit from some years in bottle.

Of the whites, the Chardonnay Reserve is silkily good, the Chenin Avec Chêne is an effective blockbuster, and the occasional Vin de Liza is among the Noble Late Harvest elite. Pioneering Kaapse Vonkel now has a little Pinot Meunier added to the Pinot Noir and Chardonnay in its blend, and is happily zestful and clean. A prestige bubbly called Cuvée Royale, usually with a much higher proportion of Chardonnay, spends up to five years before disgorgement and is all the better for that; it is undoubtedly one of the Cape's best sparkling wines, making a fitting toast for the admirable estate that produced it.

www.simonsig.co.za

SPIER

The Spier of today emerged from a complicated series of mergers in modern times, with even the property's attachment to its own name impossible for a while. The name derives from Speyer, the hometown of Hans Hattingh, who acquired the property in 1712; it had been granted to a German soldier, Arnout Jansz, in 1692, when it consisted of six separate holdings totaling 34 hectares, on which Jansz had already planted two thousand vines. The usual plethora of owners and eventual dereliction followed, until Spier was bought in 1965 by Niel Joubert, who restored the buildings and consolidated Spier with the other farms in his flourishing organization. Joubert died in 1992 and the following year Spier (the part including the cellar and old buildings) was sold to businessman Dick Enthoven. The wines were labeled IV Spears until 2001 when, after some wrangling and expense, he bought the Spier name from the Jouberts. Meanwhile Enthoven had begun implementing his grand ideas of development, and Spier soon had an amphitheater, luxury hotel, conference center, and various restaurants and other attractions to make it a prime wine-tourist resort—there's even a cheetah sanctuary on the estate, not to mention all those authentic old buildings. In 1999 Spier merged with wine company Savanha and Longridge to form Winecorp. By 2007, consolidation saw Winecorp disappear, with the Spier and Savanha brands retained under the banner of Spier Wines.

Fortunately, there has been greater continuity in the cellar (though it has been impressively upgraded), where Frans Smit has been in charge since 1996. In fact, he presides over more than his team of winemakers, in very effective manner, and is involved in the whole chain of production, including marketing at one end and, at the other, managing the relationship with the farmers who are contracted to meet some of the winery's grape needs. This is, in fact, a very substantial operation. Spier's own 193 hectares of vineyard supply some 70 percent of the grapes, with the rest sourced from farms in Stellenbosch, Paarl, and Darling. Annual production is well over a million cases.

The hallmark of this winery is a soft, rich ripeness, with every effort made to keep the tannins gentle—even the pips are removed during the fermentation process to avoid any hint of green stalkiness. They all tend to be powerful and with substantial alcohol levels—readings over 15 percent are common—but all are well crafted, with new oak lavishly but sensitively used. The reds have a rounded muscularity, with those svelte tannins well coated with flavor and creamy texture—they are at the demure end of blockbusterdom. The Private Collection name has been reserved since 2011 for single-varietal export wines only. At home, the top level is occupied by a would-be icon wine (that is, a very expensive red), released with a maiden 2004, and designed to express the best of Spier—meaning that its composition changes each year, but is dominated by the Bordeaux varieties with a little Syrah and Pinotage sometimes added. It partakes of the general character of the Spier wines, but is usually even larger, and with greater depth and intensity. It was named for the man who has helped so much with the winery's impressive perfomance, Frans K. Smit.

The high-level 21 Gables range (celebrating the many Cape Dutch gables on the property) was introduced in 2011 with a lush, oaky Pinotage and a slightly more elegant, nearly dry Chenin Blanc. In fact, the two signature South African varieties perform well at all levels at Spier. The Creative Block wines are all blends—named for the number of varieties in each wines. The largest number—more entry-level, and generally good value—are in the Signature range. A few organic wines have also been introduced.

www.spier.co.za

STARK-CONDÉ

After decades abroad, Hans Peter Schröder relocated to Stellenbosch and bought the Oude Nektar estate on the slopes of the Jonkershoek Valley in the late 1980s. Just 40 hectares are vineyards, while another 200 are maintained with indigenous vegetation. The 6,000-odd cases are the result of meticulous attention from American-born winemaker José Conde (Schröder's son-in-law) and viticulturist Pieter Smit.

The Three Pines top tier consists of two wines, Syrah and Cabernet Sauvignon, from the highest vineyards on the farm, at about 300 meters. They are both extremely good, powerful and rich, and José Conde is unafraid of forceful—though always ripe—tannins that need a few years to soften into amenability. The Syrah particularly, though, has elegance to its intensity, with a touch of perfumed florality and the fruit unobscured by its 30 percent new oak. It matures splendidly over five to ten years at least. The Cabernet (which contains up to 15 percent of other Bordeaux varieties) is more magisterial, and in some years the 70 percent new oak component can show strongly in youth.

These Three Pines bottles proclaim "Jonkershoek Valley" on the labels, but although the second tier, from the same varieties, are noted as merely "Stellenbosch," they are also from the estate. And very considerable wines too—in fact, it is misleading to call this a second tier rather than simply another range; they are made in essentially the same way and are equally serious in intent and effect.

Although the first bottlings under the Stark-Condé label were in 1998, the Oude Nektar vineyards were well established, though completely replanted in the years around 1990. Since then underperforming vineyards have been removed, and siting and plant material improved. A new 2 hectare vineyard, at about 600 meters, was planted in 2003 for a single-vineyard blend of Cabernet Sauvignon, Syrah, and Petit Verdot. The tendency on the whole farm (and in the winery) is toward natural methods, and this vineyard is being farmed organically with some biodynamic inputs. "I tend to be a skeptic when it comes to biodynamics," says Conde, "but we are trying to adapt some of the ideas to our own conditions and see how they work." On a nearby Jonkershoek smallholding (Lingen) is another 2 hectare vineyard, 400 meters lower, which he has taken on a twenty-five-year lease—and planted to match the higher vineyards to see how different a wine it would make.

This is all a welcome expansion of activity, and Conde is also making some Pinot Noir from a cool site in Elgin where he has a joint venture with the farmer. His long-held ambition to make Pinot is not surprising, he says, as his winemaking "tends to be more typically Burgundian in many ways: small lots, open fermenters, hand punchdowns. A lot of natural yeast ferments; malo in the barrel; careful racking and bottling without filtration. Nothing fancy." The Pinot joins other varieties bought in from elsewhere and marketed as Pepin Condé: Chenin Blanc and Sauvignon Blanc were the first releases in 2010.

www.stark-conde.co.za

STELLEKAYA

The name is hybridly allusive: "Stelle" for Stellenbosch as well as "stars" in Italian; *kaya* is Xhosa for "home" and also recalls Super Tuscan names like Sassicaia. IT mogul Dave Lello founded Stellekaya in 1999, though its vineyard base has shifted to 24 hectares in the Blaauwklippen Valley, where planting began in 2004. Grapes are still also bought in from other Stellenbosch locations, however, and now vinified at the modern winery in an old brandy cellar on the edge of Stellenbosch town. Various people made the first few vintages in various cellars, but since 2004 the winemaker has been Ntsiki Biyela. She came (immensely courageously, it must be said), via a scholarship for study in what were alien surroundings, culture, and language at Stellenbosch University, from Zululand—"so wine was not exactly a part of my culture." It is now, and she makes a very respectable range of red wines (supported by consultant Mark Carmichael-Green). The top blends—notably the Bordeaux-style Orion and the Sangiovese-based Hercules—tend to be fairly big and powerful, but well balanced and with good, intense, and not ultraripe fruit and a spicy vinosity, all helping them cope with perhaps rather too much new oak. I prefer the greater modesty of some of the others, such as the Merlot, which can be lovely—pure-fruited, with about 30 percent new wood, firmly but quietly and harmoniously structured. Perhaps the winery doesn't yet have an established aesthetic, but decent quality is being maintained.

www.stellekaya.co.za

STELLENRUST

This is one of the largest family-run Stellenbosch properties—two properties, really: half the 200-plus hectares are in the Helderberg Golden Triangle not far from the town, the other half in the Bottelary Hills. Some 150,000 cases are produced in a number of bottlings under their own label (from a wide range of varieties, rather more black grapes than white), other grapes are sold off, and various wines appear under the labels of clients. In fact, although the farm was established in 1928, the own-label is a newish idea, with some Stellcape Vineyards wines (initially vinified elsewhere) marketed since 2003. Then the name of the family farm, Stellenrust, was used for the main ranges. The "boutique-style" wines are made in a converted milk shed on the Bottelary property, and the larger-volume ones at a large facility in Stellenbosch. Owners Tertius Boshoff and Kobie van der Westhuizen are responsible for winemaking and viticulture, respectively. The number of wines made seems to be continually growing at both super-premium and more modest levels. I know little about them, but they are generally made in approachable, ripe, and seldom bone-dry styles and are gaining some acclaim at home as well as abroad—they export to at least thirty countries, something for which their Fairtrade accreditation and Black Economic Empowerment business status are no doubt useful. The "47" Barrel Fermented Chenin Blanc receives most accolades.

www.stellenrust.co.za

STELLENZICHT

This old farm in the southern section of the Golden Triangle area south of Stellenbosch was granted in 1692 under the name of Rustenberg; when financier Hans-Joachim Schreiber bought it (needing some radical replanting) in 1981, it was called Alphen. With those two names both then among the best known of Cape wine brands, Stellenzicht—literally, "view of Stellenbosch"—seemed a good idea. It is now part of Lusan Holdings, Schreiber's joint venture with Distell. This is traditional red wine country, and some 80 percent of Stellenzicht's 92 hectares of vineyards, predominantly on west-facing Helderberg slopes, are planted to Cabernet Sauvignon, Syrah, and Pinotage. Use of Syrah rather than Shiraz is particularly appropriate here, in fact, as Stellenzicht's famous 1994 Syrah was the first local wine to use the newly official synonym, which was prompted by an application by Stellenzicht's then winemaker, André van Rensburg, who felt his wine marked a new departure—as perhaps it did. It seemed then perhaps the iconic new South Africa red: sophisticated and irrefutably high-quality. That wine had 14 percent alcohol and was matured in just 30 percent new oak; the versions made by Guy Webber, who took over from van Rensburg in 1998, generally have alcohols well in excess of 15 percent and a gram or two more of residual sugar than a classicist would consider respectable, and they flaunt new oak. It all makes for formidable, ripe opulence, which Webber's skills keep reasonably balanced and undeniably impressive. Lush, oaky ripeness is the essence of the winemaking here, leaving little room for any terroir expression. At the apex of the range, alongside the Syrah, is the Rhapsody blend of Pinotage and Syrah, and Stellenzicht's most ambitious white, the Sémillon Reserve, is usually drier, less powerful, and more elegant than the reds.

www.stellenzicht.co.za

STERHUIS

The Afrikaans name means "star house": the story has it that back in the seventeenth century the few Capetonians who were there then could see the lonely light gleaming on this farm, high on the Bottelary Hills, and easily mistook it for the evening star. The winery's motto continues the theme, with the observation (in Latin) that "there is no easy way from the earth to the stars"—which indicates both Sterhuis's ambition and a recognition of the hard work involved in reaching it. In fact, although members of the Kruger family have been farming grapes here since 1980, it was only a few years into this century that they started making and bottling wine for their own label, and the progress has been impressive since then. New plantings were made at that time of Chardonnay, Cabernet, and Merlot, supplementing the Chenin bushvines (then already thirty years old) and mature Sauvignon and Pinotage vines. A crucial boost was Johan Kruger's decision in 2006 to give up his winemaking job at Diemersdal to concentrate on the family business (he'd been at Jordan briefly before). The range expanded, the quality improved—and both of these aspects continue to develop: Johan likes to say that he has had no training as a winemaker, except for what he learned on the job and "at Passionville," and it seems to be a perfectly adequate education.

The starry altitude that confused the early inhabitants of Cape Town is of relevance to the Sterhuis vineyards: at 300 to 400 meters in elevation they have relative coolness, something that shows in the depth of the white wines particularly. Granite-derived soils, with a little sandstone, no doubt make their contribution to the finesse of the wines. Little acidification is necessary, and in the fine 2009 vintage Johan was delighted not to need any at all, for the first time. The white wines are made with partial spontaneous fermentation. There is as yet no winery at Sterhuis, and all the wines are made at Devon Hill.

The varietal Chenin, Chardonnay, and Cabernet are all good and serious wines, but the flagships are even better. Astra Red is a firmly built but softly textured and well-fruited wine, with a balance and structure that should keep it in good shape for many years. Astra White, introduced with the 2006 vintage, has Sauvignon Blanc, Chardonnay, and Chenin collaborating harmoniously to achieve a greater and seamless whole—Viognier plantings might lead to an addition to the blend. The subsequent vintage was rather too oaky in its youth, meaning that the lovely fruit was rather hidden at least at first—but it still had a lovely citric freshness. If trained winemakers could achieve as much as Johan Kruger has—and with the same friendly modesty and confidence in his vineyards—all would be well in the Cape. We can look forward to see what he makes of the youthful Pinot Noir plantings he is excited about.

www.sterhuis.co.za

TAMBOERSKLOOF

The home of Tamboerskloof wines is Kleinood farm in the foothills of the Stellenboschberg, bought by Gerard and Libby de Villiers in 2000. The 10 hectares of vines are mostly of Syrah, with blocks of Viognier and Mourvèdre; a little Roussanne was planted in 2011. There are just two wines, made by Gunter Schultz since 2007 in the small but technologically advanced winery. The fine Viognier is an unusually restrained version, properly dry, with alcohol levels seldom reaching 14 percent, and the subtlest of oak influences. It must be hoped that the winemaking philosophy behind the first few vintages of the Syrah will not change under Schultz, for they were becoming notably elegant and restrained, and better as the vines matured—if not yet profound. The 2007 vintage (the first entirely from home vineyards; previously some grapes were brought in from Paarl) was down to just 14 percent alcohol, with lovely flavors, smart, fine tannins, and just 30 percent or so new oak. A little Viognier and Mourvèdre are cofermented.

www.kleinood.com

TEDDY HALL

Teddy Hall has been most associated with Chenin Blanc, since the great successes he achieved with it at Kanu and then at Rudera, the winery that began as a moonlighting sideline in 1999. He broke away from Kanu in 2003 to concentrate on Rudera, but in 2006 established the current label bearing his own name. Two years later a divorce meant that he lost Rudera, so here he is, without vineyards but with a fine reputation and a growing range of wines—including two or three from the variety for which he has such admiration and a clear affinity. Especially at the grander level for his white wines, Teddy goes in for oak (though not too much of it is new), and a ripe richness that usually involves an amount of residual sugar, making the wines just about off-dry, although there is also usually a balancing vein of fine acidity. The serious-level red wines, a Cabernet and a Syrah, also evidence great ripeness and fairly late picking, together with skillful work in the cellar: they are good wines in the succulent modern mode. Most of them take their names from minor but colorful characters in Stellenbosch history—Herculès van Loon Cabernet Sauvignon, for example, is named after a lovelorn, suicidal priest, and Dr Jan Cats Chenin Blanc Reserve commemorates a doctor who had the victims of his less successful treatments carried at midnight to the mortuary conveniently located across the road from his surgery.

Most of the wines in the Teddy Hall range have had only one or two releases to date, so it would be wrong to be too definitive about them, but they do accord with the aesthetic already associated with this accomplished winemaker. There is every reason to think that he will succeed with this latest venture as he did with previous ones.

www.teddyhallwines.co.za

THELEMA

The establishment of Thelema in the mid 1980s was a significant point in the modernization of the Cape wine industry, as became clear with the first white wine vintage of 1987 and more so with the 1988 reds. It was one of the modest wave of new farms to be established with fine-wine production in mind, but in addition it was one of the few that looked less to the established and recognized qualities of the great wine districts of Europe than to other virtues more associated with the New World. Certainly Gyles Webb (not long since having undergone the moment of truth that diverted him from his accounting career and sent him back to university to study viticulture and enology) was inspired by the great wines of Europe, but four months in 1983 with Joe Heitz in the Napa Valley perhaps showed him some of the virtues of a modern, different approach to winemaking. I well remember, as a Bordeaux-oriented classicist, rather disapproving of the youthful easiness, the forward pure fruit of Thelema's Cabernet and Merlot wines; there was undeniably structure there, but it seemed unlikely that the wines would mature and last for many years. I was wrong—though correct in sensing that something new was happening to Cape wine. Nowadays it is remarkable how classic—well, modern-classic—Thelema's winemaking seems, not to mention extremely good, across quite a range.

These parts at the top of the Helshoogte Pass had long been considered too elevated, and therefore too cool, for viticulture. When the 158-hectare run-down farm was bought by Gyles Webb's parents-in-law, the McLeans, the only recent farming was of fruit, although some wine had been made here earlier in the century. The name of the new farm (called Hooggelegen, "high-lying," in 1692) came from Rabelais's tales of the Abbey of Thelema. Buildings were restored or renovated; orchards and virgin mountainside were cleared, prepared, and planted with vines. Tests revealed the soil on these mainly southeast-facing slopes, at elevations ranging from 370 to 460 meters, to be deep, red decomposed granite with good water-retention capacity (a dam allowing for limited irrigation was built in 1997). Now there are 55 hectares of Cabernet Sauvignon, Merlot, Syrah, Chardonnay, Muscat de Frontignac, Riesling, and Sauvignon. In 2000 Thelema bought a farm in Elgin, with a further 40 hectares planted to Cabernet, Petit Verdot, Pinot Noir, Chardonnay, Riesling, Roussanne, Sauvignon, and Viognier. The vineyards have always been Webb's focus when it comes to high-quality wine, and he and his viticulturist since 2007, Conrad Schutte, have invoked the international expertise of both Phil Freese from California and Aidan Morton, who brought the experience of his work in Australia. As on many of the best farms, there is a combination of advanced technology and as much "naturalness" as possible, with a genuine orientation to conservation and sustainability. In 2009 two vineyard blocks were certified organic, with more in line. And, says Thomas Webb—Gyles and Barbara Webb's son, who joined the team in 2005 after completing a wine business degree at Adelaide University—"we have a new reed bed designed to further purify effluent before it is allowed back into the dam—very green, very cool. All our winery waste is now incorporated back into the vineyard."

Sharing winemaking responsibilities with Gyles Webb since 2000 has been Rudi Schultz (who also makes a very good Syrah under his own label, and in the best years, an even finer Reserve version). The Elgin wines are kept separate in their own range, called Sutherland. For some years, these were not quite as impressive as the home-farm wines, but they have been improving as the vineyards mature, and the rich but subtle blend of Roussanne and Viognier is first-class. The Thelema whites are led by a good Sauvignon Blanc and a Chardonnay that is often more than good, intense, creamy, and fine. There's also a Chardonnay called Ed's Reserve made from a single vineyard of a clone with strangely Muscat overtones, and a dry Riesling that is among the handful of decent Cape examples. But Thelema is best known for its reds, led by two Cabernet Sauvignons from mature vineyards (the original plantings), one's name prefixed by "The Mint," referring to the distinctive character given by the vineyard it comes from. Both are serious wines that deserve at least five years in bottle before broaching, and in the best vintages will mature and keep for much longer than that; and both are ripe and fairly plush, though with alcohol levels usually happily below 14 percent. The Merlot (with an occasionally released Reserve version among the Cape's best examples of this variety) and the Shiraz tend to be both more alcoholic and more exuberant. A top-priced blend called Rabelais was introduced with a 2007, with Cabernet and Merlot (mostly the former) selected from new-oak barrels; Petit Verdot was added in the superior 2008. It's a slightly showier wine than Thelema is known for, powerful and with unabashed dark fruits, all carried rather triumphantly by a convincing structure of acidity and tannin. The reliability of the whole range is well known to wine lovers; their quality and comparatively modest prices ensure that this winery has little trouble selling out early (less so at the height of recession, perhaps). Gyles Webb sticks firmly to his principle that he won't sell wine for more than he'd be prepared to pay himself, but perhaps he's too modest in assessing the value of his best wines.

www.thelema.co.za

TOKARA

It took a decade from the first plantings in 1995 to the first appearance of Tokara-labeled wines on the market; the team was determined to get things right, and even for the earlier-appearing second label (formerly called Zondernaam, meaning "nameless" in Dutch, and the original name for a portion of the farm) they were slow and very choosy. Time, as well as expense, was not to be spared, it seemed, on this 60-hectare property at the crest of Helshoogte Pass, located right next to Thelema, but just in the Simonsberg-Stellenbosch ward rather than in Banghoek. The views—across to Table Mountain in one direction and to False Bay in another—were spectacular, as was the winery, designed to perform brilliantly as well as look impressive, glowing in ultraviolet light as one catches a glimpse of it through plate glass on the way to the stylish restaurant. The smart buildings, including a dwelling, went up after the property was bought by rich banker G. T. Ferreira in 1997; it was named for his two children, Thomas and Kara.

Cellarmaster from the start—something more than a consultant, for many years—was neighbor Gyles Webb from Thelema, with young Miles Mossop (now fully in charge) coming in as winemaker in 2000, the same year that Aidan Morton arrived to take charge of the vineyards. His viticulture is thorough and precise, making use of extensive scientific resources: GPS soil mapping, aerial remote sensing, irrigation management with neutron probes. Tokara was, apparently, the first cellar in South Africa to make use of the NDVI process, which captures both visible and infrared light emitted from vineyards to create a color index indicating variances within individual vineyard blocks. Virus is fought with real dedication here (still a rarity in the Cape)—all the staff are equipped with tape to mark any virused vines, and serious testing of suspect vines is regularly carried out.

The main five red and main two white Bordeaux varieties, as well as Chardonnay, Syrah, and Mourvèdre, are planted on these Helshoogte slopes, at altitudes from 320 to 550 meters above sea level, on deep, high-potential Oakleaf soils. But now Tokara also draws in grapes from other properties bought by Ferreira (apart from an immediate neighbor), giving a total vineyard size of more than 100 hectares. A farm in Elgin—much cooler than Stellenbosch, of course—concentrates on Sauvignon Blanc, but also has some Chardonnay and Sémillon. The ripe, beautifully poised Elgin Sauvignon Blanc contrasts with the generally leaner, racier, and more mineral version that bears the Walker Bay appellation and comes, as does a Chardonnay, from the sandstone soils on Ferreira's farm in the Hemel-en-Aarde Valley.

Production in the 950-ton-capacity cellar is about 50,000 cases. The flagship Tokara wines are a very fine pair simply known as Director's Reserve Red and White. They, like all the wines, are beautifully crafted, with a good deal of polish and sophistication, in a style one could call classic modernism. The Cabernet Sauvignon–based Red, for example, is big, ripe, and powerful, but also modest in its oaking; it balances seductive ripeness with structure, depth, and subtlety, seriousness with charm, ageability with youthful appeal. The Sauvignon-dominated White tends to be more understated and elegant, but is certainly in the top echelon of the new wave of Bordeaux-style whites in the Cape. Sauvignon is also used for a good Noble Late Harvest. An ambitious Pinotage from bought-in grapes was introduced with a plush, rather oaky and hedonistic 2006—Miles Mossop letting himself off the rein, perhaps, and revealing the fun-loving surfer boy lurking within the well-mannered, smart-school exterior that seems to be a good counterpart to the unexceptionable suavity of his wines. This top range goes under Reserve labels, while the second tier are straight Tokara. Each year, I find myself more impressed by the sheer quality of Tokara, and by Miles Mossop's deftness as he reveals himself to be one of the Cape's finest winemakers.

www.tokara.com

UVA MIRA

From among Uva Mira's vines on the upper slopes of the Helderberg, standing in the warm sun but with the cool breezes off False Bay, it seems you can see almost all the Western Cape's mountains and coastline. At 420 to 620 meters above sea level, these 30 hectares testify to the urge of the past few decades to climb higher up the Stellenbosch hillsides, mostly in search of coolness. The soils are a mixture of decomposed granite and shale, with numerous aspects making for the differences that winemaker-viticulturist until 2013 Matthew van Heerden was intent on exploiting in his wines. The star at present is the Chardonnay, from a vineyard at 550 meters and planted in the mid 1990s.

Whole-bunch pressing, a natural fermentation in oak, and eleven months on the lees make for a harmonious, understated wine of refreshing finesse. The other white is a decent Sauvignon Blanc, from the highest vineyards of all. These two wines have alcohol levels up to 14 percent, and it's a pity the same isn't true of the reds—which are a percentage point higher, though admittedly they are in good balance and without obvious overripeness. The top red goes simply by the name of the estate, and is based on Cabernet Sauvignon, with some Merlot and Cabernet Franc—as well as some Syrah, which seems to work well and in fact is something of a tradition in this part of the Helderberg. Although the wine shows every sign of having the ability to age five to ten years, it is fairly accessible in youth, its impressiveness made approachable by sweet berry fruit. The tannins are firm and ripe but not imposing, and not too supplemented by oak tannins, for the oaking regime is intelligently restrained: eighteen months of barrique maturation, with only about 30 percent of the wood being new. There's also a decent Syrah. Uva Mira, established in the late 1990s, is owned by Denise Weedon, widow of a former mining magnate—and a formidable cook, something for which I can happily vouch.

www.uvamira.co.za

VERGELEGEN

This is one of the great historic wine estates of the Cape and now firmly reestablished among the finest producers of the "new" South Africa. The name means "situated far away," an outpost—which is what it was when Simon van der Stel planned it after 1685, in the mountainous wilds of Stellenbosch far from the tenuous security of the incipient colony huddled near Table Bay. The Dutch East India Company, it is claimed on the current Web site, had "bought the grounds in 1672 from the chiefs of the tribe that owned it," although the price is not mentioned. Its days as an outpost ended when Willem Adriaan, van der Stel's eldest son and successor as governor in 1699, was granted the 342 hectares of freehold land in 1700. With all the resources that were honestly and corruptly at his disposal, he set about establishing a magnificent mixed farm, including some half a million vines. By the end of his first year as owner, Vergelegen was already able to impress the visiting Reverend François Valentijn, who "saw this place with exceptional pleasure, since everything there was laid out wonderfully finely." A beautiful homestead was built, reportedly by slaves owned by the company. As it seems that Willem Adriaan was of an intelligent and experimental mind, and certainly lavish with expenditure, we can probably regret from a winemaking point of view that his tenure was doomed by his tyrannical arrogance, or else the Cape might have had a second pole of excellence as a counterpart to Groot Constantia. But bitter conflict with the expanding settlement's free burghers (especially the richer ones), over markets that Willem Adriaan sought to arrogate to himself, eventually led to his downfall and then to exile in 1706. The enormous farm was broken into four after 1708. Fortunately, orders to demolish the homestead were only partially carried out.

That was the end of magnificence—for a time. The home section of the farm, which kept the name Vergelegen, passed through a long undistinguished period with various owners. One of them, Dawid Malan, left in nearly as much of a hurry as the first, as recounted by his descendant Rian Malan in his book *My Traitor's Heart:* Dawid was discovered in flagrante delicto with the lovely female slave of a neighbor; both fled on horseback and did not return. The Theunissen family acquired Vergelegen in 1798, and it stayed in their hands for a century. A new cellar was built and, apparently, winemaking flourished. But decline set in, and by the time it was bought in 1917 by mining magnate Sir Lionel Phillips and Lady Phillips, Vergelegen was in disrepair. A good deal of money was spent in restoration (and alteration) of the buildings and gardens, and of the estate itself. Unsurprisingly, perhaps, at a time when Cape wine was at a very low ebb, the vineyards were ripped out and mixed agriculture supervened. After the death of the Phillipses, Vergelegen was bought by businessman Charles Barlow in 1941, and a little viticulture was reestablished. Then in 1987 the farm was acquired by the farming division of the powerful, locally based multinational Anglo American Corporation (now Anglo American plc, registered primarily in London), and its renaissance began.

A start was soon made on planting or replanting 100 hectares of vineyards. Martin Meinert was appointed as winemaker, and a splendid new hilltop cellar was designed by a leading Paris firm of architects, its design inspired by van der Stel's original octagonal walled gardens (the octagon is also the basis of the wine label image). Little appears above ground to disturb the environment unduly: architect Patrick Dillon thought the site the most beautiful he had ever seen for a cellar and planned the winery, whose working parts were sunk underground, to be "a small speck within the context of a valley of a vast and varied tapestry of colours, textures, shapes and forms." Meinert's early vintages, partly from bought-in grapes, attracted attention and praise, and increasingly so; but having overseen the establishment of Vergelegen as a serious wine producer, he left after the 1997 vintage to concentrate on his own winery. Burly, controversial, brilliant André van Rensburg arrived from Stellenzicht in early 1998, immediately claimed Vergelegen as his own (mere incidentals of title deeds aside), and started putting his stamp on things.

But it was not a matter of continuing where Martin Meinert left off. Van Rensburg was fairly soon certain that to meet his and his employers' quality aspirations he needed to have a substantial say in the farm's viticulture as well as its winemaking (Niel Rossouw has been the chief viticulturist here since 1995), and then that it was vital to replant virtually the whole farm in order to combat leafroll virus, which affected about 80 percent of the vines. A major replanting program was undertaken between 2003 and 2009—some new vineyards planted on soil that had not seen vines for two hundred years, some replanted on sites left fallow for three years after uprooting. The inevitable cost—aside from the great financial one—was working with the fruit of young vines (Sauvignon Blanc and Cabernet Sauvignon constituted the bulk of the remaining older vineyards), which possibly affected quality in those years; but by 2010 van Rensburg was sure that he was literally reaping the rewards of the replanting program. With rigorous monitoring, the tightest possible control is kept over the vineyards to prevent reinfection with virus. Only a minuscule proportion of the vines needs removal and replacement each year. Crucial to this success, van Rensburg is convinced, is the enormous and enormously expensive effort that has been put into removing alien vegetation and the rehabilitation of the natural fynbos on the 3,500-hectare estate, and this, for various reasons, has also helped him virtually eliminate pesticide applications and radically reduce the amount of fungicide and herbicide needed. Organic compost prepared from winery residues is used.

Plantings on the 145 hectares of vineyard include Cabernets Sauvignon and Franc, Merlot, Syrah, Chardonnay, Sauvignon Blanc, and Sémillon. They are planted at altitudes ranging from 140 to 310 meters above sea level, with slopes facing virtually all directions. Temperatures monitored at three automatic and six manually read stations indicate a two-degree Celsius difference between the lower, north- to northwest-facing slopes and the higher plateau and south-facing slopes. The proximity of False Bay (just six kilometers distant) moderates temperatures, but the wind is a source of continuing anguish to van Rensburg as it can seriously reduce the crop in some years. Twenty-one soil types have been identified on the farm, generally with a high clay content, and variety, rootstock, and planting density vary accordingly. All the vines are trained on trellis, and irrigation is available throughout the farm but its use is kept to a minimum.

Van Rensburg is a classicist in his winemaking approach, and works with classic varieties too, primarily the Bordeaux ones, both white and red. He is not interested in fashionable "wild ferments" and is convinced of the advantages of filtering his wines. Perhaps the finest of all the large, fine range is the white blend, generally with more Sémillon than Sauvignon. In the cellar a fairly oxidative regime is followed. The two varieties are separately bunch-pressed and then fermented in oak (mostly new for the Sémillon, mostly older for the Sauvignon), where they spend some ten months before being blended. The wine is intended for aging and can be tight as well as oaky in its youth, but after a few years have elapsed it reveals a growing complexity and harmony, a discreet richness, a serene intensity of flavor, and subtle power. The evidence of vintages since the maiden 2001 is that the wine should develop well over more than ten years. A vertical tasting held in late 2012 of all the vintages from 2001 to 2011 was most impressive; there seemed then no reason to think that the 2003, for example, should not happily last another decade or more. The Sauvignon Blancs, standard and Reserve, are also excellent, as are the corresponding pair of Chardonnays.

Vergelegen's top reds are similarly not designed for very early pleasure, but develop well. The flagship red is a Cabernet Sauvignon–based blend, firmly structured but with plenty of fruit—a good balance of new- and old-world styling. Vergelegen V is nearly all of single-vineyard Cabernet, and was introduced in 2001 as an aspirational "challenge to Californian cult wines," which meant it was seriously overoaked and generally flamboyant. Succeeding vintages, however, saw this approach toned down, to the great advantage of the wine, which remains, however, more immediately impressive than the blend and the varietal wines (among which the Cabernet Sauvignon usually offers particularly good value).

Vergelegen's high quality has been consistent through the vineyard changes, and there is every reason to agree with André van Rensburg that he has very good terroir to work with, and to be confident that, with financial backing for his sedulous care and work, he is going to achieve ever better results from it.

www.vergelegen.co.za

VERGENOEGD

The Faures have been here since the 1820s, with John Faure, winemaker since 1984, the sixth generation. The estate dates back to 1692, when Pieter de Vos cleared this land a mere five kilometers from False Bay. He was officially granted the property in 1696 but soon died and in 1700 his widow sold it to her neighbor, Ferdinand Appel; it is from this date that wine is believed to have been made on Vergenoegd. The name means "far enough" and implies, the Faures say, "Satisfaction has been achieved." The farm is perhaps not perfectly situated, on flat land barely 12 meters above sea level, the soils a mix of fertile alluvial loam and, for the better wines, sand with layers of yellow clay and calcareous matter. The estate has long been associated with red wines, and the 90 hectares of vineyard are planted to the Bordeaux varieties (minus Malbec) and Syrah, with Tinta Barroca and Touriga Nacional for the port. Some 10,000 cases are bottled under the Vergenoegd label, with the balance of the grapes sold off. Varietal wines are made, as well as a blend going under the estate name. Stylistically, though not exactly old-fashioned the wines seem somehow well suited to the elegant family-farm ambience of Vergenoed, with its historic manor house (now housing a restaurant) and other old buildings. They are made from ripe grapes and sometimes have robust alcohols, firmly and seriously built, now matured in well-judged proportions of new small oak, and benefiting from at least five years in bottle, though accessible earlier unless you demand fruity frivolity—in which case, look elsewhere than Vergenoegd.

Latterly, the releases have been increasingly delayed, probably as the result of a particularly slow market for this style of wine, but the extra time in bottle suits them well. A tasting in 2012 of the forty vintages of Cabernet Sauvignon from 1972 was remarkable and revealing. There are few wineries outside Europe that could put on a forty-vintage vertical tasting at all—let alone one in which there was not a single dud (or dead) wine. Moreover, the 1972 was still drinking rather deliciously, and there were many other vintages that impressed. However, while the wine showed a greater capacity for aging than, say, the Rubicon from next-door Meerlust, there were very few vintages that could compare in quality with Rubicon at its best. Many of the wines could be said to have aged well rather than matured well, and only a few could number among the best Cape examples of the relevant vintages (the 1995 was one of those).

There are signs that Vergenoegd's style is changing, with attempts to graft extra ripeness onto the sternness that is probably partly a reflection of terroir, and if that is a correct observation we shall have to wait a little to see if the strategy is successful.

www.vergenoegd.co.za

VILLIERA

This substantial and successful family-owned winery is a good riposte to those doubtful about the common pattern of offering large and diverse ranges. Villiera makes many wines, from Méthode Cap Classique sparklers to botrytised dessert wines and port, from a delicate off-dry Riesling to a serious Bordeaux-style red blend—and none is less than adequate, while some achieve much more. Quality and good value are consistent. What more could one ask? More moments of excitement, perhaps.

The property was bought by the Grier family in 1983, after undistinguished wine had been produced for less than a decade—the first Villiera release was 1976. (The name comes from earlier owners, the de Villiers.) Simon took responsibility for the vineyards and cousin Jeff for the ever-growing cellar. Extensive plantings and replantings took place in the mid 1980s, and the farm itself was to grow over the years; now about half the 400 hectares are under vine, mostly irrigated, and 175 hectares are set aside as a wildlife sanctuary: the Griers have always had a tendency to "greenness" (just as they have always been known as model employers). Insecticides have been banned for well over a decade, and there is a focus on water conservation and recycling, in addition to a greening program with indigenous trees. Varying soil conditions allow for thirteen varieties to be grown fairly plausibly, with the proportion of red grapes now rising to 40 percent.

If there is a speciality here, it is sparkling wines—about 40 percent of production is of MCC. Perhaps the finest is the occasionally made Brut Natural from Chardonnay, fermented with native yeasts and bottled without sulfur or dosage. The flagship, Monro Brut, is also at the top end of local bubblies, a rich but fresh wine from Pinot Noir and (oak-fermented) Chardonnay. Villiera used to be famous for its Sauvignon Blancs too, but while their two examples are good, especially the Traditional Bush Vine version, they do not usually stand out in today's much larger crowd. The best of the reds is the Monro blend of mostly Merlot and Cabernet Sauvignon, nowadays less classic than it was, more ripely voluptuous, new-oaked and powerful—a slight stylistic shift apparent in some of the other wines, too, such as the Traditional Barrel Fermented Chenin Blanc.

www.villiera.com

VRIESENHOF

Little is known of the early days of this farm in Paradyskloof on the slopes of Stellenbosch Mountain, just outside the town, but it seems that the farm Kafferkuil, of which it was a part, was used for hunting and grazing. Certainly grapes were being farmed here when it was bought in 1980 by Jan "Boland" Coetzee, who had combined being a famous rugby player with making wine at Kanonkop. The maiden release was the Cabernet Sauvignon 1981. Long leases, purchases, and land swaps helped consolidate Vriesenhof. A major replanting program was begun in 1995, and there are now 37 hectares of Cabernets Sauvignon and Franc, Merlot, Pinot Noir, Pinotage, and Chardonnay. A new cellar replaced the old lean-to in 1991. A decade later Coetzee was still open to new ideas and was an early advocate of such things as sorting tables and gentle pumping methods. It should be mentioned that Coetzee was long one of the more "enlightened" farmers, a leading light of the Rural Foundation who substantially improved his workers' housing conditions, helping with the issue of freehold property rights for farmworkers (1993) and assisting his employees to buy their own housing.

Coetzee remains in charge of cellar and vineyards. His wines tend to display the traditional virtues of firm body, genuine dryness, and not too much fruitiness, and require a few years in bottle to start showing their best although they are ripe and not at all forbidding. The Cabernet Sauvignon—generally released after a good few years in the magnums in which it is bottled—is perhaps the most pleasing. Also in magnums is a good, forceful, and rather delicious Grenache made from grapes brought in from Piekenierskloof. At present, it must be said, this is the best of the Vriesenhof wines: delicious, succulent, and savory, and firmly but not too severely structured. Kallista is a modest, well-balanced Bordeaux-style blend that gets thirty months in older oak. The Pinot Noir has its admirers, though I found the earlier vintages rather oaky and the more recent ones a touch rustic. White grapes are ably represented by a serious-minded, steely Chardonnay.

www.vriesenhof.co.za

WARWICK

The 100 hectares of this family-owned estate in the Simonsberg-Stellenbosch ward were originally part of the grant known as De Goede Sukses ("good success"), and the home-stead and outbuildings date from about 1791. The present name came in 1902 when one Colonel Gordon bought half of De Goede Sukses and named it in honor of his regiment. Livestock and fruit were the main farming concerns until Stan Ratcliffe acquired the farm in 1964. Until 1985 the grapes were sold to Distillers, but in that year the first certified Warwick Estate Cabernet was made by his wife, Norma. This feisty Canadian was one of the pioneering female winemakers of the Cape, and for a long time certainly the best known. Cabernet Franc and Merlot had been planted in 1984, and Norma included them in the maiden 1986 Bordeaux blend, which soon acquired its present name, Trilogy. A monovarietal Cab Franc, then pretty rare in the Cape, followed in 1988. Warwick was firmly moving away from "boutique" status.

The vineyard mix today also includes Pinotage, Syrah, Chardonnay, and Sauvignon Blanc, the total covering about 60 hectares and producing some 28,000 cases annually, about 60 percent of them red wine. Some of the vineyards are on the northwest lower slopes of the Simonsberg, but most stretch up Klapmuts Kop. Viticulturist Ronald Spies has been here since 2001 and has the benefit of having American Phil Freese—a partner of Warwick managing director Mike Ratcliffe in Vilafonté—as a consultant.

In the cellar, Norma long continued to have a significant influence and remained the public face of Warwick (much less so these days), somewhat obscuring the contributions of various winemakers, although these now get the credit—and there have been a few of them since Louis Nel left in 2007 to consult and to start his own range of ripe, lavishly fruited wines under the Louis label. Mike Ratcliffe, son of Norma and the late Stan, is doing a sterling job as an aggressive marketer of Warwick, with particular success in the difficult United States market. Mike is also something of a champion of Pinotage, which features at Warwick as a monovarietal as well as in the interesting and sumptuous Cape blend called Three Cape Ladies (the other two "ladies" being Cabernet and Merlot, and Syrah joined them recently as an unacknowledged fourth). The reds here are generally smooth, modern, and ripe, with the supple but forthright muscularity associated with the area; they tend to tread the fine line between cheerful accessibility and structure. Alcohol levels often approach 15 percent and there is no fixation with getting the classic level of dryness that Norma strove for in the heroic days of the 1980s. Acidification is less than it used to be, and oaking is generally subtle and unshowy. In many ways, Warwick is a model of how a smallish family winery can be a successful business in the twenty-first century.

www.warwickwine.com

WATERFORD

One of the first incursions of IT money into the wine lands came in 1998, when Jeremy Ord started development at this 120-hectare property in a fold between Helderberg and Stellenbosch Mountain. A splendid winery complex was built from stone and wood in a Mediterranean style, and the tinkling fountain in the central courtyard provided the design on most of the chic labels. From the start, the project involved close collaboration with Kevin Arnold, a personal friend, who remains cellarmaster and a partner in the wine company. Arnold had been at neighboring Rust en Vrede and continued to hanker after one red wine that distinctively expressed the Helderberg; the result was a diverse range of plantings, to explore what would prove most successful. There were initially 14 hectares of vines on the farm (some already planted), and 36 more to come. Now, with Cabernet Sauvignon and Syrah having the best track record, there are also blocks of Cabernet Franc, Malbec, Merlot, Petit Verdot, Mourvèdre, Grenache, Barbera, and Sangiovese, with Tempranillo to follow once out of quarantine. Chardonnay and Sauvignon Blanc must not be omitted from the list, as there are seriously good wines made from them. The maiden Waterford release was, in fact, a 1998 Sauvignon. The first reds, also 1998, were the Kevin Arnold Shiraz and a Cabernet Sauvignon from bought-in grapes (they would start coming from home-grown grapes as the vineyards matured).

The goal remained the definitive blend—in fact, as former winemaker Francois Haasbroek suggested, the terroir "seems less expressive of 'varietal' characters than other areas; by blending we can fill in 'shy' spots in all our wines" (and indeed the Cabernet has 10 percent other Bordeaux varieties and the Syrah about 8 percent Mourvèdre). Experiments led to wines in 2003 and 2004 for the annual auctions of the Cape Winemakers Guild that promiscuously blended Bordeaux and Rhône varieties. These experiments were to continue, and in 2011 an interesting Library Collection of small-volume but sometimes excellent wines started being released—mostly one-offs. The 2004 wine that was eventually released as the flagship was based on Cabernets Sauvignon and Franc, but with six other varietal components. Its somewhat inelegant name, the Jem, was taken from the familiar version of Jeremy Ord's name. It was one of the most expensive local wines, but more justifiably so than some other local wanna-bes: somewhat opulent but also fairly elegant, fresh and firmly structured, it is a fine wine. Its composition remains, however, a work in progress.

Francois Haasbroek, incidentally, can surely be given some credit for Waterford's current success—which is not to downplay the leadership role of Kevin Arnold, but to assert the skills and touch of one of the country's more questioning younger winemakers, with a passion for honesty in wine and an orientation to classic approaches. (He left, to start his own label, Blackwater, and to consult, in late 2012.) Waterford is a tight ship and intuition must substitute for information, but the reduction in overt oak, especially American oak, at Waterford over the years speaks of other influences than just Arnold's. The Kevin Arnold Shiraz has grown (from about the 2007 vintage) into a better, more expressive wine, partly because it has little new-wood influence—and no American. Anyway, under the joint regime in the cellar, Waterford is gaining a high reputation, making a small, very sound range of serious classic-modern wines (there's also a good value range of decent, untrivial entry-level wines called Pecan Stream). The Waterford Chardonnay and Sauvignon Blanc are marked by unshowy restraint—both, usually, below 13 percent alcohol—and qualitatively comparable to the reds that are the cellar's pride.

www.waterfordestate.co.za

WATERKLOOF

British wine importer Paul Boutinot acquired this handsome property near Sir Lowry's Pass in 2004, after a long worldwide search. There are 120 hectares, 70 of which are dedicated to natural vegetation, the rest under vine—most recently planted on virgin soil, but some older. Most of the vineyards are on the slopes of the Schapenberg, open to the winds of False Bay some five kilometers distant. This is clearly neither simply an investment nor a lifestyle matter, but a serious commitment from Boutinot, who is ambitious for the wines that will eventually bear the Waterkloof name. In the early years there was only a fine, serious Sauvignon Blanc (a grape that accounts for about a third of the vines), but Bordeaux and Rhône red varieties are planted and will soon produce grapes for the top label. Meanwhile two easygoing but fairly serious blends, one white and one red, go under the name Circle of Life. There is also a slightly less ambitious, though promising (and not cheap) range, Circumstance, and some grapes also go into Boutinot's False Bay and Peacock Ridge négociant ranges—themselves comprising by no means contemptible wines. The Circumstance Syrah has been a particularly good wine, the best of the reds. A splendid new winery was opened in 2009, under the control of the quietly impressive Werner Engelbrecht until 2013. The orientation is clearly toward traditional, noninterventionist winemaking: nearly all the wines are fermented without inoculation, and the majority are not acidified. The modern gravity-flow cellar contains the country's largest array of wooden fermenters outside of Capaia's. This preference for the natural approach marks the estate's viticulture, too; it is being conducted on organic principles, with a significant move toward biodynamic practices (the formal certification process as a biodynamic producer was begun in 2012). A nursery on the farm grows the plants used in biodynamic preparations, and an ever-increasing number of animals (horses, cows, sheep, and chickens) play their parts. The vineyards are all under drip irrigation, but the modest size of the farm's dam as well as the viticulturist's preference indicates how re-strainedly irrigation is to be used. Eco-friendliness is practiced wherever possible, from the perching poles for raptors to conduct rodent control to the water treatment plant running on solar and wind power. In view of the terroir, Boutinot's serious and unhurried ambition, an apparently large reservoir of investment capital, and a general devotion to quality, there seems every reason to expect Waterkloof to become fairly rapidly a leading Cape winery.

www.waterkloofwines.co.za

WEBERSBURG

Webersburg is a boutique winery on the lower slopes of the Helderberg. Although it is close to some of the grand old names of Cape wine (Rust en Vrede, Alto), it was founded by businessman Fred Weber in the mid 1990s, with elegantly restored eighteenth-century buildings testifying to old-Cape connections. A portion of the land was sold to Ernie Els to form the basis of that new estate. The old cellar now serves as a maturation cellar, and a new winery was built in 2007, where the wine is made by Matthew van Heerden (of Uva Mira) and consultant Giorgio Dalla Cia; previously the wines were made at Meerlust. For the first few years there was just one wine, a notably elegant, restrained Bordeaux-style blend going simply by the estate name. This is now supplemented by a Cabernet Sauvignon and a Sauvignon Blanc, as well as a few tiny-production sparkling wines. With so much new, it is difficult to make useful generalizations about the wines—although at least as early as 2003 they seemed to be tending to become more easily, charmingly expressive in youth, more open-structured and lighter-hearted, losing the edge of austerity that was for some admirers part of Webersburg's appeal.

www.webersburg.co.za

ZORGVLIET

As elsewhere in the beautiful Banghoek Valley, there were many more fruit trees than vines planted at Zorgvliet after phylloxera's devastation—although wine was produced here in the early eighteenth century, and probably before. When entrepreneur Mac van der Merwe took over the farm early this century, a start was made on planting some 50 hectares of vines. Plantings are mostly on the eroded coffeestone valley floor, but rise a few hundred meters up the lower slopes of the Simonsberg. An impressive gravity-flow cellar was built, large enough to provide winemaking facilities for less well-endowed neighbors and near-neighbors. From the start, with Rudolf Jansen van Vuuren in the vineyards and Bruwer Raats in the cellar—now his assistant, Neil Moorhouse, has taken over—the aim at Zorgvliet has been varietal expression and a pursuit of ripeness. The wines are, indeed, big in both alcohol and flavor, with the best marked by beautifully soft, ripe tannins: "I look for a lot of tannin," says Moorhouse, "but spectacularly fine tannin—and tannin ripeness happens at the end of the ripening process." It was for the sake of tannin structure that 10 percent Tannat was added to the blend of the expensive flagship, Richelle, which also contains the five main Bordeaux reds. This is an immediately attractive wine of the modern, ripe-fruited, spicy, and generously oaked type, but which benefits from at least a few years in bottle (the first vintage was 2004, so we can't be sure quite how many).

Equally big are red monovarietal wines from most of the grapes used in Richelle, as well as a few whites, notably a Sauvignon Blanc and the new-oaked Simoné from Sémillon and Sauvignon. Moorhouse is an accomplished winemaker, and the wines can be recommended to those who are not looking for traditional virtues. The majority of the wines are in the Silvermyn range, named for a dubious eighteenth-century project to mine for precious metals in the Simonsberg.

www.zorgvlietwines.com

7

PAARL AND WELLINGTON

PAARL

"The history of the area started in 1657," blandly announces the Web site of a Paarl winery, "when Abraham Gabemma, public treasurer of the new Dutch settlement at the Cape of Good Hope, was searching for additional meat resources." In fact, history (if by that we mean human activity) had been under way for some time already in these large valleys, which were the grazing and hunting grounds of Khoikhoi long before the arrival of the Dutch. Gabemma reported finding kraals all along the river.

Abraham Gabemma, taking the privilege of being the first historically recorded person here, not only (re)named the large hill still known as Klapmuts (meaning, approximately, a flat cap, in reference to its shape), but when he saw another, higher mountain crest with its domes of bare granite glistening in the sun after rain he called it "de Diamondt en de Peerlberg" (Diamond and Pearl Mountain). He was clearly a man of imagination as well as—we may infer from his undertaking this mission—brave. The diamond reference soon disappeared, and the mountain now sheltering the town it gave its name to soon became known more simply as Paarlberg: Pearl Rock or Pearl Mountain.

Six months after Gabemma's foray, in February 1658, a party of fifteen explorers, under Sergeant Jan van Herwaarden and including surveyor Pieter Potter to produce a record and map, made its slow way from the fort at Table Mountain through this land. Along with the human inhabitants, there was plentiful wildlife, including large herds of zebra, shy rhinoceros, and hippopotamus in the tree-shaded river pools. The valley then was filled with trees rather than vines. The major mountain range was named for

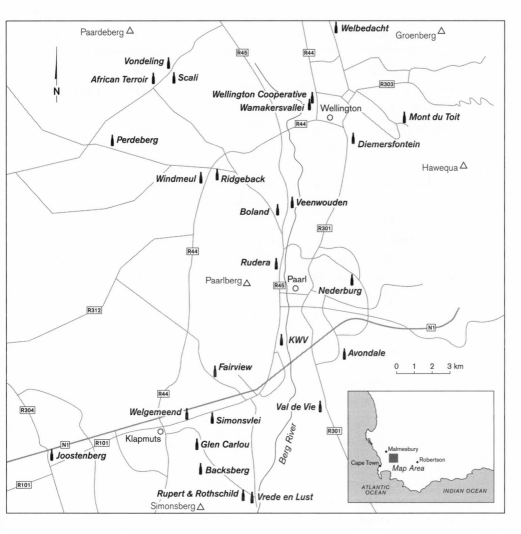

MAP 4
Paarl and Wellington

Commissioner-General van Reede tot Drakenstein, who came to the Cape in 1685; actually, there are two separate ranges—the Groot Drakenstein on one side of the Franschhoek
Valley and the Klein Drakenstein to the east of Paarl. Farther north in the mountainous
chain, after Hawequa and Groenberg, are the Limiet Mountains overlooking what was
to become known as Wellington (town and area), then but certainly not for long the limit
of territorial expansion outward from Table Bay.

Within a few decades, a settled community of farmers was established in the Drakenstein Valley. In October 1687, twenty-three farms of 52 hectares each were granted
along the Berg River—which had been named by people more prosaic than Abraham
Gabemma: it simply means "mountain river." The trees and zebra were doomed, as
were the pastoralist Khoi, who would soon provide at least some of the labor the

settlers' farming activities demanded, although slaves would make a much greater contribution.

By the time the Cape settlement was a century old, in 1753 to be exact, the Drakenstein area (boundaries are not always easy to interpret at this time) declared 1,494,000 vines—probably lower than the real figure, as the submissions were made for tax purposes. The valleys of the Berg River were proving more fruitful than many parts of the expanding colony, and this was about 36 percent of all the vines in the Cape; Stellenbosch had 24 percent, and the rest of the Cape, including the peninsula, 40 percent. By 1794 Drakenstein had forged further ahead, with well over five million vines, producing about half the Cape's wines. This was a proportion that it more or less maintained for the remainder of the eighteenth century and throughout the nineteenth, too—1860's production figures for the greater Paarl area show it contributing just over half the total volume.

Since the establishment of better communications between inland areas and the marketplace and the building of dams and irrigation systems, Paarl's volume significance for the Cape wine industry has shrunk greatly (some parts have also been reallocated to other districts). The presence of two central institutions has, however, greatly added to its importance as a wine town and area: above all, the KWV, which has long had its administrative and winemaking headquarters here, and Nederburg, an important name and presence for Stellenbosch Farmers' Winery and now for Distell.

THE WARDS

The district of Paarl—landlocked, though at present considered part of the Coastal Region—includes two wards. There were two others until recently, but the total area of poor old Paarl has been chipped away substantially. In 2010, Franschhoek Valley was granted independence, as it were, and became a district in its own right, and the same thing happened to Wellington in 2012, although it is still sufficiently associated for them to share a chapter here. The two current Paarl wards are twenty-first-century creations. Voor-Paardeberg was established, at the request of producers there and with the consent of the demarcation board, following the revivification of the area to the southeast of the Paarde-berg, at a little remove from the bulk of Paarl wineries. In many ways, in fact, Voor-Paardeberg has stronger associations with the Swartland than with the rest of Paarl. The line separating the two districts is approximately at the base of the Paardeberg itself, and much of Voor-Paardeberg is on the low slopes leading up to the mountain. With a strong cultural and viticultural orientation to the Swartland, ideally it should be incorporated into the latter—but apart from any other issues, many of the farms have long-standing relationships with Paarl cooperatives that would be prejudiced by moving to another district. It is possible, and to be hoped, that some solution to this problem might be found.

Cabernet Sauvignon is easily the most planted variety here, but Syrah is catching up fast (291 hectares) and has overtaken Chenin Blanc. Merlot, Pinotage, and Sauvignon Blanc follow in that order. If it is a few small wineries that are leading Voor-Paardeberg's quality claims, quantity is mostly in the hands of Swiss-owned African Terroir and

Perdeberg Winery. African Terroir makes large volumes of mostly very ordinary organic wines under various labels, primarily for the lower shelves of the international market. Perdeberg (with thirty grape-farmer owner-members and 2,500 hectares of vineyards) sells only a very small percentage of its wine under its own label (although there's a reserve range, most of the wines have increasingly lacked interest in recent years). The rest, mostly sold off as grapes or wine, appears under a great variety of more and less prestigious names—including the Saam range, developed jointly with the British Bibendum company—and some of those do reveal the depth of potential here.

Simonsberg-Paarl is another fairly recent demarcation within the Paarl district, based on the northern and eastern foothills of Simonsberg. The ward is warm, though cooler for plantings higher up the slopes; rainfall is good, about 800 millimeters annually; and the reddish-brown soils are based on the mountain's granite, becoming sandier and more alluvial in nature lower down. There are some reasonably good wines made at wineries here, although much of the area does not compare in standing with the southwesterly, Stellenbosch side of Simonsberg. Vrede en Lust, an old French Huguenot farm acquired by Dana Buys in 1996 and thoroughly improved since then, is an impressively energetic producer with a range of deservedly popular wines. A newcomer to the area with great ambition is communications tycoon Koos Bekker, whose 62 hectares on his Babylonstoren farm should prove interesting at least. Some of the Simonsberg-Paarl vineyards higher up the slopes are excellent, and supply Nederburg with Cabernet Sauvignon, for example, for both its Auction Reserve and its II Centuries ranges. The quality focus of the area is reflected in the vineyard plantings, with Cabernet Sauvignon (303 hectares) the most planted, followed by Chardonnay (which has performed particularly well for Glen Carlou), Syrah, and Sauvignon Blanc; only after those varieties does Chenin Blanc figure.

The majority of the wines that are simply WO Paarl, without demarcated wards, are on all the mostly granitic lower slopes of Paarlberg (except for the east, which is where the town lies), as well as south of the town toward Simonsberg and Franschhoek. There is much variation of terrain, slope, and aspect, but this is generally hot country: as ambitious wineries like Fairview have discovered, moving higher up the slopes is advantageous not only for soil types but more for a little improvement in air flow and cooler conditions. Rainfall is good, but supplementary irrigation is often necessary. The two Boland Kelder wineries (together taking in grapes from 2,650 hectares of vineyards from as far away as Voor-Paardeberg) are in this area, well reputed for the large range of wines under its own labels, including a few ambitious Reserves. Windmeul Cooperative (mostly a supplier of bulk wine) is on the sloping plains to the north of Paarlberg; Simonsvlei, one of the more dynamic and successful former co-ops, to the south, offers a good range of big, ripe, easy-to-like wines. Chenin Blanc (1,840 hectares in the district as a whole), then Cabernet Sauvignon and Syrah, are the leading varieties, with Pinotage putting in a good showing, and rather a lot of Cinsaut; Sauvignon Blanc does not generally perform well in Paarl's heat, but there are more than 600 hectares of it in the entire district.

It would be a pity not to mention a winery that in the 1980s and 1990s was one of the foremost Paarl establishments: boutique-size Welgemeend, founded in the late 1970s by a Bordeaux-loving amateur, Billy Hofmeyr. Here he produced the Cape's first Bordeaux-style red blend as well as the first red blend to declare Pinotage as a component (Syrah and Grenache the others), expressly designed to be a local take on a classic Côtes du Rhône. After many years of almost diffidently offering their increasingly old-fashioned but (or therefore?) fine wines, the Hofmeyrs sold the property in 2007 (Billy had retired from winemaking because of illness about 1990, and later died), by which time the badly virused vineyards had ceased to offer very good quality.

Numbers of new wineries have emerged in Paarl since 1994, some of them very promising, to join a handful of good older producers, but investment in the area has not been comparable to some other parts of the Cape. Val de Vie, a large and upmarket private housing estate, has a winery and is showing very promisingly with a range of wines from grapes associated with the Rhône, including a fine flagship based on Mourvèdre. But Paarl has comparatively little cachet, unfortunately—something recognized by a few producers in Simonsberg-Paarl, who have chosen to belong to the Vignerons de Franschhoek marketing group and pretend, with different degrees of assiduity, that they belong there. Their own success as wineries, and that of wineries alongside them and elsewhere in Paarl, like Veenwouden and Glen Carlou and longer-established ones like Backsberg and Fairview, should suffice, however, to indicate that it might be much preferable for many reasons to instead build the reputation of this historic area.

WELLINGTON

Chenin is the predominant variety in Wellington, which is a long-established appellation, though only recently made a district rather than a ward—which means that it could include subdivisions in the future, which might well be a good thing, considering the variability of conditions. The area was originally known as Limiet Valley (border or frontier valley), and then as Val du Charron or Wagenmakersvallei ("valley of the wagonmaker"). The town at the southern end of the area was formally established in 1840, when the name was changed to Wellington in honor of the victor of Waterloo, depriving us of a beautiful historic name for the area. There are some vineyards on the fertile alluvial terraces to the west of the town, but most wineries are to the east, in the many little valleys and on the foothill slopes of the mighty Hawequa Mountain and the slightly less imposing Groenberg. The area is generally hot (with an average summer daytime temperature over 24°C), although there is a good deal of variation even in this factor, as some vineyards on the slopes are exposed to cooling winds, or to moist air flowing down from the peaks, while aspect obviously affects the number of sunshine hours. The winter coldness of some parts (the mountains are snow-covered) ensures a good dormancy, a benefit not always conferred on Cape vines. Lower levels are shale-based, with sandstone and granite on the slopes. Rainfall throughout the area is low to moderate, and irrigation is generally the rule.

Site is very important in Wellington. It is worth remembering that one of the best-reputed modern South African wines, Boekenhoutskloof Syrah, comes from a vineyard here (though this origin is not acknowledged on the label). Much Wellington wine, however, is typical warm-country stuff, of varying quality. Two cooperative cellars on the edge of the town take in grapes from a total of some 3,000 hectares: Wellington Cooperative and the perhaps more ambitious Wamakersvallei Winery (established in 1941 but turned into a company early in this century), which markets its wines under names less challenging to supermarket buyers in Britain, including the top La Cave range, smartly and expensively packaged. Some small, independent wineries have sprung up here since 2000, many of them producing interesting wines. As mentioned, Chenin, with nearly a thousand hectares, is the main grape, but it's followed by the usual cluster of noble black grapes; and, as in the warm Paarl district, Sauvignon Blanc is, very sensibly, less planted than Chardonnay (311 hectares). Wellington is also the premier site for vine nurseries in the Cape, producing more than 90 percent of the vines for the local market.

THE WINERIES

AVONDALE

The approach to organic viticulture at Avondale has always been somewhat eclectic, which is evidence of the deep sincerity with which it is undertaken rather than anything else. All of the 100-odd hectares of vines (with a wide range of varieties) are now officially certified as organic, and it is all, in fact, farmed largely according to biodynamic principles these days. And when owner and viticulturist Johnathan Grieve explains it all, much of his approach seems compellingly logical—why, you can even eat the ducks that have munched their snail-eating way up and down the rows. The latter is my own frivolous observation, but Grieve is convincing about the benefits to the vineyards and the whole ecology of his type of organic farming, taking lessons from biodynamics that he finds useful, and also having recourse to science and technology if they too can help him understand his soils and respond to their strengths—and comprehend and correct their deficiencies through natural processes.

Grieve is part of the family (founders of a large health-foods business) that has owned Avondale since 1977. The farm is at the foot of the Klein Drakenstein Mountains and climbs the lower slopes, though the higher parts, as well as carefully planned "islands," are mostly given over to natural vegetation. It dates back more than three hundred years, and seems to have been the first in the area to be allocated specifically for wine production.

The naturalness of the viticulture is complemented by Corné Marais's straightforward approach in the fine underground cellar, with a minimum of intervention: spontaneous fermentation and avoidance of additives are the rule, for example, and the use of new wood is blissfully minimal; even in the top reds no more than 40 percent of the oak is first-fill. The spontaneous fermentation perhaps helps to account for a pleasing, fresh, mineral-earthy quality that is discernible in many of the wines. Alcohol levels are generally low, which Grieve believes is ascribable to organic farming, but certainly also reflects a policy of comparatively early picking—a practice that has sometimes led to herbaceousness in some of the reds. Overall, there is no doubt about Avondale's dedication to both responsible and terroir-driven viticulture and to producing serious wine from this slice of Paarl.

www.avondalewine.co.za

BACKSBERG

"We've had only three winemakers in twenty-five years," says young Simon Back, son of owner Michael Back and in charge of much of the marketing. True, I respond (defending the implications of my remark about the difficulty of characterizing most Cape producers in light of the changes so many of them have been undergoing), but two of those winemakers arrived and two left within the space of a few years. Since then, another has left but the previous one has returned! Backsberg is, in fact, one of the more mature of twentieth-century wineries in South Africa. In 1916, as Klein Babylonstoren, the farm was bought by Charles Back, a Lithuanian immigrant. His son Sydney was one of the proponents of estate wines in later years, and bottled his first wines under his own label in 1970; the winery took on its present name as an estate in 1973. From then and through the 1980s Backsberg built a reputation for decent quality and good value. The quality side was faltering in the 1990s, however, as Backsberg got overtaken and also rather lost its way. But a substantial cleanup of the cellar, and the arrival of Alicia Rechner in 2001, started putting things on a more modern and acceptable track. She left for Australia and was replaced by Guillaume Nel, who, to the satisfaction of many, seemed intent on using less oak and less extraction than his predecessor; he also tried to get lower alcohol levels from improved viticulture rather than tricks in the cellar. The range started undergoing some revision. Alicia Rechner returned to take up the position when Nel left in 2012, and it will be interesting to see if there are consequences.

This is a large family winery, with some 130 hectares under vines growing mostly in soils of decomposed granite on the low slopes of the Simonsberg. There is plenty of space for improved matching of variety to site, and this is increasingly happening. Matching the size, Backsberg has a number of ranges. The Family Reserves were reduced to two, which will be offered only in good vintages: the Red Blend of Bordeaux varieties plus Syrah, and a newish White Blend, mostly of Chardonnay and Roussanne. The Black Label and Premium ranges should continue to offer good value, some of them undoubtedly punching above their weight levels, including the venerable Klein Babylonstoren Cabernet-Merlot blend and John Martin Reserve Sauvignon Blanc, which was many years back one of the first ambitious local Sauvignons to be made, as it still is, with some wood influence. There is also a kosher range—although, as Simon wryly says, the farm's owners are insufficiently "good Jews" to be involved themselves, and a rabbi must come in to work under the winemaker's instruction until the wine is pasteurized; "The tanks are wrapped with a hazard tape warning, so that no one touches the wine without him." The country's first kosher Méthode Cap Classique appeared here in 2009.

Michael Back is passionately devoted to environmental issues, and in 2006 Backsberg became the country's first winery to achieve carbon neutrality through measuring its carbon emissions and taking measures to offset their impact. The concern is a continuing one and, in line with the quiet modesty of this property, both genuine and seldom trumpeted. There is every reason to believe that Backsberg will continue developing its regained reputation for good quality and good value.

www.backsberg.co.za

BOSCHENDAL

This large property has vineyards reaching across ward boundaries in Simonsberg-Paarl, Franschhoek, and Stellenbosch, but is officially located on the Paarl side, though it tends to be most associated with Franschhoek in the minds of visitors—and sometimes of its public-relations team. It does indeed share a French Huguenot past with Franschhoek. There is some dispute about when the land grant of the original Bossend-aal ("wooded valley") was made to Jean le Long: according to the publicists of the property it was in 1685, but historians seem more inclined to think it was three years later. Anyway, it was sold in 1715 to another Huguenot, Abraham de Villiers, who also acquired adjacent land belonging to Nicolas de Lanoy—both farms of some 51 hectares. The prosperous de Villiers family owned it for the next 160 years and built the manor house in 1812. The economic and viticultural problems of the late nineteenth century led to its sale, however, and very soon it was joined with numerous other farms in the area into Rhodes Fruit Farms, the fruit export–oriented project of Cecil John Rhodes. The culmination of big-business ownership came in 1969 when the mighty Anglo American Corporation became a majority shareholder (and eventually sole owner). The farm and the many historic buildings were restored, and from the 1970s wine production once more became the focus. The first wines bottled under the Boschendal label appeared with the 1976 vintage.

In 2003 Anglo American sold Boschendal (while retaining Vergelegen in Stellenbosch) to a consortium of international, local, and Black Economic Empowerment business interests. The huge property, including its many historic houses, would be developed with residential, retirement, and hotel establishments, as well as a number of smaller wine estates within it—though all are farmed as a single unit. In 2005 the Boschendal wine business—brand, winery, cellar, wine-tasting facilities, and more—was sold to the large wine group DGB. Not the vineyards, however; there are some 200 hectares of these, with a predictably wide range of soils and aspects, and a serious vineyard investment program was initiated by their owner. Boschendal produces 250,000 cases annually, a good proportion of which is exported, with DGB energetically building the brand and the premium image of its business. Boschendal is a prime tourist attraction, which does not do any harm to the image of its already successful brand.

The number of wines made is sizable. Unfortunately, they are all marketed as WO Coastal or Western Cape, rather than with more specific origins, which is too often one of the telltale signs of a large wine business in South Africa when marketing concentrates above all on brand building. They are grouped in five ranges based on price and ambition, and all tend to overdeliver in terms of quality. Sauvignon Blanc is perhaps the winery's strongest suit, though Syrah also performs well; there is one of each in the top Cecil John Reserve range, as well as in the other and larger top range, the Reserve Collection.

www.boschendalwines.com

DIEMERSFONTEIN

This Wellington farm has been in the Sonnenberg family since the early 1940s, when Max Sonnenberg (a member of the Jan Smuts government and founder of the upmarket local supermarket chain Woolworths) bought 183 hectares of land below the Hawequa mountains. Vines were first planted in the 1970s but until 2001, when current owners David and Sue Sonnenberg resolved to establish their own label, the fruit was delivered to the nearby Bovlei Co-op. They immediately made something of an impact with their Pinotages, which attracted both praise and controversy. It was during his tenure here that winemaker Bertus Fourie developed the "coffee Pinotage" style, with the clever use of yeasts and toasted oak staves. The wine remains immensely popular, even if sniffed at by most critics, and it has spawned an increasing number of copies in the Cape (and has spread like a mutating virus to other varieties, too). Other varieties in the 60 hectares of mostly red wine vineyard are Cabernets Sauvignon and Franc, Malbec, Merlot, Mourvèdre, Petit Verdot, and Syrah, with Chenin Blanc and Viognier representing the whites. Some grapes are also bought in from other Wellington vineyards.

There are two ranges of mostly varietal wines. The flagship Carpe Diem line is made from fruit grown in select vineyards. The wine receives a longer maceration period than the standard range, with mainly free-run juice being used, and a generous amount of new oak for maturation. Big, generous, and well-fruited, the wines are typical of warm and sunny Wellington, with the Chenin Blanc perhaps the standout.

There are also very satisfactory wines made here under the Thokozani label, a partnership between Diemersfontein and its employees started in 2006 (which also operates the conference and guest accommodation businesses on the farm).

www.diemersfontein.co.za

FAIRVIEW

This property on the southern slopes of Paarlberg, on which the cheesery is as economically important as the winery, is the headquarters of the thriving empire of Charles

Back, one of the great figures of Cape wine in the past forty-odd years. The farm was originally part of a larger property, which dates back formally to a grant in 1693, though vines had been planted here five years earlier. After the usual checkered history, in 1937 the farm, then uncharmingly called Bloemkoolfontein ("cauliflower fountain"), was bought by the present owner's grandfather, also Charles, a few decades after he had acquired Babylonstoren, now called Backsberg. The original homestead, dating to about 1722 and part of another subdivision, is now part of Fairview once more, well restored and home to the proprietor. The process of revitalizing the property was most thoroughly pushed by Charles's son Cyril, who inherited Fairview in 1955 (Babylonstoren went to the other son, Sydney). Cyril replaced the old Cinsaut vines with Cabernet Sauvignon and Syrah, together with Pinotage and, later, some Pinot Noir and Chenin Blanc. The wine went to the KWV until 1974, when the first 500 cases each of Cabernet Sauvignon, Syrah, and Pinotage appeared under the Fairview label, and were successfully sold at the Cape's first public wine auction—innovation and dynamism have long been apparent in the Back family.

Cyril's son Charles, trained at Elsenburg, joined the team as cellarmaster in 1978 and took over the property after Cyril's death in 1995; his skills and spirit of innovation as a winemaker (in 1985 he made the Cape's first Gamay Nouveau by carbonic maceration, for example) were accompanied by a capacity for business that has built Fairview into a most successful winery and cheesery. He continues to play a central role in the cellar, as in all facets of the immediate Fairview business—as well as doing the same in his Spice Route winery (dealt with in the Swartland chapter), along with the Goats Do Roam and other ranges. Anthony de Jager, here since 1996, is the hands-on force in the cellar at Fairview.

Undoubtedly Charles's spirit of innovation and experiment is responsible for the planting on Fairview of varieties that are still uncommon in the Cape—notably Tannat, Sangiovese, and Petite Sirah, in which last he is a great believer. In the 1990s he was one of the first to plant Viognier. He has also recently acquired neighboring land higher up the Paarlberg slopes, cooler and with more decomposed granite than the sandy loam of the lower sites, which is allowing him and his viticulturist, Thys Greeff, to drag the Fairview vineyards up the mountain, as it were, to their benefit. The home farm is mostly planted to red varieties, including Syrah, Pinotage, and Mourvèdre in addition to those already mentioned. The Fairview range also draws on other Paarl and Swartland vineyards (not only on Back-owned farms), as well as on Back's 80 hectares in the cooler Darling hills (planted to Sauvignon Blanc, Sémillon, Pinot Gris, Chenin Blanc, Riesling, and Nouvelle) and his 50 hectares on the slopes of the Helderberg in Stellenbosch (largely the red Bordeaux varieties).

It should also be mentioned that Back bought the failing Citrusdal Cooperative in the Olifants River region in 2007 and is working on improving the wines coming from the associated farmers. To meet his wine needs and ambitions he is collaborating with growers in nearby Piekenierskloof to establish Grenache, both Noir and Blanc. But, as has long been obvious, no area is immune to his enthusiasm or his fine eye for viticultural (as well as marketing) potential, and he has even been working with Cabernet Sauvignon and Syrah in the high, cool Upper Langkloof on the southern fringe of the Klein Karoo.

With Back's far reach and his substantial holdings, it is not surprising that the Fairview range is large and diverse, with wines coming from many parts. Not that everything goes into one vat—Back is far too respectful of the claims and delights of terroir for that. Many of the best Fairview wines are, in fact, from single vineyards, including a handful of Shirazes: the Beacon and Eenzaamheid from Paarl, and Jakkalsfontein from Swartland. Pegleg Carignan comes from an old Swartland vineyard, and Oom Pagel Sémillon from much younger vines in Darling. But one of the best of the wines is the Rhône-style red blend from Swartland grapes called Caldera, generous, rich, and powerful, deep and concentrated but not too showy or bold, with good structure and texture. Certainly it is the Swartland, rather than the home vineyards, that at present accounts for the majority of the best Fairview reds.

The general style of de Jager's wines is in line with what is tasted in Caldera: they are mostly ripe, sweet-fruited, a little alcoholic, but well made, showing a sensitive use of oak. It must be a question whether breadth (of vineyard ownership as well as of wine labels) does not lead to a loss of depth, or quality of focus, that could make more splendid wines off some of Back's great sites. But the average standard is undoubtedly good.

An important label in the Charles Back portfolio, particularly in the United States, where it has been one of the more successful South African wine brands, is the Goats Do Roam—whimsically and punningly named in homage and challenge to the Côtes du Rhône wines that are their inspiration. This range is now reduced to three blends (White, Red, and Rosé), while the single-varietal wines have been concentrated in a new range of cheerful, easy-drinking wines under the La Capra label—another reference to the goats of Fairview, of whom a lucky and characterfully decorative few occupy the goat tower near the much-thronged entrance to the visitor areas of the farm.

www.fairview.co.za

GLEN CARLOU

Glen Carlou was founded in 1985 by Walter Finlayson (with a group of investors), who already had something of a reputation as a good and innovative winemaker—he was still at Blaauwklippen at the time. It became an archetypal family winery, especially after son David joined and gradually started taking over the winemaking from the mid 1990s, allowing Walter to spend more time on his beloved herd of Ayrshire cattle. But an outsider bought in once more—this time in the form of Donald Hess of Napa's Hess Family Estates, who acquired a share in 1995, allowing for expansion of the cellar. A decade later the Swiss-based Hess Group took complete ownership.

David Finlayson remained cellarmaster until 2009, when he left to concentrate on his Edgebaston wines. He was succeeded by his longtime assistant Arco Laarman, and there has been little change in the style of the wine, which seemed by 2005 to have evolved in a notably "commercial" direction. Most of them had long been on the modern side of Cape wine—ripe, powerful, and oaky—but a greater degree of presumably calculated vulgarization crept in, most notably expressed through higher levels of residual sugar in the wines, and not just in the entry-level Tortoise Hill range. The standard Chardonnay, for example, one of the Cape's best examples in the 1990s, became less characterful and serious, with a particular California type as its model; it is scarcely dry, and this is obvious on the palate. The same sugar level (4.5 grams per liter) is found in the Cabernet Sauvignon introduced with the 2006 vintage, and the Pinot Noir is only a little less sweet. These are undoubtedly pleasant, smart wines, well made for a target market. The Syrah has been made in successful full-bore, sweet-fruited and powerful new-world style since the maiden 2000—the name change from Shiraz in 2003 did not mark any change in orientation in this regard. The wine now has touches of Mourvèdre and Viognier adding perfume to a good deal of fruit flavor and the sweet blandishments of its American oak component. More to my own taste is the Grand Classique, a more classically styled Bordeaux blend—though still with the 14.5 percent alcohol that is common to the wines. An expensive new range includes the Gravel Quarry Cabernet Sauvignon, named for the vineyard's gravel soils and the old quarry site where the winery now stands. It's a rather grand and superior version of the variety, still modern and powerful, but pretty dry and fully furnished with French oak. Quartz Stone Chardonnay is also from a mature, registered single vineyard, and takes off where the older standard Chardonnay left off; the new oak shows, and the wine is certainly rich, but the fruit is refined and citrusy, threaded with excellent acidity, and there's a good development potential over five to ten years; it usually stands out as the best Glen Carlou wine.

www.glencarlou.co.za

JOOSTENBERG

Most visitors buying Joostenberg wines at the modern Klein Joostenberg Deli & Bistro, just off the N1 motorway on the way to Paarl, are unaware that, although the brand has been on the market only this century, there is much history tied to the Joostenberg name and the Myburgh family. Their home, a 250-year-old (and more) manor house nearby, has been in the family since 1879. Wine and brandy had been made on the farm since the early 1800s but ceased in 1947; until 2000 the crop was delivered to the local co-op. After a couple of trial vintages with bought-in grapes, the Myburghs—patriarch Philip and his sons Philip Jr. and Tyrrel, who now own the property—launched the modern-day Joostenberg label with the 2000 vintage. Philip the younger was at that stage an advocate, Tyrrel a philosophy graduate. Philip then completed his master's degree in wine technology and marketing in Australia, while Tyrrel worked harvests both locally and in France and California—it is he who is now in charge of both cellar and vineyards here.

Joostenberg's 31 hectares of vineyard grow on duplex soils; the subsoil is heavy clay with topsoils varying from graveled or rocky weathered soils of granitic origin to ones of lighter texture. They support Cabernet, Merlot, Mourvèdre, Syrah, Touriga Nacional, Chenin Blanc, and Viognier, the aim being to produce a small range headed by the oaked Chenin-based white blend called Fairhead, and the mostly Cabernet-Merlot blend called

Bakermat (which means, in Afrikaans, "birthplace" or "cradle"). The whites are rich, and the reds ripe and big but not blockbusterish—the culinary orientation here means that they must be able to accompany food. But perhaps the best of the wines is the Chenin Blanc Noble Late Harvest—bunch-pressed, fermented with native yeasts, and matured in partly new oak.

Tyrrel Myburgh is winemaker not only for Joostenberg, but also for MAN Vintners, a useful négociant partnership between the Myburgh brothers and José Conde of Stark-Condé in Stellenbosch (the name of the wine business comes from the initials of their wives' first names). For the large range of wines they source grapes from a number of farms, mostly in the Voor-Paardeberg area, mostly unirrigated, low-yielding vines whose juice tends (or tended) to go into the enormous tanks of the co-ops and big merchants. A new, higher-level range under the Tormentoso label (named for the Cabo Tormentoso, "cape of storms," spoken of by early Portuguese navigators around the Cape) was introduced in 2011, with wines from the best of those vineyards, and has received a measure of acclaim.

www.joostenberg.co.za
www.manvintners.co.za

KWV

For much of the twentieth century, the history of the KWV was so central to the history of Cape wine that it has been discussed in earlier chapters. Its history in the past few decades, since it gave up its statutory powers and developed into simply a huge privately owned wine and spirits business, is, I fear, rather too complex—and controversial, especially in relation to the arrangements reached with the government about its conversion to a company—for a mere wine journalist to understand. An outline giving some salient features must suffice.

By 1992, when the KWV announced the lifting of the thirty-five-year-old quota system, membership had long ceased to be compulsory—though virtually all wine-grape farmers and wine producers remained members, regardless of whether they ever delivered grapes or wine of any kind to the production facilities in Paarl. As discussed briefly in chapter 2, in 1997 the once all-powerful ruler of South African wine converted (via prolonged negotiations) from a cooperative to a company. As Michael Fridjhon has put it, suddenly KWV "was no longer a national treasure, just a hustler like everyone else"—despite remaining, of course, one of the largest wine and brandy companies in the country. Early restrictions on share trading were lifted in 2003, at which point shares became available to the general public. In September 2009, ninety years after the birth of the KWV, KWV Ltd was split, unbundling its holdings in Distell (which dated back to the 1970s) to an investment company to be named Capevin, while the remainder became KWV Holdings. Shareholders are dominated by investment companies, the KWV Employees Trust, Vinpro (the service organization that had taken over many functions of the old KWV), and the consortium of black companies and organizations called Phetogo.

Until the modern era, most South Africans saw little of KWV's wines apart from the fortified wines and brandies, which were the only KWV brands allowed to be sold on the local market—apart from, somewhat controversially, those of Laborie, an old French Huguenot farm just outside the town of Paarl, which KWV had bought in 1972 and maintained as an independent estate with its own label. Now most of the KWV ranges are available locally and must battle to find a market, although the international market remains central to commercial success. The wine brands include (apart from Laborie) Pearly Bay, Roodeberg, Golden Kaan (formerly jointly owned with a German partner), KWV Wines, Cathedral Cellar, and Mentors.

It must be said that on the whole, the KWV's wines have not impressed much, until recently, at any level (apart from the Cathedral Cellar range, perhaps). There are a lot of them, of course, and my own experience of them is far from wide or deep, but this seems to be a common assessment. The nadir of the company's wine reputation came in a scandal in 2004 when two of its senior winemakers were found to have illegally adulterated Sauvignon Blanc with a flavorant. Charges were never laid against the winemakers, who were sacked and found new jobs almost immediately—and I should mention, as a kind of declaration of interest insofar as discussing KWV is concerned, that I was served with a lawsuit by KWV's then chief winemaker, Sterik de Wet, for remarks that I subsequently made about the matter, although the KWV later dropped the case. It was no doubt partly the rude shock of this scandal that revealed to the KWV that something more was needed than arrogance and the sort of wine culture that somehow allowed the idea of "improving" wine via illegal means, and in 2005 the company appointed a wine committee, or panel of mentors, under the eminent Neil Ellis and including the equally eminent Charles Back, while a senior Australian winemaker from Southcorp was contracted to serve as an adviser. Possibly of even greater significance, in late 2008 KWV's then newish CEO, Thys Loubser (who had already purged the company of most of the management appointed in the bad old pre-1994 days), set out to find a new chief winemaker to oversee the reestablished production teams in the various cellars. The job went to an Australian (an Aussie in charge of KWV winemaking—what outrage that would surely have caused in old South Africa!), Richard Rowe, who came from Evans & Tate. No doubt the hope was that Rowe would preside over the same growth in wine quality and reputation that Distell saw under its own Australian winemaking boss, Linley Schultz; in fact, there has already been improvement. (But Loubser lasted as CEO only until mid 2011, when he was ousted, presumably at the behest of investment company HCI, which had acquired a majority stake in KWV a few months earlier. At the end of 2012, HCI director André van der Veen was still acting CEO.)

The KWV's elegant headquarters in Paarl, La Concorde, has 22 hectares of production facilities behind it, overhauled and expanded into a number of different wineries under one conceptual roof around the turn of the century. Apart from the usually excellent Muscadels and moderate port-style wines, there are various ranges appearing under the straight KWV label. At the head is the Abraham Perold Shiraz, a big, bold Barossa-style example from a Paarl vineyard—oaky, opulent, and good of its type. Wines in the Reserve, Mentors, and Lifestyle ranges, widely sourced, seem not to be consistently of this style, with some tending almost to lean classicism while others aim for sweet richness.

In fact, the Mentors range started showing signs of real improvement (and expansion) by 2012. The wines, widely sourced, are modern and expertly made—mostly in a rather lush, "commercial" style. Whites outnumber reds, and are generally more interesting— particularly the fine Grenache Blanc.

Laborie Cellar makes a range of mostly varietal wines from its 39 hectares of vineyards on the southern slopes of Paarlberg, just outside the town—some 40,000 cases of red, white, and sparkling, along with the interesting Pineau de Laborie, a Pinotage fortified with pot-still brandy also made from Pinotage.

Back at the Paarl cellar complex is the splendid Cathedral Cellar, which gives its name to the flagship KWV range. Officially opened in 1930 and restored in 2005, it has a barrel-vaulted roof, stained-glass windows, and a granite and wood-inlay floor, with carved wooden vats lining the sides. The wines, from widely sourced grapes, do not quite match this fine grandeur but are very good, tending toward a polished, recognizably new-world style: ripe and rich, dense and extracted, with obvious fruit and generally obvious oak, but well if softly structured. There are single-varietal wines made from Cabernet Sauvignon, Pinotage, Syrah, Chardonnay, and Sauvignon Blanc, and a Cabernet-based blend called Triptych, although this sometimes contains more than the three varieties the name suggests, with Syrah as well as the usual Bordeaux partners.

The KWV has rekindled its ambitions, and done something about setting a route to achieving them, with every sign that the company is aware of the imperatives of quality; it will be most interesting to see if the top ranges continue to improve.

www.cathedralcellarwines

www.kwv.co.za, www.kwv-wines.com

MONT DU TOIT

Mont du Toit (pronounced in the French manner) was established in 1996 by Stephan du Toit (pronounced Toy, in the Afrikaans manner). The du Toits, of Huguenot descent, have a tradition of wine farming in the Cape for more than three hundred years—though Stephan himself is a lawyer, based in Johannesburg. The original du Toit established a (different) farm near Wellington in 1691 and introduced the first vines in the area. The 28 hectares of vineyard lie close to Du Toit's Kloof Pass, at the foot of the Hawequa Mountain (Hawequa is a Khoi word meaning "place of the murderers," referring to the San Bushmen who would raid the pastoral Khoi in the valley before retreating to the mountain).

Mont du Toit is a red-only property; plantings include the Bordeaux varieties as well as Syrah, Mourvèdre, Tinta Barroca, and, unusually, the teinturier Alicante Bouschet. These are planted on weathered granite and Clovelly Hutton soils, the sloping aspects facing a sunny and warm north and northwest. The cellar is also built into a slope, enabling the whole vinification process to be carried out by gravity.

Two of Germany's best-known winemakers originally consulted here in Wellington's very ungermanic conditions: Bernhard Breuer (until his untimely death in 2004) and Bernd Philippi. After some turnover, the local team has been headed since 2011 by consultant Loftie Ellis and winemaker Marinus Bredell. The flagship blend is the Mont du Toit, usually from Bordeaux grapes, Syrah, and Alicante. Le Sommet is produced only in exceptional vintages, and the blend is never announced. In 2010, varietal Cabernet Sauvignon, Syrah, and Merlot revivified the extremely good value range called Les Coteaux, along with an excellent Cabernet-based blend, Sélection.

True to their warm inland origin, the Mont du Toit wines are generous in size, though alcohols are well balanced by concentrated fruit and carefully judged tannins; oaking is appropriate to the aging potential for which the major wines are designed. Since the maiden vintage, they have gained in structure and balance; they are ripe but not jammy and the blends are agreeably homogeneous. They are polished and sophisticated, if not notably elegant or complex.

In 2003 Stephan du Toit started Blouvlei, an empowerment initiative, with his employees as shareholders. The easy-drinking wines are sourced and made at Mont du Toit.
www.montdutoit.co.za

NEDERBURG

As the biggest brand of the mighty Distell, this is a name that is among the most important in South African wine purely in volume terms, with well over a million cases produced annually, at all price and quality levels. It is, too, a name that resonates with history and even evokes a glorious past: those who are lucky enough now to drink one of the fine old bottles of auction Cabernet that remain (the 1974 a particularly famous and still eminently drinkable vintage) will understand why this was, in the years before the estates became most prominent as producers of fine wine, one of the most prestigious names in Cape wine. Fortunately, recent years have seen the label regaining much of the reputation it had lost as it churned out large volumes of mostly lackluster stuff: now, at all those price and quality levels, Nederburg is again a force to be reckoned with.

The land of the original Nederburg estate in Paarl was allocated in 1792—fairly late for this area—to a German immigrant, Philippus Wolvaart, and named for Commissioner-General Sebastiaan Cornelis Nederburgh, who was in the Cape at the time carrying out one of the Dutch East India Company's occasional investigations into the conduct of its servants here. Wolvaart supervised the building in 1800 of the fine Cape Dutch homestead that is now a central focus for the modern Nederburg, including providing the setting for its famous annual auction. Germans were to continue to play an important role in the property's development, and the next moment that wine history bothers to note was the acquisition of the farm, with its 93 hectares of ill-tended vineyards, by another German immigrant, Johann Graue, in 1937. He and his son Arnold were responsible for a good deal of important innovation in the years of expansion after the end of World War II, particularly in relation to the development of cooled fermentation of white wines. Success was inaugurated, but Arnold was killed in an airplane accident in 1953, which seems to have broken his father, who died in 1959, three years after merging his company with Monis of Paarl.

Advances in technology, meticulous viticulture, and an expansion of the program for blending grapes from diverse areas were refined under Arnold Graue's successor in 1956 as cellarmaster at Nederburg, Günter Brözel—the next force in the vital German influence at the company—who was to remain until 1989.

In 1966, as part of Monis, Nederburg became part of Stellenbosch Farmers' Winery, and its role in South African wine continued to expand. Complications around the Wine of Origin legislation introduced in the early 1970s meant, however, that Nederburg's name could not be attached as the name of an estate even to wines coming solely from the home property; for a few years (after which other complications supervened) those wines were sold under the Johann Graue Estate label. In fact, there were only six wines, five whites and one red. But Nederburg was now firmly established as a prestigious brand name for an ever-growing range of wines.

The prestige was only increased by the inauguration of the Nederburg Auction in 1975 to sell such wines as the groundbreaking dessert wine Edelkeur. The auction rapidly developed into a vital source for some of the finest Cape wines—not only the range of special bottlings produced by Nederburg and available to the trade only at this event—as well as a major social occasion. With the rise in the number and quality of fine wines generally available, and with less of a premium on matured wines, the Nederburg Auction was visibly losing luster some years into this century. The auction of the Cape Winemakers Guild (open to all, not just licensees) started overtaking it in all respects except sheer volume: average bottle price, total revenue, prestige. Since Nederburg's auction was an expensive exercise, where the public-relations clout was a vital component, clearly something needed to be done, but it was not clear what.

The reputation of the Nederburg brand, though, was rising as the significance of the auction was waning. As with some other parts of the Distell behemoth (notably Fleur du Cap), the rejuvenation of a somewhat tired brand was inaugurated around the turn of the century. The public face of the change was that of the new cellarmaster, the charismatic and notably self-confident Romanian Razvan Macici, who arrived in time to lead his winemaking team for the 2001 harvest. An expensive revamping of the cellar (allowing, for example, for microvinification when desired and involving large-scale automation) was a part of the transformation, as was a reexamination of the sources of grapes, with less focus on the Paarl home vineyards. The last vintage of the great old stalwart Paarl Cabernet was the 1999; thereafter it was, in common with most of the wines, declared to be Wine of Origin Western Cape—the Distell marketing machine does not pay much attention to the claims of terroir.

In fact, origin and terroir are not in focus at Nederburg, where style, varietal expression, and "quality in the bottle" are what count most—as they do for most consumers, of course. This might change, however, as ambitions to produce wines at the highest level mature. Ranges have been carefully stratified and elaborated. The dozen-odd Private Bin varietal wines made for sale at the Nederburg Auction are mostly very sound, though the reds tend, in my opinion, to be somewhat overoaked and showy. They are, in fact, big, ripe wines, more than competently made in a somewhat international style, though with a sterner structure than that much-invoked category always allows for. That assessment sounds more ungenerous than intended: indeed, they are very good wines—but just lack a little character. Reds and whites in the Private Bin range are equally good, with the Shiraz and the two Sauvignon Blancs perhaps the standouts—apart, that is, from the Noble Late Harvest dessert wines, all unoaked and invariably including the venerable Edelkeur, still made from Paarl Chenin Blanc; the Muscatty Eminence; and an occasional Sémillon, which can be brilliant.

But in fact the auction wines are no longer at the summit of Nederburg. Macici saw in—it seems to have been his pet project—a pair of blends: Ingenuity Red, a fine mix of Sangiovese with Barbera and Nebbiolo (not the sort of thing that could easily happen in Italy), and Ingenuity White, which crams eight separately vinified varieties into the charming but totally unbinnable skittle-shaped bottle that marketers perversely decided was suitable for Nederburg's most lay-downable wines. These two can often stand among the Cape's best; the first vintage of the Red was impossibly and pretentiously overoaked, but this fault was corrected with the second. The silkily elegant White is put together with particular beauty and subtlety, and represents a signal and original contribution to this important category of Cape wine. Yet another top-level label—II Centuries—came a little later, with a first-class Cabernet Sauvignon, from an excellent vineyard on the Paarl slopes of the Simonsberg, and a good but hardly revelatory Sauvignon Blanc.

Also of comparatively recent date, and also fairly expensive, is the Manor House range, very good varietal wines rather fresher, less obviously grand, more easygoing than the Private Bin wines. And at the risk of confusing (but if Nederburg is willing to do it, so must I), the Heritage Heroes range can also be mentioned. It was launched in 2010, with little clear purpose except to use some names referring to important people in Nederburg's past—or, at least, to aspects of them that allow for supposedly catchy names and appropriate images (the Motorcycle Marvel, the Young Airhawk, etc.). These wines vary from adequate to less so.

There are something like a dozen wines in the Winemaster's Reserve range, produced in very much larger quantities than the pricier wines. Good old Edelrood, which seemed the height of luxury in the mid 1970s, is now a Cabernet Sauvignon–Merlot blend of good quality and a safe bet for anyone seeking a safe, fairly serious red at reasonable price in a restaurant or at a supermarket. The Shiraz—a variety that seems to do particularly well in the Nederburg cellars—is perhaps the best of the reds, though all of them, and the whites, are good. Again an outstanding wine is the Noble Late Harvest (called simply that), generally one of the Cape's best examples, at a bargain price.

The biggest volumes of Nederburg are in the Foundation range: sound, decent wines generally overdelivering at their price point. These last two ranges are now apparently made according to a recipe calling for a little more residual sugar (the addition of unfermented juice would be the usual way) than used to be the case. This bid to make the wines that bit sweeter, softer, and richer is something that one is rather sorry to see. Nonetheless, it is a great advantage to wine drinkers to have a ubiquitous label that can be so thoroughly relied on as perhaps never before, while the top wines can stand alongside the Cape's best.

www.nederburg.co.za

PLAISIR DE MERLE

Huguenot Charles Marais was granted this land in 1693, but it was his grandson Jacob who was responsible for developing it into one of the finest estates of the region and building the lovely manor house in 1764. Two centuries later, after some other ownership changes, the property came into the hands of Stellenbosch Farmers' Winery (now part of Distell) as something of a showpiece farm, and its vineyards on the southeastern slopes of the Simonsberg were planted to meet the needs of Nederburg. But three hundred years from the date of the original land grant, Plaisir de Merle was granted independence within the large corporation, and its own cellar was built: it was described by John Platter at the time of its grand launch as merging "grand proportions and great practicality with history, whimsy and a touch of fantasy—there's a moat, suggestions of Beau Geste about the fort-like façade, gargoyles and carved friezes."

Plaisir de Merle's own identity (well, with a remarkably Venetian-looking winged lion) was stamped on a handsome range of bottles, and Niel Bester was appointed as winemaker—a position he continues to fill to this day—and he is still able to draw on the advice of Château Margaux's Paul Pontallier, who has been an adviser since those early years. He and viticulturist Hannes van Rensburg have approximately 400 hectares of vineyards from various areas to make their selection from, and the volumes are comparatively high for ultrapremium Cape wine: a total of some 40,000 cases annually.

In 1993 the Cabernet Sauvignon and Merlot were welcomed as early examples of a trend toward ripe, rich, and amenable reds with gentle tannins (no press juice used) that allowed for pleasurable early drinking. The range has grown. There have been a Chardonnay and a Sauvignon Blanc from the outset, but while they are very acceptable they have never attracted the attention that the reds have. The Cabernet label—the biggest-seller of all—has been a trifle downgraded, as most of the reds are now, by the presence of somewhat drying tannins from an oaking regime that has become assertive; but it is still smooth and ripe and not particularly concentrated. The flagship Grand Plaisir, a blend of the five main Bordeaux reds, usually plus Syrah, shows new wood aromas, but copes better in terms of structure with the oak, though the tannins are drying here, too. This is a big, bold wine, as are the Shiraz and Merlot, albeit also fairly serious. Perhaps the most successful in the range is the varietal Cabernet Franc, usually with less oaking and lower alcohol, so it shows some graceful elegance—too rare in this range.

www.plaisirdemerle.co.za

RIDGEBACK

This winery behind Paarl mountain, now with 35 hectares of vines, was acquired in 1997 by Jerry Parker, a retired farmer of tobacco in Zimbabwe and Malawi. His origins explain the new name, referring to the Rhodesian ridgeback breed of dog—a hat-carrying example of which appears as the winery logo. Fruit had previously been supplied to the local cooperative, but he began a wholesale replanting and modernization program and brought in consultant Cathy Marshall to make the wines—initially in rented space, until the cellar was built. The vines are Merlot, Cabernets Sauvignon and Franc, Syrah, Grenache, Mourvèdre, Viognier, and Sauvignon Blanc. The Shiraz has long been the flagship here, generally both elegant and rich, nicely dry and firmly structured, and modestly oaked. Renewed attention to the Bordeaux varieties produced a well-built, even slightly austere Cabernet Franc (quite powerful by this cellar's standards at 14 percent alcohol) and a Merlot-based blend called Journey. There are other wines in the range, as well as notably good value offerings under the Vansha label.

Marshall remained as consultant when viticulturist Toit Wessels also started working in the cellar, but she left about 2009. I suspect that the wines might already have started changing in character, with less influence from her classic orientation—and her knack for choosing picking dates—which made the Ridgeback wines under her aegis notable for their moderate alcohols (by the standards of this warm area, anyway) while not showing any greenness. It must be hoped that the graceful legacy of Cathy Marshall will, in fact, persist here, for the wines are very decent, if not spectacular.

www.ridgebackwines.co.za

RUPERT & ROTHSCHILD VIGNERONS

The French part of this luxurious-sounding partnership is the Château Clarke branch of the Rothschilds, the local part one of grander names in local wine (see Anthonij Rupert Wines) as well as in international capitalism; both were represented only by their initials in the first name of the winery: R&R. The original partners in 1997 were Baron Edmond de Rothschild and tycoon Anton Rupert, now both deceased; their heirs continue the relationship. Just three wines are made at Fredericksburg—a French Huguenot farm established in 1690—on the Paarl slopes of the Simonsberg, though the vineyard sources are spread across the Western Cape (and despite the public relations insistence that the farm is really in Franschhoek—deemed a sexier address). A good deal of the grapes from the large home farm find their way into other labels.

Despite the smartness of the names involved, and despite (some would say because of) the early involvement of the famous Michel Rolland as a consultant, the wines tended to fall just a little short of commensurate eminence, though the handsomely packaged and fairly handsomely priced Baron Edmond red has always had cachet in expensive Johannesburg restaurants. Until the 2005 vintage it was generally a bold, ripe, and richly extracted blend of predominantly Cabernet, with some Merlot, the showy oaking less in balance than the massive alcohol—usually at least 15 percent. But things grew more restrained, for the better, and the Baron is now much more elegant, and among the Cape elite of this style.

The "second" red, Classique, is also an ambitious wine, and privileges Merlot over Cabernet; it has always tended to be easier than the Baron, partly because less new oak is lavished on it. The quality is remarkable for a wine made in these volumes— approaching half a million bottles annually—and testimony to the skills of cellarmaster Schalk-Willem Joubert and of viticulturist Renier Theron. If offered a choice between the more expensive wine and Classique before the abovementioned change, I would have chosen the latter. Now I would reckon more on the grander wine, especially with a few years in the bottle. Baroness Nadine, from cooler-area grapes, is the sole white: a very pleasing, rather elegant Chardonnay with useful maturation potential; creamily rich, polished, and subtly oaked. This was, incidentally, the first winery in South Africa to be awarded ISO 14001 environmental management certification.

www.rupert-rothschildvignerons.com

SCALI

The farm on which this dynamic little Voor-Paardeberg winery is based is called Schoone Oord ("lovely place" in Dutch), and from its 70-odd hectares of vines it used to supply a good volume of grapes to the Boland Kelder cooperative. That link has now been broken by Willie and Tania de Waal (Willie is the fifth generation of his family to own the farm), and they now make a reasonable volume under the Scali label, while also supplying grapes to some high-quality producers outside the area—which gives them, they say, much more satisfaction than seeing them lost in the vast co-op mix: now they can at least see what happens to what they grow.

"Scali" derives from the initial sound of Schoone Oorde blended with the name of the dominant soil type of the area—*skalie* is the Afrikaans for "shale." The farm is at the foot of the Paardeberg, and the de Waals played a major role in getting the immediate area's distinctiveness officially recognized and the Voor-Paardeberg ward declared.

The cellar on the farm was built in 1912 (with, the de Waals happily point out, the "conglomerate rock which, when decomposed, forms the gravel in many of our vineyard sites"), and after long disuse was revived: the de Waals ripped out concrete fermentation tanks and replaced them with ten oak 2,500-liter open-top fermenters; air-conditioning also had to be installed, of course.

After some tiny winemaking experiments, in 1999 they made twenty barriques of Pinotage and by 2008 produced 20,000 cases of three wines. The Pinotage is an excellent example, with about 13 percent Syrah adding perfume to the typical notes of the grape; a big, fruit-sweet wine, with well-managed tannins—not exactly refined, but close. It can improve for well over a decade. The Syrah, now that the de Waals have overcome the beginners' temptation to lavish too much French oak on it, is a graceful though large wine (about 14.5 percent alcohol), revealing the dried herb aromas that often come through in the wines of the Paardeberg area. Working in the vineyard to try to bring down the alcohol levels is a priority here, especially now that the other great goal of organic accreditation has been achieved. In 2005 Scali Blanc was born, joining the growing ranks of Chenin-based blends from the area. This one adds in Chardonnay, Roussanne, Viognier, and Sauvignon Blanc, matured in older oak for a year. It is oxidatively made, with aromatic and flavor complexity and a rich texture, well cut by natural acidity.

www.scali.co.za

VEENWOUDEN

This 18-hectare property between the towns of Paarl and Wellington was bought by international opera singer Deon van der Walt in 1989; he believed its rich, ferrous clay subsoils resembled those in Pomerol, whose wines he loved. The name he chose, Veenwouden, recalls the Netherlands home of the first van der Walt to land at the Cape in 1727. Deon was the victim of a tragic family murder in 2006, and the extent to which the scandal prompted the currently somewhat diminished image of the wines is unclear. The farm and winery now belong to a family trust, and Marcel van der Walt, Deon's brother, continues to make the wine, as he did from a fairly early stage.

There are just 12.5 northeast-facing hectares planted with the Bordeaux red varieties as well as a little Chardonnay, running down a gentle slope to the river; but Syrah is brought in from Marcel's own Thornhill property nearer Wellington and for the red blend in the second-level Vivat Bacchus range.

The varieties are vinified and barrel-matured separately prior to the assemblage of Veenwouden's two best-known wines: Merlot and Classic, the latter a Bordeaux-style blend. The wines have always enjoyed some acclaim, but for many they were, in early years at least, rather too ripe, soft, and oaky, relying on added acid to achieve a simulacrum of freshness. They are now undoubtedly more refined, though still a touch less classic than their winemaker seems to believe, and good—the blend especially with some firm, well-padded tannic infrastructure.

www.veenwouden.com

VILAFONTÉ

The late Sydney Back of Backsberg introduced the well-known Californian husband-and-wife team of Phil Freese and Zelma Long to the Cape. Several further visits (including work as consultants) confirmed their belief in the possibility of making site-specific wines here, and they bought some land in Paarl in the mid 1990s—the name derives from one of the soil types (Vilafontes) on the property. Michael Back, present owner of Backsberg, was initially a partner, but now Warwick's Mike Ratcliffe is the local member of the partnership, handling marketing with his usual assertive aplomb. After some turnover, Martin Smith was appointed winemaker in 2010—Freese and Long jet in several times a year.

Viticulturist Freese believes that many South African vineyards are planted on soils with too high potential and liked their piece of land, close to the Berg River, for its low-fertility gravelly clay soils. "Low-capacity sites produce a smaller vine structure," he says, and he finds that their high-density planting (5,200 vines per hectare, where 2,400 is the norm) and careful viticulture make little remedial work such as topping, leaf removal, or excessive shoot positioning necessary. Supplementary irrigation is available.

Only Bordeaux black grapes are planted: Cabernet Sauvignon, Merlot, Cabernet Franc, and Malbec (Freese rates Petit Verdot as an unreliable performer in the Cape). Less than 20 of the available 42 hectares are under vine as yet.

The first Vilafonté vintage was 2003. Two wines are made in the simple, yet effective custom-designed cellar—at a little distance from the vineyards, on the outskirts of Stellenbosch town. There are sufficient stainless steel tanks to hold each block—the blocks being made up of different clones, rootstocks, and irrigation programs. Vinification is determined by the vintage, as is oaking—the amount of new and the length of maturation. This is altogether very careful, thoughtful winegrowing. The two stylistically different wines emerged from observation of what was produced by their sites: Series C has greater structure and power, and is based on Cabernet Sauvignon; Series M, with more Merlot, is usually more fruit-forward and accessible earlier. It's not difficult to find as much American as Cape orientation in the wines (and the United States was always intended as a significant market, of course); they are sophisticated, powerful, ripe, and pure. And big—but their power is contained in a finely managed, refined, and harmonious structure. (Vilafonté can be found on map 3 in chapter 6.)

www.vilafonte.com

VONDELING

This Voor-Paardeberg farm was granted in 1704 to Swedish immigrant Olof Bergh. The name means "foundling" (but why it was called that seems uncertain). Wine was made here until 1940, after which the grapes were delivered to the KWV and then the local co-op. It was bought early in this century by the London-based commodities and financial services business Armajaro, and the first wines under the farm's own name were bottled in 2005. A few years later the original landholding was reestablished with the purchase of neighboring Klein Vondeling, which had been split off some time in the past. There are 40 hectares of vineyards, including Sauvignon and Chenin blocks from the 1980s, but currently the plantings reflect a newer focus on Rhône varieties, with Carignan, Grenache (Rouge and Blanc), Mourvèdre, Syrah, and Viognier—as well as Muscat de Frontignan, Cabernet, Merlot, and Chardonnay. These are all under the loving care of director and farm manager Julian Johnsen, who is increasingly moving toward organic, or "biological," farming. Soils on the Paardeberg slopes are granite-derived, those on the valley floor alluvial. Vondeling is home to the Paardeberg Sustainability Initiative as well as the Paardeberg Fire Protection Association, both initiatives "focused on preserving the biological and economic welfare of all those on the Paardeberg."

Matthew Copeland has been in charge of the cellar since 2008. Thus far the Chenin-based white blends (notably the Babiana—named for a bit of local fynbos) and a

Muscat-led straw wine called Sweet Carolyn, are the most successful, but as the farm properly finds its feet the reds should also come into line. Erica Shiraz, with small additions of other varieties, looks the most promising; already it is a very decent, well-structured, intense but unflamboyant wine.

www.vondelingwines.co.za

WELBEDACHT

Although the winery bears the grander official name of Schalk Burger and Sons, Welbedacht is the name of the established farm that Schalk Burger bought in 1997, and also the name that appears on most of the labels (there's also a range of decent entry-level wines called Meerkat). Burger Sr. and one Burger Jr. have been eminent Springbok rugby players, something that does no harm to their marketing locally and is behind the name of their high-priced No. 6 (the number on the rugby jersey that both have worn). It's all very sporting, with cricket represented by a pitch outside the cellar and also providing inspiration for some labels.

The farm—which has an unpretentious, workmanlike air to it—is a large one: with something like 130 hectares of vineyards planted to nineteen grape varieties, it is one of the biggest producers of estate wines. Wines and grapes are also sold off, including grapes from a vineyard for long the source of one of the country's best-known Syrahs, from Boekenhoutskloof. Most of the Welbedacht soils, at the foot of the Groenberg and climbing its lower slopes, are of decomposed granite, which gives them some finesse, over clay, which assists water retention—although it generally requires a modest level of irrigation. Burger—who has a long history in the wine business and clearly something of a passion for viticulture (a battered copy of Richard Smart's *Sunlight into Wine* is always to hand)—is keen to stress another factor that he thinks important for his wines in this generally warm inland area: a notable variation in day-night temperatures.

In fact, the wines do not have a particularly "warm-country" presence. Burger has a taste for elegance, and the wines are not picked too ripe, with none of them exceeding 14 percent alcohol, in an area known for its big blockbusters. Some disagreement over style did seem to be the likely cause of the winemaker's exit in 2011. Oaking is restrained, with no new wood at all on the top Syrah-based reds and seldom more than 25 percent on any wine. The notably unshowy but efficient replacement cellar, built in time for the 2005 harvest, is equipped with cement fermentation tanks for the reds, as well as an array of stainless steel.

There are some interesting blends among the large range: the respectable Bordeaux-style Cricket Pitch blend is based on Merlot and has a smattering of Syrah, and the more lushly fruity Hat Trick is largely a Pinotage-Syrah combination. The No. 6 looks set to be, appropriately, a six-way blend based on Syrah with mostly Rhône varieties plus a touch of Petit Verdot, and from the maiden 2005 has been a well-structured and harmonious wine, unshowy but fairly concentrated, with supple and subtly firm tannins. Burger's stress is on red wines, but the farm has some good mature Chenin vines, from which a varietal wine is made; the same vines also contribute greatly to the ambitious and expensive Myra, an impressive, oxidatively made wine with Viognier giving half the fruit and inevitably a good deal of the character—although, in keeping with the restraint of this cellar, this is far from being an overblown, overly fragrant expression of the grape.

www.schalkburgerandsons.co.za

8

FRANSCHHOEK

BACKGROUND

The long story of human settlement in what we now know as the Franschhoek Valley is movingly told in the museum at the Solms-Delta wine estate, from the first inhabitants whose traces remain in stone tools, through the slaves who worked and died there and the European settlers, and the years of apartheid, to the hopes and the sometimes ambiguous freedom of the present. The museum is a fine way to help wine lovers penetrate, if they wish, behind the blandness of the cursory accounts generally on offer, where the brute reality of slavery is replaced by sentimental evasions or silence.

Not many years after the first establishment at Table Bay, exploratory expeditions penetrated to this valley, where they encountered both the Khoi hunter-gatherers and teeming wildlife (the area was initially called Olifantshoek because of the herds of elephants breeding there and passing through the valley). Khoi resistance in the district had been largely broken, however, and neither humans nor animals posed a significant threat to well-armed settlers; pioneer farms were established after 1687 along the banks of the Berg River and its tributaries. The Dutch East India Company's intention was, of course, that the farmers should produce meat and grain to meet pressing needs, not wine. The valley was named Drakenstein (Dragon Rock) by van der Stel, after a great estate in Holland.

There was land aplenty in the Cape, but European settlers were in shorter supply, and the company's willingness to assist the settlement of refugees from religious intolerance in France was welcomed by the governor. The prospect of freedom of worship at the foot

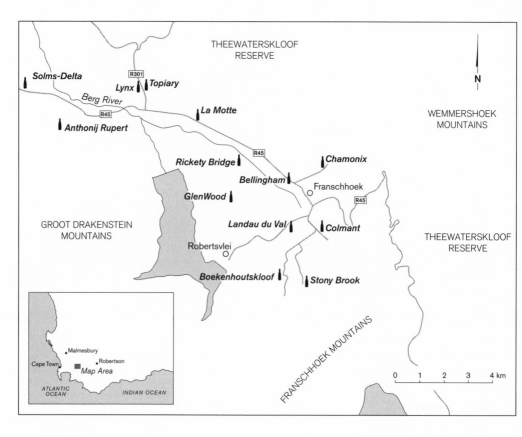

MAP 5
Franschhoek

of Africa does not appear to have excited refugees in Holland, but from 1688 to 1699 a few hundred did arrive in the main wave of immigration; they were allocated land and given some farming implements, weapons, and other necessities. They constituted about an eighth of the Cape's white population at the time.

Most of the Huguenots were settled in the Drakenstein Valley, interspersed among the Dutch. "The difficulties Commander van der Stel experienced in settling them and integrating them with the Dutch," notes Eric Bolsmann in his history of the French in South Africa, "were as numerous as the vicissitudes the Huguenots suffered during the process." But integration was achieved rapidly. The upper end of the valley, where a number of the Huguenots were settled, was initially known as Le Quartier Français, but within a generation the French language had largely given way to Dutch among the new settlers, and the name changed to Fransche Hoek. It was only in 1881, when the area became a municipality, that the village itself, previously Roubaix Dorp, changed its name to Franschhoek.

The cultural legacy of the French is found here mostly in the names of many farms poignantly recalling the regions or villages of France, which must have come to seem terribly distant to their displaced sons and daughters: La Bri, Grande Provence, La Motte,

La Bourgogne are just a few of the names that survive. The surnames of the people—du Toit, Marais, Malherbe, de Villiers, and so on, often now pronounced somewhat differently—are established in the population of South Africa. The modern winemakers of the valley play up the French connection splendidly if not entirely disingenuously: the dynamic wine producers organization is known as Les Vignerons de Franschhoek, and they participate in Bastille Day celebrations, which tourism publicists have revived. In fact, there is no evidence that more than one or two of the Huguenot settlers had any of the winemaking skills van der Stel had hoped for. Most had been cottage farmers or unskilled laborers, few with any significant connection to winemaking in their native country—although a third or so of them seem to have had occasional employment as vineyard laborers. This has not prevented a romantic legend building up around the Huguenots' contribution to winemaking, and vague claims in this regard are repeated in most brief histories of South African wine (sometimes accompanied by an equally vague assumption of the "certain cultural flair," some *je ne sais quoi,* that they—being French—must surely have brought with them). No specific winemaking contribution made by the Huguenots has been recorded, to my knowledge—the great tradition of Cape winemaking was being forged primarily in Constantia, by the Dutch. Nonetheless, the genuine French note that lives on in the names of the farms is a pleasant connection with the world's greatest wine country.

Viticulture thrived in the valley, and by the middle of the nineteenth century Franschhoek was a substantial contributor to the total production ascribed to Paarl—which was much more productive than the Stellenbosch area. But phylloxera's devastation at the end of that century prompted a substantial replanting with fruit trees. This was where Cecil John Rhodes brought together some thirty farms in a scheme to provide for the fruit export trade to Britain, and for a good part of the twentieth century Franschhoek was better known for its fruit than for its wine.

In fact, it is only as recently as the turn of this century that the area has started to regain some high reputation for wine, a reputation that postdated its claims as a "lifestyle choice" for the rich, many of whom bought properties here, including alleged mafioso Vito Palazzolo and his friend Count Agusta, and radical politician–turned–capitalist Tokyo Sexwale, who purchased a minor wine farm, which promptly disappeared from view and thus far has not returned. It used to be often sneered that the best wines coming from Franschhoek cellars were made from grapes grown elsewhere. There was an element of truth in that, although La Motte, L'Ormarins, Cabrière, and Chamonix made some fair wines during the 1990s. The problem—in the admitted context of an overall lackluster industry—was that too much of the vineyard was on the valley floor, which was not yielding fine-quality grapes. In the recent huge overhaul of L'Ormarins, the Rupert family showpiece, in the name of Anthonij Rupert Wines, an essential move has been to abandon the lower-level vineyards and effectively drag viticulture up the mountainside.

But now, well into the twenty-first century, Franschhoek is on a roll, as improved as any of the other traditional regions. The stimulus imparted by Boekenhoutskloof, which, ironically, made its first claim to eminence with Syrah made from grapes brought in from elsewhere, has been significant; Boekenhoutskloof's dynamic cellarmaster, Marc Kent, has been a vigorous promoter of Franschhoek and an influence on many of its winemakers, including Gottfried Mocke of Chamonix, which is another property showing the advantages of not only improved viticulture but of vineyards creeping up the lower mountain slopes of this magnificent valley.

Nowadays Franschhoek, including the inevitably spoiled village, is one of the most touristed parts of the wine lands, with visitors attracted by the combination of tangible history, many fine old buildings, the mountains, an array of good restaurants, and luxury guesthouses—as well as, one trusts, increasingly by the wine.

Franschhoek was a ward within the Paarl district until 2010, when, slightly enlarged, it was granted independence as a district. The valley, with the Berg River flowing through it and with high mountains enclosing it on three sides, offers a wide range of aspects and sites, ranging from the majority on the valley floor at an elevation of about 300 meters to some up to 600 meters above sea level, on variously facing slopes. Rainfall is reasonable, usually over 800 millimeters annually, but irrigation is generally necessary because of the sandy, mostly sandstone soils. The richer alluvial soils of the valley floor are generally less conducive to fine winemaking than the well-drained poorer soils on the slopes. Most of the vineyards are trellised and fairly youthful, though there are pockets of older bushvines—often Sémillon. One of the country's oldest producing vineyards, planted in 1903, is here, producing Landau du Val's fine Sémillon.

Owing to the range of soil depths and types and also the variousness of aspect, it is hardly surprising that there is no particular style of wine or type of grape associated with Franschhoek, though Sémillon can be seen as something of a signature variety—serious winemaking is anyway too young here for particular strengths to have emerged. Red and white wines are pretty equally made, and fashion obviously accounts for many of the recent plantings. Sauvignon Blanc is the most-planted variety, but with just a little more than 200 hectares, it is scarcely ahead of Cabernet Sauvignon, and Syrah is at 175 hectares, followed by Chardonnay, Merlot, and Sémillon. Most of these grapes produce at least one example of an outstanding Franschhoek wine, as does Pinot Noir at Chamonix.

There is notable attention to sparkling wines in Franschhoek, with the Cape's first winery exclusively producing bubbly (Haute Cabrière, now making a few other wines, while its sparkling wines are sadly no longer as noteworthy) and one of its most recent specialists (the excellent Colmant). Another newish winery, Topiary, surprised everyone— including itself—with a fine blanc de blancs in 2008. Though seriously made, it was originally intended as a vehicle for early-harvest fruit off a young vineyard, but acclaim for that and the subsequent vintage have made Topiary reconsider its strategy.

Among a number of other Franschhoek producers making wines worthy of note is GlenWood, particularly well known for the opulent Vigneron's Selection Chardonnay. Rickety Bridge makes a large range from its own 39 hectares and bought-in grapes. The flagship is an ambitious wine from Cabernet Sauvignon, called the Bridge, and the Paulina's Reserve prestige range includes another Cabernet, together with varietal wines from Sauvignon Blanc, Chenin, and Sémillon.

THE WINERIES

ANTHONIJ RUPERT

The home of this grand enterprise is L'Ormarins, a Huguenot-founded farm with a beautiful homestead whose neoclassical gable is dated 1811. It finds its place here less for its recent achievements than for the fact that it is a great bundle of potential. L'Ormarins was acquired by capitalist and wine dynast Anton Rupert in 1969 and passed to his son Anthonij, who was killed in a car accident in 2001. Anthonij's brother Johann took it over and inaugurated a major program of expansion. Rumors ran wild about what it was all costing; a magnificent new red wine cellar was built, and the white wine cellar was modernized. New, astutely chosen farms were added to the portfolio, notably a fine spread on the Kasteelberg in the southern Swartland (with white and red Rhône varieties plus old Chenin and Pinotage), a farm with some 160 hectares of established vineyards near Darling, and cool, high vineyards in the mountains near Villiersdorp (now, at the firm's urging, promulgated as the Elandskloof ward). At home in Franschhoek, the valley-floor vineyards were abandoned to horse paddocks, and viticulture was pulled up the granitic slopes of the Groot Drakenstein mountains. Viticulturist Rosa Kruger did a splendid job with establishing these major new plantings and with managing the existing ones during her period of employment here; she also, at Johann Rupert's behest, sought out fine old forgotten vineyards in other parts of the Cape as a source of interesting grapes—not only for themselves but to alert the country's wine producers to these largely unknown vineyards, in the hope that decent prices could be paid for their grapes and the vineyards would then stand a chance of survival. It seemed clever to invoke the help of the famous Bordelais consultant Michel Rolland at the estate, but the results must be deemed depressing, at least partly because the essential strategy seemed to be to pick ultraripe grapes and to use too much oak in vinifying them. Early vintages of the very expensive Anthonij Rupert range made little impact except to raise a number of eyebrows. Rolland has now pulled out of his international consultancies, and the policy of ultralate picking seems to have been abandoned here.

Apart from the flagships, there is also a range called Terra del Capo, featuring Italian varieties, and a larger entry-level range called Protea. Some individual vineyard sites of interest, including special blocks of old vines from up the West Coast, are marketed under the Cape of Good Hope label, and a few extremely good white wines have been made. With an extraordinarily rich owner committed to the highest ambitions (though not always finding the best advice on how to achieve them), with fine vineyards both old and new available, and new plantings coming into production as of 2009, the project should begin to fulfill potential—if the cellar can start to match the quality of the vineyards.

www.rupertwines.com

BELLINGHAM

Although the property is still there at the mouth of the Franschhoek Valley (and much expanded now, with a huge area devoted to natural vegetation), Bellingham is today known as a brand rather than the pioneering wine farm it once was. The original piece of land was granted to Gerritt Jansz van Vuuren in 1693 and expanded in the nineteenth century; but, like many other Franschhoek properties, it had become derelict when Bernard ("Pod") and Fredagh Podlashuk bought it in 1943. The Podlashuks rehabilitated the homestead and replanted the run-down vineyards. They also made regular visits to France where the untrained Pod learned more about winegrowing. It was the French dry white wines that appealed particularly to him; his optimistically named Premier Grand Cru gained many imitators over the next decades—one of several firsts that the Podlashuks introduced to South African wine-drinkers. Early bottlings included Riesling in 1950, Premier Grand Cru and (the first dry) Rosé in 1951, and Johannisberger (a semisweet white) in 1955. South Africa's first varietal Syrah came in 1957 and was for long a benchmark.

Union Wine took over the farm in 1970. Ownership changed again in 1990, when Graham Beck bought Union Wine. Beck fused his wine and spirits interests with Kersaf in 1991 to form Douglas Green Bellingham (DGB). A young Charles Hopkins (now at De Grendel) proved to be a fine winemaker. Eight years later, Beck sold DGB to company management, though he retained ownership of the Bellingham vineyards. Niël Groenewald took over the winemaking in 2004, and two years later Stephan Joubert became viticulturist.

Fruit for the four-thousand-ton crush is sourced from ten growers scattered around Stellenbosch, the West Coast, Paarl, and Franschhoek. The flagship Bernard Series range, from southern French varieties as well as local stalwarts Pinotage and Chenin, is named in honor of Bernard Podlashuk. The reds, Basket Press Syrah and Small Barrel SMV, are generally big, opulent, well-crafted wines, with plenty of new oak and tannin and about 15 percent alcohol. The Old Vine Chenin Blanc is in a similar blockbuster vein, new-barrel-fermented and a touch sweet, and usually impressive as such. The Viognier and Roussanne are similarly rich, and can be lovely.

www.bellinghamwines.com

BOEKENHOUTSKLOOF

The Afrikaans name means "Cape beech ravine"—*boekenhout* (pronounced "book-n-hote") trees are part of the indigenous vegetation here at the extreme southerly corner of the Franschhoek Valley. The farm is surrounded on three sides by towering mountains, up whose lower slopes the vineyards increasingly climb. It was bought in 1994 by Tim Rands, the dynamic founder of distribution company Vinimark, with a group of partners. There are now seven partners in the business, including the winemaker that Rands was characteristically astute enough to appoint when still young and largely untried, Marc Kent; they are represented on the Boekenhoutskloof label by seven different antique chairs (presumably made from Cape beech). A cellar was built, and a start made on new plantings of Cabernets Sauvignon and Franc, Merlot, Syrah, Sauvignon Blanc, and Sémillon. Today there are 22 hectares of vines, which achieved organic accreditation in 2010. But most of the wines under the Boekenhoutskloof label are from bought-in grapes, and the home vineyards account for only about 6 percent of the grapes needed for the various labels owned by this remarkably successful producer.

Boekenhoutkloof's maiden releases were a 1996 Cabernet Sauvignon and a 1997 Sémillon, together with a Sauvignon Blanc under the Porcupine Ridge label. But it was the release of the 1997 Syrah (from Stellenbosch grapes) that made it particularly clear that this was going to be a winery well worth watching. Unfortunately, the source vineyard was rapidly buried under an industrial park, and since then the Syrah has come from a vineyard on Welbedacht farm in Wellington. Made in open concrete fermenters and matured in barriques for about two years—with not a scrap of new oak—it is a wine whose substantial size (generally about 14.5 percent alcohol) is hidden within an elegance and focus that have given it an international reputation. Despite coming closer than most Cape wines to being "cultish," in terms of demand, it has remained inexpensive compared with any number of less well-reputed wanna-bes. Whether it is a finer wine than the Boekenhoutskloof Cabernet Sauvignon from Franschhoek grapes is debatable—I have found that the reliably excellent, densely rich but harmonious Cabernet (although it is arguably less distinctive, more international in style) seems to mature better, but we have insufficient track record as yet.

The Chocolate Block (sold without the standard Boekenhoutskloof label) is one of the winery's great successes, made in huge volumes and selling at an ultrapremium price, while gathering some critical acclaim. It is a Syrah-based blend, with other Rhône varieties and Cabernet, mostly from bought-in fruit. Again, it is matured in older oak, though for only a year to help retain the fruitiness. Another top wine that has its own distinctive label is the Journeyman, a first-rate Bordeaux-style blend. This is, in fact, the only one of the reds that is made entirely from grapes grown on the home farm.

Thus far, the only Boekenhoutskloof whites have been from Sémillon—the first a ripe, rich, and subtly oaked wine from Franschhoek grapes, with fine acidity and a good record of maturing in bottle. A more recent addition has been a Noble Late Harvest from the same variety (all home-grown grapes)—the only Boekenhoutskloof wine made in all-new oak, but coping splendidly with the responsibility; it is perhaps the most Sauternes-like of all the Cape's dessert wines, and among the best.

Remarkable as was the growth of Boekenhoutskloof's reputation in just a dozen years, to the point that it would be a serious contender for the highest position in any ranking of wineries on the basis of current performance, the breadth of its achievement and its sheer volume growth have been as impressive as the quality heights it has reached. Porcupine Ridge wines overdeliver at their price point, as do the (few as yet) wines in the later-established entry-level Wolftrap range. Considering that Boekenhoutskloof has done extremely little in the way of obvious marketing, including avoiding most competitions, the growth in reputation has been particularly noticeable. No doubt having the focused attention of a distributor like Vinimark has been significant, but much credit must go to

Marc Kent's leadership in and around the cellar. In 2009 Rudiger Gretschel, Kent's senior winemaker, moved to take overall charge of all Vinimark's wine-production interests—the company acquired Helderberg Wijnmakerij in Stellenbosch in 2009, and has financial stakes in the brands of Robertson Winery, the House of Krone, and Reyneke, as well as the fuller investment in the Swartland mentioned below. Kent, thus relieved of some outside responsibilities, returned to play a fuller role as cellarmaster at Boekenhoutskloof, assisted by a high-caliber team.

In 2009 Boekenhoutskloof bought a newish (and struggling) Swartland wine farm on the Porcelain Mountain (which will give its name in the Afrikaans form, Porseleinberg, to the label), and entrusted its winemaking and viticulture to Callie Louw, who will relish the farm's orientation to (certified) organic and (arguably certifiable!) biodynamic production. This will always be a small and independent winery, but of wider significance is that there are some 45 hectares of Syrah planted here, destined for Boekenhoutskloof Syrah.

www.boekenhoutskloof.co.za

COLMANT

Early this century Jean-Philippe and Isabelle Colmant, plus five children, made the leap from a stoneworking factory in Belgium to a Franschhoek smallholding. They planted vines and began sourcing grapes from elsewhere, intent on establishing a cellar solely dedicated to serious sparkling wines from the classic varieties. The winery was built in 2005. "According to our philosophy of hands-on quality, we designed a cellar that was both modern, small, and efficient, which allows us to control the whole production cycle," their Web site relates. And, as it continues, "probably the most important part of it is the bottle maturation room, with a storage capacity of over 100,000 bottles." The Colmants' dedication to quality is evidenced by the increasingly long time their wines are left on the lees before disgorgement—and by the wines themselves. What makes the Colmant wines even more unusual at the smarter end of sparkling wine is their lack of vintage date, which is brave in light of the general local prejudice in favor of vintaged wines. I would guess that soon there will be vintage Colmants too, but at present Jean-Philippe clearly finds it advantageous to blend in reserve wines from previous years—and quality overrides marketing advantage.

Already Colmant has established itself as among the leaders of South Africa's Méthode Cap Classique producers (they acknowledge the help of Pieter Ferreira of Graham Beck), and one feels that perhaps they have only just begun. Three wines are made, from Chardonnay off their own 3 hectares of vineyard as well as from elsewhere in Franschhoek, with a little from Robertson's lime-rich soils and Pinot Noir sourced in Robertson, Elgin, and Stellenbosch. The elegant, delicate Brut Reserve is usually of a near-equal blend of varieties. Sometimes even more impressive is the Brut Chardonnay, which includes some new oak-matured wine. These two wines have a classy, stony finesse that you won't find in, for example, the more commercial mass-produced (and much more expensive) wines of Champagne. There is also a good Brut Rosé.

www.colmant.co.za

CHAMONIX

The official name of the farm is Cape Chamonix, but Chamonix *tout court* is how it appears on the labels of the increasingly excellent wines produced here. The name is fairly new, but the property was originally part of La Cotte, the first farm granted to the Huguenot refugees in the valley, in 1688; it has been owned since 1991 (and was reestablished) by German businessman Chris Hellinger. Chamonix's 50 hectares of mostly unirrigated vineyards are on the eastern slopes above Franschhoek village, and their altitude is a good reason why Chamonix is the finest producer of a range of wines made only from Franschhoek grapes. Although Chamonix grapes are reputed to be the last harvested in the area, this relates to the vineyards' comparative coolness rather than to extreme ripeness: in fact, a classic approach is dominant, and alcohol levels are moderate.

Young Gottfried Mocke took over winemaking and viticulture in late 2001, and since then the reputation of Chamonix has grown steadily, to the point that it is certainly among the top few dozen wineries in the Cape. Mocke's serious involvement in the vineyards (which are increasingly going organic) is probably of even more importance in this quality growth than his sensitivity and technical expertise in the cellar. There, all of the most serious wines are made at least partially with spontaneous fermentation, and there is no acidification. The most convincing explanation (one that the winemaker insists on) for the improvement in the Chamonix reds, however, is the improved quality of the grapes coming into the cellar. There is a decent Bordeaux blend, Troika, and a rather good Pinotage made in a complex way involving a mix of early-picked and desiccated grapes, but it is the Pinot Noir Reserve that best marks the revolution here. Few Cape wines have improved so much in the space of a few years, with the real transformation beginning with the 2004 vintage. That and subsequent vintages stand well alongside the best of the Cape. A new high-altitude Pinot vineyard seems destined for a separate bottling.

Probably more eminent are the Sauvignon Blanc and Chardonnay Reserves (both also made in very good standard versions), but that has been the case for some time. Jancis Robinson was on a panel at an important local competition in 2007 that awarded a Museum Class trophy to a decade-old Chardonnay Reserve and asked afterward, "Where else [other than South Africa] outside Burgundy could field a 1997 in such great condition?"

The Sauvignon Blanc Reserve is wooded, made in a subtle mode, offering more than the usual winning, simple charm of a combination of ripeness and greenness: there is a restrained, elegant steeliness and earthy minerality too, and the oak maturation is beautifully calculated. A Reserve White was introduced with the 2011 vintage, and immediately found a place among the elite of Sauvignon-Sémillon. The very good Cap Classique sparkling wine made from Chardonnay should also be mentioned, and Chamonix also offers a good pair of "restaurant wines" that are much more than the dumbed-down stuff that constitutes so many second-label wines. All the Chamonix wines in fact, could probably count as good value, even the pricier ones.

www.chamonix.co.za

LA MOTTE

This farm was originally granted to German immigrant Hans Hattingh in 1695 and was used for grazing cattle, but it came into the hands of a French Huguenot in 1709. Pierre Joubert gave it a name recalling his Provençal birthplace, La Motte-d'Aigues, but it took another change of ownership before vines would be planted here, in 1752. Further ownership changes followed, until it was acquired in 1897 by Cecil John Rhodes and later became part of Rhodes Fruit Farms. In 1970 La Motte was bought by the immensely rich Rupert family, who restored the fine old buildings of the late eighteenth century. These buildings are all now national monuments, and the owner is well-known mezzo-soprano Hanneli Koegelenberg, daughter of Anton Rupert.

The first wine to be made under the La Motte label was, apparently, Château La Motte Cabernet Sauvignon—probably of the 1969 vintage, but this is uncertain. Major changes and replantings were undertaken and the property was reestablished as La Motte Estate in the mid 1980s. A modern cellar was built in 1985, when maiden crops of Cabernet Sauvignon, Pinot Noir, and Syrah were harvested; those first Estate reds were released in 1989. La Motte became the first Bergkelder estate to bottle its own wine—and even, by 1991, allowed tastings and sales on the farm, which was unusual at the time.

This is one of the larger properties in the Franschhoek Valley, with some 108 hectares of vineyards. Under viticulturist Pietie le Roux (who has been with La Motte since 1986), the farm has converted to organic production. The vineyards run from the fertile, alluvial soils close to the Berg River up the rocky, infertile south-facing slopes of the Wemmershoek Mountains. Grenache, Chardonnay, Sauvignon, and Viognier have joined the original plantings—and Pinot Noir has been removed, after a few vintages were offered to no great acclaim. La Motte also has a farm in the Bot River area, organically certified and planted to Sauvignon Blanc, Syrah, Cabernet, Petit Verdot, and Sémillon. But grapes are widely sourced for the wines, which helps account for La Motte's success.

La Motte has the money and the will to improve, and has embraced modern technology in the cause of growing the best possible fruit: GIS satellite scanning is used to monitor the effects of slopes, radiation, micro- and macroclimates, and soil classification, while infrared scanning pinpoints stress and irrigation requirements. On a micro-scale, the farm's weather station and temperature monitoring system determine humidity and temperature in the grape bunch zone.

With all this dynamism, the wines are indeed improving—not that they have ever been poor. Indeed, for much of the 1990s the Shiraz was generally at least as highly regarded as any in the country, and the Millennium was also among the leaders of local Bordeaux blends, a lightish, modestly elegant wine, as it still is. But with the rise of smart new properties and smart new styles, La Motte lost something of the prestige it had enjoyed.

Jacques Borman had been the highly regarded cellarmaster from the outset, and when he decided to leave for vineyards new he was succeeded by his assistant, Edmund Terblanche, who took over for the 2003 harvest. This (and a rebuilt cellar, which opened in 2008) probably helped allow for change. Now, in addition to the established Classic range—the Shiraz (a good, elegant wine), Millennium, Cabernet Sauvignon, Chardonnay, and Sauvignon Blanc—there is also the prestige Pierneef Collection. The Sauvignon Blanc (from the Bot River farm) is always impressive, and the Shiraz-Viognier is one of the more refined exercises in this genre, from cofermented grapes, generally including about 10 percent Viognier (the grapes are kept very cold and under a blanket of sulfur until the Syrah is ripe in its turn, and picked). A supple Shiraz-Grenache was later added to the range. Both of these reds are from widely sourced vineyards and generally, like most of the La Motte wines, are bottled at less than 14 percent alcohol.

www.la-motte.com

LANDAU DU VAL

In 1689 this piece of land in the Franschhoek Valley was granted to French Huguenot Jacques de Villiers, who named his new property after his home village, La Brie (near Champagne). More recently, land and vineyards were restored by Basil Landau, a retired businessman, and when the first wines were released in 1996 he put a new name on the labels to avoid confusion with a neighboring farm named La Bri (without the *e*). The farm has 15 hectares of vineyard, but is most notable for its old Sémillon vines: the bushvines, producing grapes for what is now the only wine Landau du Val makes, were planted in 1905. The wine has always been made offsite by different winemakers; it is now being made at Rickety Bridge. The character of the wine has remained pretty constant, however. Barrel-fermenting and -maturing, with a mix of older and new oak, adds silky opulence to the serenely complete and lovely Sémillon, offering citrus notes from lemon to tangerine, incipient waxiness, and subtle, elegant concentration.

LYNX

This is Franschhoek's smallest estate, with 11 hectares producing some 3,500 cases annually under its own label. The size of the wines themselves is some compensation, however! Somewhat unusually for the valley, the focus at Lynx is on red wines, with only Viognier planted (and bottled varietally) among the Cabernets Sauvignon and Franc, Merlot, Grenache, and Syrah. Owner and winemaker Dieter Sellmeyer (a former engineer) has enjoyed great success since 2002, his earliest vintage, with wines that are very ripe and sweet-fruited, with firmly plush tannins—certainly admirably crafted, even if not to my own taste. There are, remarkably, fourteen wines in the range, inevitably made in small quantities. Leading the pack is the Lynx itself, a Cabernet-dominated Bordeaux-style blend.

www.lynxwines.co.za

SOLMS-DELTA

This is an old farm, dating back to 1690—as is made wonderfully clear in the modern estate's museum, which tells the story of the human presence on this land from ancient times, through the colonial presence and slavery and then apartheid, to the latest and hopefully more hopeful chapter. The context is always the broader history of South Africa, and it was in that context, after the democratic elections of 1994, that its then largely expatriate owner, renowned neuroscientist Mark Solms, reestablished the neglected farm. The social commitment of the energetic and deeply humanistic Solms, together with that of his British friend and partner in the project, philanthropist Richard Astor, who owns the neighboring jointly farmed property, is remarkable. The third element in the partnership is the trust they established, with their own farms as equity, of which the direct beneficiaries are the established farmworker-tenants of the property. The rebuilding of community here and the attempt to redress the evils of the past and present is unique in the wine lands. One of the happiest results and symbols of that is the wonderful revival of music here (a special project of Richard Astor's), drawing on the traditions of the Afrikaans-speaking colored people. The annual *oesfees* (harvest festival) has this sort of music at its large heart; it was started for the primary benefit of the farmworkers of the valley and still has that orientation, though the gates are crowded with others trying to get in.

There are some 23 hectares of vines on the property, at the Paarl end of the Franschhoek Valley, planted to white and red Rhône grapes as well as Muscat varieties and Sémillon. The first bottling of the revived wine estate (grapes had not been grown here for very many decades) was in 2004. Solms had become fascinated, as he attempted to come to grips in libraries with the idea of producing wine, with ancient techniques of desiccation—drying the grapes on the vine by crushing their stems when ripe—and he wanted this to be a part of the new Solms-Delta. His first winemaker, Hilko Hegewisch, was delighted to experiment, and the wines they have produced have been extremely successful and interesting—if not always easy for the authorities or an unaccustomed public to appreciate. Young Jacques Viljoen took over as winemaker in late 2012, probably to have a beneficial effect on the consistency of quality from the cellar (or cellars—the home one, with its fine exterior mural, is too small, and vinification happens also in rented space in other wineries). The wines in the Solms-Delta range are all from the Rhône varieties that Solms had decided were most appropriate to the area (although in the earlier years the grapes had to be widely sourced while the home vineyards matured) and include components of vine-dried grapes. Hiervandaan is from Syrah, and the particularly good Amalie is from well-oaked Grenache Blanc and Viognier, a serious and even austere wine. Most of the names of the wines, incidentally, are Afrikaans and in some way invoke the history and culture of the Cape.

Two table wines are made entirely from desiccated grapes; effectively they share some of the character of the Amarones of Valpolicella. Africana is a dramatic wine, full of power but beguilingly appealing, with enough sternness and well-integrated oak to set off the hint of sweetness and a promise of complexity. The Koloni, also with alcohol levels unsurprisingly over 15 percent, is from Muscat varieties and Riesling—though one would never guess this, and varietalism is not what this wine is about. The controlled oxidativeness of the winemaking is apparent (and brings frequent anathemas from the certification body), but the fruit flavors are concentrated and brilliantly partnered by a tangy, bone-dry minerality. There is also a Solms-Astor range of easier-drinking wines. Goemoedsrus is a bizarre but successful take on port, a desiccated Syrah wine fortified with husk spirit (grappa) from the same grapes, rather than with brandy or neutral spirits.

Social and winemaking ambitions are high here—including a comparatively rare desire to make interesting, characterful wines. The wines already achieve that goal, and they are fortunately also good. Rosa Kruger's arrival as a fully involved consultant viticulturist in 2011 can only bode well. The winery has come from nowhere to be a significant part of the ever-brighter Franschhoek scene and should prosper, along with its worker-tenants, in this splendid project.

www.solms-delta.co.za

STONY BROOK

Nigel McNaught was a doctor in Grahamstown in the Eastern Cape before he and his wife, Joy, moved to Franschhoek in the early 1990s. In 1995 they came to Stony Brook, a 22.5-hectare property on the lower slopes of the Franschhoek mountains, crushing the first grapes in 1996. Medicine finally yielded to wine full-time for McNaught in 2003. Orchards have made way for 14 hectares of Cabernet Sauvignon, Malbec, Merlot, Syrah, Mourvèdre, and Pinot Noir among reds, while whites are represented by Sémillon, Chardonnay, and Viognier, planted on soils varying from decomposed granite to sandy loam.

A cellar was created from the old fruit-packing shed. The range has expanded to a current eclectic nineteen (though the total production is only about 5,500 cases), varietal and blended. McNaught has proved an adept winemaker. The Sémillon from old bush-vines is probably the best of the whites, and the single-vineyard Cabernet Sauvignon called Ghost Gum, new-oaked and fairly serious, the best of the reds. An interesting and pleasant oddity, now abandoned, was the semisweet Rose de Vert, the first wine in modern South Africa to be made from the red-skinned version of Sémillon, which used to be vastly more common than it is now.

www.stonybrook.co.za

9

DURBANVILLE TO DARLING

BACKGROUND

The busy town of Durbanville—virtually continuous with Cape Town, and no farther from the city center than is Constantia—began life with a much homelier name: Pampoenkraal ("pumpkin kraal"). It was a resting and meeting place for travelers, wagoners, and local farmers. The little village was obsequiously renamed D'Urban, for a colonial governor, in 1838, but the growing fame of the Natal port of Durban prompted a retreat to Durbanville fifty years later. Now, with much farming land already lost to urbanization, the inevitable struggle continues to defend the interests of agriculture against housing, golf courses, and gentlemen's vineyard estates.

The area's wine-producing history is a long and honorable one—though surprisingly without prominence until recently, as a substantial proportion of the best grapes went into leading wines of the giants like KWV and Stellenbosch Farmers' Winery (component of the future Distell). Indeed, Durbanville produced one of the most quietly illustrious Cape wines of the twentieth century (though it was not widely known, because it was made only in 1966 and 1968): the GS Cabernet Sauvignon. Little is certain about the making of the wine, but it was probably vinified on the Durbanville farm where the grapes were sourced. The location of the vineyard is contested, but in all likelihood it has long since been covered with concrete and asphalt.

GS might possibly have come from Altydgedacht, which dates to the late seventeenth century, as do two other Durbanville estates, Meerendal and Diemersdal. Altydgedacht's cellar was built in 1705, and inventories record wine sales from 1730 at the latest. But

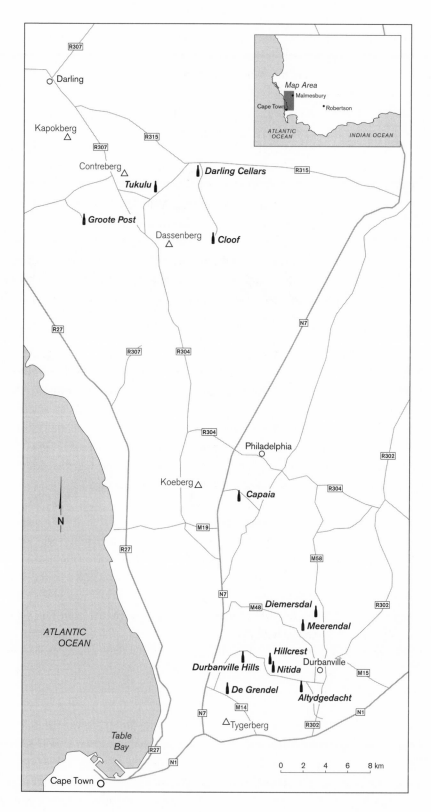

R307

Darling

Kapokberg △

R307

R315

Contreberg △

Tukulu █

Darling Cellars █

R315

Groote Post █

Dassenberg △

Cloof █

Map Area
Malmesbury
Cape Town
Robertson
ATLANTIC
OCEAN
INDIAN OCEAN

N7

R27

R307

R304

R304

Philadelphia

R302

Koeberg △

Capaia █

R304

M19

N

M58

R27

N7

M48

Diemersdal █

R302

ATLANTIC
OCEAN

Meerendal █

Hillcrest █

Durbanville Hills █

Nitida █

Durbanville

M15

De Grendel █

Altydgedacht █

N7

M14

N1

R302

Table
Bay

△ Tygerberg

R27

N1

Cape Town

0   2   4   6   8 km

MAP 6
Durbanville to Darling

surplus wine for domestic consumption was certainly being produced in Durbanville many years before. Altydgedacht is typical of the region in that in modern times its grapes all went to Nederburg, before the owners started making wine to bottle under their own label in the mid 1980s.

THE WARDS

If Durbanville town is an extension of Cape Town, Durbanville country abuts the Swartland, and wheat and pastoral farming are also important agricultural pursuits. Nitida, for example, was a cattle and sheep farm before Bernhard Veller decided to plant vineyards in the early 1990s. Today there are nine producing cellars in Durbanville, as well as a number of grape producers contributing either to the big-brand wineries or to Durbanville Cellars.

What is special about Durbanville—and unites it to the other areas discussed in this chapter—is its proximity to the Atlantic Ocean, as little as ten kilometers distant (and in Durbanville's case there is also exposure across flatlands to False Bay). The area is hilly, with vineyards mostly on east-facing slopes, at altitudes of up to 350 meters. It can be hot in summer, but the sea breezes have a marked cooling influence on exposed vineyards, making Durbanville one of the cooler areas of the Cape. Rainfall is low at about 450 millimeters annually and, with limited water catchment and storage potential, possibilities for irrigation are fairly limited; many vineyards are dryland-farmed. The soils of Durbanville are based on forms of weathered sandstone, not acidic like most Cape soil, but sometimes with rather too much vigor-producing richness. Generally on the lower slopes they are deep and red, while shallower shale soils are found higher up. Varieties preferring cool conditions, such as Sauvignon Blanc, Chardonnay, and Sémillon, are grown on south-facing slopes, while Cabernet Sauvignon, Merlot, Syrah, and Pinotage prefer the warmth of the north-facing slopes.

Durbanville's current reputation is above all for Sauvignon Blanc, and this grape constitutes its largest plantings: 400 hectares at the end of 2011. At about a quarter of that hectarage, Chardonnay is the only other white variety grown with some seriousness, as Chenin vineyards have declined recently. Recognition for the area's possibilities in terms of often comparatively elegant red wines is reflected in the surface area devoted to Cabernet Sauvignon (282 hectares), Merlot (234), and Syrah (216).

Farther north, among the wheatlands, are vineyards in the youthful ward of Philadelphia, which combines with Durbanville to make up the Tygerberg district. The cooling exposure to the Atlantic continues here, as do the hills, with most of the vineyards at altitudes up to 250 meters. Red wine grapes predominate, with Cabernet Sauvignon overwhelmingly leading (225 hectares) and Merlot, Syrah, and Cabernet Franc far behind; Sauvignon Blanc is, though, inevitably significant, with 140 hectares. The two wineries here are comparatively new, and have shown that the viticultural potential of the area is enormous—expansion is limited only, one suspects, by the lack of water for irrigation.

The district of Darling is a little north of Tygerberg, with some vineyards less than ten kilometers from the Atlantic. Until viticultural ambitions set in during the mid 1990s it was an undistinguished part of the Swartland, known more for its dairy cattle feeding on the plains of natural grass. It was probably the fine Groenekloof Sauvignon Blanc of négociant Neil Ellis that drew attention to the cool-climate possibilities of the area. The Groenekloof ward was declared, but clearly the climatic conditions required a separation from the Swartland, so the district of Darling was subtracted from the Swartland in 2003, with Groenekloof as its ward. The only winery not within Groenekloof is Groote Post, the winery closest to the sea: some 120 sloping and particularly cool hectares of unirrigated vines set in a huge farm of livestock, dairy cattle, and cereals. The first bottling here was in 1999 and the estate offered much promise, but it did not entirely deliver on that promise. Something more than a decade later, however, there are clear signs that the white wines are being made in a less clumsy, sugar-dependent way; the Shiraz and Pinot Noir have also made strides, and the winery has many admirers. Nevertheless, it would be fair to say that there is little stunning coming out of the district, although Darling Cellars is certainly one of the best former cooperative wineries in the country. Nearby, at Cloof, a good deal of effort goes into marketing the deftly made wines, which are unabashedly commercial—and unabashed in all ways, in fact, from very ripe grapes, with big alcohols and big, up-front flavors. As the winery Web site once cheerfully remarked about the Cellar Blend (made from Tinta Barroca, Pinotage, and Syrah), "This is not a wine that will be revered for its subtlety." Much the same could be said of the Very Sexy Shiraz, and Daisy Darling. Tukulu, the property owned by Distell and a few Black Economic Empowerment companies, makes some attractive organic and Fairtrade wines.

The Groenekloof wineries are on the eastern flank of the range of hills of that name, and are therefore more protected from stronger winds. But the coolness generated by the Benguela ocean current still reaches the more exposed slopes, and there are many wines made with a good natural acidity reflecting this and complementing a ripe richness—both traits characteristic of the Sauvignon Blancs from the area, which are perhaps the best wines produced there. Apart from the vineyards of Groote Post, where white grapes are in the majority, red wine grapes predominate, with Cabernet Sauvignon in 2008 having by far the most extensive plantings at 566 hectares. Syrah is at 431 hectares but is beaten into third place by Sauvignon Blanc with about 500; then comes Chenin Blanc (273), followed by Pinotage. The still somewhat old-fashioned nature of the vineyards here (remember that Darling Cellars, not long ago a typical cooperative, accounts for by far the largest proportion of vines) is indicated by the fact that Cinsaut can still muster more than a hundred hectares. Rainfall is generally fairly low in Darling (under 550 millimeters annually) and there is little potential for water catchment, so most vines are unirrigated and cultivated as low-growing bushvines, which have lower water demands.

THE WINERIES

CAPAIA

If Capaia doesn't eventually become a leading winery, it won't be for lack of capital, or of expertise invoked, but because it lost its way. The 140-hectare Philadelphia estate on the northeast flank of the Olifantskop was bought in 1997 by German wine importer Alexander Baron von Essen and his baroness, Ingrid, of the extraordinarily rich Miehle family. No expense was spared. The 60 irrigated hectares of vines were planted with advice from Jan Coetzee of Vriesenhof and Daniel Schuster of New Zealand. The 80 percent carrying red Bordeaux varieties (bar Malbec) was planted with material imported from Bordeaux—such was the concern to obtain genuinely virus-free stock. Sauvignon Blanc, local virus-free material, was planted in 2002. Hungarian Tibor Gál was the first winemaking adviser and guided the building of the elegant winery—completed with the installation of a world-beating array of fifty-six oak fermentation vessels of five thousand or eight thousand liters each. The first harvest was 2003. Gál died two years later, but Alexander von Essen has friends at the highest levels of the European wine world and soon afterward Stephan von Neipperg was brought in as consultant. Then Austrian Manfred Tement came to advise on the Sauvignon Blanc. The aristocratic (even feudal) tenor of the establishment and the importance accorded to high-profile European consultants are more than possibly the reasons for the problematic high turnover of resident winemakers.

The flagship used to go by the name of the estate but was renamed ONE; it is made from the main Bordeaux red grapes, with a little added Syrah in recent years. It started off extremely well, and has been good in some vintages but apparently affected by a lack of care consequent upon the flurry of winemakers. It looks as though this problem might now be resolved and we can look forward to more of these dark-fruited, soberly handsome, and suave wines, with smoothly ripe and gently convincing tannins. The fruit does seem to be improving a little each year as the vineyards mature. The blend is led by Cabernet or Merlot, with Cabernet Franc and some Petit Verdot. The Sauvignon Blanc was undistinguished, but showed signs of improvement from about 2010. This is undoubtedly a winery to watch, and even better things can be expected from it.

www.capaia.co.za

DARLING CELLARS

This winery was formerly the Mamreweg Co-operative, established in 1948, and since its conversion in 1996 has been one of the most successful of the conversions from co-op to company, producing a number of ambitious wines at the head of its enormous range. For this the primary credit must no doubt go to the terroir and to the farming practices of the twenty or so farmer-shareholders, supported by the cellar's viticulturist (Jaco Engelbrecht since 2008): the vast majority of the 1,300 hectares of mostly unirrigated vineyards consists almost entirely of low-yielding bushvines on a range of soil types. Cabernet, Cinsaut, Merlot, Pinotage, Syrah, Chardonnay, Chenin, and Sauvignon Blanc predominate, though smaller pockets of other varieties are grown, too. The presence in the cellar of Abé Beukes, who had built a good reputation at the once-prestigious Lievland estate in Stellenbosch before coming here in time for the 1998 harvest, is also of clear significance—and so too must be some intelligent management. Since the transformation in the 1990s, the cellar's 350,000 cases annually (70 percent red) have been progressively consolidated into various ranges (with various names over the years), of which the Darling Cellars Premium and Reserve ranges are the core, and the Limited Releases the most serious. The majority of the top wines come from a smaller number of selected vineyards, mostly in the Groenekloof ward. They are generally rich, ripe, and alcoholically powerful, but not excessively so, and pack a lot of oak—but this is also well-judged. The well-structured Cabernet Sauvignon was perhaps the finest of these until a few ultrapremium blends were added: the most notable are the Sir Charles Henry Darling, a Cabernet-led Bordeaux-style blend, and Lime Kilns, a fine entry in the category of rich Chenin-based blends characteristic of the West Coast.

www.darlingcellars.co.za

DE GRENDEL

This is surely the winery with the best view of Table Mountain, across Table Bay. De Grendel (the name of this very old farm is Dutch for "lock" or "latch"), on the slopes of the Tygerberg hills, is just twenty minutes' drive from central Cape Town, and less than ten kilometers from the sea. Some 110 hectares of the huge farm, largely of well-drained decomposed shale soils, are planted with vines. This is a fairly recent transformation, as the farm was devoted to wheat, cattle, and horses until the present owner, Sir David Graaff, inherited the property in 1999 from his father, politician Sir De Villiers Graaff. The land has been in the family's hands for nearly a century. Winemaker Charles Hopkins (previously at Bellingham) oversaw the building of the new wine cellar in 2005. The Sauvignon Blanc vines here have given probably the best results so far. Hopkins and the viticultural team use satellite images to monitor and classify the vineyards according to growing patterns and help set picking times. The generic Sauvignon is good, but the Koetshuis, mostly from one special block but supplemented by a more mature vineyard elsewhere, is finer and more serious. Hopkins's recognition of the greater concentration available from older vines also led him to source the majority Cabernet for De Grendel's first Bordeaux-style blend from elsewhere, in this case a thirty-plus-year-old block of bushvine Cab in Stellenbosch, blended with some home-farm Malbec and a few drops each of Cabernet Franc and Merlot. The maiden Rubáiyát 2006 was a serious but delicious if not profound wine, with a balanced 14.3 percent alcohol and, less discreetly, all-new oaking. There are also very acceptable varietal examples of Merlot, Syrah, Viognier, and Pinot Noir, and an attractive blend called Winifred, of Chardonnay, Sémillon, and Viognier. With winemaking in such capable hands and with an interesting terroir, there's every reason to expect the standards of wine here to rise as the vineyards mature.

www.degrendel.co.za

DIEMERSDAL

This Durbanville farm was granted in 1698 but took its present name from a Captain Diemer, who married the widow of the grantee. Wine was made here from the start, as an inventory from the first years of the eighteenth century attests, with its mention of forty-five wine barrels, a wine press, and glass bottles. The property has been owned by the Louw family since 1885 (current winemaker, young Thys Louw, is the sixth generation) and has the unpretentious, authentic air of a family farm. Until Tienie Louw, the present owner and Thys's father, took over and decided to concentrate on wine, Diemersdal was a mixed farm. Early vintages from 1979 onward were finished elsewhere, until the end of the 1980s when he could complete the winemaking process on site. Today Diemersdal is one of the larger privately owned wine farms. The dryland vineyards on the northern and southern slopes of the Dorstberg, cared for since 1980 by Div van Niekerk, occupy 180 of the farm's 340 hectares of land, with the rest for grazing or conservation. Production grew dramatically in the early years of this century, with Thys taking production from 30,000 bottles annually to 400,000.

If it were left to Thys, all 400,000 would undoubtedly be Sauvignon Blanc. Not only are there (at last count) five different and excellent straight Sauvignon bottlings, some stylistically conceived while others demonstrate terroir diversity, but also a Sauvignon rosé (with a dollop of Cabernet for color), and Thys has even experimented with a port-style Sauvignon. His intellectual and sensual curiosity about his beloved grape is endless—the MM Louw version, for example, is fermented with a beer yeast, and then bottled unfined and unfiltered (but certainly not unoaked). It's an interesting wine, less orthodox in character than, for example, the 8 Rows Sauvignon Blanc, which tends to showy New Zealand style, with a lot of juicy fruit and breadth. Red wines are not neglected at Diemersdal, however, and even account for the majority of plantings and of labels in the large range. While the white wines are made in a new state-of-the-art cellar, the reds are more traditionally made, in open fermenters. The MM Louw Red Blend is a fine Bordeaux-stye wine. Various varietal bottlings are also good, showing the versatility of Thys's enthusiasm, skill, and feeling for wine.

Thys also owns, with partners, an interesting property called Sir Lambert, up the West Coast at windy Lamberts Bay. Although a Syrah (untasted) was released mid 2010, the star is, of course, Sauvignon Blanc—delicate and intense, with thrilling mineral raciness to its compact structure.

www.diemersdal.co.za

DURBANVILLE HILLS

Durbanville Hills was established in 1998 as a joint venture between the forerunner of Distell and farmers who supplied the wholesaler with Durbanville grapes (and generally produced their own wine, too). In addition to giving a substantial recognition boost to the Durbanville area, the venture created benefits all around: the wholesaler provided technology and capital, the farmers the resources from long-proven sites. There are now eight participating farms with, since 2000, workers from the farms and the central cellar having a 5 percent equity stake in the business via a trust.

The maiden harvest was crushed in 1999 in the eight-thousand-ton-capacity, state-of-the-art cellar (though it was still, said harried cellarmaster Martin Moore, essentially a construction site) designed to allow for specialized treatments: speeds for destemming, crushing, and pumping over can all be adjusted according to variety and style, and forty stainless steel fermentation tanks of varying sizes allow for small-batch fermentation. The wine is moved as little and as gently as possible. This was one of the first wineries in the Cape to make a serious attempt to establish "green" credentials, and in 2004 it received ISO 14001 accreditation for its environmental management system. Within the limits of the demands of commercial viticulture, Durbanville Hills also shows concern for the much-endanged local flora—a variety of fynbos known as renosterveld. Preservation is well managed, and new vineyards are planned to avoid disturbing the little remaining renosterveld.

The area's topography is as hilly as the label suggests, with varied aspects, altitudes, and soils across the 770 hectares of vines from which the winery draws grapes. Of the winery's own-label production of 150,000 cases annually, a majority is Sauvignon Blanc. In the Rhinofields range there is a more ambitious version than the good-value standard one, designed to offer a satisfying balance between green and tropical flavors, and in the best vintages there are two others aiming to reflect in their characters the terroirs of the "inner valley" and "outer valley" areas they take their names from. The top-level Biesjes Craal Sauvignon Blanc draws fruit from 1970 bushvines on a steep, south-facing vineyard on Bloemendal.

There are two reds in the Single Vineyard range: Luipaardsberg Merlot ("leopard mountain," as the early settlers called the hills where the patchwork effect of the indigenous shrubs reminded them of a leopard skin) and a blend, Caapmans Cabernet Sauvignon–Merlot. The lack of wooding for all those Sauvignons gets an outlet in perhaps a little too much enthusiasm for new oak in these reds. Merlot is also the most favored red variety in the other ranges, and it does seem that the variety can do a little better here than in most parts of the Cape—that is, moderately well. Varietal wines from Chardonnay and Syrah complete what is a very useful and reasonably priced, if not immensely exciting, range.

www.durbanvillehills.co.za

HILLCREST

It's always pleasing when there's an element of concordance between wines and their winemaker, as there is here. Graeme "Curly" Read and his wines both have a direct, straightforward likability, a reserved friendliness, honesty, and modesty. The farm itself was bought in 1984 by a construction company, initially for business premises and a stone quarry; but then vineyards were planted, and the grapes sold to Durbanville Hills when that winery was founded. Read (a marine biologist) turned up in 2001 and persuaded the company to let him start a cellar. He has been winemaker here ever since, though a good load of the grapes off the 25 hectares of vines still goes to Durbanville

Hills. Merlot is the signature variety here, though it can often show a green-tinged leanness. But the herbaceous tendency in the Quarry, where it takes on a dollop of Petit Verdot, is part of an elegant freshness, balanced by a bit of richness and a firm structure. The other wine in the flagship Metamorphic range is Hornfels (named after a particular kind of rock on the farm), and includes all five of the major Bordeaux red varieties; it's also generally restrained and good, richer and more intense than the Quarry. There are a few other wines in the standard range, including a typically lively, fresh Sauvignon Blanc, which promises well for a planned blend of Sauvignon and Sémillon.

www.hillcrestfarm.co.za

MEERENDAL

There were vines recorded at Meerendal as early as 1716—tended by the widow of Jan Meerland, who had been granted land in the Tygerberg Hills in 1702. He died on a voyage to Holland, as part of the deputation that was to put the free burghers' complaints about governor Willem Adriaan van der Stel to the Lords Seventeen. Meerland's widow later doubled her farm size to some 85 hectares. From then until the twentieth century the property was to change hands many times until it was bought by William Starke in 1929, and it belonged to his family until it was sold to a consortium of businessmen in 2004—one of whom, H. N. Coertze, now owns it outright.

In 1929 just 28 of the farm's now 400 hectares were planted to vines, the rest given over to wheat and livestock. More vines were planted and the grapes sold to the KWV—including port varieties and the Syrah on which the well-known Roodeberg blend was based. William Starke was joined by his son Kosie in 1948. The early Pinotage vineyard Kosie planted in 1955 is now among the country's oldest, and starting in 2005 the wine it produced has been bottled alone, as Heritage Block. With the rise in interest in estate wines, the KWV began to bottle small quantities of Meerendal wines under its own name in 1969—it was the first farm in the area with its own name on bottles—but because the KWV was not allowed to sell on the local market, a switch to the Bergkelder was made in 1974.

Meerendal has always been best known for its red wines, and 80 percent of the vines are Cabernet Sauvignon, Merlot, Pinotage, and Syrah; but Chenin Blanc, Sauvignon Blanc, and Chardonnay are also made into single-varietal wines—though one never feels that Meerendal's heart is in them, and the Sauvignon is not always up to the area's high standard. Winemaking—the responsibility of Liza Goodwin, who has worked in the cellar since 1998—is in some ways rather old-fashioned, making use of old open concrete vats, with fermentation temperature moderated by cooling coils. The wines tend to be made from ultraripe grapes, heavily extracted, with big, bold fruit and new-oak flavors. But how could such a historic property be omitted from a survey of Durbanville?

www.meerendal.co.za

NITIDA

The first wines to come off this former cattle and sheep farm (named after a protea that grows prolifically in the area) were of the 1995 vintage. Since then Bernhard Veller, owner and hands-on viticulturist and winemaker, has built what appears to be a highly successful business, supplying wines off his 15 hectares of irrigated vineyards that many people want to drink, and using innovative ways of selling it to them directly. In fact, this is an extremely good white wine cellar, which in 2009 even added a Riesling (from Darling vineyards) to its range. Sauvignon is one of the stars, both the standard one and the Club Select, which adds some steely, mineral elegance and concentration, to make a consistently good example. The wooded Sémillon and the Sémillon-Sauvignon blend called Coronata Integration are more impressive, however. There are a few reds, which are cheerful and easygoing without being trivial; the fleshy and ripe Bordeaux blend, Calligraphy, is a little more ambitious than the others.

www.nitida.co.za

10

THE SWARTLAND

BACKGROUND

The colonizing Dutch called it Het Zwarte Land, the Black Country—not, it would seem, because of the soil, which is not black, nor because of the San hunters they skirmished with on their early invasive investigations and tentative settlements, but probably because of the indigenous vegetation, which is characteristically dark in some seasons. Nowadays the predominant summer color of the broad, open, mostly gently undulating landscape is the gold of wheatlands, with areas of green vineyards on the foothills and lower slopes of the isolated mountains. There are always other mountains on the horizon, and the skies are enormous. This is not the dramatic beauty of Stellenbosch, Franschhoek, or Constantia, but the Swartland is a place that can tenaciously grip the imagination and the heart.

The history of viticulture in this area north of Durbanville and Paarl goes back nearly three hundred years, though it is little documented. One of the first French Huguenot refugees to come to the Cape was granted a farm on the lower slopes of the Paardeberg, at the southernmost part of the Swartland, in 1685. The land must have been teeming with wildlife at the time. Some memento of that lives on in the name of the Paardeberg, which means "horse mountain" (the Dutch spelling and the modern Afrikaans version, Perdeberg, are used interchangeably now), named for the type of zebra that was to be driven into extinction by the settlers, so much more efficient at slaughter than the San. In the editor's notes to Bird's 1822 account of conditions in the Cape Colony, "Paerdeberg" and "Riebeck Kasteel" (a nearby mountainous outcrop) are mentioned as among the

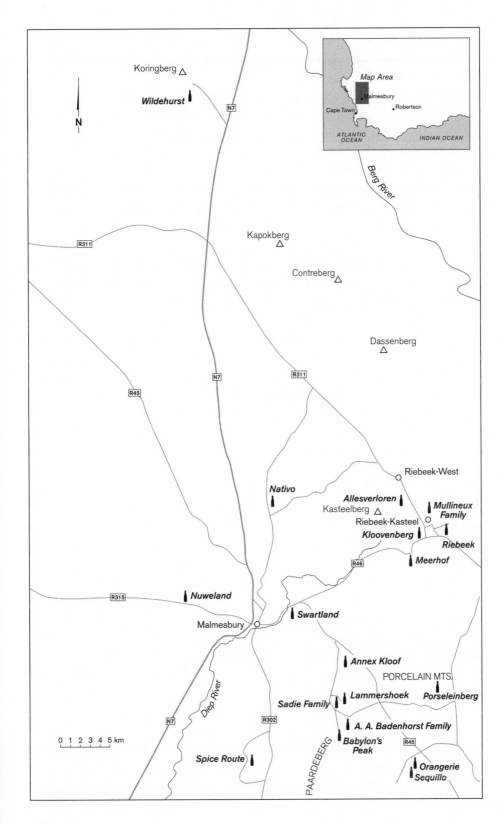

Koringberg △

Wildehurst

N7

N

R311

Kapokberg △

Contreberg △

Dassenberg △

Berg River

Map Area
Malmesbury
Cape Town
Robertson
ATLANTIC OCEAN
INDIAN OCEAN

N7

R311

R45

Riebeek-West ○

Nativo

Allesverloren

Mullineux Family

Kasteelberg △

Riebeek-Kasteel ○

Kloovenberg

Riebeek

R46

Meerhof

R315

Nuweland

Malmesbury ○

Swartland

Annex Kloof

PORCELAIN MTS.

Sadie Family

Lammershoek

Porseleinberg

A. A. Badenhorst Family

R45

Diep River

N7

R302

Babylon's Peak

PAARDEBERG

0 1 2 3 4 5 km

Spice Route

Orangerie Sequillo

MAP 7
The Swartland

areas providing the best wine and used to justify his probably valid observation that the quality of Cape wine was limited by the usual practice of planting on valley floors rather than hillsides. By 1860, Malmesbury-Piketberg (which would have covered most of the present Swartland district) was producing about 4 percent of the Cape's wine.

We can take the Lammershoek farm as in many ways emblematic of the Swartland's viticultural history. It is now one of the largest and most significant winegrowers on the Paardeberg, and the cellar the owners revived only about 2000 bears the date 1762 above its door. The farm was proclaimed in 1718, and vineyards were planted in the middle of the eighteenth century. In the later part of the twentieth, Lammershoek's grapes mostly went to the cooperative; now the vineyards supply grapes for its own-label wines and for some important producers based locally and elsewhere. Farming is overwhelmingly organic, with a tendency to biodynamic practices.

Until almost the turn of the millennium, the Swartland district's name appeared on few interesting or fine bottles, and wine production was overwhelmingly from cooperatives. Now the Swartland is among the most dynamic contributors to the rebirth of South African wine. Significantly, though, the co-ops of the region—Perdeberg, Swartland, Riebeek—have always been among the country's best. Charles Back of Fairview, the man who pioneered the rediscovery of the Swartland at his Spice Route winery, did so because he had remembered for twenty years the postuniversity year he spent making wine at the Perdeberg Co-op (technically in Paarl, but on the border of the more northerly district and sharing much of its essential character): "Quality happened so easily there!" he says, and when the chance came to return, he did so. He was seeking a vineyard site that would be expressive of the Cape's Mediterranean climate, especially for red wine. He found one in the combination of mixed clay-gravel laterite and deep, red, decomposed-granite soils of Klein Amoskuil, where the winery was established.

It is very much still a markedly rural-feeling area, with many of the farms accessible only by gravel roads. Just as Malmesbury is a poor town compared with, say, Stellenbosch, so too are the farms, and the comparatively few wineries are modest and unsophisticated— without the grand homesteads and manicured lawns that mark Stellenbosch district.

Quality of the highest order is now emerging from new and old Swartland vineyards. If Charles Back was the pioneer, the young man he was clever enough to appoint as Spice Route winemaker has become an even more important and inspirational figure in the region as a deeply well-informed and talented winemaker and viticulturist. Eben Sadie was too dynamic, too ambitious, too large to remain more than a few years at Spice Route before moving out on his own—taking and then developing the understanding his explorations of the region had given him. He took, for instance, Back's insight into the Swartland's potential for the red Rhône varieties, and started creating his Syrah-based Columella, which rapidly established itself as one of the Cape's foremost wines. As far as reds go, the growing association of the area with the Rhône varieties, especially Syrah, owes much to Sadie's success, but even more to a genuine affinity. In fact, it would be true to say that the idea of "Swartland wine" has probably more stylistic and varietal coherence than is offered by many areas—and that applies to white wine, too.

Sadie's focus was largely on the Paardeberg, and with his white wine, Palladius, he transformed an old tradition into a hugely ambitious project that has already led to a new, autochthonous style of white blend (as discussed in chapter 3). Sadie recognized that the numerous vineyards of old-vine Chenin Blanc—mostly planted to feed the demand for off-dry white wine in the 1960s and for the brandy industry—constituted something of a national treasure. It was a treasure threatened by the low yields and high viticultural costs of the vines, which were being rapidly pulled out. Others had worked with varietal wines; Sadie showed Chenin's potential in a blend with other grapes, including Chardonnay and the Mediterranean varieties.

To understand the split character of the Swartland, the old and the new, it is instructive simply to stand amid Sadie's unirrigated, organically treated, gnarled old bushvines (leased from Lammershoek), knowing what they produce, and to see on a neighboring hillside the thick green of long hedges of the same variety—knowing that they are grown to produce abundant, easily harvested crops for Distell. One of the differences in the resultant wine is lesser concentration, of course; another is that such viticulture means that ripeness comes at the price of extremely high alcohol levels. Powerful alcohol is to an extent inherent in warm-country winegrowing, but Sadie and a few others are trying to solve the problem in the vineyards rather than with machines. Both old and new vineyards frequently, in fact, show evidence of experimentation and of lessons learned in Europe, especially in Spain's Priorat region, where Sadie was also a leading producer, and the Rhône valley: methods of pruning the bushvines, for example, and the Syrah vines each trained to its own pole, *en echelas,* in the manner of Côte-Rôtie.

Meanwhile, the cooperatives continue to produce decent-quality stuff—and sometimes much more than that—the overwhelming majority of which tends to be bought in by other producers for their own labels.

Much of the obvious early excitement of the Swartland centered on the Paardeberg—although some important wines sourced grapes on the other side of the R46, the road linking Malmesbury and Tulbagh. There too, near the twin villages of Riebeek-West and Riebeek-Kasteel, a mountain or two and a valley provide the conditions for high quality. It was in this area that Johann Rupert of Anthonij Rupert in Franschhoek acquired extensive vineyards—but has not made any commitment to establishing a winery, instead transporting the grapes to the home winery's splendid facilities. Increasing numbers of other grape farmers in the area are now making a few wines for themselves, and it was in the charming village of Riebeek-Kasteel that Chris and Andrea Mullineux set up the home base of what is emerging as one of the star producers of the Swartland. This location was a significant one: to an extent it was effectively a declaration of independence from the cluster of Sadie-struck winemakers based on the Paardeberg, but, more significant, it came from a wish to widen the revolution and encourage ambitious small producers to look in this other important area of the region.

The process of dynamic change in the Swartland is, in fact, continuing to spread as well as deepen, with wineries emerging from the wheatlands, generally on the occasional hillsides or small mountains. So there is now a tiny, isolated vineyard and winery called Wildehurst farther north, in the hamlet of Koringberg ("corn mountain") and, more important, Porseleinberg, the farm established by Boekenhoutskloof on the Porcelain Mountain south of Riebeek-Kasteel.

Apart from the larger producers, the new winemakers that are making this unquestionably among the most exciting regions in the new South Africa are basically of two types. First, there are the tiny labels often belonging to winemakers working in the area or elsewhere and making their own Swartland wines from bought-in grapes. More often than not, each makes a white, either a varietal Chenin or a blend based on it, and a red blend, usually based on Syrah. Among the finest (and that means very good indeed) of these microproducers are Intellego, made by Jurgen Gouws, who assists at Lammershoek; Tobias, made by Bryan MacRobert, who was for many years Eben Sadie's right-hand man; Rall Wines, the fairly well established garagiste label of Donovan Rall, since 2011 winemaker at Vuurberg in Stellenbosch; and David, the label of David Sadie (no relation to Eben), who is winemaker at Lemberg in Tulbagh. It is, however, almost invidious to list just these out of so many.

The second group of producers is characterized by ownership of substantial properties that continue to produce grapes for the large merchants or co-ops, while inspired by what they've observed happening around them to set aside special vineyards dedicated to their own wines. Kloovenberg started making some own-label wines off its 130 hectares on the Riebeekberg as early as 1998—but it is not really associated fully with the new-wave winemakers, as indicated by the presence of grapes like Cabernet and Sauvignon Blanc in its pleasant, solid range. But Babylon's Peak, for example, makes a modest amount of newer-style wine under this label, off 230 hectares of vineyards. Annex Kloof makes less wine (but including one of the Cape's most delicious varietal Malbecs, rather oddly) off individually farmed vineyards on a number of farms separately owned by Toeloe Basson and his four sons. At Orangerie, one of the oldest farms on the Paardeberg, young Pieter Euvrard has a tiny cellar in which he makes his own appealing versions of white and red modern Swartland wines, though most of the farm's grapes go elsewhere—no doubt, however, there are ambitious dreams in his head. Juan Louw's dreams finally started attaining reality when in 2008 he converted an old chicken coop into a cellar and started making some wine under the Nuweland label off the family farm's vineyards. Wonderful old vines are giving some gratifying results in a surprisingly large range—including a vibrant Pinotage and successful blend of thirteen different varieties (some, but by no means all, overlapping with the thirteen famously grown in Châteauneuf-du-Pape.

Another producer likely to make a signal contribution to the area is Meerhof. It had been around for a decade, doing only dull stuff, when it was revived, partly under the inspiration of the self-confessedly eccentric Krige Visser, who has a passion for Cinsaut in particular, the winemaking methods of Alain Graillot in Crozes-Hermitage, and interesting wine in general. With Johan Meyer as winemaker for Meerhof and for a separate label in which Krige is part-owner, Mount Abora, interesting wines are starting to emerge: naturally made reds and whites, beautifully fresh, dry, and declining to rely for their effect on oak or alcoholic power. In the vineyards, new plantings of Spanish and Rhône varieties have been made. Unquestionably these are labels to watch. Furthermore, Meerhof is large enough to be able to host some of the smaller producers that lack their own wineries but wish to vinify within the Swartland so that their wines can qualify to carry the imprimatur of the Swartland Independent Producers (SIP) organization.

This grouping, to which most of the above-mentioned producers belong, is yet another manifestation of the ambitious and innovative spirit that has gripped the area. The aim of this voluntary body is to guide winemakers to express better the Swartland terroir. An evolving set of rules and guidelines is modeled on the appellation systems of Europe—with some stricter, some looser than those. These include the requirement that all wines to bear the SIP logo should be made in the district. Permitted varieties (largely the Mediterranean ones, plus Chenin and Pinotage) are named, though others may be used minimally in blends; various rules for viticulture and winemaking are concerned with keeping processes as natural as possible—no yeast inoculation or acidification, for example, and a maximum of 25 percent new oak is allowed for maturation; vineyards must be farmed sustainably, irrigation minimized, and so on. There seems to be considerable willingness from many of the newer Swartland producers to abide by this unprecedented and often troublesome set of rules—although there is a clear recognition that theirs is not the only voice in the region.

As for official appellations, there are only two defined Swartland wards—Malmesbury, a large but largely blank area to the north of the town of that name; and Riebeekberg, on the eastern slopes of the Kasteelberg near Riebeek-Kasteel. Neither of them is actually of relevance to producers or consumers, and their names do not appear on any labels. A ward within Paarl, Voor-Paardeberg, starting at the lower southern slopes of the Paardeberg, does have an independent identity—as well as strong associations with the southern Swartland—but for various reasons there is little immediate prospect of a union.

The cooler, more coastal district of Darling is an enclave within the Swartland and used to be one of its wards, but became independent some years ago in recognition of its different and distinctive character. It is considered in chapter 9, together with Durbanville.

LAND, CLIMATE, VITICULTURE

Although much of the viticultural land of the Swartland is well inland, the influence of cool Atlantic sea breezes continues to be significant on the slopes and foothills of the Paardeberg, for example. On the whole, however, this is hot-country viticulture, with an average summer daytime temperature of nearly 24°C. Even so, temperature variation between hot summer days and cool nights can be marked, and is probably significant for the high natural acidity found particularly in grapes from the higher-located vineyards. Some of the higher east-facing vineyards on the Riebeek-Kasteelberg get respite from hot afternoon sun.

Water is scarce in most parts of the Swartland, and many vineyards must perforce go unirrigated, although on the southern slopes of the Paardeberg rainfall is somewhat higher and dams more plentiful. The traditional vineyards are almost entirely low-yielding bushvines, with some experimentation with single-vine staking, and some of the newer plantings (such as Viognier) are on trellises—which is also the predominant method, of course, for the majority of the intensively grown, high-producing vines providing large and cheap volumes to the cooperatives and big merchants.

The soil is varied throughout the district. Paardeberg and some other outcrops are granitic, with increasingly weathered soils on the lower slopes; the sandy topsoils are well drained, but a much deeper layer of clay serves as something of a reservoir during the mostly dry summer. There are also gravelly, iron-based soils in the area. The soils on the Riebeek-Kasteel and Porcelain mountains are based on shale, which also characterizes the area to the north of the Paardeberg—giving good drainage, but again with a clay content that helps retain moisture. The new-wave producers are very conscious of the different characters given by these soils.

By far the most planted variety throughout the Swartland is Chenin Blanc, with some of it mature bushvines—even old, by Cape standards, although these low-yielding vines are still being lost at an alarming rate despite the increased awareness by some producers of Chenin and Chenin-based blends throughout the Cape of their irreplaceable value. At the end of 2011 there were 2,675 hectares of Chenin (mostly, of course, higher-yielding younger and trellised vines). Chardonnay, some of which goes into serious blends, is the next most common white grape, a long way behind at 780 hectares, with Sauvignon Blanc, no doubt a trifle opportunistically responding to fashion rather than terroir, only a little behind.

Of the black grapes, Cabernet Sauvignon is the most planted, at 1,656 hectares, supplemented by other Bordeaux varieties, notably Merlot at 677 hectares. These, on the whole, produce very little wine of interest or distinction. Syrah, identified by the new generation of winemakers (as well as by some of the older producers, such as Allesverloren) as key to serious Swartland red wine aspirations either in blends or alone, is rapidly catching up to the Bordeaux varieties, with 1,550 hectares. Pinotage follows with 1,390. There are few varieties grown in the Cape, however, that are not represented at some level in the Swartland.

THE WINERIES

A. A. BADENHORST FAMILY

Cousins Hein and Adi Badenhorst aroused some surprise when they bought an old run-down farm called Kalmoesfontein in the Paardeberg area, and Adi aroused even more when he made it clear, by resigning as winemaker at the grand Stellenbosch estate of Rustenberg, that it was not a part-time venture. There was a great deal to do. Adi tells how his father-in-law, Jan Coetzee of Vriesenhof, on visiting the property for the first time, took a good look around and announced gloomily (in Afrikaans, of course), "There's forty years of work here!" They've made a good start, with strictly limited resources: the neglected cellar, last used in the 1930s, has been revamped and extended, and rehabilitation of the vineyards is well under way. Adi's aim is perhaps best deduced from his announced inspiration: "the great old wines of South Africa and the discarded varietals, the bottles of which can be found in the forgotten corners of old cellars before modern methods and fame came along and changed the purity of the wines."

The prime vehicle for this return to better ways is Kalmoesfontein's 28 hectares of unirrigated bushvine vineyards, including Chenin, Cinsaut, and Grenache, some sixty years old and planted on variously facing granitic slopes. Fruit from other sites within the Swartland region is brought in to complement the home vines. Fermentation (with native yeasts; winemaking is essentially "natural") takes place in old oak or concrete tanks, and a lengthy postfermentation maceration in variously sized oak, including some large *foudres*. There are two main wines (maiden vintage 2006) bearing the characteristically quirky, unusual, and brilliantly successful Badenhorst labels. The White typically blends nine or ten varieties, usually with Chenin the largest contributor, while the 2009 Red modestly has a maximum of only four: Syrah, Mourvèdre, Grenache, and Cinsaut. Both are what is coming to be understood as typical southern Swartland wines, with excellent structures and incipiently complex and pure-fruited characters, edged with dried herbs.

Adi also makes occasional wine for sale at the Cape Winemakers Guild auction, and he initially seemed to use this vehicle to keep his hand in with the Bordeaux orientation of his previous career in Stellenbosch. Red blends have been in the tradition of the understated John X Merriman he made for Rustenberg rather than the blockbusters he also perpetrated there, and there have also been excellent Sauternes-type dessert whites. His full infection by the Swartland became clear, however, when he chose rather to offer a delicate, modest, delicious Cinsaut in 2012—with little prospect of it doing nearly as well as the full-bore reds generally prevailing at the auction (it didn't). Even more unusually, Adi is also experimenting with sherry-style and other *flor*-influenced wines.

A quite separate Badenhorst-owned label is Secateurs—also with a traditional winemaking philosophy, but seemingly more easygoing—the equivalent, it looks like, of a second label, though mostly from other Swartland vineyards than his own. Adi is probably not joking (it's not always easy to tell) when he describes it as "the smallest, most quality-focused cooperative around" and invites other, similarly minded producers to join in. Secateurs is proving a great success, and is sold in comparatively large quantities for the non-co-op Swartland, offering particularly good value for money.

www.aabadenhorst.com

ALLESVERLOREN

When the first Malan arrived at this farm on the slopes of the Kasteelberg in 1870, there were already a few vines growing here, though it was predominantly wheatland. The farm had been granted in 1704 and acquired its bleakly anguished name later that century when its then-owner returned from a long and arduous visit in Stellenbosch to find that San raiders had razed the buildings and stolen the cattle: all is lost! Incidentally, the older son of the first Malan owner, both named (like many descendants) Daniel François, became the country's first National Party prime minister. The younger son took over the farm in 1904, but did little to develop viticulture there. When his two sons inherited and split the farm in 1945, it was another Daniel François who received the part with the old homestead and started taking wine production seriously on his 500 hectares. But in 1961 the farm was split again between two sons. The smaller and more viticulturally attractive portion, with the homestead, went to Fanie. He concentrated on red wine, though retaining the port varieties that his father had made a famous port with.

Today the port-oriented tradition continues, with another Danie Malan the owner, winemaker, and viticulturist since 1987. Even after all those splits, Allesverloren is a large farm of 227 hectares of shale and weathered sandstone, with 187 of them planted to Cabernet, Syrah, and various port varieties. Seven of the latter are in fact used in the port, made in Vintage style, but usually less grippy and with a lower alcohol (17.6 percent in 2006) than many, and very delicious even in youth. The table wines are modest in the best sense of the word, the Syrah being the best of them, with the firmly graceful tannins that characterize good Swartland Syrah, and a forceful restraint. The varietal Tinta Barocca and Touriga Nacional are unassuming, a little rustic, fresh, dry, and food-friendly. Joining in the new wave does not seem likely for Allesverloren.

www.allesverloren.co.za

LAMMERSHOEK

This large farm, in the Aprilskloof fold of the northern slopes of the Paardeberg, has been highly significant, not only because of the increasingly fine quality of wines under its own label, but also because its 80-odd well-managed hectares of vines used to supply grapes to a number of big-name outside producers convinced of the quality of Paardeberg fruit. But now, as Lammershoek uses more and more of its own fruit, the supply for outsiders has dwindled—though Eben Sadie continues to manage some vines for his own wines. Many of the vines are old by Cape standards, notably a good deal of Chenin Blanc dating back to the 1960s, with some Clairette, Carignan, Hárslevelü, and Chardonnay of the same age, joined by newer plantings of the Rhône varieties that perform so well in the area: Syrah, Grenache, Viognier, and Mourvèdre. Cabernet Sauvignon and some varieties less suited to the area are being pulled out. There is some irrigation potential, though many of the vineyards are dry-farmed, and by and large now organically managed by Paul Kretzel, whose pleasure in his heavy labor has manifestly increased since the organic route was taken. Aspects and altitudes vary with the undulations of the land.

The farm was first proclaimed in 1718. The name means "lambs' corner"—apparently, ewes would take their lambs to the forests surrounding the farm to shelter from the black eagle. Vines were planted by about 1750. The cellar goes back to the mid nineteenth century but was extended and renovated in 2000, and it now rambles most pleasingly, with three levels that prove useful to a winemaker keen on utilizing gravity flow as much as possible. The cellar had not been used for more than fifty years when the farm was acquired by former businessman Paul Kretzel and his wife, Anna, together with a partner in Germany. At that time, grapes went to the cooperative.

Until 2010 Lammershoek wines—improving annually—accorded well with the new Swartland wave, gradually relying less on oak, the richness of the whites less marked by the residual sugar that came with stuck fermentations of extremely ripe, potentially alcoholic grapes. But then new young winemaker Craig Hawkins arrived with radical ideas. He'd been influenced in Europe by the "natural wine" movement, and locally by the example of Tom Lubbe, now vigneron at the esteemed Domaine de Matassa in the Languedoc, but an early associate of Eben Sadie and maker of fresh, early-picked wines at the Observatory, a modest Paardeberg farm (recently acquired by a new owner, fortunately, after having become more or less defunct). Lubbe had shown that it was possible to make both red and white wines in the area that were marked by high natural acidities and low alcohol—and yet without green, vegetal flavors.

The Kretzels supported—and loved—this revolution, and it is these characteristics that now mark Lammershoek's wines. The really radical, experimental stuff happens in the "natural" winemaking of Hawkins's own label, Testalonga: eschewal of sulfur additions being the least of it, barrels stuffed with whole bunches and left for two years being the most way-out—and, incidentally, far from unsuccessful. For Lammershoek, Hawkins can be maturely pragmatic, though sulfur is reduced, picking of grapes is done early enough to produce much lower-alcohol wines than are general in the area, and there are some experiments with skin contact. Definitions in the matter of "natural winemaking" can be fraught with problems, of course, but by most of them this is what Lammershoek is involved in. Whole-bunch pressing is universal for the white wines, and at least partially used for most of the reds. There is a small range of more experimental wines called Cellar Foot, made in very small quantities and becoming fixtures if they prove successful—as happened with the maiden releases in 2010, a spicy, almost austere but completely fascinating Hárslevelü of penetrating length and just 11.5 percent alcohol, and a succulently thrilling Mourvèdre.

Above all, the Lammershoek wines are all wonderfully fresh. The primary whites in the standard range are a Chenin Blanc and a blend called Roulette Blanc, which adds some Viognier and Clairette to Chenin. Both are subtle, deliciously dry, even steely wines, with more penetrating focus than breadth and richness. The Syrah and the Rhône-style blend Roulette, which were also good wines under the previous regime, are now finer, more elegant expressions of the Paardeberg, with alcohol levels generally not much more than 13 percent.

Lam is a less expensive, quirkily labeled, excellent-value range, often from younger vines or at least those offering less intensity of fruit, made in the same way as the Lammershoek wines. It surely need not be added that there is now no new wood to be seen in the rambling Lammershoek cellar—only older barrels and casks of various sizes, a little stainless steel, and a number of large cement fermentation tanks.

It must be said that a good deal of the work that makes possible such balanced wines with comparatively modest alcohol levels in this warm climate is done in the vineyards, to produce vines themselves in balance. Early picking then becomes more viable. Altogether, what is happening at Lammershoek is surely as significant and exciting as anything in Cape wine.

www.lammershoek.co.za

MULLINEUX FAMILY

Chris Mullineux got to know and love the Swartland when sourcing grapes for the négociant wines at Tulbagh Mountain Vineyards (now Fable), where he had his first winemaking job starting in 2002. The influence of Eben Sadie inevitably was, and remains, important. It was no great surprise when he left for the Swartland to go solo in 2007—duo rather than solo, in fact, as he got married the same year to his Californian assistant winemaker. Mullineux Family Wines was formed, with a couple of other wine people coming in as financing partners. Chris and Andrea Mullineux set about finding and securing vineyards (to be managed, though not owned, by them, and farmed as organically as possible) for the small portfolio of wines they were contemplating: a Chenin-based blend; a Syrah that would include small proportions of other varieties, notably Mourvèdre, Cinsaut, and Grenache; and a straw wine. The vineyards are scattered widely across the southern Swartland; some are old bushvines, some younger trellised ones.

The first vintage (2008) was vinified at biodynamic Reyneke in Stellenbosch, where the two Mullineux were at the time contracted to make the wines; the next few at Quoin Rock; and then—much closer to home—at Meerhof. A small cellar in leased premises was established in early 2010—though only for maturation purposes, as well as sales—in picturesque Riebeek-Kasteel. They will use rented space for vinification in the meantime, but the pair plans to buy land in the area and put up a cellar (by 2014, they hope)—and plant vines, too, though the majority of grapes will always be bought in.

Those who admired the maturity, confidence, and sheer excellence of Chris Mullineux's work at Tulbagh and Reyneke have no doubt that Mullineux Family Vineyards is going to become a force in the Swartland and indeed, in the Cape—particularly since Andrea's contribution appears to be significant: they seem to work, somehow, in complementary and mutually strengthening ways, although Chris is the leader in the vineyards and Andrea in the cellar. The first vintages only increase confidence, though one hopes that finances will soon allow their wines to be held back for another year or two before release. The Syrah, only lightly oaked, is elegant and assured, a fine expression of the scattered vineyards on shale, schist, and granite. In fact, from 2009 there has been a further pair of (very expensive by local standards) Syrahs produced from single vineyards, each bearing the name of the soil type involved: Schist and Granite. They are remarkably different in character, though made in exactly the same way—a triumphant vindication of the concern with terroir that characterizes Chris and Andrea's work. They are also arguably the most elegant Syrahs in the country. Alcohol levels of these wines are generally below 13.5 percent.

The White Blend is Chenin-based with small proportions of Viognier and Clairette, and stresses minerality and restraint. Finely textured and subtly rich, it comes from grapes picked earlier than is often the case in the Swartland, with (as for the reds) a consequently lower alcohol level and better acidity, less showy in youth but probably destined for a long development in bottle.

The very successful straw wine that Chris Mullineux made at Tulbagh emerged from a splendidly original solera system, and although the first-rate Mullineux version, also from Chenin, is released with a vintage date, the winemakers are holding back a proportion each year and establishing a new solera—which is, like just about everything at this winery, good news.

There is also a good-value second-tier range under the Kloof Street label—a Rouge, blending Mediterranean red varieties, and a Chenin Blanc. Meanwhile, another winemaking venture called the Three Foxes, which began in 2004 as little more than a hobby with two friends to make wines for themselves from various interesting vineyards, has shown distinct signs of growing.

www.mullineuxwines.com

NATIVO

This is the brand name used by Hughes Family Wines. Billy and Penny Hughes's farm—north of Malmesbury and thus set a little away from the nerve centers of the revived Swartland—has an importance beyond their own wines, rewarding as those are, for the 27 hectares of mostly Rhône varieties in addition to Chenin Blanc supply grapes to a number of leading local winemakers. The vineyards were fully accredited as organic in 2012. Billy, a moonlighting engineer, makes the wines himself, and is doing so with increasing deftness—although that is perhaps the wrong thing to say for someone who avoids cellar interventions as much as possible. There are two wines, a red and a white blend, with 2004 the first bottling. The latter is less oxidative in style than many new-wave Swartland whites, and somewhat unusual too in that the majority component is oaked Viognier (but a well-disciplined, unexuberant Viognier) supplemented by Chenin—reversing the more usual mix. The pure-fruited red is led by Syrah, with four minor components, and is delightful. Both wines improve with some years in bottle.

www.nativo.co.za

PORSELEINBERG

The name is the Afrikaans version of Porcelain Mountain, where the vineyards and winery are located—although the mountains in this part of the southern Swartland are little more than substantial hills, with sweeping views across wheatlands to the Paardeberg and Riebeekberg. Here Franschhoek winery Boekenhoutskloof bought a struggling but promising small farm making organic wines under the Schonenberg label, and a major planting program was begun in 2009, with plans to plant at least 100 hectares eventually, mostly to Syrah. The destiny for most of the organically, even biodynamically, grown grapes will be Boekenhoutskloof's own wines, but a small proportion of the vines will go under the

Porseleinberg label. Organic farming is made easier by the relative isolation of the vineyards and by the fact that they are planted—on all slopes of the hill—on soil previously unused for vines. In some parts, in fact, the soil is not easy to see beneath the characteristic shale rocks. Planting and establishing vines is not easy here, and would have been almost impossible without pumping irrigating water from the Berg River, for distances up to seven kilometers. Presiding over the vineyards and the simple cellar, with its egg-shaped cement tanks and old *foudres* (and also over the cattle, sheep, and chickens he has brought in to help him farm), is Callie Louw—though *presiding* is really too grand a word for such a literally down-to-earth young man, whose experience was mainly gained at Vondeling and Tulbagh Mountain Vineyards (now Fable). The first Porseleinberg wine, from the older vineyards established here starting in 2005, was the 2010. It was a very fine effort indeed, fresh, delicately forceful, and beautifully structured, but we must wait a little longer to see the best that can come off these hills. Whether the wine will remain monovarietal is uncertain (there are some plantings of Cinsaut and Grenache), but the early vintages, and indeed the example of Schonenburg Syrah, its predecessor, suggest that it is totally viable that it should.

www.porseleinberg.com

SADIE FAMILY

Eben Sadie's first wines were made while he was still winemaker at the pioneering Spice Route, but independence was inevitable for his restless and enormous winemaking ambition, and by the time Columella 2001 was released he had a tiny home in an old shed on Lammershoek farm on the Paardeberg. The white blend Palladius came the following year. Sadie was later able to buy the shed, together with the bit of land around it (a few hectares are now planted to a wide assortment of unusual Mediterranean varieties), and to build a larger winemaking facility shared by Sadie Family Wines and his joint venture, Sequillo. The growth of his business in such a short time, from virtually nothing and with little in the way of financial backing, is testimony not only to the brilliant international and local success of his wines, but to Sadie's rare blend of vision, intelligence, and strategic competence, and perhaps above all to a capacity for extremely hard and effective work. In the same years that he was building Sadie Family Wines he was also establishing vineyards and a winery, Terroir al Limit, in Priorat in Spain which has received even greater international acclaim than his home project.

Sadie owns no vineyards of his own, but meticulously tends the vines on the parcels he leases, most of them scattered across the Swartland and Olifants River regions. Those for Palladius have historically been all on the Paardeberg: separate blocks of old Chenin (generally 40 percent of the blend), Chardonnay, and up to another half-dozen varieties. But Sadie wants a range of origins to give Columella the complexity he requires of it, and the eight or nine separately vinified Syrah components (as well as the nearly 20 percent Mourvèdre complement), from different soils and aspects, show remarkably different characters before they are blended, each with strengths contributing to a whole that is greater than the sum of its parts.

Both of these celebrated wines have remained to an extent works in progress, with the blend of Palladius significantly changing a good deal over the years (particularly with the decreasing role of Viognier): Sadie is now managing to make the wine, though from fully ripe grapes, drier and a little less alcoholic than it was in the first few vintages, partly through work in the vineyards. Older oak and cement "eggs" play an increasing role in its maturation. The changes in Columella have been subtler, but there was something of a breakthrough in the 2008 and especially 2009 vintages, with the grapes now earlier-picked for more freshness and less new-oak influence—Sadie is generally moving toward traditional large-format, well-used oak containers.

In 2009 Sadie made six fascinating wines in an Old Vines series ("Ouwingerdreeks" in the Afrikaans that is used on the labeling), each in minuscule quantities. The wines of the initial vintage were sold as a composite pack, with labels featuring specially produced artwork by South Africa's leading artist, William Kentridge. Subsequent vintages were sold separately, in varying quantities. Three new wines were added as of the 2011 vintage. All in the series come off old unirrigated bushvines—some of them on their own rootstocks—from as far afield as Stellenbosch and obscure reaches of the Swartland and Olifants River. There are five dry whites, from Chenin Blanc or Sémillon (the standard and the red versions), or field blends of those varieties plus Palomino. There is one dessert Muscat (but that is destined to be withdrawn from the range shortly) and three reds—from Cinsaut, Grenache, and Tinta Barroca, respectively. They are made using the simplest of old-fashioned techniques (certainly not a whiff of new oak) and designed partly to show the value of these rapidly disappearing old vineyards. As ever, Sadie's commitment to large values—to the wonder of wine, perhaps, and to a wider wine culture—is an integral part of his work.

www.thesadiefamily.com

SEQUILLO

The first bottling under the Sequillo label was a red blend in 2003, bottled at Anura in Stellenbosch, with whose owner Eben Sadie had established a partnership. By the time a white blend arrived with the 2006 vintage, that partnership had been dissolved in favor of one with wine lover and wine collector Cornel Spies (a doctor who has since moved to Australia, but retains his interest). And the wines were then being made in the new cellar the winemaker had built for them and for his Sadie Family Wines. Later a maturation cellar was established for barrels of Sequillo (both White and Red, but just about all older wood) in a lovingly restored three-hundred-year-old barn elsewhere on the Paardeberg. It must be stressed that this is not a second label for Sadie: the vineyards used (also leased, but under Sadie's vigorous control) are distinct, and differently managed—less expensively, for one thing. The Red usually has about 70 percent Syrah, with Mourvèdre and Grenache; the White blends Chenin, Grenache Blanc, Roussanne, and Viognier. So these wines are not very different in composition from the Sadie Family ones, though made in larger quantities, and in fact are usually little inferior—the White particularly being a splendidly mineral, fresh wine with good aging potential, and probably preferred by those who find Sadie's Palladius a little funky at times. The Red is also a very fine, rather beautiful wine, though less profound than Columella. Both Sequillo wines are good value, especially in comparison to Sadie's other wines and some of the other ambitious new wines of the Paardeberg area.

www.sequillo.com

SPICE ROUTE

As discussed in the introduction to this chapter, Charles Back of Fairview, in search of a new quality and a new style of red wine that would uniquely express the soils and climate of the Cape, bought a farm called Klein Amoskuil near Malmesbury and started to establish the winery that he and his partners in the venture called Spice Route, in poetic tribute to the fifteenth-century mariners who passed the Cape of Storms. (Soon Back—who likes doing things at his own pace and in his own way—bought out his partners.)

If the combination of mixed clay-gravel laterite and deep, red decomposed-granite soils was appealing, much of the existing vineyard was not: some forty-year-old blocks of Chenin Blanc and Pinotage were kept, but for the most part he planted anew, a wide range of Mediterranean reds—mostly those of southern France, but also Tempranillo, Barbera, and Zinfandel. Back was responding with his customary intelligence and insight to the conditions of this part of the Swartland; there was no water for irrigation, so bush-vines would do best in the hot weather (though the nights are often comparatively cool, beneficially slowing the ripening process).

Within a few months he had created a cellar by converting an old tobacco-drying shed. It's worth noting, too, that all the cellar employees and farmworkers at Spice Route own their own houses. Eben Sadie was appointed as winemaker and, from the maiden 1998 vintage, Spice Route started attracting attention. Sadie left after the third vintage and was replaced by Charl du Plessis.

There's an element of irony in the fact that although Spice Route has its admirers, there is now more excitement generated by Swartland wineries that have emerged since Charles Back broke the ground, as it were. Back, one feels, would dearly love to produce the world-renowned wines (here or at Fairview) that his erstwhile protégé does, and yet (like Elijah on Pisgah) he seems doomed to be the prophet and the leader unable to enter that particular bit of the promised land, even though his reputation as an industry leader in South Africa remains high.

The red wine that occasionally comes closest to brilliance at Spice Route is Malabar, a Syrah-based blend that varies from vintage to vintage, with Mourvèdre plus usually Grenache and Petite Sirah. It's a generous, warm wine, but fresh and beautifully balanced when it is not picked overripe. A second-label version of this wine was introduced with the 2007 vintage, called Chakalaka.

There are also two varietal Syrahs, from the same vineyard but made very differently: the exuberant Shiraz stresses the sweet fruit, with mostly older American oak used, to make a well-balanced new-world-style wine of some charm. The Flagship Syrah, on the other hand, looks to the Rhône, with more oak, all French, half of it new; at its best it is more complex, fine, and deep, with something approaching elegance despite the 14.5 percent alcohol that is typical of it (and of the other wines in the range). Three whites are regularly made: the Sauvignon Blanc is made from Darling grapes, and presumably there because customers want a Sauvignon; it's a decent, ripely tropical example. The Viognier, fermented in older oak, is a fairly restrained version, pleasantly underplaying the apricot perfume and lush structure of the variety, often with a little residual sugar (which makes for ease, perhaps, and also keeps the alcohol level down just a bit). Altogether more interesting, altogether more superior, is the Chenin Blanc, from mature bushvines; barrel-fermented with a very small new-oak component, it is intriguing and subtly forceful, with a good vein of acid.

www.spiceroutewines.co.za

11

BREEDE RIVER VALLEY

BACKGROUND

This is the Western Cape's most wine-productive area, a long, wide valley with the Breede River and its tributaries as lifeblood. A great mountain barrier separates most of it from the coastal areas, leading the river to the ocean east of Agulhas. The three districts—Robertson, Worcester, and Breedekloof—together have something like a third of the country's vines and produce rather more than a third of its wine, thanks to their high yields. A good deal of the annual harvest is destined for grape juice or distillation—as the large preponderance of Chenin Blanc and Colombard (some 11,000 hectares in 2008) indicates. But there's plenty of just about everything here: if one thinks of Constantia, Elim, and Elgin, say, as the areas most associated with Sauvignon Blanc, one must reckon with the fact that the Breede River Valley has close to 2,900 hectares of it, while the smaller regions can muster only some 600 hectares among them. Quality is a different matter, but in addition to ordinary and less-than-ordinary wines there are some good and very good wines made and bottled here, primarily from estate producers—of which there are a surprising number in this heartland of large wineries feeding the distilleries and the merchant houses.

Substantial wine production is a comparatively modern component of Breede River Valley farming, however, as the northerly reaches had to wait for viable commercial access to Cape Town until the middle of the nineteenth century and, for its great production explosion in the next century, for irrigation from the Brandvlei Dam near the town of Worcester and the development of cold-fermentation techniques after World War II. Early

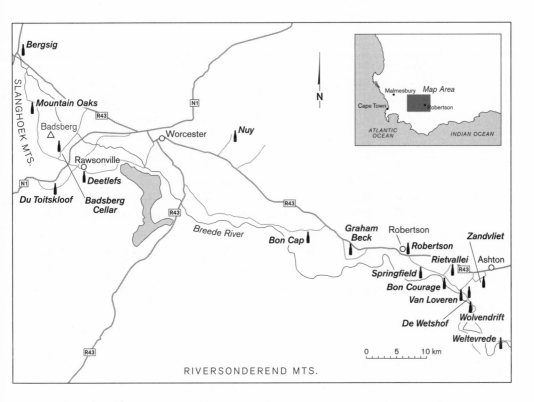

MAP 8
Breede River Valley

in the history of the settlement at the Cape, Swellendam had been approached through the Overberg area, but the main northerly route across the mountains was via the valley of Tulbagh, which then gave access in the southeast to the Breede River Valley. A road through the Bain's Kloof pass, completed in 1853, opened the way from Paarl and Cape Town to Worcester.

By 1875 Robertson and Worcester (the latter would have included the district now known as Breedekloof) had a total of some eleven million vines, rather more than half as many as greater Paarl, and more than two-thirds as many as Stellenbosch. Later, the (generally low) 1909 harvest was cited in a report, which gave Paarl's production as 5,053 leaguers while Worcester's was 4,206 and Robertson's, 3,059. So already a hundred years back, the figures were climbing tremendously and the valley was coming into its own. The 1913 collapse of the ostrich industry, which was significant especially around Robertson, and then the rise of the KWV system rewarding quantity over quality, along with dams and a developed transport infrastructure easing connections to the main markets, encouraged large-scale wine production even more. The crucial elements in the success of contemporary viticulture in the whole hot, dry valley (mostly with rainfall under 300 millimeters annually, and the Breede River often runs dry in summer) were, to repeat, enhanced irrigation possibilities, the growth of the brandy industry, and cold-fermentation techniques.

THE WARDS

The Breedekloof district has some twenty-two wineries, ranging from large cooperatives to a few quality-ambitious boutique establishments, mostly disposed along the Breede or its tributaries flowing from the mountains that form its western and southern boundaries. The alluvial soils and boulder beds on the valley floor, where most of the wineries are, are darkly rich and sandy, while the lower slopes of the mountains feature sandstone. The lovely Slanghoek Valley, which forms one of the district's two wards (seldom mentioned on labels), has good summer rainfall and summers that are less hot than in the other ward, Goudini, centered on Rawsonville. A relative newcomer to the area, which does use the WO Slanghoek name on its labels, is Mountain Oaks, owned by Christine (the winemaker) and Mark Stevens. Their small, certified-organic farm is a pleasant surprise in an area known best for qualitatively modest, large-scale, and certainly chemically assisted production. As for the wines, they're pleasant enough—particularly the Pinotage—but the range is somewhat anarchically unstable.

Scattered among the many, hugely productive cooperatives of Goudini (Du Toitskloof probably today the best known, with excellent-value wine appearing under its own label, including a good Chardonnay-Viognier and, rather remarkably, an equally good Nebbiolo in its Reserve range) are a few estates, with Deetlefs among the most ambitious. The Deetlefs family built the homestead in 1863 and, in the same period, a winery with five concrete tanks—still in use today, now suitably epoxy-coated—and eleven vats. They have 100 hectares under vine at the foot of the Du Toitskloof Mountains, planted with just about everything from Riesling to Petit Verdot. Bergsig (whose splendid mountain views at the narrowing of the valley give the estate its name) is another old family farm, dating back to 1843, with the sixth generation of Lategans now involved in farming 253 hectares of vineyards, producing some 50,000 cases under their own label, including an interesting wine called Icarus, a blend of Cabernet, Touriga, and Syrah.

Among other examples revealing the potential of some Breedekloof sites must be mentioned two Pinotages made by Bruce Jack's Flagstone: the regular Writer's Block and an occasional first-class Reserve, which originate in a single vineyard block high in the Waaihoek Mountains. Bizoe, a small producer based in Somerset West, also finds a good red in the area, in its case a Syrah. And a remarkable treasure-house of top-quality dessert wines (botrytised and Natural Sweet as well as fortified) can be found at the Badsberg Cellar cooperative, where winemaker Henri Swiegers splendidly exercises his international experience in, and love for, such wines.

As elsewhere along the Breede River, white grapes predominate in Breedekloof, substantially for distillation. They occupy the top four positions in the local grape league table, from declining Chenin (more than 2,000 hectares in 2011) through Colombard, Chardonnay, and Sauvignon Blanc (947 hectares). But red wine grapes are not a negligible presence, with some 800 hectares of Cabernet Sauvignon, and Syrah, Merlot, Cinsaut, and Ruby Cabernet not all that far behind.

The Worcester district, centered on the historic town of the same name, has a basically similar planting pattern on a reduced scale (1,700 hectares of Chenin, 300 of Cabernet). Production for brandy is, again, a vital part of the viticultural program. Here too most vines are trellised, though there are plenty of bushvines, mostly older ones. Moving eastward, rainfall steadily diminishes compared with Slanghoek: at Nuy, forty kilometers away, the annual total is roughly a mere 200 millimeters. Irrigation is vital. In recognition primarily of different soil types—mostly derived from alluvium and shale—there are four declared wards within the Worcester district, but these seldom appear on wine labels: this is not the sort of area that generally prompts producers to seek terroir expression. The land and climate do speak in general terms through the wines, of course, not least in the delicious and long-lived Muscadels made at the Nuy cooperative alongside a number of other good-value but modest wines made under its own label. Muscadels and Jerepigos there are aplenty, of course, in this warm area, among the most renowned of which are those of Rietvallei, near Robertson, most notably the tiny quantities of 1908—made from the small vineyard of gnarled old low-yielding bushvines planted in that year.

The town of Robertson, which gives its name to the qualitatively most important winegrowing district along the Breede River, was named after Dr. William Robertson, a minister who emigrated from Scotland in 1822. He was based at Swellendam but every three months would hold services at the home of Johannes van Zijl on a farm called Roodezand ("red sand"). Robertson was one of those who in 1852 assisted in the purchase of that farm in order to establish a town, and the community named it after him in recognition of his services.

Although the Robertson area is also predominantly devoted to white wine, it has both a larger proportion of good-quality black grapes than do Breedekloof and Worcester (not all that much less Cabernet than Chenin, which has just over 1,500 hectares, and about a thousand hectares of Syrah) and a rather different ranking of the white grapes. In fact, Chardonnay vies with Colombard as the most-planted variety at roughly 2,000 hectares. Robertson has a rich vein of limestone, making for an unusual variation from the generally acidic Cape soils, and parts of the district have thus proved as well suited to Chardonnay as they have to the breeding of horses. Danie de Wet of De Wetshof Estate has been the great pioneer and exponent of the variety here—and his interest in improving his vines and wines led him, of course, into being one of the original Chardonnay smugglers of the 1980s, as described in chapter 2.

The building of the Brandvlei Dam in the first decades of the twentieth century (it was completed in 1937 and extended in 1989) was here, as elsewhere in the valley, important for viticultural spread. The district is warm, with an average summer daytime temperature of 23°C and a number of extremely hot days always likely, but southeasterly winds do bring in cooling, moisture-laden air from the Indian Ocean a hundred kilometers distant. The Langeberg range to the north and the Riversonderend Mountains to the south of the valley look harsh and barren from the vineyards and orchards of the irrigated valley floor. Some viticulture is practiced on the slopes of the foothills, where the soils are heavy and reddish-brown. Otherwise, apart from the limestone outcrops, they tend to be sandy with boulder beds, or lighter-textured alluvial soils prompting more vigor than is commensurate with the highest quality. Vines are mostly trellised and widely spaced. Soil varies, as elsewhere in the Breede River Valley, and is the factor prompting the large number of wards in Robertson: there are nine of them, but you will struggle to find a reflection of them on bottles.

Most of the wineries discussed below are located in Robertson. Although there are rather more private producers here than elsewhere in the valley, there are a number of cooperatives, too. Particularly interesting and dynamic is Robertson Winery (in which distributor Vinimark has a substantial interest), established as a cooperative in 1947 and one of the first few to bottle and market its own wines instead of selling it all in bulk to wholesalers. More than 1,900 hectares, owned by thirty-five growers, provide grapes for the enormous winery complex, where some two million cases per year are produced (about half for export). Robertson was perhaps the first of the co-ops to start recognizing and rewarding outstanding individual growers, and to start isolating vineyards especially capable of producing fine wine in order to vinify their grapes separately. There is now, in addition to the other ranges under the winery's own name, a selection of half a dozen such wines, named for their vineyards and offering estate quality.

Among the family wineries in the district offering good quality and value is the Retief family's Van Loveren, which now produces something like a million cases per year, making it the largest privately owned wine business in the country. Van Loveren also initiated one of the more significant and real Black Economic Empowerment schemes, and in 2008 was given the top award for empowerment in South African agriculture. Despite the Breede River Valley being seen by some as a stronghold of "old South African" social values (some depressing stories have come from the environs of Rawsonville, for example), Robertson has a better history of social concern than some more obvious areas: in the late 1990s Weltevrede initiated the area's first empowerment scheme, and De Wetshof Estate has long been recognized for its (arguably paternalistic, but effective) concern for its workforce.

Also not lacking in Robertson is the spirit that has seen so many ambitious grape-growers around the country turn to making and bottling some wines on their own account. At the deciduous fruit and wine-grape farm Wolvendrift, on the Breede River between Robertson and Bonnievale, fifth-generation Lourens van der Westhuizen has, working with his father Frikkie, planted a dozen hectares of prime varieties on carefully selected soils. The old cellar on the property is now the tasting facility for Arendsig ("eagle view"): in 2009, said Lourens, "I moved my winery into my dad's old table-grape packhouse." It is early days yet—his first wine was bottled only in 2004—but his sumptuous Shiraz is so far the most promising of his range.

The little-planted district of Swellendam is no longer included in the Breede River Valley district, but finds itself in the newer Cape South Coast district.

THE WINERIES

BON CAP

Roelf and Michelle du Preez represent the sixth generation of the family to farm this land. Their organic approach is nothing new: "The du Preezs have been farming organically for years," says Roelf, who manages the lands; "from the start we could see the benefit to the soil." They received full organic status from SGS in 2002, the year the first wines were made here; for many years their grapes had gone to a local cooperative. The first eighty-ton harvest was vinified in a converted tractor shed only just big enough to cope, but the next year a new winery was built, and today capacity is 500 tons from the farm's 45 hectares of Viognier, Chardonnay, Syrah, Cabernet, and Pinotage. Both the Bon Cap and the Ruins ranges are good advertisements for organic wine; the varietal wines show purity, while the blends (including the Cape's first bottle-fermented organic Méthode Cap Classique) are carefully constructed to offer an extra dimension. All are balanced and pleasant-drinking on release, though as yet they show little ambition for lengthy aging or great complexity.

www.boncaporganic.co.za

BON COURAGE

Bruwer (pronounced "Brewvair") is a name with strong associations in the Robertson area. Current winemaker Jacques Bruwer represents the third generation on this farm, whose Afrikaans name, Goedemoed, translates into the French Bon Courage. Jacques's grandfather bought the property in 1927, and for many years the crop was sold as bulk wine to the KWV. Son André took over in 1965 and modernized the farm. In 1983 he registered it as an estate and started moving increasingly to producing premium-quality wines. About 150 hectares are planted to vineyards, on soils varying from alluvial—the property lies at the confluence of three rivers—to limestone on the slopes. Numerous varieties are planted, and a large range of mostly unambitious, good-value wines is made. Less modest all around, at the top level are the Inkará Cabernet and Shiraz—big, very ripe, generously oaked wines with high alcohol and a little residual sugar: not made to appeal to subtle palates, but rich and velvety, and flamboyantly successful in this style. The winery is better known for its MCC sparkling wines that invoke the old French spelling of the family name: the Jacques Bruére *[sic]* Brut Reserve Blanc de Blancs is from Chardonnay, and the Brut Reserve has 60 percent Pinot. Both are light, dry, and fresh, with some oak influence giving a round richness.

www.boncourage.co.za

DE WETSHOF

De Wet is one of the oldest names in Cape wine (the first de Wet settled here in 1694, apparently), and Danie de Wet, owner of this large and progressive Robertson estate, has been one of the modern industry's leading figures, a force in many important organizations. Danie it was who established the property's reputation. The de Wets had been in the Robertson area since the early 1800s, but bought this farm only in 1952. In 1968 Danie went to Geisenheim in Germany, returning three years later to put into practice the viticultural and enological lessons he had learned, and the ambitions he had nurtured.

Cold-fermentation equipment was installed, and new plantings were made—notably of Sauvignon Blanc, Riesling, and Pinot Gris, as well as of Chardonnay, the variety for which De Wetshof was to become best known. In 1972 the farm became the first estate in Robertson under the new Wine of Origin legislation, and in 1973 came the first wines under the De Wetshof label. The Chardonnay clones Danie had at his disposal were heavily virused, and in the early 1980s (as described in chapter 2) he took what are now described as "unorthodox" steps to bring in new planting material—although it unfortunately turned out to be Auxerrois. But in due course—and notwithstanding some great success for wines from the older vineyards, including highest honors at Vinexpo for his 1985 Chardonnay—the vineyards were replanted. Further work on vineyards has meant careful soil mapping to match variety to terroir, from the alluvial soils near the Breede River to the lime-rich higher slopes on the valley sides. Advanced technology also monitors water needs within the irrigated vineyards. There are now 180 hectares under vine; the majority are for white wine varieties (overwhelmingly Chardonnay, but also Riesling, Sauvignon Blanc, and Sémillon), but red wines joined the portfolio in the early years of this century, so Cabernet Sauvignon, Merlot, Petit Verdot, and Pinot Noir are also planted.

All of the Chardonnays are good and soundly made (Danie de Wet still presides over the cellar, with Mervyn Willams as winemaker and next-generation Peter de Wet also involved since 2007), and occasionally the expensive, seriously oaked Bateleur has challenged top examples of this variety in the Cape. The differentiation between the six or seven versions on offer (spread across the De Wetshof and more modestly priced Danie de Wet ranges) seems to be more stylistic than expressive of terroir—although another version (perhaps the finest yet), called the Site, was introduced with the 2009 vintage and represents a single mature vineyard planted (uniquely in South Africa) with the Burgundian 119 clone. Chardonnay d'Honneur is also new-oaked, while there is less wood influence on the more citrusy Finesse, and the Bon Vallon is unwooded—indeed, it was the first in this style in the Cape, further testimony to Danie de Wet's innovative spirit and his alertness to market possibilities.

This is a serious estate, where commitment (and not just to narrowly interpreted wine matters) runs deep: De Wetshof has been a forerunner in qualifying for national and international certificates relating to quality management systems as well as safety and hazard standards; it has an admirable sense of responsibility to the well-being of its employees; and Danie de Wet and his wife, Lesca, took conservation matters to heart long before it became de rigueur to do so, setting aside 422 hectares of pristine natural habitat on the property.

www.dewetshof.com

GRAHAM BECK

For a generation Graham Beck was a formidable—if publicly unassertive—force in South African wine. With a considerable fortune from coal mining, he became a racehorse owner, and in 1983 bought a large property in Robertson, Madeba. Planting began in 1985 with Chardonnay. Fruit and paddocks for racehorses also do well on the lime-rich soils, and the balance of the extensive estate is given over to indigenous vegetation—it became the second Biodiversity and Wine Initiative champion in 2006.

The first Madeba cellar, largely dedicated to sparkling wine production, took in its first harvest in 1991, having already generated some excitement with its orange walls and curved green roof—an image of modernity far from the whitewashed gables of Stellenbosch, but one well suited to this environment.

In 1990 Beck also bought Bellingham in Franschhoek. When he sold the majority of DGB (Douglas Green Bellingham) to company management in 1999, he retained the Bellingham property and the recently built red wine cellar there, while the old cellar was revamped to cater to white wines. Meanwhile, by 1997 the production and maturation cellars had been completed at the Robertson estate.

The last years of the 1990s also saw Beck buying two farms near Firgrove in Stellenbosch. He consolidated his four farms and two production centers into a unified 300,000-case operation. The substantial total hectares of vineyard include a wide range of red varieties as well as Chardonnay, Sauvignon Blanc, and Viognier. Some grapes are also bought in, notably Chenin Blanc. This enables a large range of still wines across three quality ranges, as well as the MCC sparkling wines for which the house is best known. Some of the wines originate entirely from the vineyards of just one property, and there are even some single-vineyard wines, but there is also a good deal of blending.

Graham Beck died in 2010, and the wine business (including Steenberg in Constantia) is owned by a family trust. There have been some changes since Beck's death, including the sale of the Franschhoek property to neighbor Johann Rupert. Facilities at Steenberg were expanded for cellarmaster Erika Obermeyer to handle many of the premium still wines under the Graham Beck label. The Robertson facility is devoted to sparkling wines and the Robertson terroir wines, still under cellarmaster Pieter Ferreira—there since 1990 and probably the country's most experienced and skillful maker of MCC wines. His first bubbly for Graham Beck, a blanc de blancs, was produced in 1991; it remains one of the foremost Cape examples, from Chardonnay off Robertson's limestone soils, half fermented in oak (10 percent new barrels added each year), and disgorged only after at least thirty-six months. There are also a nonvintage Brut and Brut Rosé, and a vintage Brut Rosé, all from Pinot and Chardonnay. In 2008 the prestige label Cuvée Clive (named for Graham and Rhona Beck's late son) was introduced with the 2003 vintage after some five years of maturation on the lees, an immensely elegant and by local standards expensive Chardonnay-based wine.

The numerous wines are spread across half a dozen ranges. Many are perfectly decent reds and whites of reasonable value, with most interest coming, of course, at the top level.

The reds have for the most part been big, very ripe, and rather alcoholic (generally approaching 15 percent), though mostly not overoaked, and serious-minded in their new-world styling. But some rethinking has apparently been taking place, and some detectable movement will probably have been the consequence. A new Cabernet-Syrah blend called Ad Honorem was introduced with the 2007 vintage and was certainly impressive. The Chalkboard range, of wines from bought-in grapes, was introduced in 2011, also perhaps in response to some new thinking—although they offered not much that was new. Of the more established wines, the Ridge Syrah is generally the most elegant of the smart reds, though still undeniably opulent. The Joshua adds a little Viognier to Syrah, and many enjoy its lavish, ripe lushness. The Andrew is a big, generous blend of Bordeaux varieties, while the William has been the Beck red that I have most enjoyed—a blend of mostly Cabernet with varying proportions of Pinotage, rather lighter-footed than its big alcohol implies, with fresh, sweetly juicy fruit. (It will be noticed that Graham Beck was the arch-proponent of the rather twee custom of giving family names to his wines; he also prefixed them with a definite article.) All these reds will undoubtedly benefit from at least three years in bottle, perhaps more. The Chardonnays seem to be lightening up on the new oak, which had on occasion been a touch excessive; the barrel-fermented Bowed Head Chenin Blanc, introduced with the 2008 vintage, is ambitious, weighty, and sumptuously powerful; Pheasants' Run is a typically very good Sauvignon Blanc balancing greenness, minerality, and tropical fruit.

www.grahambeckwines.com

SPRINGFIELD

This is one of the most interesting wineries in Robertson—indeed, in the whole Breede Valley—because Abrie Bruwer is one of the most interesting winemakers and farmers: a believer in terroir and allowing it express itself by intervening as little as possible, an experimenter who would prefer to make what he calls a "monumental stuff-up" than safe but mediocre wine. What he knows he taught himself or learned by working with his father. The Bruwer family's association with winemaking on this farm goes back four generations, but Abrie is proud to trace his ancestors five generations more, to the Bruères, Huguenots from the Loire.

There are 150 hectares of vineyards here, on lime-rich soils varying from unforgiving rock to clay to sandy stretches by the Breede River. Varieties include Sauvignon, Chardonnay, Pinot Noir, Merlot, Petit Verdot, and Cabernets Sauvignon and Franc. All vine rows run east-west, to encourage more evening ripening while offering protection against the sun—and in the hope of catching a cooling southeasterly wind coming up the valley from the distant ocean. Viticulture is aimed at sustainability, with minimal chemical spraying, and ducks cheerfully roam the vineyards to keep down the snails.

The natural approach continues after harvest. White and black grapes are vinified and matured in separate cellars (the red wine cellar gravity-fed), and neither crushers nor pumps are used. Only Sauvignon Blanc is inoculated with yeast. The extreme expression of Abrie's naturalism and his risk-taking, and his greatest triumph (when it succeeds), is his Méthode Ancienne Chardonnay. Fermentation in barrel on native yeasts—a process that may take up to two months—is followed by malolactic fermentation, after which the wine remains unsulfured in oak for a year on the original lees, and is then bottled unfined and unfiltered. It makes for a subtle, multilayered wine of minerality and richness, usually able to mature for at least ten years. The downside is that only about half of the attempts have succeeded. The Méthode Ancienne Cabernet Sauvignon is made in the same way and is more regularly successful, if rather oaky and not quite as distinguished a wine.

Springfield's two Sauvignons are also remarkable, if only because this variety in Robertson should not give these cooler-climate characteristics. They speak eloquently of Abrie Bruwer's viticultural sensitivities. In fact, the comparatively early picking practiced here leads to all the wines having alcohols that are moderate by all Cape standards, let alone hot-area ones. Life from Stone Sauvignon Blanc, with less than 13 percent alcohol, comes from a single rocky vineyard planted about 1980; it has a racy minerality, with citrus and passion fruit. The differently charactered and more substantial Special Cuvée version, also from a single mature vineyard, grows closer to the river, on sandier soil with a rocky base. Both mature happily for a good few years. Without winemakers like Abrie Bruwer, South African wine would be decidedly poorer and less interesting.

www.springfieldestate.com

WELTEVREDE

This farm is one of several that helped to make Chardonnay the calling card for limestone-rich Robertson. It was a subdivision of a much larger farm granted in 1831 and sold to Nicklaas Jonker in 1911 as a mixed farm. Further subdivisions followed among his sons, and in 1933 the portion including the family homestead went to Japie Jonker, father of current owner, Lourens Jonker. Lourens had studied in both Stellenbosch and California, and took over when his father died in 1969; the year before he had replaced the old cellar with one equipped with cooling to produce high-quality white wine. In 1975 Weltevrede was the first in the area to bottle its own wine and sell directly to the public; it was also an early planter of red varieties here, and in 1976 marketed the first estate Red Muscadel—the pioneering fortified dessert wine in the Nederburg Auction. Weltevrede was also among the early experimenters with small French oak. In addition to expressing his dynamism on the home farm, Lourens Jonker became a director of the KWV and then its chair.

Further properties were added to Weltevrede over the years, crucially bringing slopes and a variety of soil types to the alluvial flatland. There are now 160 hectares, of which 100 are under vines: Cabernet Sauvignon, Merlot, Pinot Noir, Chardonnay, Colombard, and Sauvignon Blanc. The emphasis is on the Chardonnay, which now accounts for nearly 40 percent of the vines. Twenty different clones are planted, a third of them experimental, on a wide variety of soil types and slopes.

Lourens's son, Philip, took over the winemaking in 1997 and has put his own stamp on Weltevrede's wine, notably in his splendid obsession with terroir expression for the Chardonnays, as well as his successful focus on sparkling wines. The first Chardonnay vintage under the Weltevrede label was 1989. Unsurprisingly, Philip's three Chardonnays are the most interesting of the still wines. The Rusted Soil version, off the red-topped limestone soils, produces wines with plush yellow peach and pine-apple tones and a citrus twist—a fairly typical profile for Robertson Chardonnay. It is matured in less new oak than the Place of Rocks, from the shale slopes, which is less obviously fruity and more mineral, with a richer, more oxidative character. Philip's belief in the effect of soil is vindicated here, as the same clone is responsible for both of these wines. Poet's Prayer Chardonnay is a tiny blending of fruit from both terroirs, but not necessarily more successful or harmonious than either. Other wines in the Estate range that reflect specific terroirs are Bedrock Syrah and the Travelling Stone Sauvignon Blanc. Chardonnay also features in a new and expanded (in 2009) range of MCC sparklers, among which the Entheos looks most promising—a nonvintage blend of Chardonnay and Pinot Noir. There are also some entry-level wines and a few Muscadels.

www.weltevrede.com

ZANDVLIET

If Robertson is the land of wine, racehorses, and roses, as the PR people have it, then Zandvliet is typical to a high degree. Certainly the stud has produced great champions, the wines are not bad, and the roses are lovely. Zandvliet was founded in 1838 and Jacobus de Wet bought it in 1867; on his death, subdivision reduced Zandvliet to 1,000 hectares. The current owners are the farm's fourth generation of de Wets, Paul and Dan. Syrah was planted, as the farm's first red variety, before World War I and was used for fortified wines. When Paul de Wet (father of the present owners) took wine production in hand in the early 1970s and decided that the estate's prime red wine should be a Syrah (against conservative advice, which thought the area suitable only for white wines), he replaced the older stock with material from Durbanville. The first wine bottled under the Zandvliet label was the Shiraz 1975. Paul also installed cold fermentation in his newly built wine cellar and pioneered the making of dry white table wines in Robertson. Until 1994 Zandvliet was one of the estates for which the Bergkelder matured, bottled, and marketed the wine.

Syrah is now the majority variety, covering 40 of the 150 hectares of vineyard, with further plantings planned; also planted are Cabernet, Merlot, Chardonnay, Colombard, Sauvignon, and Chenin. Initially, the Syrah was grown on alluvial soils, but later plantings were on the less-vigorous *kalkveld,* with its gravel and clay or limestone slopes. Growth is regulated by irrigation and canopy management, crop thinning, severe winter pruning, and organic fertilizers. As well as a straight Syrah, two versions are made with Kalkveld in the name; these are differentiated primarily by the type of wood used (and as both are marked by the use of all-new oak, it is not easy to discern subtler differences). The Kalkveld Shiraz is matured in French oak; the Hill of Enon version is all-American. Both are fairly powerful and concentrated, but not overextracted or heavy, with spice and fresh minerality, and benefit from a good few years in bottle. There are also pleasant Chardonnays in the Estate range, and two lesser ranges.

www.zandvliet.co.za

12

WALKER BAY AND CAPE AGULHAS

BACKGROUND

The land along the most southerly coastline of the Western Cape had to wait for the KWV quota system to be abandoned in 1992 before its potential for winegrowing could start to be fully explored. True, there was a very small premodern history of wine production in parts around the fishing village of Hermanus, and inland around Bot River there was some viticulture: an old property named Beaumont was revived as a fully functioning winery in 1994 after some years of more or less desultory grape-growing. Generally, however, vineyards would have been planted and wine made only for domestic use and sometimes to supply passing wagoners.

The richer valleys of the mountainous interior had a long history of pastoralism, and the land there was used primarily for herding from the early days of white settlement too, and also for wheat. Bot River was known by the original pastoralists as the Gouga (meaning "abundance of fat"). The word was apparently used for the butter that early Cape merchants used to come trading for; they referred to the river as the Botter (Dutch for "butter") as early as 1672.

After the devastation from phylloxera, there was little replanting of the few vineyards in the hinterland of Hermanus. The cooler climate (near the coast, and substantially south of Stellenbosch or Paarl), which is now an attraction, was a disincentive when large and reliable crops were the only desiderata. Coolness was important to Tim Hamilton-Russell, a rich and serious wine-lover with ambitions to grow the great grapes of the Côte d'Or, who in 1975 decided to settle in the Hemel-en-Aarde ("heaven and earth") Valley. The pioneer's regret was that the country did not extend another two hundred kilometers southward, but Hamilton Russell Vineyards was for some time the Cape's most southerly wine producer.

The chain of valleys of what has come to be known as the Hemel-en-Aarde area (after some bickering over the extent of the Hemel-en-Aarde Valley as such) is still rural, in marked contrast to the fashionable and now sizable seaside resort of Hermanus, whose ugly fringes are only starting to threaten invasion. There is not much agricultural activity apart from the expanding vineyards. The Atlantic is nearby—a few kilometers at its closest—separated from the scattered patches of viticulture by a range of modest mountains. Sea breezes flow in, giving the famous coolness (which term must be understood in a South African context rather than, say, a New Zealand one). This applies even to the part farthest inland, but here conditions are a little more continental, giving warmer days but often cooler nights, and definitely colder winters and the risk of frost. Rainfall is generous at about 750 millimeters annually, but a good deal is lost through runoff and drainage in parts where clay does not provide water-holding capacity. Particularly in the most inland sections, the most recently developed in terms of viticulture, expansion is limited to areas near hillsides from which runoff water can be dammed for supplementary irrigation. Soils are mostly of shale, clay, and sandstone, with decomposed granite as well in the middle section. The soil-mapping done so assiduously at Hamilton Russell Vineyards has bequeathed to the area as a whole a wider carefulness of matching variety to soil—though adjustments are still necessary.

Until fairly recently, the authoritative influence of pioneering Hamilton Russell Vineyards has been extraordinarily important and immediate. Viticultural development in the area spread out from there—and not only through the little empire of the family's three adjacent estates. In the great tradition of settlers and pioneers, the Hamilton-Russells have spread their winemaking genes, as it were, throughout the district. It seems that their winemakers leave only to set up shop elsewhere in the Hemel-en-Aarde. In 1990, the first to do so, Peter Finlayson, became a partner in a new winery nearby. The second, Storm Kreusch-Dau, moved on to establish a cellar for her Whalehaven label at the foot of the valley, where she made mostly Burgundian-style wines from bought-in grapes (after some vicissitudes Whalehaven is under new ownership, and undergoing regeneration). Kevin Grant was next in line at the pioneer winery, and he too moved on, in 2004, escaping only as far as the next valley, still within the Hemel-en-Aarde area. The second generation in direct succession has come with one of the most recent—and immensely promising—new wineries being established by Peter Finlayson's two sons.

At the close of the twentieth century, however, the only addition to the Hamilton Russell and Bouchard Finlayson estates were Newton Johnson Vineyards and Sumaridge (the latter not yet bottling wine, but at least effectively doing away with what was looking strangely like a requirement for double-barreled names in the valley). Thirteen years later there were more than a dozen—not including Hermanuspietersfontein and Whalehaven, which are wineries with no vineyards in the area. It is not likely that there will be many more, owing to the lack of easy access to water. Expansion farther eastward is particularly

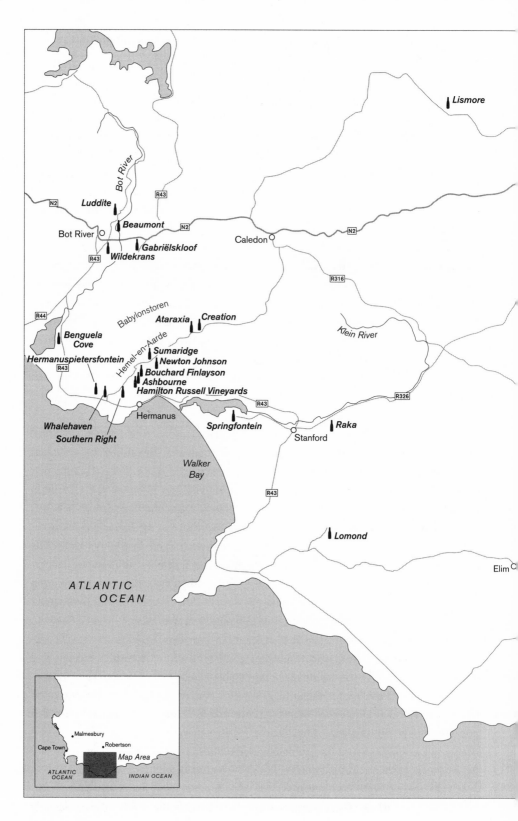

MAP 9
Walker Bay and Cape Agulhas

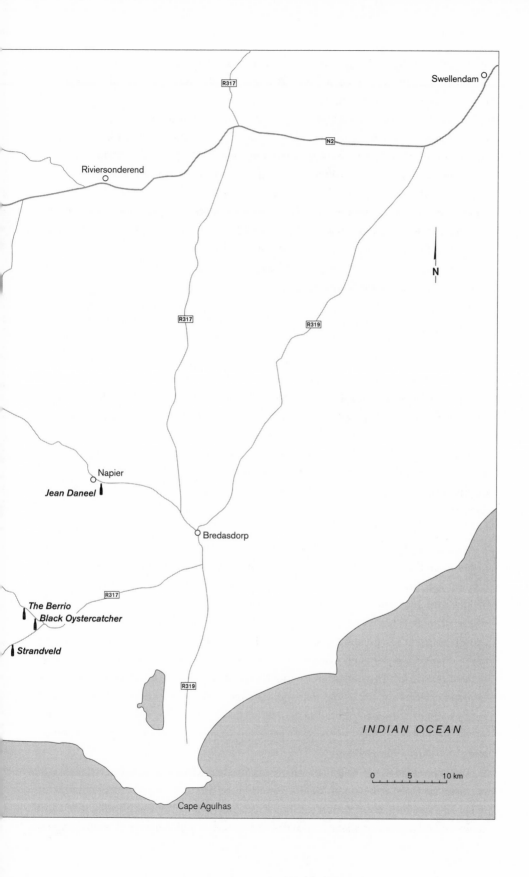

Swellendam

R317

N2

Riviersonderend

R317

R319

N

Napier

Jean Daneel

Bredasdorp

R317

The Berrio
Black Oystercatcher

Strandveld

R319

INDIAN OCEAN

0   5   10 km

Cape Agulhas

unlikely—although cooling sea breezes do penetrate to the farthest inland winery in the area, their significance would be much reduced over the next set of mountains, barring a wind sweep down a contiguous valley.

Tim Hamilton-Russell had been concerned to emulate Burgundy, and the Burgundian varieties remain something of a signature for the area, with most of the producers having at least some planted, and a few specializing in them. Fashion and the market dictate an increasing proportion of Sauvignon Blanc, however, and it covered about 268 hectares in 2011 (plantings having doubled in the three years leading up), compared with 107 for Pinot Noir and 92 for Chardonnay. While this is the largest proportion of Pinot Noir for any area in the Cape, and while most local wine-lovers would most associate Hemel-en-Aarde with Pinot and vice versa), in fact it is not an overwhelming part of the Cape's total of 1,019 hectares. Syrah is the only other variety with a really significant presence, though a number of other varieties are also grown.

THE WARDS

Until fairly recently, Hemel-en-Aarde was simply part of a much larger district, Walker Bay, which itself was only subtracted from the Overberg district in this century. Considering the attention paid to terroir here, however, it is appropriate that its claims for difference were rewarded by the promulgation of three wards (though whether consumers are ready for such fine distinctions is another matter). Two are within the valley as such: that closest to the sea in the west taking its name, the next inland called Upper Hemel-en-Aarde Valley. For a while the establishment of the most easterly of the wards was delayed by a dispute over the name—about whether the sacred "Hemel-en-Aarde" bit could also be applied to what, it was argued, was a separate valley, on the far side of a significant watershed. Agreement was reached in 2009, and Hemel-en-Aarde Ridge was named.

Within the Walker Bay district, the ward of Bot River stretches from the Bot River Lagoon into the foothills of the Groenlandberg and Babylonstoren mountain ranges, on mostly shale and sandstone soils with a variety of aspects. Apart from Beaumont and Wildekrans—the latter established in 1993 and starting a promising regeneration some fifteen years later under new ownership—the other half-dozen wineries date from this century. Most are in the more inland part, though still exposed to the cooling influence of the Atlantic, but Benguela Cove, which is part of a large housing estate, is on the banks of the lagoon itself. There seems to be much promise in the area, which will not take long to reveal itself more fully. Different conditions have called for a rather different array of grape varieties than is found in the Hemel-en-Aarde: Syrah vies with Sauvignon Blanc as the most planted, and there is also a generous planting of the red Bordeaux varieties, and some older Chenin Blanc.

The other ward in the Walker Bay district is Sunday's Glen on its eastern edge, wedged between the Overberg ward of Klein River and the Cape Agulhas district and partaking of some characteristics of both areas: higher altitude and the prevailing wind give some coolness, and Sauvignon Blanc dominates and does very well, but westerly slopes happily accommodate the Bordeaux red varieties. There are no wineries here, but this is where the farms of Hermanuspietersfontein are to be found. Between the Hemel-en-Aarde wards and Sunday's Glen, a few wineries are located not far from the town of Stanford.

In some ways more continuous with the Hemel-en-Aarde, continuing along the Atlantic coast, is the district of Cape Agulhas, which makes it a fair partner in this chapter. This is the larger of the two districts, in fact, but younger and with a smaller number of wineries. It has one ward demarcated within it, Elim, where most of the wineries are to be found—only Quoin Rock, just to the north of that ward and on the southern slopes of the Bredasdorp mountains, and Lomond, in a very separate valley, are outside it. The district takes its name from that of the southernmost tip of Africa where (according to most authorities, but it is a somewhat vexed question) the Atlantic and Indian Oceans meet. The quaint little town of Elim was founded in 1824 by Moravian missionaries (and today is largely inhabited by members of the Moravian Church). After the effective ending of slavery in 1838, the mission took in freed slaves, and a century later the country's only monument commemorating slavery was built here.

The sober missionaries needed sacramental wine and were thus local pioneers of winemaking, but viticulture ceased at some stage (it seems the Moravians never applied for a KWV quota) and was resumed only in the mid 1990s. The story goes that Johan de Kock, who had recently bought a farm with the Nuwejaarsrivier running through it, was persuaded that access to water was the only real problem in an area perfect for winemaking. Stellenbosch Farmers' Winery considered a joint venture, but the southeasterly wind was blowing when the inspection was made and it came to nothing. De Kock got a few of his neighbors, along with some winemakers from elsewhere, interested in the viticultural idea, however, and the Land's End project planted its first vines in 1996. Over the next half-dozen years, four other wine producers were established within the area that was to be demarcated as Elim, as well as two others nearby. The prospects for fine-wine production here look excellent, and have not gone unnoticed by established producers elsewhere—already David Nieuwoudt of faraway Cederberg makes elegantly racy wines from Elim grapes, for example.

The sea wind—as the doubting big-business investors had noted—is a problem that has to be taken into account (Merlot quickly showed its unwillingness to cooperate, though it performs much better in more protected Lomond). Other problems include salinity from those winds, grape-predatory birds, and frequent soil variation—though the basic types are shale and laterite.

Sauvignon Blanc is, thus far, the unquestioned success, and at the end of 2011 it represented the largest plantings in all parts of the Cape Agulhas district, with some 115 hectares. Sémillon and Nouvelle are present, primarily as blending partners for Sauvignon. Syrah is the variety most are pinning their red-wine hopes on (with some real justification, as is becoming increasingly clear), with more than 60 hectares planted. Lomond has a good whack of Merlot, and there's Cabernet Sauvignon in Elim, as well as a little Pinot Noir (an exciting prospect) coming into production. Apart from those, a dozen other varieties are present in only minuscule quantities.

It's worth noting that the farmers of Elim are very conscious of the biodiversity around them and, as the Elim Winegrowers, have established the Nuwejaars Wetland Special Management Area Initiative to protect the ecosystem and preserve the unique animal and plant life of the Agulhas coastal plains. It seems, fortunately, most unlikely that the area will become a grape-growing monoculture—but the range of South African viticultural terroir has been most interestingly extended by this adventure in the southernmost reaches of the continent. The limits of viticulture along the south coast have not been fully explored. One of the more surprising and exciting developments in recent years has been the planting of vines at the estuary of the Breede River (in the otherwise little-planted Swellendam district), as far east of Agulhas as Agulhas is east of Hermanus (see the discussion of Sijnn under De Trafford in the Stellenbosch chapter). Windy terra incognita lies in between, and beyond—all the way to some adventurous plantings at Plettenberg Bay.

THE WINERIES

ASHBOURNE

The 113-hectare property that Anthony Hamilton-Russell owns on the eastern boundary of his eponymous estate was renamed Ashbourne (after an Irish ancestor) in the early years of this century and dedicated to the production of two wines. The red is simply called Ashbourne, and is one of the Cape's more noteworthy wines made primarily from Pinotage. While some other refined, restrained examples of Pinotage tend toward a Burgundian style, the vintages thus far of Ashbourne (the first was 2000, but it has not been made every year since then and tends to be released late) have shown more affinity with Bordeaux in terms of structure and even of flavor profile; this sophisticated and polished wine has included some Syrah and Cabernet since 2007. Also somewhat adventurous, and convincingly good, is the white wine, called Sandstone. Though a work in progress, it is likely to remain an unoaked blend based on Sauvignon Blanc, with Chardonnay and Sémillon (partly fermented in amphoras). It is also released late, which is a good thing as it can show remarkable development over a good few years. There are some 25 hectares of vineyard on Ashbourne. Viticultural experiments—testing what is, after all, new terroir—include planting bushvines on virgin soil. Until a planned cellar is built, winemaking is on the parent property.

ATARAXIA

Kevin Grant had been making wine for Hamilton Russell for something like a decade when he, like his predecessors there, felt impelled to make his own wines and, like them, did not want to move away from the area whose terroir he had come to believe so well suited to fine Pinot Noir and Chardonnay. In 2004 he established his own property farther inland, to become a pioneer of the Hemel-en-Aarde Ridge ward. For winemaking,

Grant is "still squatting in friends' cellars." The first crop from the new 12 hectares of vines came in 2010, and some of it was used for Ataraxia Chardonnay 2011. Grant plans in the medium term to progressively plant some 25 hectares. The focus is, inevitably, on Chardonnay and Pinot, with Sauvignon as a serious accompaniment. Until the vines come into useful production Grant is sourcing grapes from elsewhere in the valley and from other cooler-climate sites. Because of its nascent state, this winery must be categorized as one to watch, but the Chardonnay is so fine that there is early accomplishment to acknowledge as well as future brilliance of which to be fairly confident. The Sauvignon also leans to the richly austere, with a flinty core to its fruit. There has been no accompanying Pinot, as Grant could not source the quality he required, but he continued "with experiments from bought-in Pinot, to keep the eye sharp and the hand in." He also vinified but did not commercially release small batches of young-vine Pinot from his own vineyards. There is a red blend mixing very ripe plushness and refinement, from a variety of grapes and areas; called Serenity, it's another moment in the rhetoric of the winery, whose Greek name means, apparently, "a serene state of freedom from worry and preoccupation."

www.ataraxiawines.co.za

BEAUMONT

The Compagnes Drift farm on the eastern slopes of the Houw Hoek mountains, at the northern end of the Bot River ward, on which the Beaumonts grow their grapes and make their wine, had been an outpost for the Dutch East India Company in the middle of the eighteenth century. It's now a real family farm, a warm refuge from pillared entrances, rolling lawns, and smart PR. The old rustic cellar, last used forty years before and a place of vaults and alleys, was refurbished and reintroduced to use when Raoul and Jayne Beaumont decided in 1993 that their grapes should start being vinified and bottled under their own label. The maiden bottling was in 1994, with Jayne the first (pretty successful) maker of the Pinotage. Niels Verburg, now a neighbor at his own Luddite property, was winemaker from 1996 until 2003, when the Beaumonts' son, Sebastian, took over.

Only 34 of the farm's 400 hectares are under vine, the rest left to the natural mountain vegetation. They manage to squeeze in thirteen varieties, however. Chenin Blanc vines are among the oldest and provide grapes for two versions, of which the sensitively oaked Hope Marguerite is the more compelling—and an outstanding example of the less showy but still rich style. The Beaumonts were the first in the Cape to bottle a varietal Mourvèdre, a big and bold wine that has been good in some years, though the blend with Syrah tends to be more convincing. Mourvèdre also appears in the flagship Vitruvian, along with Pinotage and some dashes of other varieties. The Pinotage is serious and good, and Ariane (named for Sebastian's sister, who helps with the winery's marketing) is an elegant blend of all five Bordeaux red wine grapes. Goutte d'Or is a pleasant botrytised Sémillon-Sauvignon dessert wine. Raoul's range, named for the family patriarch who died in 2008, comprises three modest introductions to a selection of wines that is always pleasingly individual and interesting—and, seemingly, improving in quality.

www.beaumont.co.za

THE BERRIO

Francis Pratt pioneered wine farming in the Elim region when, against a lot of advice and struggling even harder against the winds, he made his first plantings in 1997. The Berrio (named for a caravel in Vasco da Gama's expedition that rounded Cape Agulhas in 1497) released a Sauvignon Blanc in 2001, followed by a Cabernet of the same vintage, both marketed as a joint venture with Pratt's old friend Bruce Jack, then the owner as well as the winemaker of Flagstone, where the wines were made. The label is now fully based in Elim, from the cool vineyards to a cellar built in time for the 2011 harvest; Pratt makes the wines. The fine, flinty Sauvignon was joined in 2006 by a near-equal blend of that grape with Sémillon in the Weather Girl (the name a typical bit of Jackish whimsy), sold at the Cape Winemakers Guild Auction; the subsequent 2008 was the first under the Berrio's own label. So far these whites are the undoubted stars, although there has also been a full-flavored Cabernet Sauvignon, which was joined in 2009 by a Pinot Noir, a Syrah, and a Bordeaux-style blend (including Cabernet Franc, Malbec, Merlot, and Petit Verdot off the property's 40 hectares of vines). This winery will certainly help the second decade of the century reveal definitively whether the most southerly winegrowing area in the Cape is going to be as propitious for red wine as it undoubtedly is for Sauvignon Blanc and Sémillon.

www.theberrio.co.za

BLACK OYSTERCATCHER

Members of the Human family have farmed around Elim for generations and were among the earliest to introduce vines in recent times, the first plantings being made on the family farm, Moddervlei, in 1998. The name of their wine range comes from a seabird found only along the Namibian and South African coasts. The 18.5 hectares of Cabernet Sauvignon, Merlot, Syrah, Sauvignon Blanc, and Sémillon are planted on a ridge of laterite and broken shale. So far it is the whites that have proved most interesting. The Sauvignon is restrained and tight but flavorful, with green notes dominant, though at 14 percent alcohol not without pretensions to ripeness. A lightly oaked blend with Sémillon, called White Pearl, is predictably that much more interesting—and in fact winemaker-viticulturist Dirk Human says he is finding that blending generally results in greater complexity. He's doing it with the previously stand-alone Syrah too, bringing a majority of Cabernet and a little Merlot into the equation of Triton. It is also, sensibly, very modestly oaked, and a good deal of the pleasure to be got from the Black Oystercatcher wines is their avoidance of the blockbuster route—unlikely to work well in this area anyway. Things can only improve with the winemaking moving on-site as of 2009, following the renovation of a building on the home farm.

www.blackoystercatcher.co.za

BOUCHARD FINLAYSON

In 1990, a decade or so after helping to establish Hamilton Russell Vineyards, where he was the first winemaker, Peter Finlayson set out on his own to create the valley's second winery. The French part of the name is that of one of his early partners in this venture, Paul Bouchard of Bouchard Aîné, the first Burgundian to invest in the Cape. He is no longer there (the hotelier Tollman family now has a major investment), but the Burgundian influence is substantial, beyond the central concern with Pinot Noir and Chardonnay. Finlayson had Burgundian experience himself on top of his years at Hamilton Russell, but Bouchard was no doubt important in the decision to adopt, for example, double Guyot trellising and high-density planting patterns (more than nine thousand vines per hectare) that are more typically French than South African. Irrigation, however, is a concession to a warmer climate, and green harvesting is regularly practiced.

Much of the property's 125 hectares is mountain land set aside for the indigenous flora. There are 20 hectares of vines on the west-facing slopes of the mountain separating the valley from the Atlantic. More than half of these vines are Pinot, with the remainder Chardonnay, Sauvignon Blanc, and a few more unusual varieties. The wines, like the viticulture, are firmly oriented to Europe, aiming at classicism rather than fruity exuberance. The regular Galpin Peak Pinot Noir is named for the mountain overlooking the vineyards; Tête de Cuvée is a barrel selection made in the best years only, and matured with a greater percentage of new wood—about 75 percent, while the standard version gets about 30 percent. Both have had very good vintages, but that is by no means a certainty. There's an unexceptional Sauvignon Blanc and two good Chardonnays. The first, Kaaimansgat ("crocodile's lair"), comes from another coolish area near Villiersdorp, also in the Overberg district; the late-ripening, unirrigated vineyard, at an altitude of 700 meters, produces a vibrant, mineral wine. Missionvale Chardonnay (the name refers to the Moravian mission station of which the farm formed a part in the earlier nineteenth century) is from home grapes. It is perhaps a little richer, but also elegant. Both wines tend to have little more than 13 percent alcohol; both are made in classic style, fermented in oak, and kept on the lees for seven or eight months.

Rather less French in inspiration is Hannibal, a delicately powerful red, bizarrely blending Italian varieties (Sangiovese, nearly half of the total, Nebbiolo, and Barbera) with French (Pinot Noir and Syrah). It was the first wine in the Cape to make substantial use of Italian grapes in a blend, and is still one of the most successful.

www.bouchardfinlayson.co.za

CREATION

This is one of the pioneering wineries of the easterly Hemel-en-Aarde Ridge ward. It was virgin land when bought in 2002 by Swiss winemaker and viticulturist J.-C. Martin and his wife, Carolyn—niece of Peter Finlayson of Bouchard Finlayson (Peter had long noted the viticultural potential of this area). Swiss viticulturist and friend Christophe Kaser joined the project a few years later. They grow a remarkable range of varieties on their 22 sloping vineyard hectares (and also bring in a neighbor's grapes), convinced of the area's potential for just about everything from Grenache and Viognier to Sauvignon and Sémillon—of course taking in Chardonnay and Pinot along the way. This is not the specialization that one might have expected from Europeans—though perhaps the liberation from the legal and climatic restrictions of Europe is precisely what leads to this exuberance when it's climatically possible to indulge it. The wines are all worth trying, and will no doubt become even more attractive as the vines get a few more years on them and, Martin points out, as the vignerons learn more about them. I have enjoyed the whites particularly: a ripe and stony Sauvignon Blanc and a lively, fresh Chardonnay with subtle pear and hazelnut notes and a harmonious balance. Of the reds, the generous but fairly elegant Syrah Grenache has usually appealed more than those from red Bordeaux varieties. Early vintages of the Pinot Noir (its debut was 2008), in a robust modern style, augur well for the area's signature red grape in J.-C. Martin's hands.

www.creationwines.com

CRYSTALLUM

Whether it's through the power of genes or of example is uncertain, but we happily have the next generation of Finlaysons established not only at Creation (Peter Finlayson's niece), but now also at this new setup in the Hemel-en-Aarde area, owned by Peter's sons. Peter-Allan is the winemaker; Andrew, an architect, designed the eco-friendly winery made of straw bales, local clay and stone, and recycled stuff ranging from paper to steel. It is not only the genes that give confidence in Crystallum's future: the maiden 2008 wines were extremely promising, and that promise has been fulfilled in subsequent vintages. A single-vineyard Pinot called Cuvée Cinéma is the finest, absorbing plenty of new oak, but the Peter Max version, with much less new oak, is also good. The name of the impressive Clay Shales Chardonnay better indicates the interest in site-specific wine; Agnes Chardonnay is from widely sourced grapes. The brothers have no vines of their own ("and are in no hurry" to make that investment, says Peter-Allan), but have been sourcing grapes mostly from the Hemel-en-Aarde Ridge ward—though Peter Max has been partly from Elgin fruit. Stylistically, although there is at present more similarity to New Zealand than to Burgundy in the immensely appealing and easily approachable Pinots, Peter-Allan seems to be looking beyond the plenteous fruit in new-world Pinots and aiming for more structure—vineyard age permitting—partly through using a larger proportion of whole bunches in the fermentation than the 10 percent to 20 percent of the early vintages. It must be said, in fact, that the younger generation of Finlaysons is triumphing.

www.crystallumwines.com

GABRIËLSKLOOF

It's early days yet for this Bot River winery, which released its first wines from the 2008 vintage, but the prospect of something special is there; everything is being very well done, and the releases have been good and promise even better. The first vines were planted in 2002—the first in the modern era, that is, for the estate is named after Gabriël le Roux, who apparently made wine and brandy here in the nineteenth century, for domestic use and passing trade. Businessman Bernhard Heyns has invested deeply in this project, and wisely, I'd say. The buildings, including a restaurant for today's passersby, are attractive and elegantly understated—rather like an unpretentious Waterford, with not a shred of pseudo-Tuscan. The estate's grand wine, called the Five Arches because it has all five red Bordeaux varieties, is ripe, rich, and showy, though not overdone (except perhaps in oakiness). The second label, rather desperately called the Blend, can be more attractive to those who prefer a wine modest in demeanor, fruit-centered and drinkable though also well structured and, being less oaky, better balanced. The Reserve Shiraz is also appealing. Of the white wines—in fact, of all the early releases—most impressive has been the classic blend of Sauvignon and Sémillon, called Magdalena in honor of Bernhard Heyns's (nondrinking!) sister. The winemaker is Kobie Viljoen, working with Barry Anderson in the vineyards. Gabriëlskloof is an ambitious winery, and one to watch in the years to come.

www.gabrielskloof.co.za

HAMILTON RUSSELL VINEYARDS

For a decade and more after 1975, the Hamilton-Russells were almost the only, and certainly the most passionately eloquent, spokespeople for terroir in South Africa. In that year advertising executive Tim Hamilton-Russell bought this southerly, cool land in the Hemel-en-Aarde Valley, just three kilometers from the Atlantic but protected from too much salt-laden wind by the intervening mountains. For many years, while some observers were still shaking their heads at the eccentricity of the choice, and while Tim and his winemaker, Peter Finlayson, were establishing a winery and learning about their young vineyards, a continuous struggle had to be fought against the provisions of the quota system, which made labeling a nightmare. Happily, they won in the end, and the wines, notably the Pinot Noir and Chardonnay, quickly started winning a fine local and then international reputation. The estate has ceased to grow other varieties, which are now the province of two nearby properties in the valley (see Ashbourne, Southern Right), as Anthony Hamilton-Russell (son of Tim and current owner) decided that two wines were the maximum that a serious producer should market from one estate. For some time in the 1990s they were—deliberately—the most expensive South African wines. Crowds of wines with aspirational prices have more recently overtaken them in that department, though seldom in terms of reputation. The Chardonnay is unquestionably one of the foremost Cape whites.

In a sense, the very success of the wines has made for one problem: rather too many successive winemakers. Since 1975, three have been inspired to leave in order to start their own operations in the valley. The current incumbent is Hannes Storm, here since 2004. The development in the winemaking process (as with the viticulture, always genuinely centered on how best to express the vineyards and hobbled only by the significant presence of virus) has been to increase the proportion of the wines made without inoculation of commercial yeasts. So, despite more than thirty years of production, the winemaking regime is, surprisingly, still not fixed. More recent experiments have involved the use of amphoras lined with local clay for fermentation and aging, especially for the Chardonnay. Inevitably, then, the character of the wine is subject to change. But generally, both wines are marked by restraint, by dryness and a serious mineral acidity (natural acidity, of course), by moderation in oaking—Burgundian barrels are used, about a third of them new—and by a concern for longevity. And both have, indeed, a track record of beneficial development over a decade at least, the Chardonnay being the more convincing in this respect—for example, a well-stored 1989 tasted in 2012 was drinking superbly; the Pinots have shown more variation in quality, if not in their Burgundian, unfruity character, but at their best they are very good.

www.hamiltonrussellvineyards.com

HERMANUSPIETERSFONTEIN

This extremely good winery, based at the entrance to the Hemel-en-Aarde Valley, was given the original version of the name of the nearby seaside town, now—surely to everyone's relief—known more succinctly as Hermanus. (Hermanus Pieters was a nineteenth-century Dutch schoolteacher.) This is a partnership between experienced winemaker Bartho Eksteen (best known before this venture as a négociant) and the owners of a pair of farms in the Sunday's Glen ward, near Stanford. For the fairly large range of wines, one farm, with westerly slopes, supplies Bordeaux varieties and the other, with easterly slopes, supplies those associated with the warmer climate of the Rhône. Prevailing southeasterly summer winds and the highish altitude of the vineyards (220 to 230 meters) make for relative coolness. Soils vary from weathered shale to weathered granite, with a gravel topsoil and a clay subsoil.

There is no doubting the speciality here—Sauvignon Blanc, the grape with which Eksteen has long been particularly associated. From the 21 varied hectares at his disposal now he makes (at last count) five different versions: the tropical No 3; the more austere, green-flavored No 7; a wooded version, No 5; and the flagship Die Bartho, a splendid, harmonious marriage of the three styles. All had an admixture of Sémillon and Nouvelle, but the latter seems to have been mostly dropped as of the 2012 vintage; Die Bartho 2011 has 28 percent of wooded Sémillon and 7 percent Nouvelle. A finely balanced, unoaked, lowish-alcohol dessert version called Sauvignon Blanc No 2 was launched in 2012.

The red wines are impressive in a ripe and rather alcoholic, modern, heavily wooded style, and manage to retain a litheness that is not a million miles from elegant. In the flagship range, Die Arnoldus is a Cabernet-based blend, with the other four main Bordeaux red varieties also taking part; Die Martha is mostly of Syrah, with some Merlot and Cabernet. (It perhaps needs to be pointed out that *die* is Afrikaans for "the," rather than a persistent reference to death; it is one of the idiosyncrasies of the winery that all the labeling is only in Afrikaans, while the Web site is in English!)
www.hpf1855.co.za

LOMOND

Looking now at the low hillsides bearing (so far) some 120 hectares of vineyards, with a beautiful stretch of water that is more of a lake than a reservoir (and also supplies a nearby village), it's hard to believe that when engineer Wayne Gabb first came across this valley near Cape Agulhas in 1999 it was virgin land, with the then-choked Uilenkraals River scarcely trickling through it. Development was rapid and impressively thought through, with expert soil analysis and careful matching of variety, planting orientation, rootstock—also taking into account the varied aspects. The property is at a little remove from the cluster of wineries in the Elim ward, but like them it also stretches inland from just eight kilometers away from the sea, with similar benefits and challenges as a consequence—summer coolness, serious winds, and some summer rainfall and humidity—that impose limits on the organically oriented viticultural methods. In addition to the soils derived from sandstone and shale, there are useful granitic intrusions and patches of clay.

The original partners, including Gabb, who remains general manager, later formed a joint venture with Distell, which makes and markets the wines and takes some 65 percent of the grapes for its own purposes. The Lomond label concentrates on Sauvignon Blanc, Merlot, and Syrah, with Sémillon, Nouvelle, and Viognier available for a Sauvignon-based blend called Snowbush (most of the wines are named for local indigenous plants); new plantings of Pinot Noir could produce something interesting. The Conebush Syrah has suffered a little from excessive ambition, being picked very ripe and matured in all-new oak, which tends to dominate it. The Merlot is adequate, and might be matched with Cabernet Sauvignon when those vineyards start producing—but ripening red grapes adequately here is not easy. There is no doubt about the quality of the white blend and the Sauvignons, however. In addition to a generic version of the latter, there are two single-vineyard offerings: Sugarbush, which tends to display the variety's greener characters, and Pincushion, which shows more tropical notes—both doing their thing in much more than satisfactory fashion.

A substantial part of the property is left to nature, and there's a program to remove alien vegetation. Tall poles dot the vineyards, providing perches for the peregrine falcons and steppe buzzards that are often to be seen there, looking handsome to us and no doubt terrifying to their prey.

www.lomond.co.za

LUDDITE

The tiny winery of winemaker Niels Verburg and Hillie Meyer lies on the slopes of the Houw Hoek Mountains near the village of Bot River, not far from Beaumont, where Verburg made wine until 2003. The 17-hectare farm was bought in 1999, and ten years later little more than 5 of a planned 10 hectares of unirrigated vines had been planted—mostly with four clones of Syrah, plus a little Cabernet Sauvignon and less Mourvèdre. A small vineyard of Chenin Blanc joined them in 2011. The winemaker's wife, Penny, is in charge of the vineyards. They built a cellar in time for the 2009 harvest. Only a Syrah is made under the Luddite label (the maiden 2003 came out as Mudge Point Shiraz), though Verburg has made blends with Cabernet that were sold at the auction of the Cape Winemakers Guild, and a Chenin Blanc is a real possibility once that vineyard matures a little. He makes 2,500 cases of Syrah, buying in grapes from elsewhere to supplement his own until the 2008 vintage, the first made entirely from the home vines. The wine is intense, spicy, ripe, and warm, but always fairly refined and under 14 percent alcohol, with just a quarter of the oak barrels new—a pleasant combination of typical new-world richness with the more old-fashioned style suggested by the winery's name.

www.luddite.co.za

NEWTON JOHNSON

When Dave Johnson and his wife, Felicity (née Newton), planted their first vines, completed building a new winery, and crushed their first grapes from bought-in fruit in 1997, the Hemel-en-Aarde Valley was still viticulturally uncrowded. Ten years later, after they had their first harvest in the larger winemaking facility and farm to which they had relocated farther up the valley, they had many more winemaking neighbors. Son Gordon and his wife, Nadia, were long established in charge of the cellar. On the home farm there are now 15 hectares of vines on north-facing slopes, with a further 3.6 more recently acquired on south-facing slopes on the other side of the valley. The latter comprises just Chardonnay and Pinot Noir, while the former site also has Syrah, Grenache, Mourvèdre, and Sauvignon Blanc. More plantings are foreseen, and eventually the larger part of the winery's needs will be met from their own vineyards, but long-term relationships with owners of vineyards elsewhere in the valley and in Elgin and even the Swartland will continue, and grapes will be bought in.

Newton Johnson's reputation had grown well over the years, based on a range of wines made mostly from outsourced grapes, and it leaped ahead in 2009 when they released the first Pinot Noir and Chardonnay bottlings entirely from their own (virus-free and pesticide-free) vineyards, then seven years old. These two wines now have the variety name prefixed with the Family Vineyards tag. The Pinot especially stood out, and continues to do so, as one of the best from an area with a fine reputation for the variety, seeming to happily combine new-world fruit concerns with structure and elegance more reminiscent of Burgundy—not that the established version from Elgin fruit is hopelessly the lesser by any means. Just as the approach in the vineyards is to avoid as many interventions as possible, so it is in the cellar, where yeast inoculation and chemical additions are avoided. The result is wines of firm delicacy, restraint, balance, and freshness. The Chardonnay, Sauvignon Blanc, and a Savignon-Sémillon blend called Resonance are very attractive, but almost most interesting of all is the success the Johnsons are having with Rhône-inspired blends from grapes off rocky soils on the bottom slopes of the estate. Full Stop Rock (named for a feature apparently famous to surfers—like many local winemakers, these two are as often as possible on their boards) is from Syrah with a little each of Grenache and Mourvèdre; 2010 saw the birth of a second blend of these varieties, this one based on Grenache. The finesse and charm of the two wines probably owes much to lessons learned by the Johnsons as they struggled (so successfully) to master Pinot, and represent fine additions to the other unshowy range from an unshowy but deeply rewarding family domaine.

www.newtonjohnson.com

SOUTHERN RIGHT

The third of the Hemel-en-Aarde Valley wines from the Hamilton-Russell pair has started finding its home in the large Patryskloof farm on Hamilton Russell Vineyards' western border. This was acquired by a consortium including Anthony Hamilton-Russell in 2006, just over a decade after the Southern Right wines first appeared. Its own cellar was opened in time for the 2010 vintage and will eventually be fed by 50 hectares of new vineyards. Southern Right has thus far been sourcing fruit for its two wines, varietal Pinotage and Sauvignon Blanc mostly from the home valley, especially Ashbourne, but also from elsewhere in the Walker Bay district. In the first decade of this century, however, the wines were perhaps more typical of their varieties than of anything else, though showing their comparatively cool-climate origins. But the Pinotage is a much more exuberant, typical example than Ashbourne's, though still fairly serious-minded; the ripe, sweet fruit is not jammy, the substantial tannins (some of them oak-derived) do a good restraining job without overwhelming. The Sauvignon Blanc has lots of tropical, passion-fruit notes, with a capsicum edge and a big, luscious acidity.

SPRINGFONTEIN

Johst and Anja Weber of Germany, with a group of friends, bought the pristine 500 hectares of Springfontein, near Stanford, in 1996, and released 2004 as their maiden vintage off an initial 25 hectares of vineyards. Perhaps to gauge potential, large numbers of varieties were planted, but Chenin Blanc and Pinotage dominate and are bottled as varietal wines, with Cabernet Sauvignon, Merlot, Mourvèdre, Petit Verdot, Syrah, Chardonnay, Sauvignon Blanc, and Sémillon going into blends. Those first 2004s were vinified by Anja Weber, with no doubt excellent advice from Kevin Grant and David Trafford. After a change or two, Christo Versfeld took over as general manager and winemaker for the 2007 vintage. All the wines are barrel-aged, the whites also oak-fermented, and all are bottled unfiltered. Most impressive so far have been the two single-vineyard wines. Jil's Dune Chenin Blanc has all-new oak well absorbed into a rich and mineral-driven whole. Jonathan's Ridge Pinotage, also matured in new oak, leans toward its Pinot parentage, with an appealing freshness and lightness of touch. There are a dozen other wines—disconcertingly many, perhaps, for a new small property—and it will be interesting for us as well as the owners, no doubt, to see which endure. Apparently already some vineyards are being regrafted for a range shift; and for all the vineyards the process of converting to organic viticulture had begun by 2012.

www.springfontein.co.za

STRANDVELD

This was, they say on the Web site, a "somewhat rundown sheep/wheat farm of about 800 hectares a few kilometers from the tip of Africa" until a group of friends got together to buy it in 2001 and started planting vines and building a winery. There are now more than 70 hectares of Pinot Noir, Syrah, Sauvignon Blanc, and Sémillon, and recent years have shown just how successful red grapes can be in these cool conditions—especially Syrah; it is still early days for Pinot, but things look promising.

For a number of years only wines under what is now the second-tier range, First Sighting, were produced, but a 2007 Sauvignon showed that consulting viticulturist Andrew Tuebes (Tienie Wentzel is now permanent in the position) and winemaker Conrad Vlok were doing all the right things, and Strandveld appeared set to become the leading winery in this burgeoning winegrowing area on the windy Agulhas plain. Adamastor, a fine blend of Sauvignon and Sémillon, followed. The Syrah (the maiden 2006 was called Shiraz, as the First Sighting version still is) has a little Grenache and Viognier admixed; it is a ripe, attractively perfumed, and rather elegant version despite robust alcohol levels. A Rhône-style blend called the Navigator, with less Syrah, more Grenache, and some Mourvèdre was introduced with the 2010 vintage, and it looks likely that this will be the red wine flagship. None of the wines is overdone in any respect—Vlok's oaking is modest and admirable, for example—and this is undoubtedly a winery to watch with great interest.

www.strandveld.co.za

SUMARIDGE

Things were rather unsettled at this winery in the Upper Hemel-en-Aarde Valley for a good few years from the first bottling in 2001, with a rapid turnover of winemakers—who did manage some good Chardonnay at least. But with the arrival in 2005 of Zimbabwean expatriate Gavin Patterson to manage the vineyards and the winemaking, it started to look as though Sumaridge would soon live up to the undoubted potential of its site. New British owners Simon and Holly Turner seem to be happily supportive of his management. Patterson reckons that while the soils of Sumaridge are significant, including a decomposed granite portion that is unusual in the valley and a good underlying layer of free-draining clay allowing for minimal supplementary irrigation, mesoclimate is more so: of all the Hemel-en-Aarde farms, this one, he suggests, is most affected by the vagaries of weather, being more open to winds from sea and land. At present 38 hectares are planted to Merlot, Pinot Noir, Pinotage, Syrah, Chardonnay, and Sauvignon Blanc, and that is nearing the maximum possible. Decent varietal wines are made from all of these— with the Pinot Noir, after some lackluster years, looking from 2006 onward as though it might be the most promising, especially when Patterson's drive to elegance gains full control of the tannins and wood use. He has also introduced very promising blends "designed to express a sense of place." Epitome is a blend of Syrah, Pinotage, and Merlot; Maritimus, from Sauvignon, Chardonnay, and Sémillon, draws on "sites most affected by the climate and interesting soils."

www.sumaridge.co.za

13

ELGIN AND OVERBERG

BACKGROUND

A track across the mountain range that the Dutch settlers called the Hottentots-Holland certainly long preceded their first brave and tentative penetrations through to the interior. The Khoikhoi knew the track and called it the Gantow, meaning "the way of the eland." Not long after the arrival of the European settlers a wagon road overlaid it—presumably the least of the devastating problems being caused for the eland and other wild animals of the region. The land to the east of the Hottentots-Holland—as far as the Breede River—was *over 't gebergte,* "over the mountains," now more tersely known as Overberg.

The settlers first sought meat here, bartering with the indigenous pastoralists, but the expansion of the early eighteenth century saw them increasingly arrogating the land to their own use for pasture, crop cultivation, and timber cutting. The first group of Europeans in the Overberg settled along the Zonder End River, not far from what is now one of the youngest of the Overberg's wine wards, Greyton. The indigenous inhabitants, militarily defeated and also devastated by European diseases, as elsewhere in the burgeoning colony could do little other than increasingly supply the settlers with what they immediately needed most: land and labor. This process was, of course, proceeding everywhere; it is mentioned here as an illustrative example. By the time the Dutch East India Company's rule was coming to an end at the end of the eighteenth century, the assimilation of the indigenous population into the service of the farmer was established. Russell Viljoen has written a pamphlet about the concerns of Moravian missionaries with the

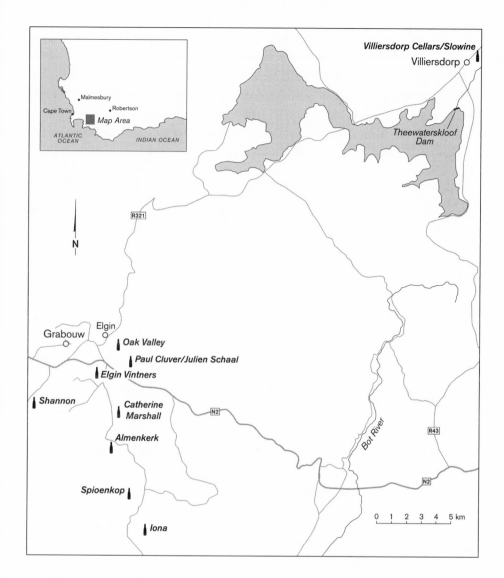

MAP 10
Elgin and Overberg

souls and bodies of these laborers in the Overberg at that time, and it is worth reminding ourselves of the contemporary socioeconomic context of farming. A poor farmer (owning no slaves) from Swellendam complained about refuge given to their "deserting" laborers: "How are we to have work done, for we have no slaves; the Hottentots have been for many years the farmers' servants. . . . You who live in the River Sonderend may have Hottentots enough, but what are we to do?" The government did not meet farmers' demands for action but, Viljoen says, the relevant official in Swellendam took matters into his own hands, supplying his field cornets with arms and ammunition to carry out raids among the Khoisan to recruit labor. Furthermore, the tot system was in full force at the time, helping to keep the workforce docile and badly paid through regular measures of wine or brandy.

There seems to have been little notable viticulture in the more westerly parts of this large, mountainous, and in general terms vaguely defined region (the Breede River Valley, including Swellendam, is now generally considered apart, certainly in terms of wine production). As far as the Wine of Origin scheme is concerned, the Overberg district is, of course, clearly defined—though the definition has been in flux in recent years with the development of new areas. The coastal stretch, which was the ward of Walker Bay, seceded as a district and is considered elsewhere. In 2011 Elgin, increasingly important as a high-quality wine-producing area, was changed from a ward to a district (meaning that it will in time be able to subdivide into wards itself).

THE WARDS

There are now four wards in the Overberg, mostly separated by mountains, or by valleys largely planted with wheat and fruit—and themselves sparse in terms of vineyards. It must also be said that not a great deal of distinction has emerged from them, and few of the wineries are discussed below. The newest ward, Elandskloof, near the town of Villiersdorp, is perhaps the most promising. It is a very beautiful enclosed valley, mostly planted to apples but with the well-established east-facing Kaaimansgat vineyard, which has long been a source of fine Chardonnay for, especially, Bouchard Finlayson and Newton Johnson in the Hemel-en-Aarde area. This is a high-altitude but almost continental area, where there is always snow on the surrounding mountain peaks in winter— and occasionally on the vines, too; it is cool in summer, without the heat waves that can be such a problem in much of the Cape. Now more vineyards are being planted in the valley's rich, red, water-retentive soils on south- and west-facing slopes by Anthonij Rupert wines of Franschhoek. Eventually some 35 hectares of mostly Chardonnay, Sauvignon Blanc, and Pinot Noir will be planted, and it is going to be very interesting to see what comes off them: the potential is possibly great.

Theewater, from which Elandskloof was subtracted, seems unlikely to produce fine quality from the valley floor, but there are a few small wineries and a thirty-eight-member cooperative, Villiersdorp Cellars, which since 2009 has also had full control of the Slowine brand. Newer vineyards on the higher slopes might prove much better.

Klein River, with a little more influence from the Atlantic and with Africa's most southerly range of mountains occupying a good deal of the ward, also has little viticulture and few wineries. The Greyton ward is named for the deservedly much-touristed mountain village near which the ward's few wineries are to be found. Lismore Estate (belonging to a California expatriate, Samantha O'Keefe) has its own vineyards now well established (see the Walker Bay and Cape Agulhas map in chapter 12) and produces some serious cool-climate wines—including Chardonnay, Sauvignon Blanc, and a Viognier, but also a decent Syrah—from what must be one of the most magnificently sited mountainside farms in the Cape. There is every chance that something very interesting will emerge from a farm where rain and cold add their toll to the challenges of Cape viticulture.

With the exception of some isolated vineyards, Elgin has nearly as short a history of grape growing as most of the Overberg. Despite indications that grapes had been grown in the past, as early as 1813 on the De Rust estate, there was no official production quota for the area when a little interest in viticulture started being shown in the 1980s. So quickly has Elgin become established as one of the country's important cooler-climate areas that it is hard to remember that, despite having proved its potential with some serious wines, as recently as the turn of this century it was still being talked about as a place that might—should!—take off as a wine-producing area. The number of substantial wineries in the area is increasing, and a few outside producers—notably Tokara and Thelema in Stellenbosch—have bought farms here and make Elgin ranges.

Elgin has long been associated with apple production; if vicissitudes in the international apple market have encouraged some to turn to viticulture, the area is still much more important for fruit production, with the town of Grabouw as its commercial center. It was a rare bit of insight and adventurousness that prompted the giant Stellenbosch Farmers' Winery and the Nietvoorbij research unit to have the idea that valley might have potential for wine, and to do something about it in the early 1980s. They approached two of the largest farms there, De Rust (now home to Paul Cluver) and Oak Valley, and between them they planted Gewürztraminer, Riesling, Pinot Noir, Chardonnay, Sauvignon Blanc, Merlot, and Schönburger. The last of these has essentially disappeared, but the other varieties—even Merlot in some parts—have thrived. Nederburg did release Cluver wines under the Elgin Wine of Origin designation in the late 1980s and early 1990s, and in 1990 the prescient négociant Neil Ellis released a Sauvignon Blanc from a vineyard planted in the early 1980s by another apple grower. The Cluver project soon involved building a cellar, once quota restrictions were a thing of the past, and Oak Valley, which for a long time has supplied grapes for some prestigious wineries, now also bottles its own wines—with remarkable success.

The next crucial step in the emergence of Elgin as a wine producer was when Andrew Gunn established what he suggests is the coolest farm in the country. His success at Iona with a racy Sauvignon Blanc, its first vintage 2001, undoubtedly encouraged the development of other Elgin vineyards and the area's increasingly recognized affinity for Sauvignon. An arguably more exciting match—because that much more rare—is with Pinot Noir. Bouchard Finlayson's first Pinot grapes came from Elgin, and it remains a source for some other well-known wines; but increasingly the Elgin producers wish to make their own Pinots, and are doing so to some acclaim.

In addition to grapes being taken from Elgin to the home cellars of Tokara and Thelema, other producers have started emerging, either from local fruit farmers turning some orchard land to vineyard (such as Shannon), or outsiders coming in—like well-known winemaker Cathy Marshall. An interesting model is Elgin Vintners, which brings together half a dozen local producers, mostly fruit farmers diversifying into wine. One of the partners is viticulturist Paul Wallace, who oversees the vineyards; the wines are made by different winemakers in their own cellars—each working with a variety in which he has a particular interest, like Jeff Grier of Villiera (Sauvignon Blanc), Niels Verburg of Luddite (Syrah and Viognier), and Kevin Grant of Ataraxia (Chardonnay and Pinot Noir). It would be a substantial bonus for the Elgin area to have more actual wineries locally (Shannon, for example, is making its wines elsewhere)—but that is something that will happen over time. The process has started, in fact, with wandering Cathy Marshall now putting down roots here, and the smart new Almenkerk winery owned by Belgian lawyer Joris van Almenkerk, who moved to South Africa in 2002. He pulled out most of the apple trees on the farm he bought and planted nearly 15 hectares of vines—a very wide range of them, from Malbec to Viognier. A pair of good 2009 Sauvignons marked Almenkerk's arrival on the local market. Spioenkop is another Belgian venture, by Koen and Lore Roose, who have been importing Cape wine into Belgium for well over a decade. It is still too early to make firm predictions, but the earliest releases off young vines looked promising.

On the whole, apart from Pinot Noir, Elgin is widely seen as white wine country. Paul Cluver estate, for example, has abandoned other red varieties from its own bottlings. But inevitably there are red wines made, and they cannot be written off: the Merlot from the latest Elgin star, Shannon, is among the country's best, and Oak Valley makes a respectable Bordeaux-style blend. In fact, although Sauvignon Blanc is by an enormous stretch the most planted variety in Elgin (with nearly 350 hectares in 2011), Syrah (80 hectares) is not far behind Chardonnay—a grape that has proved to do extremely well here. In fact, Chardonnay seems to be on the increase, as is Pinot Noir, now also at just under 100 hectares. Cabernet Sauvignon and Merlot are not far behind Syrah, but fairly static. Time will tell whether Syrah will perform here or owe its place in the vineyards primarily to the dictates of fashion.

Unlike some areas, Elgin is neatly delimited by geography: an inland valley—or, more properly, a plateau at a general elevation of 200 to 300 meters—in the Hottentots-Holland range of mountains, whose rims and peaks form the boundaries of the mountain basin. Prevailing southerly winds off the Atlantic—just three kilometers from Iona—and the elevation make for much cooler conditions than in most Cape vineyards: the average temperature in February is just 19.7°C. Harvests are, correspondingly, generally some weeks later than most areas. The more elevated parts, like Iona at 420 meters, are even cooler. In fact, there is substantial variation of conditions within the area, particularly because of aspect and elevation, with more vineyards now being planted on the higher slopes, and not all parts of Elgin perform as well as others. Direction of slope and consequent exposure to sunlight are frequently an important consideration; temperature can also vary greatly from one part to another. The mostly gravelly shale soils, with some sandstone, and clay beneath the topsoil, are of low vigor. Rainfall is comparatively high (1,000 millimeters annually, with summer dampness that necessitates extra vigilance in the vineyards but helps produce a couple of fine botrytised dessert wines), and supplementary irrigation is generally not required.

THE WINERIES

CATHERINE MARSHALL

After quite a bit of moving around, Cathy Marshall, one of the early garagistes of the 1990s, seems more settled now, at the Valley Green Winery in Elgin, for which she has also been consulting cellarmaster since 2011. It means, apart from anything else, that she has at last a fully equipped cellar to make the 3,000 or so cases of wine she produces for her partnership (though production might now rise). It's a good few years since this feisty, independent winemaker left her last full-time winemaking job (at Ridgeback in Paarl, where she brought the brand some renown), and her own venture was boosted by the deserved acclaim for her 2008 Pinot Noir, her first from all-Elgin fruit. Cathy is a great believer in the charms of Elgin Pinot, though she has no vineyards of her own and all the grapes are bought in. Starting in 2009 she produced three Pinots: a barrel-selection Reserve and two standard versions, one for a smart supermarket. While the coolness of Elgin is ideal for Pinot, Cathy sources grapes for her other top red, SMG (Syrah, Mourvèdre, Grenache), from warmer Swartland—and the wine does show a typical sweet warmth alongside her customary refinement. The generosity is seldom from an excess of alcohol, however, as Cathy Marshall tends to pick early and extremely well, and there's never more than a touch of herbaceousness in this wine. She has mentioned an ambition to make a white blend in the Swartland style; one senses that her heart and soul, of which she has plenty, are not in the perfectly adequate Sauvignon Blanc, now made from Elgin grapes.

www.cmwines.co.za

IONA

Andrew Gunn's decision in 1997 to buy and plant vineyards on this old apple farm was brave and farsightedly pioneering; the substantial international reputation he has built for his Sauvignon Blanc has been important for stimulating interest in Elgin viticulture. Gunn's farm (named after the Scottish island to recall his family history, as does the Viking longboat emblem on the labels) is probably the coolest in the area— the coolest in the Cape, Gunn insists, with an average growing-season daytime temperature of 17.2°C. The 35 hectares of vines (in the midst of the Kogelberg Nature Reserve) are at an altitude above 400 meters and just three kilometers from the Atlantic. Initial plantings were of Merlot and Sauvignon Blanc, and the first Sauvignon wine was harvested in 2001. Initially the wines were vinified in the Tokara cellar (Stellenbosch), and then in the new home cellar by Niels Verburg; since 2008 there has been a full-time winemaker to deal with the increasing range of wines being produced—a signal stage in the winery's growing maturity. In 2011 Werner Muller took charge, fresh from working with the brilliant Gottfried Mocke at Chamonix, which can only mean good things for Iona.

For many years, Iona's high reputation rested on the Sauvignon Blanc—a classic, clean, fresh wine, looking neither to tropicality nor to greener characters, but to flinty minerality. Its alcohol level is moderate, about 13 percent, but the wine is flavorful and fairly rich; it matures attractively for five years and at ten usually still drinks well. But the poised, taut, mineral Chardonnay now rivals it for quality. Whether the Viognier, its early vintages very overtly lush and alcoholic, is suitable for this area is another matter entirely. As to the reds, they have their admirers, although for me they have tended to be too richly ripe and fruity (I look forward to seeing the Muller versions). The Syrah is there because a nursery accidentally supplied 600 Syrah vines interspersed among the Cabernet Sauvignon. But the results pleased the team, which led to more being planted in 2004. The Gunnar is a blend of Merlot, Cabernet, and Petit Verdot, which can have a herbal element. In 2012 an eclectic blend was made of a selection of all the black grapes on the farm plus Viognier (Syrah especially, with Merlot, Cabernet, Petit Verdot, and Mourvèdre), intended to be Iona's best possible red; it's predictably big, ripe, very sweet-fruited, and polished.

www.iona.co.za

JEAN DANEEL

The pleasant little town of Napier is little more than ten kilometers from the easternmost point of the Klein River ward and even less than that north of the Cape Agulhas district, and now with a ward of its own. Highly regarded veteran winemaker Jean Daneel (he'd served at Buitenverwachting and Morgenhof) set up on his own here in the late 1990s but waited to apply for a WO Napier area until 2009, when the first crops came off his as yet few hectares of Chenin Blanc, Merlot, Sauvignon Blanc, and Syrah. The climate is fairly cool, but, says Jean, the soils are "not the greatest," although they "could be quite sustainable because of the structure. It starts with a sandy loam, and pebbles with a layer of clay at about 60 centimeters, and after that loose rocks and then sandstone. Irrigation will be needed until vines are established." In 2012 a small range off these vineyards was introduced, labeled Le Grand Jardin, at a comparatively modest price. Grapes for the top ranges continue to be bought in, most notably Chenin Blanc from old Swartland vines, which are vinified in the little cellar here, for some years now by son Jean-Pierre. The top Signature range includes a pair of powerful, tannic, and sometimes rather oaky blends of Cabernet, Merlot, and Syrah, of which the more expensive, but not necessarily better, one is prefixed "Directors" ("definitely not for the fainthearted," agrees the wine-maker). The same name distinction applies to the two Chenin Blancs, which are the winery's most persistent claim to excellence. Both are sophisticated, smartly oaked wines. The Directors version is matured in all-new barrels for about seventeen months, and shows it—but the Daneels have a track record of successful aging with Chenin made in this sort of way, and a good few well-deserved years in bottle do help. It is a rich, complex, and supple example, made only in the best years, which gives much satisfaction to those who like quite oaky wines, and is remarkably convincing even to many who have doubts. There's also a Brut sparkling wine from Chenin grapes, and the good-value but seriously made JD Initial range, which no doubt do sterling work in the country restaurant

Daneel and his wife, Renée, have established here. (See the map for Walker Bay and Cape Agulhas, in chapter 12, for the location of this winery.)

www.jdwines.co.za

JULIEN SCHAAL

This is one of the less-noticed but greatly to be welcomed stories of involvement of a foreigner in the Cape. Julien Schaal, from a family domaine in Alsace, visited in 2003 to gain Southern Hemisphere harvest experience at Bouchard Finlayson. When, a year later, his local venture was born, it drew on a friendship with another Hemel-en-Aarde winemaker, Gordon Johnson, in whose winery Schaal vinified his bought-in grapes. He now visits the Cape at least a few times each year—the longest stay being at harvesttime, naturally. With the expansion of the Newton Johnson range, Schaal recently shifted his vinification to the Paul Cluver cellar in Elgin. It's from this estate that he was already sourcing grapes for the excellent Julien Schaal Chardonnay—a little more vibrant and steely than the richer example made by his hosts. The 2010 Syrah comes from Hemel-en-Aarde vineyards and is one of the more elegant, subtle local Syrahs for, fortunately, unlike some French winemakers in the Southern Hemisphere, Schaal is fixated on balance and freshness rather than extreme ripeness, and his use of new oak tends to be correspondingly modest.

www.vins-schaal.com

OAK VALLEY

This is an enormous property, its 1,786 hectares intensively farmed, with operating divisions for fruit, cut flowers, and beef cattle—and now a growing one for wine grapes. It has been in the hands of the Rawbone-Viljoen family since the middle of the nineteenth century, with Anthony Rawbone-Viljoen the dynamic current director and his son Christopher, a wine business graduate of Adelaide University, increasingly involved. While Paul Cluver Estate was quick to follow up on the 1980s experiments in Elgin's viticultural potential, only in 2003 did an Oak Valley wine appear; grapes had indeed been produced for a few decades, but they had been sold off, notably Pinot Noir, to prestigious Hemel-en-Aarde producers. Now there are 48 hectares of vines, in gravelly sandstone soils over a structured clay layer, at an elevation of 480 to 520 meters on southwest-facing slopes. Sauvignon Blanc leads the plantings with 42 percent, followed by Bordeaux reds (especially Merlot) and Pinot Noir, with some Syrah, Viognier, and Sémillon.

A winery is envisaged, but until it happens Pieter Visser makes the wines at Paul Cluver. The 2003 Sauvignon Blanc attracted much interest at a time when wine lovers and critics were becoming alert to the fine wines starting to trickle at a faster rate out of Elgin. It proved itself to be a typical Elgin Sauvignon, with flinty minerality and a subtle intensity of flavors conforming to neither the tropical-fruit nor the capsicum model. In 2005 an even finer version, Mountain Reserve, came from the fruit of just the highest vineyard, but starting in 2007 those grapes were used for an excellent blend with oaked

Sémillon, called the OV. The Pinot Noir, from a vineyard established on the same cool slopes in 2000, looks very promising at its best, with a lovely fresh charm now that uncertainty around oaking seems to have been resolved. Perhaps when the vines have matured the grapes will be able to benefit from all-new oak; in 2007 they were thwarted by it. There seems to be something erratic, in fact, about the Pinot, as none was made in 2008 or 2010; 2009 was very good indeed, 2011 rather less so. The other red is the Merlot-based Oak Valley Blend, with a succulently firm tannic structure and a herbaceous hint as a reminder of its coolish origins. The Chardonnay is as fine and incisive a wine as the other whites from the cellar, not overconcentrated, with a good balance and modest oaking (40 percent new barrels). There seems every reason to have high expectations for Oak Valley's future as a wine producer.

www.oakvalley.co.za

PAUL CLUVER

The farm De Rust is one of the largest properties in the Elgin region (Oak Valley the other), owned by the Clüver family since 1896. But only in 1986—under neurosurgeon Paul Clüver—was a collaboration begun with Stellenbosch Farmers' Winery, and Sauvignon Blanc, Chardonnay, Gewürztraminer, and Riesling planted. In the early 1990s Cabernet Sauvignon and Pinot Noir were added. The grapes went to Nederburg (with a few under the Paul Cluver label in the early 1990s), but in 1996 former Nederburg cellarmaster Gunter Brözel guided the building of a winery on the farm, and Paul Cluver Wines released its own 1997 wines. Only two-thirds of the vineyards are devoted to estate production, however. Projected plantings over the next years should bring the total area of vineyards for their own wines up to 100 hectares.

This remains very much a family affair. Dr. Clüver has pulled back and the estate is run by Paul Clüver Jr., with his sisters also involved and brother-in-law Andries Burger as winemaker (fortunately for family relationships and for consumers, he is a first-rate one). The estate makes varietal wines from most of the varieties grown, but reds other than Pinot were phased out a few years ago. Fashionable Sauvignon Blanc already constitutes nearly half of the Cluver production, and the wine is a good typical Elgin example, with a pebbly minerality, good body, and hints of green pepper and citrus. Pinot Noir is the second-largest in terms of volume, and has built a good reputation. In 2007 a version called Seven Flags was introduced, from fruit off the oldest Pinot vineyard, which produces the finest, smallest-berried grapes and the lowest yields. It has proved to be a significant step up from the standard version (although this also is steadily improving), and is one of the Cape's best examples.

The other white varietal wines are also very good. The naturally fermented Chardonnay in the past tended to be fairly rich and bold and flourished its half-new-oak maturation, but recently it has moved toward greater elegance, with 13 percent alcohol and a fine acidic structure; it is frequently one of the country's leading examples. There are few Gewürztraminers in South Africa, and Cluver offers one of the best—all the aromatic charm one's entitled to expect, some finesse, and generally a scarcely detectable 10 grams per liter of residual sugar. The Riesling is also one of the best produced locally, with the same sweetness level as the Gewürz and a fairly racy core ensuring maturation for three or more years. A later version, called Close Encounter Riesling, is sweeter, and some find it convincing in a German Auslese style; to me the acidity is inadequate for an exciting balance. Even better is the Weisser Riesling Noble Late Harvest. Botrytis arrives regularly with the cool, moist southerly winds, and this wine is now made most years. The style is somewhere between the Germanic (some old casks the only oak) and the French (higher alcohol), and in the best vintages it has a thrilling tension of sumptuous fruit, sweetness, and nervy acid, with honeyed botrytis augmenting the notes of peach and pepper.

This is perhaps the place to mention the Thandi project, which expresses, as the Clüvers say, a commitment to "the greater farming community . . . a unique partnership between the state, the community and private enterprise whose aim it is to create owner-ship, empowerment and a sustainable business entity for the community." In 1996, when privatization of the nearby state forests was threatening to make many workers redundant, a 200-hectare farm was created by combining uncultivated land on the Paul Cluver Estate with newly felled forestry land. The initial focus was on fruit, but wine has grown in importance, and it is expected that there will be 80 hectares of vineyard. Thandi was, in fact, the world's first wine brand to be accredited by Fairtrade. There are a half-dozen very pleasant wines for which no apology or excuse is needed. The brand is owned by the Company of Wine People.

www.cluver.com
www.thandiwines.com

RAKA

It's easy to see in Piet Dreyer the weathered skipper of a fleet of squid boats that he once was. He bought this farm in 1982 and named it after his favorite boat, in turn named after the half-man, half-beast in a poem by N. P. van Wyk Louw. Ten hectares of vines joined the livestock and citrus in 1999, and the first bottling was in 2002. Now 65 of the farm's 740 hectares are planted to a wide range of grapes: the quintet of Bordeaux reds, along with Mourvèdre, Pinotage, Sangiovese, Syrah, Sauvignon Blanc, and Viognier. Raka and Boschrivier are the only two wineries in the Klein River ward, which has mountains to the south but still derives a cooling influence from the Atlantic. Cold winters ensure proper vine dormancy, but summer rainfall can cause headaches. The property lies in the narrow valley through which the river flows, and vines are planted on both sides. Sauvignon and Syrah occupy the highest slopes on decomposed sandstone; most of the reds are planted on lower-lying shale, with Viognier and Sauvignon in sandy soils along the riverbank.

This is a family concern, with Piet, wife Elna, three sons, and a daughter all involved. Elsenburg-trained Josef has run the cellar since 2007. Raka's range is large, despite the total 15,000-case production for its own label, with the reds best known. They tend to be sweet-fruited, rich, and ripe, with little profundity and a new-world-style bias, though recent vintages have been pretty dry, and alcohols rarely go much above 14 percent. It was early competition successes for Biography Shiraz, which includes small amounts of Mourvèdre and Viognier, that first drew attention to Raka, and subsequent show success has not been lacking. Other reds in this sound, easily appealing range include the Quinary (as the name implies, a full house of Bordeaux varieties), varietal Cabernet Franc, and a muscular, meaty Figurehead Cape blend, which adds Pinotage to the Bordeaux grapes. (See the map for Walker Bay and Cape Agulhas, in chapter 12, for the location of this winery.)

www.rakawine.co.za

SHANNON

The Downes family had been farming in Elgin for four decades before brothers Stuart and James at the beginning of this century replanted some 15 hectares to vineyard, meticulously matching grape variety and rootstock combination with the variety of soil types and aspects. Much of the fruit is sold off to a few serious wineries. There are twelve vineyard blocks of Pinot Noir, seven of Sauvignon Blanc, a five-clone Merlot vineyard, and pockets of Sémillon and Viognier. Just twelve kilometers from the sea and at high altitude, these are all cool-climate vineyards. The Shannon wines are made at Newton Johnson in the Hemel-en-Aarde by the team there. The three maiden releases in 2009 immediately suggested that Shannon was likely to prove an immense asset to the area. The Sanctuary Peak Sauvignon Blanc, including a little oaked Sémillon, might have been expected to be as well balanced, mineral, and racy as it is, and the Rockview Ridge Pinot Noir is decent and improving (though I haven't enjoyed it as much as some other Pinots taking grapes from these vineyards, including the Newton Johnson)—but it has been the Mount Bullet, from Merlot, that aroused the most interest. There's none of the choc-mint lushness that characterizes many Cape examples of Merlot, but instead a fresh, perfumed intensity and elegance well supported by oak. These are fine vineyards, admirably farmed by James Downes and Kevin Watts, and a range of wines to watch with great interest.

www.shannonwines.com

14

TULBAGH AND CERES

BACKGROUND

It was first called the Land of Waveren—a deep inland rocky basin, enclosed on three sides by impressive mountains. Inhabited by, of course, San and Khoikhoi, it had first been seen by exploring white settlers in 1658, but they had found nothing to compensate for the heat and the distance from Table Bay. They were anyway ill with dysentery, and at last even van Riebeeck's surveyor, Pieter Potter, turned his back on the view from the mountaintop. But by 1699 there was more pressure for expansion, and governor Willem Adriaan van der Stel rediscovered the valley and named it after an important family to whom he was related back home in Holland. The great eastern range of mountains he named the Witzenberg in honor of Amsterdam's burgomaster, but those on the western side of the valley got a more homely and indigenous name: the Obiekwaberg, as the Khoikhoi apparently regarded them as the home of San hunters, whom they liked to think of as robbers *(obiekwa)*.

Wine was never the main concern of Tulbagh; the early settlers whom van der Stel dispatched to the lands he had named in such lordly (or Adamic) fashion scratched a living from grazing sheep and cattle. It was, in fact, the first Cape settlement where conditions, combined with the distance from Table Bay, dictated a chiefly pastoral rather than mixed farming economy, bringing the settlers into direct conflict with the pastoralist Khoikhoi. No doubt there were some vines to provide some sort of wine—and to send to the primitive stills to make brandy—for the settlers, but this was too far from Cape Town, and the way too arduous and slow, to allow for commercial production for the

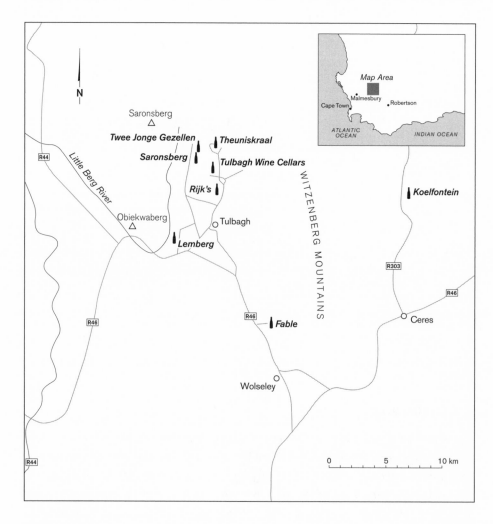

MAP 11
Tulbagh and Ceres

general market. The Twee Jonge Gezellen estate claims to have a grape-growing tradition going back to the very early eighteenth century.

It was in some ways a confirmation of isolation when the Land of Waveren was formally separated from Stellenbosch for immediate administrative purposes and given the name Tulbagh, after an earlier governor Rijk (or Ryk) Tulbagh. (The first syllable of the name is pronounced more or less as "till," the second as "Bach," as in the great musical family of the Baroque.)

The village is quaint and charming to this day, with a famous number of national monuments—many of which needed major restoration after the most severe earthquake ever recorded in South Africa struck in 1969.

The land around the town is now mostly used for fruit and wheat farming. The wine produced in Tulbagh was long a small and undistinguished contribution to the Cape's output. An 1882 survey gave a number of 2,206,918 vines for Tulbagh, less than

Malmesbury and the Cape, half as much as Robertson and Oudtshoorn. In 1906 one of the country's first cooperative cellars was formed here, in the context of the overproduction and severe depression affecting the wine lands: it was called the Drostdy Co-operative then (*drostdy* being the name for the local magistrate's court, where the proposal for a cooperative was first discussed by six anxious farmers). It changed its name to Tulbagh Co-operative Wine cellar in 1989, and in the year of its centenary merged with Porterville Cellars of the Swartland as Tulbagh Wine Cellars, with 126 members.

One of the country's great old estates is here: Twee Jonge Gezellen, founded in 1710 and with an unbroken line of family ownership going back to 1745 (and with *Jongegezellen* one word until the early 1990s). Theuniskraal is just about as old, though it first bottled a wine under its own label only in 1948: the famous (or notorious) Theuniskraal Riesling, made from Crouchen and since 2010 obliged to call itself Theuniskraal Cape Riesling—a long overdue requirement, but one carrying an element of sadness for those with a sense of tradition. Another notable bit of history associated with Tulbagh is that the tiny Lemberg (undergoing some desirable revitalization under new ownership as the second decade of this century began, after some very lackluster years) was the winery of Janey Muller, the first woman generally recognized as a professional winemaker in South Africa (although there were occasionally women in charge of winemaking in the bad old days, and certainly during the years of World War II—including Marie Furter, who very successfully made Zonnebloem wines for a few years starting in 1940).

At the turn of the century there were eight wineries releasing Tulbagh wine, and it could fairly be said that only Twee Jonge Gezellen produced wine of any real interest or distinction. The valley was generally ignored, or dismissed as a hot country making only a few decent white wines (red wine production generally seems to be seen as vital for South Africans to take a region seriously). Ten years later the number of wineries had a little more than doubled, with a small handful prominent (making successful red wine, too!) and no doubt some of the newest-comers also destined to make their mark. The most significant force behind the new Tulbagh was the establishment and growing reputation of Rijk's, whose first vintage was, auspiciously enough, 2000. Unsurprisingly, owner Neville Dorrington was cautious about advertising the origin of his wines because of Tulbagh's lackluster image, and for the first few vintages they were labeled WO Coastal. Their widespread success not only allowed this to change, but also alerted others to the area's hitherto largely untapped potential.

In fact, of course, Rijk's wine should never have been allowed to use the large catchall Coastal appellation, since Tulbagh is emphatically inland, with no coastal influence—but the fault is that of the appellation authorities, not of any winery, and is likely to be favorably resolved sooner or later in a reorganization of the regions. Incidentally, in an appellation used solely for fortified wine, Tulbagh has combined with Paarl to form the Boberg region. There is a good deal of soil variation in the area, with boulder beds similar to those found in the Rhône valley, as well as soils derived from sandstone and shale. Aspect and altitude vary, too, with many of the best vineyards lying on the foothill slopes, others on the floor of the valley through which the Little Berg River runs. Higher altitudes and mountain shadow also have an effect on mesoclimate (this, as usual in South Africa, having a more noticed influence on wine than does soil). At Fable, for example, where the vineyards are at 400 to 500 meters and receive morning mountain shadow, the average temperature is about 2°C lower than on the valley floor. Generally the climate is continental, with marked diurnal differences of temperature—and seasonal ones: winters tend to be cold, with lingering frost and snow on the high mountains. Summers are warm, with an average summer daytime temperature of 24.3°C—though this can be shortened, and the heat is anyway moderated, by the entrapment of cool night air within the valley. Rainfall is comparatively low, with a total per annum of 550 millimeters, a third of which falls in summer; supplementary irrigation is necessary.

The valley's traditional association with cheap white wine is reflected in the vineyard: Chenin Blanc (with 255 hectares) and Colombard dominate plantings, but Cabernet Sauvignon and Syrah have made big advances in this century, and now both are at nearly 140 hectares (all figures as of the end of 2011). Chardonnay, Pinotage, Merlot, and Sauvignon Blanc fill the next slots, some way behind.

A little inland from Tulbagh is the minuscule, unattached ward of Ceres, which is included here as it seems to have, vinously speaking, slightly more in common with Tulbagh than with the Breede River Valley, with which it might also be grouped. This valley is firmly associated with deciduous fruit production, and the little bit of wine production comes as a small by-product of fruit farms. But there is definite promise here. Callender Peak's few hectares of vines near the snow line were actually planted on a fruit farm in the early 1990s, though the first bottling under the farm's own label was only in 2007. The Chardonnay is made by Johan Kruger at Sterhuis, the Pinot Noir, Merlot, and Cabernet Sauvignon by Clive Torr at Topaz in Stellenbosch. The vines are ungrafted, undiscovered by phylloxera—which is perhaps anyway unwilling to venture into what is one of the coolest sites in the country, at an altitude of 850 meters.

Koelfontein is the slightly larger producer here, with less than 10 hectares of Chardonnay, Syrah, and Merlot vines (just 2 percent of the area of the fruit-growing farm), and there are plans to plant Sauvignon Blanc and Pinot Noir on the highest, coolest reaches. Dewaldt Heyns of the Saronsberg estate in Tulbagh is the consultant winemaker. The Chardonnay shows a fine cool-climate precision and, when it is not picked too ripe (this varies), the Shiraz also shows great promise.

It is unlikely that much of the valuable fruit-growing land of Ceres will be turned over to viticultural production under present circumstances—which is a pity. It could be amazing to see the results of a full-scale commitment to wine; for now we must be grateful for what essentially counts as an experiment, and hope for more.

THE WINERIES

FABLE

This, arguably the most "serious" winery in the area and certainly the one with the most classic approach, has a good chunk of Tulbagh's enlarged reputation for real quality riding on its success. The chances became even better with the purchase of Tulbagh Mountain Vineyards in 2010 (when the new branding was introduced) by the United States–owned Terroir Capital, led by Charles Banks, former part-owner of the California cult winery Screaming Eagle. In the few years before then a lack of investment by its British banker owners had started leading to problems that threatened its growing reputation.

In the early years (the vineyards and winery were established in 2000), success depended at least partly on the excellent TMV range of négociant wines (mostly from Swartland grapes) made by winegrower Chris Mullineux (who has since moved to the Swartland himself), but the commitment to Tulbagh terroir always ran deep.

There is increasing experimentation with biodynamics from the young duo in charge of production since 2009, Paul Nicholls in the vineyards and Rebecca Tanner in the cellar. I think I'm right, however, in gathering that Charles Banks himself views biodynamics much as I do, as evidence of a serious concern for vine well-being rather than a serious enterprise in itself.

The vineyards are SGS-certified as organically farmed (their creation on virgin soil and their current isolation from other farms make this easier). The arrival of Nicholls and Tanner slightly predated the new ownership, incidentally. In the cellar there is minimal use of sulfur and no yeast inoculation; gravity is used insofar as possible, and the proud claim is that the wines are unacidifed, unfined, and unfiltered.

Higher than most in the valley, the mountainside vineyards, facing northwest at an elevation between 400 and 500 meters, are less warm in character, particularly at night. Cabernet was ripped out under the new regime, which immediately started a program of planting some 20 hectares of Syrah, Grenache, and Mourvèdre in addition to what was already there. The cellar, too, was extended and refitted, and should be able to respond more sensitively, especially through multiple vinifications of smaller lots of grapes, to the development of terroir-based wines.

The first release under the Fable name was of an excellent Swartland Chenin Blanc–based white and two homegrown reds from the 2009 vintage, the 2008s having been abandoned. Branding is based on animal fables (genuine or created), in a new twist on the "critter" labels that have proved successful particularly in the United States, which is probably where these wines will be most assiduously marketed—the pre-Banks name of the winery was thought to be unpronounceable there. The new labels are controversial (ugly, in my opinion, and as equally to be regretted as the names, which evoke marketing decisions rather than the commitment to terroir that is undoubtedly behind the wines). The white is called Jackal Bird, while Bobbejaan (the Afrikaans word for baboon, and presumably not expected to cause problems for North Americans) is a sumptuously delicate Syrah—the 2009 probably the finest yet from this property—and Lion's Whisker is a Syrah-Mourvèdre blend, also extremely good, and rivaling in quality and style the best new-wave wines of the Swartland.

Charles Banks clearly has a genuine belief in the potential of this farm—he found it more or less by accident, he and his wife "fell in love with it," and he is confident that "one day he will be stunned" by its wines. Certainly, if Tulbagh as an area is to prove that it has a real potential for serious and world-class terroir-driven red wine, it is probably going to be Fable that will do it.

www.fablewines.com

RIJK'S

Rijk's takes its name from Rijk Tulbagh, after whom the valley itself was named, and it deserves the association, as it was this property that gave a much-needed boost to the area and, in particular, showed its potential for producing good red wines. Businessman Neville Dorrington bought the 136 hectares of virgin land in 1996, and although a hotel was part of his plan he took the establishment of the wine estate very seriously. Soil profiles and drainage analyses convinced him and his advisers that a wide range of grapes could happily be grown in the 300 millimeters of topsoil, with a thin layer of clay underpinned by deep vertical shale. Just about all the major varieties were planted (up to a hectare of each), from Sauvignon Blanc to Cabernet Franc, with the aim of monitoring and evaluating the wine each produced. The selection is interesting in that red varieties outweigh whites (the current mix is 65 percent to 35 percent), whereas in the past Tulbagh had always been thought of as white wine country—by the KWV at any rate—a strange viewpoint, as it is one of the Cape's hotter areas, with no access to any of the famous cooling summer breezes of the maritime regions. A total of 36 hectares of vines is now planted. Since 2002 the cellar has been the domain of Pierre Wahl, who has produced a large range of wines, many of which have achieved acclaim—not least in the form of competition awards.

As Wahl and his consultant viticulturist achieve a better understanding of the maturing vineyards, he is turning more toward blends, but most of the range is single-varietal. Ripeness is much, if not all, and Rijk's wines are notable for being rich and having a generosity of both fruit and alcohol; but these are generally well balanced by a freshening thread of (necessarily adjusted) acid. Concentration in the vineyards is increasingly on Rhône varieties, Chenin, and Pinotage, as evidenced by replantings (while weaker performers are abandoned).

In 2010 there was an experiment in splitting the wine offerings between two very distinct labels: the majority continuing as the Rijk's Private Cellar, with a few top selections of red wines as Rijk's Estate, which would be treated as a separate property with its own small winemaking facility. A few years later, however, they were reunited, as simply Rijks. There is a so-called Estate range, restricted to Shiraz (with a dash of Viognier) and the Master, a Syrah-led blend with Mourvèdre and Pinotage, along with smaller amounts of Carignan, Tinta Amarela, and Viognier. These are made in the typical Rijk's style, very ripe, alcoholic (about 15 percent) but well enough made for balance to be retained. Generally, opulence is matched by supple silkiness, a feature common among the reds. Wahl's oaking is always carefully judged—altogether he is a most intelligent winemaker, who is achieving much-deserved success.

The Reserve range includes Shiraz, Pinotage, Chenin Blanc, and Chardonnay from bought-in grapes—all varietal wines, all very good of their generous type, with the Chenin being frequently an excellent example of the rich, oaked but dry style. For many wine lovers, however, Rijk's is particularly associated with Pinotage, the Reserve being more opulent and lavishly oaked than the rather more elegantly styled version in the Private Cellar range, or that in the entry-level Touch of Oak range. Altogether, Rijk's makes a remarkably successful riposte to those skeptical about Tulbagh as a producer of red wine.

www.rijks.co.za

SARONSBERG

Saronsberg is another of the new-wave Tulbagh wineries leading the area's turn to rich, ripe red wines, mostly from the Rhône varieties. Pretoria businessman Nick van Huyssteen bought two farms in 2002 (both historically part of Twee Jonge Gezellen) and named his new estate after the mountain towering above it. Just two months later, fire destroyed most of the 100 hectares of vineyards and orchards, leading to an unplanned but carefully considered replanting program accompanying construction of the cellar. Winemaker Dewaldt Heyns crushed his first grapes, Sauvignon Blanc, in 2004.

By 2009, 41 hectares of vines, planted in 1-hectare blocks, had been established on the mountain slopes: one site has south- to southeast-facing vineyards with weathered red and yellow clay loam soils bearing a high percentage of fine gravel and some stone, while on the other site there is Malmesbury shale on lower and east-facing slopes.

The varietal spread is large. Syrah accounts for half of all plantings, together with other red Rhône varieties as well as all the main Bordeaux black grapes. There is Viognier too, and some Sauvignon Blanc and Chardonnay (the latter for a sparkling wine) are bought in from elsewhere.

Two ranges are made, Provenance and Saronsberg, the former aiming at accessibility with expressive fruit, the latter more ambitious. It is the reds that have achieved the most success, however, particularly the Shiraz, the Full Circle (Syrah with Grenache, Mourvèdre, and Viognier), and the Bordeaux-style Seismic. All are muscular, ripe, and full-bodied with multilayered flavors thanks to sensitive extraction and oaking—but definitely in the modern, internationalizing camp.

www.saronsberg.com

TWEE JONGE GEZELLEN/THE HOUSE OF KRONE

"Two young bachelors" is how the name is usually translated, although sometimes they are "companions"—but they were, in any case, the two young Dutchmen who in the early eighteenth century took over part of the large property that had not long since been granted to a Huguenot settler. By 1745 the farm, retaining the unusual name, passed into the Theron family (still a very common name in the district), and has subsequently been handed down through the generations—but because, unusually, daughters were included in the line of inheritance, the owning family until very recently was the Krones. Financial problems (at least partly occasioned by hugely expensive litigation against a bottle producer, which eventually had to be abandoned) led to the sale of the farm and business in 2012 to major distributor Vinimark, which had already owned a half-share in the brand for some years. The new owners are investing substantially in revitalizing and expanding the business. The Krone family will remain to manage the farm.

The first Krone involved was the son of a Dutch immigrant, who married into the family in 1916. But it was his son, "N. C." (father of the present cellarmaster, Nicky Krone, and grandfather of assistant winemaker and vineyard manager Matthew), who established the reputation of the farm after 1939. He also made some important contributions to Cape winemaking—notably as a local pioneer, with international reputation and significance, of modern techniques of cold fermentation. In 1959 he won thirteen first prizes from his fifteen entries in the National Young Wine Show, a feat that convincingly demonstrated to his confrères the fruitful advantages of this technique. The Krones also pioneered night harvesting in 1977, with pickers wearing miner's helmets, allowing for grapes to be harvested at about 18°C compared with anything up to 37°C during the heat of the day, when oxidation is a real danger.

N. C. also developed vineyards on the mountainsides, away from the alluvial riverside soils where they had been concentrated. Today the farm has 100 hectares of vines, extending from those on the banks of the Little Berg River up the stony lower slopes of Saronsberg. Those on the slopes are mainly east-facing, receiving morning sun but sheltered by mountain shadow from the great afternoon heat; the mesoclimate also means that they get higher rainfall than those on the flatland.

Production is now devoted to the sparkling wines for which the estate has always had a very good reputation. It's a useful style for this area, as it calls for grapes with lower sugars and therefore harvested early in the season, before the heat waves arrive. In fact, most of the table wines were discontinued about 2009, and the bubblies are branded as House of Krone rather than Twee Jonge Gezellen, which for a while remained the brand for a few minor wines. The first Méthode Cap Classique was from the 1987 vintage, and called Krone Borealis, punning on the name of the constellation Corona Borealis, partly because both *corona* and *krone* mean "crown." It has always been an approximately equal blend of Pinot Noir and Chardonnay, and one of the most attractive and classic of the local sparkling wines, with older vintages often displaying good development with brioche biscuity notes. These wines spend longer on their lees than many other local versions; an underground cellar was built especially for this purpose. There is also a Pinot-dominated Brut Rosé. In 2009 a new prestige multivintage wine was introduced: the Nicolas Charles Krone, named to honor the great man, who died in 2007. Marque 1, the maiden bottling, came from the 2001, 2002, and 2003 vintages, with some held back for later disgorgements, making for an unusually and agreeably mature South African wine release.

www.houseofkrone.co.za

15

OLIFANTS RIVER, WEST COAST, AND CEDERBERG

BACKGROUND

What generalizations are possible about this vast area? It would be difficult even if one excluded isolated wards outside of the Olifants River area (Lamberts Bay, with just one patch of vines where brusque Atlantic winds brush the heat of the interior; mountainous inland Cederberg, with some of the Cape's highest vineyards). One can find here rare old vineyards on farms producing mostly rooibos tea and wheat, capable of producing superb wines from juice that normally disappears into box-wine blends from cooperatives— Sadie Family, Botanica, and Cape of Good Hope (Anthonij Rupert) are among those making wines from dryland Sémillon and Chenin Blanc grown on the bleak Skurfberg. And there is the vastness of Namaqua Wines (an amalgamation of the former Vredendal and Spruitdrift cooperatives), with two hundred grape-farmer members, making the equivalent of perhaps ten million cases annually from 5,000 hectares of, overwhelmingly, intensively farmed vineyards. Water, heat, fertile soils, and the agrochemical industry give heavy crops and lush canopies to protect the grapes from the shriveling sun.

The Olifants River makes its long, winding way from the inland mountains to the sea, providing sustenance to an often inhospitable landscape. Everywhere in this region— except for higher mountain sites and those close to the sea—is more or less hot. Soils vary from dark alluvial to red sandy. Rainfall is low, from 220 to 450 millimeters; at any distance from the river and its dams, bushvines must find their own balance and manage without irrigation. Low cropping levels from those few vineyards mean that they are seldom viable for farmers who might do better with rooibos or buchu tea—unless their

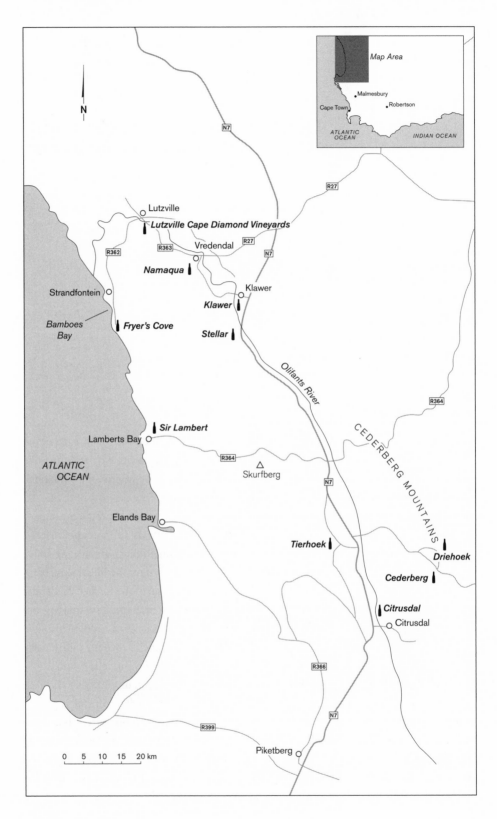

MAP 12
Olifants River, West Coast, and Cederberg

value is noticed by ambitious and curious winemakers and viticulturists from farther afield. It's a sad truth that, with few exceptions, the best wines from Olifants River are made from grapes taken to wineries much farther south—though Namaqua is trying to give itself a classier image with the Spencer Bay Winemakers Reserve range.

Klawer Winery and Lutzville Cape Diamond Vineyards are the other very substantial former cooperatives in the area. The Lutzville Valley is an official Wine of Origin district, with a ward called Koekenaap; Vredendal and Spruitdrift are wards directly within the Olifants River region. None of these appellation names is relevant to wine drinkers.

In these parts the vineyards are overwhelmingly dominated by Colombard and Chenin Blanc; Namaqua Wines takes in about 70 percent white grapes, Lutzville closer to 90 percent. But there are plantings of a great many other varieties, both white and black, on a much reduced scale. The Koekenaap ward in Lutzville Valley, which is somewhat cooler, produces Sauvignon Blanc that is sought after by many winemakers elsewhere.

A valuable addition to the winemaking scene in the Olifants River region came with the establishment in 1998 of Stellar Winery, taking advantage of the semiarid conditions that make fungus comparatively easy to manage, to become the country's largest producer of organic wines (as well as a good deal of other wine), and the first organic winery to gain Fairtrade certification. Stellar is also, it claims, the largest producer in the world of "commercially viable no-sulfur-added wines." The social concerns of the founders are reflected in the 26 percent worker shareholding in the cellar and a larger shareholding in Stellar Agri—a table- and wine-grape farming operation.

Two small coastal wards were declared earlier this century: Bamboes ("kelp") Bay and Lamberts Bay. The latter is wedged in the large triangle of no-wineman's-land between the Olifants River and Swartland regions—presumably it didn't occur to the early drafters of the regions that anyone would plant vineyards here. But in 2004 they did, and Sir Lambert Wines has made a racy Sauvignon Blanc from 10 hectares planted close to the cool Atlantic.

Farther south in the Olifants River region—where rooibos tea and oranges meet—are two districts, their names reflecting the dominant agricultural pursuit of the area: Citrusdal Mountain and Citrusdal Valley, both plunging down alongside the northern Swartland. In the former region, the only winery is that of the erstwhile Citrusdal cooperative. The winery was bought by Charles Back of Fairview in 2006, and quality should rise. The mountains of the Piekenierskloof ward of Citrusdal Mountain, where altitude can provide respite from the heat, undoubtedly contain excellent sites, some with older vines—including some ungrafted ones—planted in the mostly sandstone and shale soils. There is little irrigation available for vines, and most of the farming is dryland. Strong diurnal temperature differences seem partly to account for the elegance frequently achieved in Piekenierskloof wines. This is where Stellenbosch producers like négociant Neil Ellis and Ken Forrester have sourced Grenache for impressive varietal and blended bottlings; others—including Swartland's Eben Sadie for his Old Vines Series Soldaat— have followed suit; and Jean Engelbrecht of Rust en Vrede in Stellenbosch makes his excellent Donkiesbaai Steen from a Piekenierskloof vineyard. The only winemaking that takes place here, though, is at Tierhoek.

Virtually on the same latitude as Piekenierskloof, but high and cool among a wilderness of mountains on the eastern side of the Olifants River, is the Cederberg ward, containing just two wine producers.

THE WINERIES

CEDERBERG

Five generations of Nieuwoudts have lived on the farm (since 1893), though the first wine was made only in the 1960s by the grandfather of present winemaker David Nieuwoudt. The grape was Barlinka, a table variety, though other varieties were soon planted. A cellar was built in the 1970s; the proud story is that the grapes here ripen too late to be acceptable for the program of the local co-op. At more than 1,000 meters above sea level the area is certainly comparatively cool (*Vites Altae*—"high vines"— proclaim the bottle capsules). Rainfall is low, necessitating some irrigation. Weathered shale and slate with clay are suited to red varieties, whites favored by lightly structured soils with sandstone. Just 53 of the property's 5,500 hectares have vines, the remainder are left to nature.

Since Elsenburg-trained David Nieuwoudt took over in 1997, the wines have improved dramatically and the range has expanded greatly. The two wines in the flagship Five Generations range are a Cabernet and a Chenin, originally from the farm's oldest blocks (1978), but the Chenin now also originates from younger vines, too. Like the other reds, the Cabernet tends to international styling and is designed for early pleasure: ingratiating, with a rather soft structure, plenty of sweet fruit, and as much new oak—and charm. The Chenin is also quite oaky, but rich and silky, with sustained flavors, a fine acid bite, and some early complexity that seems likely to develop for a good few years. There are usually two Shirazes, one often selected for the Cape Winemakers Guild Auction: a supple, ripe blockbuster, with big alcohol, and usually a touch too much residual sugar and oak for classicism, but beautifully structured. Among the others is a delicious off-dry Bukettraube.

In 2008 Nieuwoudt purchased land in Elim from which he produces a Sauvignon Blanc and a Sémillon under a separate label, Ghost Corner, named for a south Cape coastal shipwreck. They show typical cool minerality and bracing acid.

Cederberg also makes two wines for a neighbor in the Cederberg ward, Driehoek Family Wines, established in 2009. It's rather too early to judge definitively, but both the Sauvignon Blanc and the Shiraz look very promising.

www.cederbergwine.com

FRYER'S COVE

Fryer's Cove Vineyards (the cove was named for a British settler who was the first commercial farmer in the area) is the sole winery in the tiny ward of Bamboes Bay—a splendid but isolated experiment in terroir. The gestation period of this tiny property was something like twenty years. The idea that here, less than a kilometer from the beach at Strandfontein, were (apart from a lack of fresh water) ideal conditions for vines came to a holidaying Wynand Hamman (then studying winemaking) and the wine-involved men of the van Zyl family he had married into. The soils were suitable, but irrigation water had to be brought from nearly thirty kilometers away. In 1999 the vital pipeline was built, and the first plantings were made. There are now 4 hectares of Sauvignon Blanc and 2 of Pinot Noir. The vines cope with the salty conditions; the seaside breezes make for genuine summer coolness, giving a long ripening period, after which the grapes meet their destiny at Hamman's hands in Stellenbosch. Sauvignon Blanc is the star here. The wine has intensity, character, and finesse, with an aromatic complexity and a steely tension. A second version, called Bay to Bay, is made partly from other West Coast vineyards, and is perhaps a little easier and fruitier, but still with a bright minerality supporting its succulence. There were early experiments with reds, but now there's only a pleasant enough Pinot Noir, which could improve as the vineyards mature.

www.fryerscove.co.za

TIERHOEK

When Tony Sandell, a wealthy Capetonian, and his now-widowed wife, Shelley, acquired this Piekenierskloof farm in 2001, gigantic boulders had to be moved in order for new vineyard plantings to be added to the sixty-year-old ungrafted Grenache and forty-year-old Chenin vines already here. There are now 16 hectares planted on the 300-hectare property—among the more isolated vineyards in the country, and wonderfully beautiful, with magnificent mountain views. Things are still developing here, and a good move was to replace the Syrah with a rich, muscular blend including Grenache and Mourvèdre. The monovarietal Grenache is also powerfully built and rather delicious, while the flintily fresh Sauvignon Blanc and gorgeously rich—yet simultaneously steely—Chenin Blanc are more than a match in terms of quality for the reds. There's also a good straw wine from Chenin. As increasing interest is paid to the Piekenierskloof as a source of fine grapes to be vinified elsewhere, it is useful that there is a winery here to be among those staking a claim. Unfortunately, winemaker Roger Burton left for personal reasons at the end of 2012, leaving Shelley Sandell mulling over various strategic possibilities for the future.

www.tierhoek.com

16

KLEIN KAROO AND ADJACENT WARDS

BACKGROUND

The Klein ("little") Karoo is perhaps the largest of the Wine of Origin regions in terms of area, but it has only scattered pockets of vines. Neither fact will surprise anyone driving through the long, semiarid basin that stretches eastward from the mountains defining one edge of the Breede River Valley. Vines are, in most parts, a vastly less likely sight than sparse vegetation and the occasional sheep cropping it under a blazing sky. Yet high in the mountains at the Klein Karoo's edges—the Langeberg and Outeniqua to the south, and the Swartberg to the north—are some of the coolest Cape vineyards. The Langeberg-Garcia district is a very narrow strip along the Langeberg Mountains, and the Upper Langkloof ward another such strip farther east, together with Outeniqua on the northern side of the Outeniqua Mountains; these are still within the Klein Karoo region, but Swartberg and Prince Albert Valley are tiny wards just outside its boundaries.

For the most part, the Klein Karoo is hot and dry, with low and unreliable rainfall and little water available for irrigation, so most vineyards keep to the alluvial soils alongside rivers. Comparison to the climate of Portugal's Douro Valley is often (and hopefully) made, especially for the area around the town of Calitzdorp, in the recently minted district of the same name, where many of the Cape's best port-style wines are made. Here the richer alluvial soils are generally eschewed in favor of poorer ones with a good clay component. East of Oudtshoorn are just two isolated wineries, largely specializing in the Muscadels and Jerepigos characteristic of the region as a whole. At and near Montagu in the west of the Klein Karoo and at Oudtshoorn are former cooperatives of

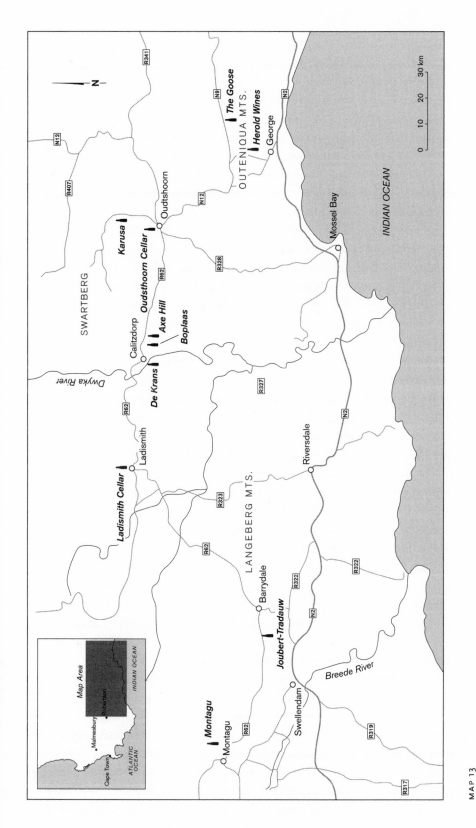

MAP 13
Klein Karoo and Adjacent Wards

little distinction—another co-op, Rietrivier, abandoned the struggle to sell any wines under its own label around 2008, to concentrate on bulk sales.

It's possible, indeed, that more wine and brandy were made at Oudtshoorn 150 years ago than today. A government report of 1882 actually showed that the area in 1875 had more vines than any other apart from Paarl and Stellenbosch—more than a third as many as the latter, and more than either Robertson or Worcester. The Riversdale area, south of the present Klein Karoo district, had about half as many vines as Oudtshoorn. Between that period and now intervened for a glorious half-century or so the Klein Karoo's great ostrich-feather industry, which caused farmers of just about everything, certainly including grapes, to turn to lucrative ostriches and their foodstuffs. A government commission into the wine industry in the early twentieth century reported on the production figures for 1909 and gave for Oudtshoorn, "the ostrich capital of the world," a resounding zero (and a relieved one, in light of the pervasive overproduction). The fashion for big, showy feathers had probably already started declining by then before finally crashing in 1913, and at various stages some farmers returned to vines, although demand for ostrich leather and meat ensure the continued presence of these strange, big birds in the area.

Interestingly, most of the cooperative wineries are comparatively young. Winemaking at Kango Cooperative at Oudtshoorn started as recently as 1976, when the tobacco cooperative founded in 1926 began to take in wine that had previously gone to a large wholesaler. The Ladismith Cellar was purely a distillery starting in 1939, but expanded to include wine in the 1970s, and Montagu produced only fortified wines until 1968.

There are exceptions to the emphasis hereabouts on fortified wines. De Krans and Boplaas, the leading port producers of Calitzdorp, do also make fairly successful ranges of unfortified wine, and there are a few Klein Karoo wineries worth mentioning that make no fortified wines at all. In fact, Jacques Conradie, winemaker and co-owner at Karusa, a small operation in the foothills of the Swartberg north of Oudtshoorn, has been quoted as claiming "the sole purpose" of Karusa as "to change the sweet wine perception of the Karoo." With minimal use of pesticides, fungicides, and herbicides, he aims to take as organic as possible an approach in the 8 hectares of vineyards, which are devoted to the Rhône varieties as well as Sauvignon Blanc, Chardonnay, and Pinotage. The first vintage bottled was 2004, and the Syrah-Viognier and Chardonnay-Viognier in the Fifth Element range, as well as the Terre Noir Syrah, are now indication enough that this is a serious winery in the making, and a revelatory addition to the region.

At Joubert-Tradauw in the Tradouw Valley near Barrydale, Meyer Joubert is making some good, honest, and rather elegant wines off his stony soil, notably Syrah and Chardonnay. In this more elevated area around Tradouw and Barrydale, in the lee of the mountains, average summer temperatures are a few degrees lower than in most parts of the region, and there is every likelihood that Barrydale could have an interesting wine future. There are even cooler conditions prevailing in the isolated and mountainous Upper Langkloof, where international pro golfer Retief Goosen in 2007 joined business-man Werner Roux and viticulturist-winemaker Morné Jonker in a wine business. They called the winery the Goose after its most famous owner, but it is based on a Jonker family farm where Morné had established vineyards and already made a few wines. There are 21 hectares of Cabernet Sauvignon, Syrah, and Sauvignon Blanc, and the results so far are satisfactory.

As for the tiny wards just beyond the Karoo's borders, rain, snow, and frost are not uncommon problems at Herold Wines, the sole, brave occupant of the Outeniqua ward, at the top of the pass between the hot, dry Karoo and cold, coastal George. The high vineyards are cool (and often wet) in summer; unsurprisingly, the Sauvignon Blanc is the most successful wine, but the Pinot Noir is charming, unshowy, and very drinkable. The first Herold bottling was in 2003—this is yet another of the many adventurous wineries to have sprung up this century in unlikely parts of the Cape, revealing possibilities undreamed of just a few decades before. On the other, northern side of the Klein Karoo is the Swartberg ward, where Howard Booysen sources grapes for his German-style Riesling (vinified in rented space in Stellenbosch) at an altitude of 1,000 meters and makes one of the better Cape wines from this variety, capable of being more bitingly nervy than the gentler maritime versions.

Plantings in the Klein Karoo reflect the predominance of wines for brandy making (a few superb estate brandies are produced in the area), making for large hectarages of Colombard and Chenin Blanc, which are also used for table wines, of course. Vineyards also reflect the importance of fortified wines. Most of the traditional port-variety plantings are around Calitzdorp—although Colombard and Cabernet Sauvignon are more quantitatively significant there, and Hanepoot (Muscat of Alexandria) easily trumps them all. The Muscat varieties are generally important in the warm areas, and there are scatterings of most of the other well-known varieties.

THE WINERIES

AXE HILL

This Calitzdorp-based port specialist punches well above its size, a tiny 1.3 hectares planted to traditional port varieties—Touriga Nacional, Tinta Barroca, and Souzão, the last of which started contributing to the wine with the 2003 vintage. The property was bought and planted in 1993 by Tony Mossop, one of the Cape's best-known wine writers and judges at the time; he named it for the stone hand-tools he found there, some as much as 400,000 years old. There is just enough water to provide irrigation for the rocky hillside vineyard—which bears netting to protect the harvest from hungry birds.

The first bottling was in 1997—Vintage Port, as it was then simply called, in an elegantly innovative 500-milliliter bottle. It was one of the earliest of the new wave of traditionally made and classically styled ports in the Cape, and has always been reckoned among the best, with enough grip and intensity to mature beneficially ten years or so in the best vintages, though always accessible in youth (when most bottles are drunk).

Tony Mossop died in 2006 and his son Miles, winemaker at Tokara, took over the winemaking, an arrangement that continued for a while after Axe Hill was sold to two Johannesburg businessmen—though one of them, Mike Neebe, fully assumed that duty as of 2009.

Vintage used to be the only style made each year, as the crop is scarcely large enough to warrant division. The alcohol level now is generally 20.5 percent, and residual sugar around 95 grams per liter. The wine is bottled unfiltered and unfined. Since 2003 a pleasant, dryish white port has been made in solera style from Klein Karoo Chenin Blanc. The new owners have acquired another property in Calitzdorp—giving them, most crucially, further water rights—and an expansion of the range has followed. Now there is not only a Cape Ruby as well, but also a burgeoning offering of unfortified reds: the first two were a Shiraz and a blend of Syrah with the estate's trio of port varieties.

www.axehill.co.za

BOPLAAS

The Nel family has been well established in the Calitzdorp area since Louis Nel settled on a 5,000-hectare farm in 1760. Boplaas ("upper/top farm" in Afrikaans) was bought in 1936 by Carel Nel (the current Carel's grandfather) to produce raisins as well as grapes for the local cooperative. He already owned Die Krans down the road. Some nine years after Carel's death in 1955, two of his sons, Danie and Chris, built a cellar on Boplaas to produce their own wines, and acquired a new farm just outside the town. In 1980, Danie and his son Carel took over these two properties, with Chris getting Die Krans.

Soils on Boplaas itself are alluvial and fertile, while those on the other property, Welgeluk, are of red Karoo soil and sandy loam, producing smaller crops and better quality. An added benefit of the latter site is that it faces southeast, meaning that the prevailing southeasterly wind often brings some cooler air from the sea eighty kilometers distant—providing some afternoon respite from summer heat. A total of 70 hectares is now under vine: Cabernet Sauvignon, Merlot, Pinotage, Syrah, Souzão, Tinta Barroca, Touriga Nacional, Chardonnay, Colombard, and Sauvignon Blanc.

In 1984, Carel Nel (who was to inherit the property) took over the winemaking. The following year, he and his father ventured over the Outeniqua Mountains to plant vines in cooler coastal climes at Ruiterbosch, near Mossel Bay, but the viticultural problems of summer rainfall prevented success. Vastly more rewarding were the port-style wines for which Boplaas has become best known. The maiden 1982 was in fact made from Pinotage, but traditional port varieties were introduced into the vineyard starting in 1992, and in 1995 came the the first Boplaas Vintage Reserve Touriga Nacional Port. Early wines contained about 18.5 percent alcohol and just over 100 grams per liter of residual sugar; today, in rather more traditional balance, the analysis shows 20 percent alcohol and 90 grams of sugar—at least for the various ruby styles; the tawnies are more in the older-fashioned mold. In a further reaching for authenticity, Carel Nel was the first local producer to install a lagar, the trough in which port grapes are—or customarily were—trodden.

The current range of ports is astonishing—there are often ten produced (they generally have the word *Cape* preceding, and included the word *port* until legislation made this impossible starting in 2012: Vintage, Vintage Reserve, Cape Winemakers Guild Auction Reserve, and four variants of tawny, as well as a ruby and a pleasantly trivial pink. These are all blends of Touriga Nacional, Tinta Barroca, and Souzão. There's also a Cape white port based on, of all things, Chardonnay. Boplaas is consistently one of the best local producers of ports, and Carel is unrivaled for his superb, richly elegant tawnies. Going even more alcoholic, the Boplaas brandy was the Cape's first estate brandy in 1989 and is undoubtedly one of the best.

But fortified wine (and there are also a few in Jerepigo style) is heavily outweighed—in terms of volume and labels, if not of reputation—by the table wines: Carel's interest in such wines is hinted at by the name of his winemaker daughter, Margaux. Realizing that the home farms were unlikely to produce sufficient wine of sufficient quality to meet his ambitions, Carel in 1998 abandoned the concept of estate wine and started sourcing grapes from all over the wine lands, including the cooler Langkloof. Cabernet Sauvignon and Syrah dominate the more than adequate reds in the top Family Reserve varietals, though Touriga plays a role with Cabernet and Merlot in the Ring of Rocks blend. A typical Sauvignon Blanc from Darling fruit is also in the range. There is a large standard range of pretty ordinary wines.

Cool Bay is a venture started by Carel and Margaux with the 2009 vintage. Grapes sourced from both the West Coast and along the Garden Route are for the time being crushed and vinified at Calitzdorp.

The Nels are also respectably and keenly "green," actively supporting protection of the great biological diversity of the Succulent Karoo Biome that surrounds them, and part of which they own.

www.boplaas.co.za

DE KRANS

Danie Nel purchased the farm then called Die Krans—a portion of the original Nel farm mentioned in the Boplaas entry—in 1890, and became a successful producer of ostrich feathers, sweet wine, and brandy. (The name became De Krans in 2002, in deference to English speakers' confusion over the meaning and pronunciation of *Die*—meaning "the." A *krans* is a cliff-face, or crag.) Carel, one of Danie's five sons, inherited Die Krans and developed the vineyards on the fertile, alluvial soils to make sweet wine, brandy, and raisins. As explained in the Boplaas entry, this farm passed into the hands of Carel's son Chris in 1980. When Chris died a few years later, De Krans gained its present owners (and winemakers), Boets and Stroebel Nel.

De Krans's 45 hectares of vineyard lie on flattish land by the river (handy for irrigation in an area where annual rainfall averages a mere 200 millimeters) on fertile sandy loam overlaid by a deep layer of topsoil.

The farm is another of the handful of excellent port producers in the Calitzdorp area. A wood-aged vintage version from Tinta Barroca, fortified with brandy and regular spirits, was part of the original range; in the early 1980s the variety switched to Pinotage, and then to a blend of both varieties. In 1990, the first Vintage Reserve was produced from Tinta Barroca alone, and in 1997 more traditional port varieties—Touriga Nacional, Tempranillo (Tinta Roriz), and Souzão—were introduced. In common with other serious producers of this style of fortified wine, the alcohol level has risen a little since the early days, and sugar-sweetness has dropped.

In addition to the Vintage Reserve from the best years, which deserves—if not demands—at least a decade's maturation, there's a regular Vintage (also very good), a nonvintage ruby, and a fine, luscious tawny. A pioneering, frivolous pink port was introduced in 2008, and there's a white made from Chenin Blanc.

The range of table wines is smaller here than at the Nels' cousin's Boplaas, but more interestingly committed to the port varieties. Boets bottled the Cape's first Touriga Nacional table wine with the 2000 vintage, a full-bodied, modestly oaked wine reflecting the growing international interest in table wines from the Douro. Further experiments resulted in Red Stone Reserve (named for the color of the *krans* itself), which blends Touriga with the Cabernet Sauvignon that the winemaker finds gives a more satisfactory result than other port varieties. A few other wines are made from fruit brought in from Elgin, Durbanville, and Stellenbosch.

www.dekrans.co.za

APPENDIX

The statistics presented in the following table add detail to the story of change that started in the early 1990s, discussed in chapter 1. Taken in conjunction with the fuller account in chapter 4 of the shift in the constitution of the Cape vineyard, these figures tell much of the story of the South African wine revolution up to 2011—up to November 2011, to be precise, as November is the closing month for the annual collection of statistics by SAWIS (South African Wine Industry Information and Statistics), from whose annual booklets—and those of its predecessor, the KWV—this table has been harvested. Those hungry for further statistics will find many on the SAWIS Web site: www.sawis.co.za.

The numbers in the table mostly get larger, of course, over this period, and along with indicating some change in shape of the industry in South Africa (private producers vis-à-vis co-ops, for example) they inevitably tend to reflect quantity rather than quality; qualitative change can be inferred from some of them, however, as well as from the vineyard figures referred to above). Of the numbers that diminish in size, the depressing one is that indicating a continuing decline in wine consumption by locals.

Synoptic Table of South African Wine Production, 1993–2011

	1993	1996	1999	2002	2005	2008	2011
Number of wineries (all types)	242	298	337	428	581	585	582
Private wine cellars	170	223	260	349	495	504	505
Producer cellars (co-ops and former co-ops)	70	69	69	66	65	58	52
Producing wholesalers	4	5	8	13	21	23	25
Number of primary grape producers	4,607	4,602	4,515	4,346	4,360	3,839	3,527
Number of bulk wine buyers (wholesalers, exporters)			65	104	118	118	101
Total wine-grape vine area (hectares)	84,103	95,721	92,601	96,233	101,607	101,312	100,568
White varieties as percentage of total area	81.1	79.4	70.7	56.2	54.3	56.1	55.6
White wine as percentage of total produced		86.9	83.7	72.1	61.1	62.4	65.0
Producing area four years and older (hectares)			75,892	79,073	87,284	92,503	92,621
Total production (thousands of liters, incl. for distillation and grape juice)	811.0	899.3	914.1	834.2	905.2	1,089.0	1,012.8
Production of wine (thousands of liters)	395.0	576.7	595.9	567.2	628.5	763.8	831.2
Percentage of total harvest crushed by private wine cellars				11.7	13.3	14.0	17.0
Percentage of total harvest crushed by producer cellars				82.8	78.7	78.9	75.2
Percentage of total harvest crushed by producing wholesalers				5.6	8.0	7.1	7.9
Certified wine (incl. fortified and sparkling; thousands of liters)	48.6	112.0	146.3	247.4	332.5	450.0	440.7

Certified wine from producer cellars (thousands of liters)	8.6	28.9	35.7	53.4	62.4	102.6	109.9
Certified wine from wholesalers (thousands of liters)	24.7	54.4	68.8	153.3	216.2	271.4	251.7
Certified wine from private wine cellars (thousands of liters)	15.2	28.8	41.8	40.7	53.8	76.1	79.0
Average yield (tons/hectare)			15.46	13.66	13.42	15.41	
Consumption per capita (liters) of South African wine	8.37	9.4	9.2	8.9	7.4	7.3	7.0
Exports (millions of liters)	24.6	99.9	129.1	217.7	281.8	411.7	357.4
Exports as percentage of wine production	6.2	17.3	21.4	38.3	44.7	53.9	43.0

As for statistics for the past half-century, the control exercised by the KWV at least resulted in a great deal of reliable information, and it published an annual booklet, *KWV Statistics Survey*. Since the KWV relinquished its quasi-statutory powers, this statistical function has been taken over by South African Wine Industry Information and Statistics (SAWIS), whose annual booklet is now titled *South African Wine Industry Statistics;* the current one is always available online at www.sawis.co.za. SAWIS also separately publishes fuller annual statistics related to the South African vineyard, also available on the Web site.

Material consulted on grape varieties, wineries, and wine production, as well as some other twentieth-century aspects, includes the following:

De Klerk, W. A. *The White Wines of South Africa*. Cape Town: Balkema, 1967.

Fridjhon, M. *The Penguin Book of South African Wine*. Harmondsworth: Penguin, 1992.

Hughes, D., P. Hands, and J. Kench. *South African Wine*. Cape Town: Struik, 1992. [There have been later editions of this encyclopedic work, less satisfactory in many ways.]

James, T. 2009. "Red Semillon: Return of the Wine Grape." *The World of Fine Wine* 25 (2009): 70–73.

———. "The Ghost Grape and Other Mysteries of Constantia." *The World of Fine Wine* 29 (2010): 82–85.

Knox, G. *Estate Wines of South Africa,* 2nd ed. Cape Town: David Philip, 1982.

Maxwell, K. *Fairest Vineyards*. Johannesburg: Hugh Keartland, 1966.

May, P. F. *Pinotage: Behind the Legends of South Africa's Own Wine*. St. Albans: Inform & Enlighten, 2009.

Orffer, C. J., ed. *Wine Grape Cultivars in South Africa*. Cape Town: Human and Rousseau, 1970.

Perold, A. I. *A Treatise on Viticulture*. London: Macmillan, 1927.

Swart, E., and I. Smit. *The Essential Guide to South African Wines,* 2nd ed. Green Point: Cheviot, 2009.

INDEX OF WINERIES

GENERAL INDEX

Sadie Family Palladius, as new style of white blend, 8, 74, 233
Saintsbury, George, on drinking Constantia, 93
Sangiovese, 58–59
Sauvignon Blanc, 69–71; in blends, 73–74
Schapenberg area of Stellenbosch, 112
seasons in the vineyard, 4
Sémillon (Greengrape), 38, 71–73; in blends, 73–74
Sexwale, Tokyo, 17, 100, 209
SFW (Stellenbosch Farmers' Winery): acquisition of Zonnebloem brand, 41; amalgamation in Cape Wine and Distillers, 46; introduction of cool fermentation technology, 41
Sharpeville massacre, 42
sherry, 78, 80–81; early experiments, 80; establishment of industry, 40
Shiraz. *See* Syrah
Simonsberg-Paarl ward, 185
Simonsberg-Stellenbosch ward, 110–11
single vineyard within Wine of Origin scheme, 89
Slanghoek Valley ward, 248
slavery and slaves, 3, 16; abolition of, 30; increased importation to supply labor, 25, 27; number of slaves (1770 to 1820), 28; wine farm ownership of slaves in early nineteenth century, 30
social transformation: Black Economic Empowerment, 18; charter for the wine industry, 18; land and brand projects, 17–18; limited extent of, 17
South African Wine and Brandy Company, 9
South African Wine Industry Council, 9
South African Wine Industry Information and Statistics, 9
South African Wine Industry Trust (SAWIT), 9; failure to empower farmworkers, 18; involment in KWV Black Economic Empowerment deal, 18
sparkling wine. *See* Méthode Cap Classique
Steen. *See* Chenin Blanc
Stellenbosch, 87*map*, 108–9*map;* decline in late nineteenth century, 107; educational institutions of, 107–8; first settlement and early history, 25, 106–7; soils and climate, 110; wards and other areas, 110–13. *See also individual wards and areas*

Stellenboschkloof area of Stellenbosch, 112–13
straw wine, 77
Sunday's Glen ward, 262
Sutherland Karoo district, 84
Swartberg ward, 303
Swartland district, 87*map*, 231*map;* early history of, 230–32; in rebirth of South African wine, 232–34; viticultural conditions, 235–36
Swartland Independent Producers, 235
Swellendam district, 250, 87*map*
Syrah (Shiraz): history of plantings and nature of wines, 56–57; importance of blend in Swartland, 13, 232, 236; as synonym for Shiraz, 56

Tannat, history of plantings and nature of wines, 58
Teinturier, 54–55
Tempranillo, 59
terroir, 20, 22, 110; significance of for appellations, 13, 88
Theewater ward, 278
Tinta Amarela, 59
Tinta Barroca, 59
Tinta Roriz, 59
tot system, 2, 16–17, 29, 42
Trincadeira, 59
Tulbagh district, 87*map*, 288*map;* early history and character of, 287–90
Tygerberg district, 222

Union of South Africa, founding of, 38
University of Stellenbosch: Department of Viticulture and Enology, 6, 40, 107; Institute for Wine Biotechnology, 107
Upper Langkloof ward, 302

van der Stel, Simon: early actions in wine industry, 25, 106; establishment of Constantia, 26
van der Stel, Willem Adriaan, founding of Vergelegen, 27, 172
van Rensburg, André, on international competition, 5–6
van Riebeek, Jan, on first harvest, 24
varietalism, versus geographical naming, 50
varieties. *See* grape varieties
Verdelho, 74

TEXT: 9.5/14 Scala
DISPLAY: Scala Sans
COMPOSITOR: IDS Infotech, Ltd.
CARTOGRAPHER: Bill Nelson
PRINTER AND BINDER: Maple Press